Landscapes of the Norman Conquest

Landscapes of the Norman Conquest

Trevor Rowley

PEN & SWORD
ARCHAEOLOGY

First published in Great Britain in 2022 by
Pen & Sword Archaeology
An imprint of
Pen & Sword Books Ltd
Yorkshire - Philadelphia

ISBN 978 1 52672 428 1

Typeset in Ehrhardt by SJmagic DESIGN SERVICES, India.
Printed and bound in the UK by CPI Group (UK) Ltd.

Pen & Sword Books Ltd. incorporates the Imprints of Pen & Sword Archaeology,
Atlas, Aviation, Battleground, Discovery, Family History, History, Maritime, Military,
Naval, Politics, Railways, Select, Transport, True Crime, Fiction, Frontline Books,
Leo Cooper, Praetorian Press, Seaforth Publishing, Wharncliffe and White Owl.

For a complete list of Pen & Sword titles please contact

PEN & SWORD BOOKS LIMITED
47 Church Street, Barnsley, South Yorkshire, S70 2AS, England
E-mail: enquiries@pen-and-sword.co.uk
Website: www.pen-and-sword.co.uk

or

PEN AND SWORD BOOKS
1950 Lawrence Rd, Havertown, PA 19083, USA
E-mail: uspen-and-sword@casematepublishers.com
Website: www.penandswordbooks.com

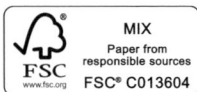

MIX
Paper from
responsible sources
FSC
www.fsc.org   FSC® C013604

Contents

Preface		vi
Acknowledgements		vii
Introduction		viii
Chapter 1	The Making of England	1
Chapter 2	The Landscape of Invasion	30
Chapter 3	Rebellion and Retribution	52
Chapter 4	The Kingdom Changes Hands	70
Chapter 5	Castles in the Landscape	95
Chapter 6	The Impact of the Conquest on Towns	138
Chapter 7	The Impact of the Conquest on the Church	169
Chapter 8	The Spread of Monasticism	196
Chapter 9	Woodland, Forest and Park	232
Chapter 10	Landscape and Empire: The Impact of the Roman World	259
Chapter 11	The Cultural Landscape of Anglo–Norman England	288
Conclusion		310
Endnotes		313
Bibliography		322
Index		340

Preface

I was brought up in Shropshire, a border county, where the imprint of Roger de Montgomery is still writ large in town, castle and church. My first degree was in geography at University College London, where the head of department was the great Domesday scholar H.C. Darby. Subsequently, I was privileged to have the father of landscape history, W.G. Hoskins, as my postgraduate tutor. Given that background it was perhaps inevitable that I would eventually try my hand at a book on the Norman landscape. In some respects, I wish I had written it thirty or forty years ago, when it would have been a relatively straightforward fieldwork-based narrative account of the Norman contribution to the English landscape. Although at that time there were still doubts in some quarters about the very existence of a distinctive Norman element in the landscape.

Today landscape history is a much broader, more complex discipline. In addition to a greatly expanded repertoire of technological aids, it incorporates the analysis of the importance of gender, mind and belief, display and spatial awareness. The male domination of Norman society reflected in the history is starkly illustrated in the Bayeux Tapestry, where out of 623 human images, just six are female; yet almost certainly the tapestry was mainly the work of seamstresses. Only in recent years has there been any serious attempt to redress this glaring gender imbalance. Where possible I have taken note of these and other developments, but cannot pretend that I have done them justice.

The Bayeux Tapestry has provided an invaluable source for illustrations. In the absence of other relevant contemporary material, I have used examples from both before and after the Norman era, and from outside Normandy and England. This book largely follows conventional landscape traditions, covering town, countryside, defence, the Church and so on, but it also looks at the historical geography of England in 1066 and the landscape of the invasion. The continuing influence of Rome on the Anglo-Norman world is acknowledged with a chapter of its own. The Norman landscape is construed in the broadest sense to include cultural landscapes of the arts as well as architecture. Due to the inter-related character of the main topics there is inevitably some overlap between chapters. The book concentrates on the Norman impact on England, with some attention given to Wales. Scotland is only dealt with superficially, and there is no attempt to cover the 'Normans' in Ireland, although all three countries are, of course, more than worthy of independent treatment.

Trevor Rowley
Appleton, Oxfordshire
March 2022

Acknowledgements

I am grateful to many people for the information, ideas and advice imparted to me during the writing of this book, notably – Martin Biddle, James Bond, Bill Bower, Giles Carey, Michael Fieldsend, Jeremy Haslam, Martin Henig, Linda Kent, Robert Liddiard, Jane Rowley, Richard Rowley, Michael Sibly and Jan Ure. As always, any omissions, mistakes or misconceptions are entirely my own responsibility.

I would like to thank the city and people of Bayeux for permission to reproduce images from the Bayeux Tapestry. The authors of other photographs and plans are acknowledged in the text, while the Ordnance Survey map extracts are all taken from the first edition 25-inch series, *England and Wales* (1841-1920).

Introduction

*[King William] implanted the customs of the French throughout England, and
began to change those of the English.*

(Hermann of Bury St Edmunds, *c*.1090)[1]

The Norman Conquest is the most celebrated watershed in English history.
Its political and cultural consequences are well rehearsed, leading as it
did to a new monarchy, aristocracy, architectural style and social system.
1066 represents a significant change in historical perception; it marks the point
from which the present line of English monarchy is normally traced. It is also
when there is a change from talking about peoples – the Romans, the Saxons
and the Vikings, to a dynastic compartmentalization of history – the Normans,
the Angevins, the Plantagenets, the Lancastrians, the Yorkists and the Tudors.
Yet uniquely among this latter group, the Normans were also a 'people' from the
Continent, albeit one whose rule, strictly speaking, only extended from 1066 to
1154, and whose numbers were limited. The Norman Conquest was achieved by
a relatively small Continental aristocratic elite and was not associated with any
large-scale folk movement; in the first instance it was essentially the transposition
of an aristocracy.

The short-lived Norman dynasty blended into a much longer line of earlier
Saxon and later Angevin and Plantagenet monarchs. The 'people' of this
particular invasion were not really Norman but were native Anglo-Saxons,
Anglo-Scandinavians, Welsh and Scots, whose world was changed in response
to the innovations and impositions of the Normans. The Normans were directly
responsible for introducing relatively little that was completely new into the
English landscape, but the political, social, economic and cultural changes they
introduced acted as catalysts which induced the distinctive Anglo-Norman
landscape of the late twelfth century, as well as establishing the template for the
later medieval landscape. The Norman Conquest may have been more like earlier
'people' invasions than it first appears; the transmission of new ideas from a small
number of newcomers on a much larger native population was probably more
common than is generally accepted. Such a transmission was certainly true of the
Romans and may well have been the case of the Anglo-Saxons and Vikings.

Normandy compared to Anglo-Saxon England was a newcomer to the
European political map. During the ninth century the Carolingian Empire, which

earlier had covered much of central and western Europe, fragmented into its constituent duchies and counties. Some of these territorial units developed into strong principalities, under the control of a militant Frankish aristocracy who assumed the powers and functions of monarchs – minting coins, collecting taxes, holding courts, appointing clergy, summoning armies, erecting fortifications and founding towns. By the millennium the western Carolingian rulers had been succeeded by the Capetian kings, based in Paris, who controlled a vastly reduced territory. In theory the individual principalities still owed allegiance to the French monarchy, but in practice many were as powerful as, if not more powerful, than the Crown itself. Normandy had not itself been a constituent county of the empire, but was carved out of the western subkingdom of Neustria, with its geography corresponding roughly to the ancient diocese of the Archbishop of Rouen.

The conventional creation story for Normandy is that it was established as a buffer territory against Viking incursions. The River Seine provided ready access to central France and in the mid-ninth century, Vikings are recorded as raiding as far east as Paris and beyond. To begin with, Norsemen raided and looted churches, monasteries and villages, but later began to settle and intermarry in the Seine Valley and along the coast. According to the traditional story, through the Treaty of Saint-Clair-sur-Epte (911), the king of the western Franks, Charles III 'the Simple', ceded territory around Rouen in the Seine Valley to a Viking warlord, Rollo, and his followers. The outcome of this semi-legendary event was confirmed in 918 by a grant by King Charles to the abbey of Saint-Germain-des-Prés, which records the land 'we have granted to the Northmen at the Seine, that is, Rollo and his companions, in order for them to safeguard the kingdom'.[2] Rollo became the Count of Rouen, and the founder of the line of the dukes of Normandy that led directly to William the Conqueror. The Pays d'Auge, the Caen Plain and the Bessin were added in 924, and in 933 the Cotentin and the Coutances Bocage finalized the shape of Normandy until the mid-eleventh century, but full ducal control of the whole region was probably not achieved until after 1000.

The Franks used the term 'Normand' to describe the Viking peoples and this was the name that became synonymous with the duchy that developed out of the original territory granted to Rollo. Despite having Viking rulers, plus there being a significant influx of migrants from Scandinavia, the Normans were essentially a Frankish people. Surprisingly, the Viking impact on the landscape in Normandy seems to be restricted largely to place names; overall the Scandinavians appear to have made far less impression in Normandy than their counterparts in England.

By the middle of the eleventh century, despite significant setbacks, Normandy was established as a well-organized state with a powerful army. Rapidly shedding most of its Viking associations the duchy increasingly resembled its Frankish neighbours. Normandy's military forces enabled its dukes to participate effectively in the politics of north-western Europe and intervene both politically and militarily in the affairs of other principalities. Normandy was able to develop a new and powerful aristocracy, Church and culture. 'As a result, the Normans had produced a new state and new society which no longer belonged to the Scandinavian world, but was in the forefront of the military and cultural development of the French.'[3]

More generally between 1000 and 1200 there was a significant movement of Franks, largely minor lords, from their homelands into new areas where they settled and frequently increased their fame and fortunes. This can be seen in the Norman takeover of southern Italy and Sicily, the militant spread of Christianity into Spain and the Baltic, and most dramatically in the 'Frankish' crusades to the Middle East. The Norman conquest of England in the mid-eleventh century represents part of a wider Frankish 'diaspora'; during the eleventh and twelfth centuries, men of Norman descent and others who joined with them became lords not only in all parts of Britain, but also in Italy, Sicily, Spain, Syria and briefly in Anatolia and North Africa.

These political movements coincided with far-reaching economic, social and landscape changes in western Europe. Although the vast majority of the people remained rooted in agriculture, as the population grew steadily in size the economy of the political territories of north-western Europe increasingly involved trade and commerce. Ports, markets and fairs flourished in response to an increase in exchange, together with the measures taken to control and monopolize it. Ancient

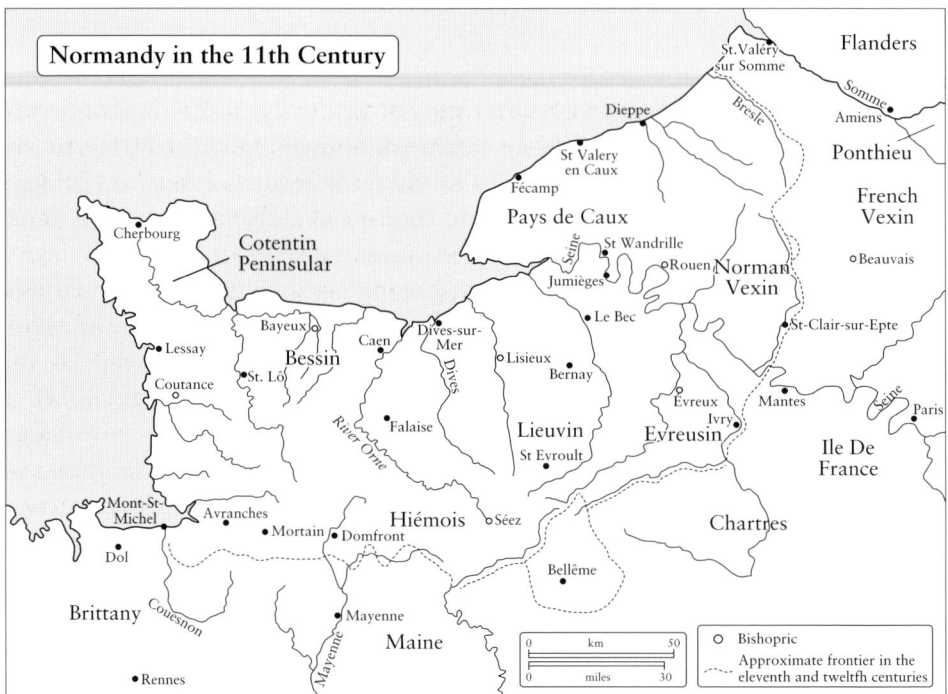

Map of Normandy in the eleventh century.

The Norman World c.1130

Map showing the Norman world c.1130.

towns were rejuvenated, sometimes taking on new roles, and new towns were created, often with commerce as their principal function. Other new towns were founded in politically marginal areas as fortified strongholds and administrative centres. In the countryside too there were fundamental changes, many of which had been in process before the millennium, and in much of Europe, forest, moor and fen were cleared or drained and brought into agricultural use. There was a move from dispersed to nucleated rural settlement, accompanied by the adoption or adaption of open-field systems. The role of the Church changed, as the landscape of western Europe was enhanced with a steadily increasing number of new monastic foundations, cathedrals and parish churches. In Normandy before 1066 these developments were accompanied by the concentration of political and military power in the hands of dukes and a new, enlarged nobility, often exercised from the security of a new form of private defence – the castle.

Since W.G. Hoskins wrote *The Making of the English Landscape* in 1955, hundreds of books have been published on every imaginable element of landscape history.[4] It is therefore perhaps surprising that no single volume has been dedicated to the impact of the Normans on the towns, rural settlements and countryside of England in the eleventh and twelfth centuries. This omission does

W.G. Hoskins (1908-1992), the father of English Landscape History, was no great admirer of the Normans.

not result from the absence of diagnostic Norman elements in town and country, and many topic-specific and regional studies have been published on one aspect or another of the Anglo-Norman contribution to the British landscape.

Hoskins, in his groundbreaking book, had relatively little to say about the specific Norman contribution to the landscape, apart from the creation of royal forests. Indeed, he viewed them largely as 'plunderers' and described William the Conqueror as behaving like some 'avenging maniac' in Yorkshire. Other aspects of the Norman era were contained within chapters on 'The Colonization of Medieval England' and 'Towns'. Hoskins anticipated the reluctance of subsequent landscape historians to detach those landscape elements that are specifically Norman from those that can be accommodated within a more general 'medieval' envelope. How far is it possible to distinguish between changes seen in England after 1066 that derived directly from the imposition of Norman rule and those associated with broader patterns of continuous national and international culture and exchange?[5] Landscape historians along with archaeologists have preferred to place the Norman era firmly in the basket labelled 'medieval'. They have used 1066 as a convenient point for the start of the Middle Ages, but baulked at the Normanization of landscape history because many of those features associated with the Normans had a much longer lifespan than the eighty-eight years of Norman kingship.

The most obvious examples of Norman contributions to the landscape are in the form of castles, cathedrals, churches and abbeys – essentially elite sites, synonymous with the projection of Norman power and authority in England, Wales and to a lesser extent Scotland. Such structures were responsible for initiating fundamental changes in the topography of many places, particularly towns. Their scale, design and decoration in itself introduced major landscape changes, as did the extensive use of stone, not only in church, but also in secular buildings. In the countryside too there were recurring echoes of powerful kingship and lordship, in the form of palaces, manor houses, abbeys, forests and parks.

The Conquest represented much more than a short-lived dynastic appropriation; it was a military, political and cultural takeover, with short- and long-term consequences – a takeover whose character and complexion altered as the Normans blended with the far larger native Anglo-Scandinavian population. It is therefore important to uncouple the Norman landscape as a whole from the timeline of the four Norman kings of England. The Norman influence on what we see about us began before 1066 and lasted long after; thus it is necessary to establish a text for the Norman contribution to the landscape which overrides the political headlines. The more indirect and longer-term impacts of the Conquest on the landscape were a result of more gradual tenurial, social and political change. Some time ago John Le Patourel recognized the need to see the Norman period as evolutionary and he placed it within a broad time frame of 1000 to 1200. He identified a military phase, followed by a phase of colonization – these phases overlapped chronologically and impacted different regions over different timescales.[6] A stabilisation phase can be added to this model, during which Norman elements bedded down with pre-existing Anglo–Scandinavian landscape features. Recent scholarship has demonstrated that the Norman Conquest was far more nuanced than has been traditionally portrayed, its precise complexion dependent on the character of specific regions and how the Normans reacted to the different regional circumstances they encountered.[7]

Chapter 1

The Making of England

When William the Conqueror seized the English crown, he became the ruler of an ancient realm. England was already an old country.[1]

The England that Duke William of Normandy conquered was indeed an old country. Layers of prehistoric, Romano-British, Anglo-Saxon and Scandinavian occupation overlapped and blended to produce a well-used landscape of towns, villages, farmsteads, fields, woods and tracks. The boundaries that defined counties, and the sub-divisions within them, hundreds, estates and parishes, incorporated features that were more than two millennia old. Many of these divisions were themselves based on elemental landscape features such as rivers, streams, hills and watersheds. Within England there were marked regional variations in settlement patterns, agricultural regimes and the distribution of woodland, marshland and open wasteland. In addition to geographic and political regions, there were distinct cultural and economic divisions.

There were ports, markets, monasteries and industries, all contributing to make up a relatively wealthy country, which had only recently been loosely united into a single kingdom. Its strategic, commercial and administrative centres were joined by a web of routeways, including many of the old Roman roads that still formed the backbone of the national communication network. London, although not yet the capital of England, was at the centre of the web, with major roads radiating to many parts of the kingdom. The city with its international trading links enjoyed geographic, political and commercial superiority, and it was already the predominant urban centre in the country.

Contemporary chroniclers describe England as a country of agricultural fertility and commercial sufficiency. Eadmer of Canterbury (d.*c.*1126) enthused that: 'England has great native and imported riches, not only does it have quantities of worldly goods, but it thrives with a great abundance of most holy men; as a result of their merits God has adorned the island munificently.'[2] The Flemish monk Goscelin of St Bertin, writing about 1100, was moved to eulogize on the glories of England: 'You must know that all earthly riches and delights, which in other places exist only individually, are here found gathered together.' And he went on to extol its 'fertile fields, flourishing meadows, broad swathes of arable land, rich pastures, flocks dripping with milk, spirited horses and flocks'.[3]

Map of Norman England and Wales.

The *Liber Eliensis* (*c*.1170) observed that the Isle of Ely was 'most delightful for charming fields and pastures … remarkable for beasts of the chase … fertile in flocks and herds'[4] and goes on to describe the variety and abundance of fish and wildfowl. Such accounts are not necessarily attempting to reflect a geographical reality but are portraying an idyllic impression of

England. They marked the beginning of what Gillingham calls 'the English view of history, the great English historical myth'.[5] Nevertheless, these claims do contain an element of truth; in the words of one Anglo-Saxon scholar: 'On the eve of the Norman Conquest, England had become an exceptionally wealthy, highly urbanized kingdom, with a large, well-controlled coinage of high quality.'[6]

The political geography of the country was the sum of past invasions, migrations and settlements, and this was reflected culturally, particularly in language and custom. Anglo-Saxon England had been subject to military, political and cultural contact with Scandinavia from the late eighth century onwards. As a result of Danish invasions in the late ninth century, the Danelaw was established in thirteen counties in eastern England between the rivers Tees and Thames. Language, laws, place names and personal names were all affected by Scandinavian practices in areas under the Danelaw.

English monarchs had close dealings with other parts of Continental Europe from the mid-ninth to the mid-eleventh century, particularly through marriage alliances with the aristocratic rulers of West Francia, Flanders and Normandy. Most famously, William the Conqueror's great-aunt Emma (c.985–1052), daughter of Duke Richard II of Normandy, had married two kings of England, Aethelred II (the Unready) Unready (d.1016) and Cnut (1016–35). Ironically, Aethelred married Emma as part of a plan to safeguard his southern shores against Scandinavian incursions. Emma no doubt brought an entourage of Frankish courtiers with her, and her son Edward the Confessor spent over a quarter of a century in exile on the Continent, much of the time at the Norman ducal court, and was clearly moulded by his long exposure to French culture. There was a small but growing number of Frenchmen in England during the first half of the eleventh century, as a consequence of the closer political and commercial ties between France and England. These incomers tended to be assimilated as 'Englishmen'; Englishness in the eleventh century 'just meant being in England'.[7]

The death of Edward the Confessor (d. 5/6 January 1066) without an immediate heir prompted another invasion, from the north in September 1066. This was in the form of a largely Norwegian force led by King Harald Hardrada, a contender for the English throne, together with King Harold's half-brother, Tostig. The decisive defeat of these invaders at Stamford Bridge, just three weeks before the Battle of Hastings, did not signify the end of Scandinavian interest in England, but it was a turning point. Thereafter, Danish expeditions to Norman England were faced with overcoming a far more heavily defended country and tended to demand payments instead of territorial control. The Norman Conquest marked a significant change in the axis of European influence in English politics and culture. After 1066 the Scandinavian impact on England did not disappear entirely, but it decreased and was replaced mainly by that of the Franks.

Landscapes of Governance

On the eve of the Norman Conquest, England, albeit somewhat politically unstable, was the most well-organized state in western Europe, with a bureaucracy that had developed out of various Anglo-Saxon, Scandinavian and Celtic administrative structures. It is worth outlining the anatomy of these arrangements as they generated much of the information on which our understanding of the landscape is based. On 12 July 927 Aethelstan was recognized as king of the English, when the surviving Anglo-Saxon kingdoms of Wessex, Mercia and Northumbria had joined together to establish a united England. However, England was not a nation state in the later sense of the term and there remained profound regional differences and divisions, particularly between the predominantly Anglo-Saxon south and the Anglo-Scandinavian north and east. Under King Cnut the country was divided into earldoms – mini-kingdoms that roughly reflected the old order – Wessex, East Anglia, Mercia, Northumbria, Kent, Essex and Middlesex, and Northamptonshire and Huntingdonshire.

By 1066 central administration was in the hands of the king and his council of advisors, the *Witan*, which consisted of the archbishops of Canterbury and York, bishops, abbots, earls, kinsmen of the king, plus the great magnates. The *Witan* met at least once a year but normally more frequently, and was held wherever the king was at the time, be it Winchester, Gloucester, Oxford or Westminster. The different trajectories of England and France in the tenth and eleventh centuries point to the fundamental importance of these royal assemblies in attracting leading members of the nobility on a regular basis. In England, the landed elite travelled long distances when summoned by the Crown, which was not the case in the diminished kingdom of France. The English nobility were drawn by the access to power such meetings gave them, where kings were made and crowned and their position was confirmed at crown-wearing ceremonies performed during the principal religious festivals. Laws were passed, state trials were heard and decisions were made relating to war, peace and taxation as well as the management of the Church. A second and even more compulsive reason was that their presence at such assemblies gave them access to wealth and a forum to compete for royal patronage. (See Plate 1)

Wickham has argued that the basic difference between England and France at this time was that the Frankish royal demesne had contracted to a relatively small core area around Paris in the tenth century, as the Crown's functions were taken over by dukes and counts in the different principalities. In contrast, the English royal demesne had grown rapidly through the conquest of Danish-controlled parts of lowland Britain. By the acquisition of these widespread landholdings the English Crown was immensely wealthy, and therefore had much more to give away and bargain with than its French counterpart. The Domesday Book shows that on his death in January 1066, King Edward was an order of magnitude richer than any other lord in the kingdom. The king enjoyed extensive powers of patronage, not only because of his personal wealth but also because he retained considerable control of the wealth of the earls and the main holders of office, who held their positions on a temporary *ex officio* basis.[8]

Next to the king the earls were the most powerful men in England, military leaders who commanded levies on behalf of the king.[9] The earldoms were not rigid geographical areas and in practice their boundaries were fluid and fragile. The events of 1066 can indirectly be attributed to a delicate power structure, in which factional and family rivalry was endemic. In 1051 the *Anglo-Saxon Chronicle* reported that civil war was only averted because wise men argued that this would open 'a way for our enemies to enter the country and to cause great ruin among ourselves'. The defeat of the English at Hastings led to the immediate decline in the importance of the earldoms, and with the execution of the last of the English earls, Waltheof, in 1075 the title became largely honorific, except for those in the Welsh Marches.

England south of the Tees was divided into administrative shires. Some shires represented older units such as the Anglo-Saxon kingdoms of Kent, Sussex, Surrey, Essex and Middlesex, while others were ancient administrative regions like the shires of Wessex – Berkshire, Dorset, Hampshire, Somerset and Wiltshire. Others had developed around the headquarters of Danish armies at Lincoln, Derby, Nottingham and Leicester. Most of the remaining Midland counties had been created in the early eleventh century as the power of Wessex kings spread into Mercia, but even then, they were often based on older tribal territorial units.[10] Each county was in the charge of a 'shire-reeve' or 'sheriff', the representative of the Crown who executed writs, collected taxation and supervised the maintenance of the king's peace. Between them, earl and sheriff oversaw a reasonably well-integrated system of local government. The primary forum in which they operated was the shire court, to which the greatest landholders of the shire paid suit. This was where the king's pleas were heard, felonies tried and other matters that affected the interests of the king were determined. More mundane business, both judicial and administrative, was delegated to local courts.[11] With the establishment of counties came the shire capitals – towns, part of whose function was to administer local government, including the collection of taxes. These tended to be larger settlements with mints, markets and in some cases demarcated by a defensive circuit.

The extensive county of Yorkshire was a successor to the Viking kingdom of York and in the Domesday Book it covered what later became northern Lancashire and parts of Westmorland and Cumberland. The remainder of these counties remained part of Scotland until 1092: Cumberland, Westmorland, Lancashire, County Durham and Northumberland were only established as English counties in the twelfth century. There were few towns of any significance to the north of York, apart from the ecclesiastical centre at Durham.

The shires were divided into hundreds, or wapentakes and carucates in the old Danelaw counties. These were established for military, taxation and judicial purposes, and each one theoretically contained 100 hides. In the Midlands, the hundreds, which were created at the same time as the shires, were of a fairly uniform size, but they ranged from 4.6 square km (Worth, Kent) to 982 square km (Salford, Lancashire). According to Edward the Elder's early-tenth-century law code, assemblies were to be held every four weeks, an interval that could be charted according to the lunar cycle.

The 'hide' may have originally represented the area of land sufficient to support a family, but varied in size from 60 to 180 acres (24–73 hectares) from region to region, depending on the quality of the soil and on local customs and usage. By the time of the Conquest the hide had become the basic unit of taxation across much of England and was used by the Normans to fix feudal dues. Under the Anglo–Saxon kings, every five hides of land owed the Crown one armed and

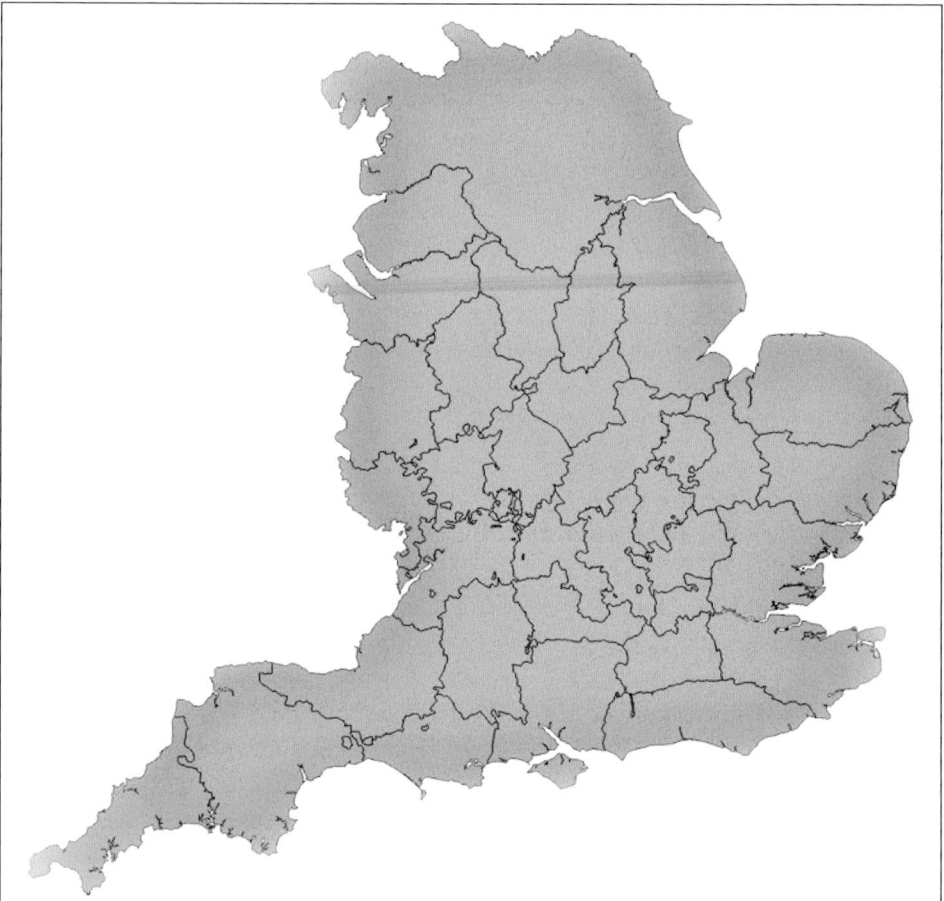

Map showing the Domesday counties.

Map of the Domesday hundreds. (Eljas Oksanen, research assistant at the Portable Antiquities Scheme at the British Museum, uses the shapefile of Domesday hundreds investigating the development of markets, fairs and commercial organization in medieval England and Wales.)

provisioned soldier for sixty days of military service in the royal army (*fyrd*), when the king went on expedition. Thus, landowners – thegns – were required to recruit and arm soldiers on the basis of their landed wealth. This arrangement was adopted and developed by William after the Conquest as part of what is conventionally known as the feudal system.

Manors

In the mid-Saxon era, the Anglo-Saxon subkingdoms of Britain had been divided into 'multiple' estates, which consisted of widely dispersed holdings with a mix of land quality and resources from whence royal, aristocratic or monastic households were provided with the commodities they required. Though such estates survived into the later Anglo-Saxon period in the north in particular, from the tenth century onwards, and possibly earlier, many of these estates were broken up into smaller, discrete holdings, known as manors after 1066. Some of the large land units found in the Domesday Book were vestiges of these estates and it is clear that they formed one of the most significant building blocks of the later English Medieval landscape.

After the Conquest much of England was divided into small, landed estates called manors (L. *manerium*). Although manors first appear in the Domesday Book, important elements of the manorial system were already in place before 1066, with Saxon thegns instead of Norman lords as chief tenants. The manor defined the relationship between the lord, be it king, bishop, abbot or baron, and the serfs and peasants, who worked the land, under his control. The manor was an economic, political and judicial unit and was the basic element of tenure between 1066 and 1300. Normally, the manor would comprise the lord's manor house, chapel and demesne, that is, land retained for the lord's own profit, plus land farmed by his tenants, namely, common ploughland and meadowland, and common grazings, woodland and wasteland. The manor was governed by the manor court where various taxes and fines were imposed, but free tenants enjoyed rights beyond those laid down by the manor. By 1200 there were a range of elected or salaried manorial officials, according to the size and wealth of the manor; frequently, these were drawn from among the manorial tenants. These could include forest haywards, rent collectors, warreners, parkers, woodkeepers and grangers, all of whom would have been supervised by a reeve or bailiff. The responsibilities of the officials included the purchase and sale of livestock, decisions upon the combination of crops to be sown on the lord's demesne, the leasing of mills, the supervision of the harvest and policing the labour obligations of the tenants.

Manors varied considerably in size and shape, and although most were compact and easily identifiable units, frequently coextensive with an ecclesiastical parish, others consisted of land in different villages or even counties. Some had no demesne or villeins or even manor house. The manor was a volatile unit and could be amalgamated, divided and subdivided over the generations; in the longer term, the ecclesiastical parish proved to be a more robust local administrative unit and over time increasingly took on secular functions.

There were numerous regional variations and customs within this system of administration and landholding, but it was sufficiently uniform to provide a degree of organizational coherence to English local government in the mid–eleventh century. It also provided a working link between the centre of royal government and the regions. Having said that, royal control was significantly weaker in the north and the west than in the south. The Anglo–Norman chronicler Orderic Vitalis (1075–*c*.1142) went so far as to claim that when William the Conqueror came to England, he found that 'in the northern and western extremities of the kingdom an unchecked savagery ruled until now and under Edward the Confessor and his predecessors, those areas had disdained to obey the king of England unless it suited them'.

The Church in Late Saxon England

By 1066, England was split into the two large metropolitan sees based on Canterbury and York; these in turn were divided into regional bishoprics, such as Winchester in the south and Durham in the north. The bishops were spiritual leaders of the Church as well as royal officers in their diocese. Many of the English dioceses were much larger than their counterparts in France and Flanders, having been linked to former kingdoms rather than long-established Roman administrative territories, found in much of western and southern Europe. Consequently, many of the English diocesan centres did not control secular government, as several cathedrals were sited in remote, inconvenient locations. For example, Dorchester on Thames was the seat of a diocese that extended over 350 kilometres northwards, from the River Thames in the south to the River Humber in the north. Dorchester had been a Roman town and was an ancient centre of Christianity, but it was little more than a village by 1066 and had been chosen for political and strategic reasons as the centre of a vast Midland diocese. Soon after the Conquest the cathedral was moved north to the former Roman city of Lincoln.

At the close of Aethelred II's reign (c.1016), categories of churches were described as 'head minster, minster, lesser church with graveyard, field church or country chapel'. The head minsters were the cathedrals, while the minsters were mother churches with responsibility for large territories. Such minsters were staffed by groups of clergy, trained as part of the bishop's staff or *familia*, who served the area over which the church had responsibility. In general, the minster clergy were priests living in communities with the task of carrying religion to the ecclesiastically unorganized territories dependent on the minsters. They were

Pre- and post-Conquest dioceses, AD1000 and AD1200.

authorized to baptize, marry, bury the dead and celebrate mass, and carry out other necessary pastoral work.

In the second half of the tenth century, parts of the English Church were reformed by Saxon clerics such as Dunstan, Oswald and Aethelwold. Before this, cathedrals and major monasteries were staffed by secular clergy, who could own property, marry and follow a variety of rules governing how they should live their lives. The reformers promoted the much tighter rule of Benedict of Nursia, already found in many abbeys in Continental Europe. The Benedictine Rule emphasized the importance of education and art, literature, book production and musical composition, and Aethelwold, in particular, insisted that all churchmen and women should be celibate monks or nuns.

By the end of the tenth century at least twenty-five new monasteries had been established at places such as Cerne, Eynsham and Abbotsbury, while many ancient centres such as Peterborough, Abingdon and Muchelney had been refounded after the disruption brought about by the Vikings. Because of the great Norman rebuilding that was to follow, few physical remains of these establishments remain to be seen above ground level. Their plans were less regular in layout than after 1066; formal cloisters were not introduced until after the Conquest and there seem to have been a series of free-standing buildings, sometimes with more than one church. Many of these late Saxon monasteries were laid out on level or gently sloping ground adjacent to a river that supplied water throughout the site.

During the tenth century, abbeys such as Abingdon were able to reclaim large estates that they had lost during the Viking era. At Ely, for instance, the *Anglo-Saxon Chronicle* records that Abbot Aethelwold (d.984) 'bought many villages from the king and made it rich'. The monasteries were also enticing wealthy patrons to endow them. Byrhtnoth (d.991), an *ealdorman* of Essex, gave land to Ely, as did the two subsequent generations of his family. Such was the scale of land accumulation by the late Saxon monasteries that it is estimated that by the early eleventh century one-sixth of land revenue was in their hands.[12]

The Domesday Book

The Domesday Book provides a picture of England in 1066 under Anglo-Saxon stewardship, and then in 1086, when it was in the hands of its new, essentially French, lords. Although it is a Norman construct, this great survey was compiled using Saxon administrative tools. It is particularly important in terms of local and landscape history, not least because it marks the first historical appearance for the names of the majority of English villages and hamlets. It incorporates the first record of 95 per cent of the 13,418 places listed in 1086, making the Domesday record the natural starting point for most local historians researching the history of their area. Its value can be seen in the East Riding of Yorkshire where only four place names are recorded before 1086; the Domesday Book names another 437.

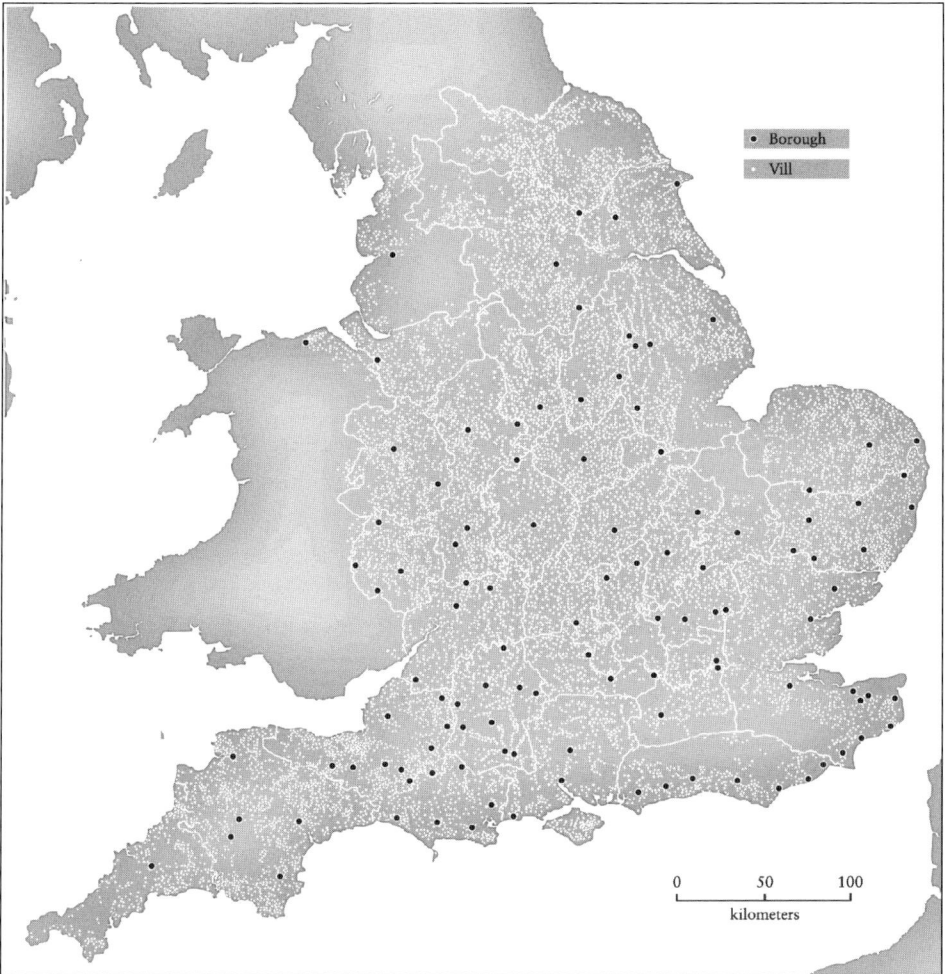

Map of Domesday settlements.

For almost four decades in the mid–twentieth century, the historical geographer H.C. Darby undertook the mammoth task of mapping the geography of the Domesday Book, using traditional cartographic techniques. Although the *Domesday Geographies* have aged with time they still provide a valuable starting point for the landscape historian trying to understand the character of late Saxon England.[13] In the decades that have passed since the last of his surveys was published in 1976, there have been dramatic changes in the interpretation of the Domesday Book and how it was made; not least in the application of digital interrogation and map–making software to enable geographical interpretation and mapping of Domesday materials, taking analysis to a new level.[14]

Historians and historical geographers have new tools with which to work, but we are still some distance from having a comprehensive new Domesday geography

Sir Henry Clifford Darby (1909-1992).
(*Department of Geography, University College London*)

of England. It is an immensely detailed and complex document with which generations of scholars have wrestled in order to interpret its contents: 'The resulting literature is as controversial as it is voluminous' observed one historian recently.[15] Another historian, Knowles, was moved to observe that Domesday studies have come to resemble 'one of the more abstruse branches of nuclear physics'.[16] Historians have for long ceased to take everything in Domesday at face value as the survey is far from a comprehensive account of the conquered land, and is normally interested in only taxable items. Landscape historians have to work hard to extract topographical details; indeed, 'Domesday evidence supplies us with an image of eleventh-century England which has been refracted through a complex series of lenses.'[17]

In the late eleventh century in the countryside, manorial land was rented out by the lord to peasants, who were categorized as either free or unfree. The free peasantry was made up of freemen and sokemen, who formed about 12 per cent of the population in 1086, which represented a significant decline from 1066. Free peasants were largely restricted to the north and east of England, in the area approximately corresponding to the Danelaw. The largest and wealthiest category of unfree peasants were the villeins, who formed about 40 per cent of the recorded population. Villeins could hold up to 30 or 40 acres, but were required to work on the lord's land for a specified period each week. Bordars and cottars (cottagers), who made up about 30 per cent of the recorded population, held smaller plots of land and owed a greater length of service to the lord. At the bottom of the social scale were the slaves, who formed about 10 per cent of the population and were literally owned by their lord. The number of slaves varied regionally, with a higher proportion in the west and south-west of England. There were other categories of specialized countryside workers, such as millers, swineherds, vine dressers, foresters and stockmen, whose numbers were recorded erratically in the Domesday Book. Additionally, there were specialists such as engineers, steersmen, stonemasons and oddly a female jester, employed by Earl Roger of Hereford.

A recent review of aspects of the Domesday coverage of Suffolk demonstrates how new approaches can be used profitably to understand the mid-eleventh-century landscape.[18] This elegant study uses data contained in the Little Domesday, which was the first draft or 'circuit summary' covering the counties of Essex, Norfolk and Suffolk. Because the information from Little Domesday was never entered into Great Domesday, Little Domesday was kept as the final record for East Anglia. Among other conclusions it finds that carucates were not Danish as is normally argued, but were probably introduced after the reconquest of the Danelaw. Furthermore, Barlow claims that the carucate was specifically a record of 120 acres of actual arable land rather than a financial device as often argued. Detailed analysis of meadowland shows that it was much more extensive in the middle and upper reaches of the main river valleys and their tributaries than towards the coast. This was a factor of grass having shallow roots, making it very susceptible to drought in soils such as peat which dry out quickly. Overall, Suffolk meadow appears to have formed narrow riverside ribbons of land partitioned into chains of small acre and half-acre enclosures. Another conclusion suggests that the most efficient plough teams were operated by slaves, who were trained to be skilful ploughmen, exacting maximum yields from the soil.

Some elements of Darby's Domesday England are revisited briefly below in order to establish a framework for landscape discussions in later chapters.

The Saxo-Norman Village

The Norman Conquest straddles the period in which nucleated villages are established in many parts of the kingdom. Our understanding of the development of the English medieval village is still not complete, but it seems clear that villages in midland England and beyond were coalescing out of a spread of hamlets and isolated farms within the multiple estates into nucleated units between the ninth and thirteenth centuries.

The break-up of an ancient, large estate at Fawsley (Northamptonshire) resulted in the creation of four small manors between 944 and 1023, and two of these had been split up into eight by the time of the Domesday Book.[19] One of the most detailed examinations of the evolution of settlement was undertaken by Aston and Gerrard at Shapwick in Somerset. The estate had been given to Glastonbury Abbey in the eighth century as part of a larger, sixty-hide grant, which included what was to become the manor of Wilton. In the second half of the tenth century, Shapwick was divided up into six separate estates, of around five hides each; these became the villages of Woolavington, Cossington, Chilton Polden, Edington, Catcott and Shapwick. The division seems to have been carefully planned and designed to ensure that each of these smaller units had access to water, pasture and other necessary natural resources. At the same time, numerous scattered settlements were abandoned and new nucleated villages established. In what was to become the village of Shapwick itself, earlier settlements strung out along the higher ground were succeeded by a single village, aligned roughly north–south, to the west of the pre-existing church. Two open fields were established to the east and the west of the new village, and much of the woodland to the north was cleared to provide meadows and pasture.[20] The importance of the restructuring of the landscape cannot be overestimated; in the opinion of one scholar: 'This revelation of a great replanning of the midland countryside in the late Saxon period, at least equal to that which followed the enclosures of a millennium later, is one of the great discoveries of British archaeology of the later twentieth century.'[21]

Aerial view of Shapwick, Somerset, showing the earthworks that constituted part of the nucleated medieval village. (*Mick Aston*)

There was no significant change in the form of village houses during the immediate post-Conquest period, although the manor house and manor farm assumed a greater significance in the village than their Saxon predecessors. Excavations at Goltho (Lincolnshire) demonstrate the fundamental way a late Saxon thegn's house changed to become a Norman manor. The manorial establishment comprised a substantial hall, which was rebuilt several times in the tenth and eleventh centuries, together with an area defined by a simple boundary bank and ditch, which was not defensive. The Normans built a defensive ringwork with a large bank and ditch within which there was a smaller hall and a defensive tower. The farm buildings were built in an outer enclosure and so separated off from the main living accommodation. The difference between life under the Norman lord and that under the Saxon thegn living in his hall, set in the middle of farm buildings, bounded only by a slight earthwork, is demonstrated here. After 1066, when an alien lord took up residence among a potentially hostile population, the living and farm activities were separated from one another and the Norman lord was set apart in a defended enclosure. By the twelfth century, as times became more settled and relations between seigneur and peasant had become more relaxed, the ringwork was levelled to form a platform for a large aisled hall. Within the ditch there was only room for the hall, kitchen and another small building; therefore, with the need for a larger, more compact establishment in the thirteenth century, the manor was moved about half a mile to a new site to the south where a moated manorial complex was constructed.

Domestic artefacts found on Norman village sites show relatively little change from the Saxon period, although the range and sophistication of items, particularly in relation to dress, become larger in the second half of the twelfth century. The range of pottery forms also becomes greater and there is evidence

Cooks watching a pot suspended above the flames, in the Norman manner from the Bayeux Tapestry. (*McClain and Sykes, 2019*)

of imported wares being brought into eastern England. In some western parts of England, locally fired pottery makes a reappearance at this stage, after an absence of several centuries. It has been pointed out that even if there was no significant change in domestic artefacts after 1066, such items were sometimes used in different ways. For example, before the Conquest, cooking pots tended to be placed directly on to the fire to heat, while afterwards they tended to be suspended above the hearth, as illustrated on the Bayeux Tapestry.

Agriculture and Field Systems

The references to over 80,000 plough teams in 1086 highlight eleventh-century dependence on arable farming, a proportion of which would have been carried out in the open fields that were a central feature of later medieval farming. At the time of the Domesday survey, approximately 35 per cent of England was under arable, 25 per cent was pasture, 15 per cent was covered by woodland and the remaining 25 per cent was under moorland, fens and heaths. Wheat was the most important arable crop, but rye, barley and oats were cultivated extensively. In the most productive areas, such as the Thames Valley and East Anglia, legumes and beans were also grown. Meadow, pasture and woodland are also recorded extensively and specialist agricultural activity is mentioned in some regions; for example, stock-rearing was important in the south-west. Meadowland is recorded in a belt of country stretching from Wiltshire in the west to the Fenlands in the east.

There is no consensus about the evolution of the field systems in which crops were grown and animals were kept.[22] In a recent comprehensive review of the topic, Hall warned: 'There can be no historically satisfactory account or proof of the origin of open fields – their creation is lost in time without written records.'[23] The predominant system which was found in one form or another in England by the thirteenth century relied upon a division of land into strips – normally scattered throughout two, three or more open fields. The method of organizing the agricultural regime involving rotation of cultivation depended upon a wide variety of different customs and obligations. The question that has exercised historians, geographers and archaeologists is, when and over what length of time did this system supersede the 'Celtic' or Romano-British system of square and rectangular enclosed fields? The view that the open-field system was brought in by Anglo-Saxon settlers has long been discarded. It seems unlikely that the changes were ethnically linked, although some historians have suggested that they represented a response to Scandinavian political advances. Hooke and others have argued that there was open-field agriculture in parts of the Midlands by at least the late ninth and early tenth centuries, and this was linked to a replanning of the whole landscape. 'The bringing together of estate tenants from scattered farms and small hamlets into larger nucleated settlements may have occurred at the same time as the creation of new, integrated, arable landholding patterns, the great open-field systems of medieval England.'[24] Another study, in west Cambridgeshire, indicates that a proto-open field system was laid out over four contiguous parishes in the Bourn Valley in the eighth or ninth century. The author suggests that this was the work of a central authority operating within an extensive estate.[25]

A switch occurred during the late Anglo-Saxon period from a plough suited to the needs of individual farmers, to one best used collaboratively with up to eight farmers combining their oxen and cultivating more productive, heavier soils. The adoption of the mouldboard plough enabled the cultivation of heavier land and thus maximized the area under cereals. There was, however, a need to use it efficiently, establish holdings of the right size, reorganize farms into strips spread evenly across several fields and impose a system of crop rotation capable of delivering fallow. The presence on some Domesday manors of far more ploughs than ploughlands suggests that these economies were not always realized. At Gunthorpe (Nottinghamshire), land for six ploughs supported four demesne ploughs and a further sixteen ploughs in the hands of the forty-seven manorial tenants, so a total of twenty ploughs, of which only six were required.

Recent analysis of late Saxon and Norman agricultural practices has emphasised the essential role domesticated animals played in society. Sheep, cattle, oxen and pigs were the main livestock reared.[26] Work on animal bones found on a variety of sites indicates subtle changes in the eating habits of different elements in society, with increased meat and fish consumption amongst the elite. Apart from the oxen who were used for pulling plough teams and pigs which were recorded as a measure of woodland, livestock is only chronicled erratically in the Domesday Book. We do hear that some parts of the country were devoted to sheep-farming, with flocks in excess of 1,000 recorded in 1086. More sheep than all other livestock put together are documented in Domesday, even so this is a gross underestimate.

January ploughing scene from a late Anglo-Saxon calendar (*BL., Cotton Julius A vi*)

Sawyer has argued that there were more sheep in England in 1086 than during the height of the wool boom in the later Middle Ages.[27] If sheep were farmed on this scale, then their wool was probably even at that date the major English export. Henry of Huntingdon marvelled at the foreign earnings of the 'flocks without number' and 'their precious wool'.

In Essex, pasture for sheep is frequently mentioned, but pastures that are assigned to some inland villages actually lay on coastal marshland in detached portions of their manors. The coastal areas of East Anglia and land adjoining salt marshes and fens were also used extensively for sheep-rearing. At Stallingborough (Lincolnshire) there was a shearing house, while sheepfolds were recorded at Eynesbury (Huntingdonshire) and Kempsford (Gloucestershire). In the early twelfth century the Abbey aux Dames in Caen kept flocks of sheep at Avening and Minchinhampton in the Gloucestershire Cotswolds. Sheep were also valued for their milk and manure and in East Anglia there are frequent references to fold-soke, the obligation for a tenant's sheep to manure his lord's demesne land. In addition to sheep, cattle and swine and a surprisingly large number of goats are mentioned, with the greatest concentration in Devon, Somerset and Suffolk.[28]

After the Conquest, in the twelfth century we hear of dedicated cattle farms, vaccaries, often located in forests such as Windsor and the New, but Domesday also mentions such farms in the upland areas of northern England, at Denby, near Penistone in the Pennines, for example. At Buckland, Berkshire, a dairy farm with 220 acres of meadow produced 10 weys of cheese, a wey being roughly 182lb (82.5kg). The monks of Pershore Abbey in Worcestershire were also attributed with a dedicated cattle farm in 1066.[29]

Tending sheep in May from a late Anglo–Saxon calendar (*BL., Cotton Julius A vi*)

Fishing

Large numbers of freshwater and coastal fisheries are described in the Domesday Book, although coverage is uneven. The importance of fishing in the late Saxon world is revealed in the conversation of Aelfric, the Abbot of Eynsham Abbey, Oxfordshire (*c*.955-1010):

> I am a fisherman … I lay down nets in the stream from my boat, and I set baited hooks and creels.
> I catch eels, pike, minnows, burbots, trout and lampreys, and whatever swims in the flowing stream.
> Sometimes I go to sea and there I catch herring, salmon, porpoise, sturgeon, oyster crab, mussels, winkles, place, soles and lobster; but I do so rarely because a large ship is needed on the sea.
> And I do not join the whalers because it is too dangerous, though I may receive a high price for whales.[30]

Quantities of herring, smelt, flatfish and whiting bones found at Westminster Abbey point to the consumption of considerable quantities of sea fish during the late Saxon period, but the Domesday survey concentrates mainly on inland fishing along rivers and streams.[31] The Thames, Trent, Nene, Bedfordshire Ouse, Wye, Avon, the Severn estuary, the Fens and the Somerset Levels were particularly important fish-producing locations. At Tidenham (Gloucestershire), on the northern shore of the Severn estuary, there were nearly seventy fisheries in 1086. Inland fishing is documented in relation to renders and to the infrastructure of fishing, such as weirs and fish traps. The flow of water through millponds would also have suited barbel, trout and grayling. Although millers and fish farmers required different regimes of water storage and release, undoubtedly some millponds would also have been used to breed fish and significantly 100 Domesday mills paid rent in eels. Weirs are referred to in Cambridgeshire, Hertfordshire and Middlesex, while a 'new fishery' at Monkton (Kent) is also likely to indicate the presence of a fixed structure.

There are rare references to fishing boats, as at Peterborough, Ramsey and Thorney abbeys, and a toll of 6 shillings was placed on fishing nets at Swaffham (Norfolk). Eels are the most commonly mentioned species, and there are a few references to salmon and renders of herring from the east coast. The *Urbanus Magnus*, a twelfth-century poem attributed to Daniel of Beccles, mentions a wider range of fish and seafood including herring, red mullet, salmon, eel, roach, pike, perch, turbot and dace, as well as whale and seal.[32]

Devices for trapping fish in non-estuarine rivers included nets, weirs or 'weres' and traps, both permanent and portable. Some of these devices may have used artificial islands or islets to anchor one end of a net, and many river islands may

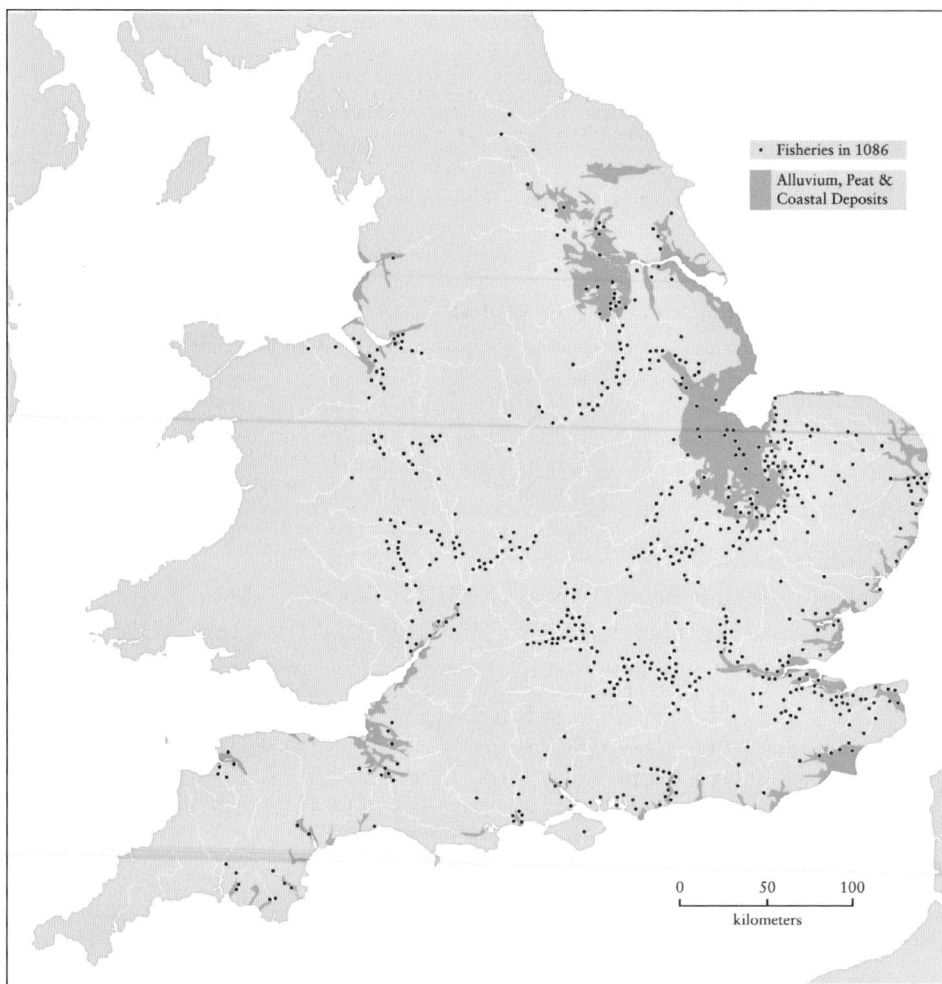

Map of Domesday fisheries, mainly located along rivers.

have originated in this way. Weirs were barriers set up often in intertidal zones and designed to channel fish into traps. They were constructed with stone walls and wattle or timber fencing. The most common form of weir was a simple V-shaped arrangement of walls which could stretch up to 100m in length. At the point of the 'V' there would have been a basket, normally pointing towards the sea in order to draw fish in from the receding tide. Most of this category of weir, such as those at Tidenham, were placed on gently shelving coastal or estuarine locations and would become sufficiently exposed at low tide for the fish to be collected. The Domesday Book refers to a foreshore fishery as a 'sea hedge' belonging to Bury St Edmunds Abbey at Southwold. There is evidence, notably from the River Witham, Lincolnshire, indicating that some fisheries had associated buildings, sited on mounds, where the catch was processed.[33]

The remains of about 500 fish weirs (of all dates) survive around the coast of England. A well-preserved fish weir with large sections of protruding timber can be found at Mersea Island in the Blackwater and Colne estuaries to the south-east of Colchester in Essex. This weir could be one of the three fisheries recorded for Mersea Island in the Domesday Book. Mersea was already under the control of Normans before 1066 as it had been given to St Ouen Abbey, Rouen, by Edward the Confessor in 1046.

One element curiously missing in the late Saxon landscape is the dedicated fishpond, which was a feature on thousands of post-Conquest manors. There is little field evidence for fishponds prior to 1066, which is difficult to explain given that water management of various types was well established in late Saxon England. We know, for instance, that the monks of Abingdon Abbey were involved in diverting the Thames at Abingdon and digging an artificial navigation channel called the Swift Ditch before the Norman Conquest, and there are many other examples of Saxon canals and other artificial watercourses at places such as Glastonbury Abbey.[34]

There are no documented pre-Conquest fishponds, although the Utrecht Psalter does depict a 'pool with fish'. The Domesday Book records fishponds at two abbeys, and it is probable that they were there before 1066: St Albans Abbey held a park for wild beasts and a fishpond in St Albans and Bury St Edmunds Abbey held two fishponds in the town. A writ of Henry II permitted the monks of Selby Abbey to have a fishpond 'which existed when the abbey was founded', i.e. before 1070. At Sharnbrook (Bedfordshire), the holding of Osbern the fisherman included a *vivarium piscium*, where there is still 'a kind of dock … which, if controlled by a sluice would make an excellent stewpond'.[35] There are several

Medieval fish trap at West Mersea, Essex. (*Ron Hall*)

other variations on the term *vivarium piscium* in the survey, which probably refer to short-term storage ponds for fish caught in rivers and intended for consumption. Many early medieval moats and artificial lakes built for defence or fashion would have contained water suitable for pike, bream and eel. One much-quoted early reference to the creation of a pool that served as a fishpond was in relation to the building of a dam across the River Foss between Layerthorpe and Foss Bridge at York. This created a lake called the King's Fishpool, constructed by William the Conqueror in 1069 and stocked with bream and pike. It was built in order to make approaches to the city from the east more difficult and its construction resulted in severe disruption of the townscape, including the inundation of property, 50 hectares of arable land, meadows and gardens, the clearance of two new mills and the rerouting of roads.[36]

Industry

Industry, like some agricultural activities, would have been temporarily disrupted in the years after the Conquest, but in the longer term would have expanded to meet the needs of the explosion of building activity and growing population that were features of the twelfth-century economy. Quarrying and mineral working would have been present in the late Saxon landscape, but were only erratically recorded in the Domesday survey. This may reflect their relative unimportance or may point to a system of *ad hoc* quarrying, where pits were opened as the need arose for specific building works.[37] The only Cotswold stone quarry recorded in the Domesday Book is that at Taynton, Oxfordshire, while there is no mention of those at Barnack, Cambridgeshire, or the Lincolnshire limestone quarries, which must have been active. There is evidence to show that stone was being imported from northern France. One of Bishop Odo of Bayeux's vassals, Vitalis, was transporting ready-worked Caen stone for the new royal palace at Westminster, and Abbot Scolland imported stone from Marquise near Boulogne for St Augustine's, Canterbury.[38] Millstones were also carried considerable distances, some from the Continent and others from the English deposits of millstone grit, such as those in the Derbyshire Pennines. The quarries at Bignor (Sussex) and Whatton (Nottinghamshire) produced millstones from the Upper Greensand (a fine-grained sandstone) and Keuper beds (sandstone), respectively.[39]

Clearly when substantial Anglo-Saxon buildings were destroyed, in advance of the great rebuilding of cathedrals, their stone was reused and, in some cases, as at Winchester and St Augustine's, Canterbury, their foundations were dug up and used as well.

Ploughshares, farm implements, horseshoes and weaponry were universally used, yet iron ore extraction and ironworking are only recorded for a handful of counties. There is a single reference to ironworking at Grinstead in the Sussex

Weald, which must have been an important manufacturing area, while Cornish tin-working is not recorded at all.

Lead-working is recorded in the Mendips, the Peak District of Derbyshire, the Cheviots and the Welsh Marches. William the Conqueror seems to have taken a particular interest in the Derbyshire lead mines, entrusting the custody of the Peak Forest to William Peverel, who built Peveril Castle on a dominant site overlooking the Derbyshire Peak District. The 'Carlisle Mine' in the northern Pennines

Above: Peveril Castle, Derbyshire, with Lose Hill in background. The castle was originally built in the eleventh century to control the Peak Forest, which contained valuable silver, lead and timber resources. (*Darren Copley*)

Left: Image of an early medieval lead worker, known as the T'owd Man, carrying a pick and basket, originally from St James, Bonsall, Derbyshire (*Toni Watts*)

dominated the English market during the twelfth century, experiencing a boom between 1130 and 1180. Lead was produced not only for home consumption, but was also exported in large quantities to France. Henry II sent lead from the Carlisle mine to Grandmont Abbey in the Limousin and the castle at Gisors in the Norman Vexin, and two hundred cartloads were shipped to Clairvaux Abbey in Burgundy via Newcastle and Rouen in 1179.

Salt

One industry which is well represented in the great survey is salt manufacture. Salt was a vital commodity used in the preservation of meat and fish, for some tanning and cloth-dyeing processes and for glazing in the pottery industry, and it was the most fully recorded industry in the Domesday Book. King William's half-brother Robert of Mortain held the largest number of salt works, 148 in four counties, while the monarch held only marginally fewer in seven counties. Twenty-nine monastic houses held 403 salt works between them; Fécamp Abbey held the largest concentration in one location of any owner, with 100 at Rye. St Augustine's, Canterbury, held forty-eight works in Kent, one of which at Thanet was linked to two fisheries.

Salt was obtained by evaporation either from inland brine springs or from seawater, and large numbers of brine pits and salt pans are recorded in the survey as well as salt workers. Domesday also mentions lead pans, a lead smithy, furnaces and requirements for firewood. The inland centres of production were based on brine springs at Droitwich in Worcestershire and Middlewich, Nantwich and Northwich in Cheshire. Droitwich, which was the most important inland producer, had thirteen salt houses and numerous pits (*putei*) and salt pans (*salinae*), from which three salt workers paid 300 measures of salt to the king. Salt was transported considerable distances from Droitwich and other production centres, by way of a network of dedicated salt ways. Salt production in some places, such as Cheshire, was severely interrupted following the post-Conquest rebellions, but subsequently there would have been a steady increase in production to meet the demands of a growing population during the twelfth century. For example, all seven new monastic houses that were founded in Cumbria between 1088 and 1150 were granted rights to build new salt works; presumably, these would have been concentrated around Morecambe Bay, where there is extensive evidence of medieval salt-working.

There were more than 1,223 coastal salt works recorded in the Domesday Book and they are recorded in every county with a coastline, stretching from Lincolnshire to Cornwall. The chief areas of production of maritime salt were along coastal marshes and estuaries; Caister-on-Sea in eastern Norfolk, for example, had forty-five salt pans, and at Lyme (Dorset), twenty-seven salt workers were recorded. Some inland manors had coastal salterns; for instance, Castle

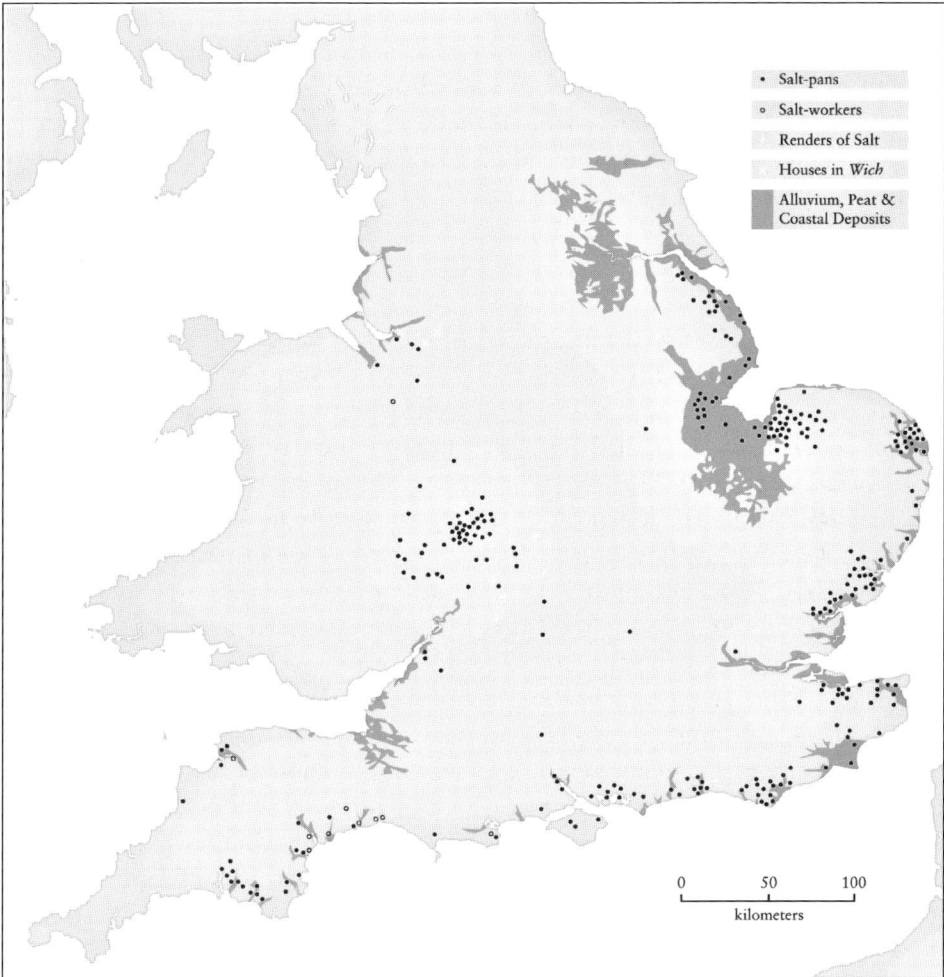

Legend:
- Salt-pans
- Salt-workers
- Renders of Salt
- Houses in *Wich*
- Alluvium, Peat & Coastal Deposits

Domesday map of salt making located along the coast and salt springs in Cheshire and Worcestershire..

Rising, which lies 8km from the sea, had thirteen salterns. Around the time of the Conquest, coastal producers maintained a significant export trade in white salt to the Continent, but later, as the population grew, England became a net importer of salt, mainly from western France.

A salt works consisted of an area of foreshore, which was divided into strips, a salt house of clay or cob, and mounds of debris from the process of salt manufacture; these are known as 'fitties' in Lincolnshire and 'red hills' in Essex and can reach a conspicuously large size. The spoil heaps gradually raise the level of the land, pushing the high-water mark and newer salt works seawards. Evidence of settlements and even churches built on top of derelict salt works can be found along the east coast.[40]

Aerial view of saltern mounds at Marsh Chapel, Lincolnshire. They are of medieval and post-medieval date and the sub-rectangular markings on some mounds may represent the outlines of former workshops. (*Historic England, monument number 81907*)

Grain Mills

Agricultural industries such as milling and viticulture are also well-represented in the Domesday folios. Watermills used for grinding corn had been a feature of the Romano-British landscape and seem to have been reintroduced to England around 700. By the time of the Norman Conquest there were over 6,000 mills, many of which were very small. Most mills were situated on a millstream or leat, an artificial channel that allowed the flow of water that drove the mill to be controlled. In other cases, the mill stood on a natural watercourse, modified with a dam and a bypass channel. The mill race often fed a millpond, and one of the most common surviving earthwork features is the dam built to retain a pond, the size of the pond and dam varying with the topography and the size of the mill to be powered.

By 1086 most communities had ready access to a corn mill. There were particularly large numbers recorded in Norfolk, Suffolk, the Cotswolds and Dorset, and low numbers in the Fens, the Somerset Levels, the Weald and the south-west of England. A lord or even a prosperous commoner would have had his own mill, and less affluent landowners would have jointly owned or shared a mill. Milling time was divided between the owner of the land on which the mill was situated, the owner of the land from which water was drawn, the owner of

Early depiction of an overshot medieval water mill *c.*1220 (*BL. Cotton MS Cleopatra C.XI, fol. 10*)

the land in which the millpond was situated and, if applicable, the operator and constructor of the mill. Such an arrangement, which must have been difficult to manage in practice, as well as divisions of property through inheritance, may have existed in late Anglo-Saxon England and may account for the shares or fractions of mills that are a feature of most counties recorded in the Domesday Book. Some mills, such as those at Frodsham and Golborne in Cheshire, are described as 'winter mills', reflecting the seasonal nature of the streams that powered them.[41]

Viticulture

One area where the Normans appear to have made a significant change is that of viticulture. In Normandy, both Mont-Saint-Michel and Fécamp are recorded as having vineyards before the Conquest, while in England, King Eadwig (d.959) confirmed Glastonbury Abbey's rights to a 'certain small portion' of a vineyard at Panborough Hill, where south-facing slopes looked out over the marshes of the Vale of Somerset. In 962, King Edgar gave 'a vineyard sited near Watchet [probably in Berkshire], with its workers' to Abingdon Abbey.[42] The tenth-century religious reforms might have led to an increase in the acreage of monastic vineyards, but the first substantive evidence for vine-growing in England comes in the Domesday record, where about forty-five places with vineyards are recorded. Of these, only that at Lorimer (Hampshire), which provided wine to St Peter's, Winchester, can unambiguously be identified as pre-Conquest. The historian Round claimed that as the majority of vineyards were measured in 'arpents', a unit in use in Normandy but not in England, most of the Domesday vineyards must have been planted after the Conquest. (An arpent roughly equates to 3,420 square metres or 1 acre.)

The growth in the number of religious houses after 1066 undoubtedly led to an increase in demand for wine, both from England and from France. Surprisingly, only fifteen of the vineyards recorded in Domesday were on monastic lands and four of these were held by secular lords. All the vineyards were on prosperous estates held by tenants-in-chief and several lords held more than one. For example, Aubrey de Vere, who appears to have been actively expanding viticulture in Essex, held four vineyards, of which two were recorded as being new in 1086. The Domesday vineyards were located to the south of a line joining the River Severn to the Wash, in three broad clusters in Essex/Suffolk, Middlesex and Somerset/Dorset. Walter, the first Norman abbot of Evesham, planted a new vineyard at Hampton (Worcestershire) between 1074 and 1086.

Vine cultivation in England seems to have reached its greatest extent between *c*.1100 and 1220, coinciding with a warmer climatic phase in western Europe.[43] The *Malmesbury Abbey Chronicle* records a vineyard being planted on south-facing slopes adjacent to the abbey by a Greek monk, who joined the community about 1084. In 1108, when the Ely Abbey estates were divided between the monastery and the new bishop, the monks retained the old vineyard and a new one was established for the bishop. The locality became known to the Normans as *l'Isle des Vignes*. One of the last entries in the Peterborough text of the *Anglo-Saxon Chronicle* records Abbot Martin of Bec planting a new vineyard there in 1137.

Map of Domesday vineyards.

emento quod anno bissextili lunae februarii xxx dies computat
ut tamen luna martii luna xxx dies habeat sic semp habeno
paschalis lunae ratio uacillet:

Workers pruning vines in February from a late Anglo–Saxon calendar. (*BL., Cotton Julius A vi*)

William of Malmesbury described the method of vine cultivation at Thorney Abbey (Cambridgeshire), where some trailed over the ground while others were supported on stakes.[44]

William also claimed that in the Vale of Gloucester, 'the vines are thicker, the grapes more plentiful and their flavour more delightful than in any other part of England ... yielding nothing to the French in sweetness'. Nevertheless, wine continued to be imported from France, the Rhineland and Burgundy after the Conquest. Wine from Normandy was associated with red painted jugs from the duchy, from Rouen in particular, which are commonly found in ports and other parts of southern England. Imports increased after 1154, when the marriage of Henry II and Eleanor of Aquitaine brought the vineyards of the Garonne region under the English Crown and much greater quantities of Gascon wine were shipped from Bordeaux to England through the ports of Bristol and Southampton.

The Domesday Book records many other landscape features, including deer parks and forests, which are discussed in later chapters.

Chapter 2

The Landscape of Invasion

Then King William came from Normandy into Pevensey.
(Anglo-Saxon Chronicle)

Invasion landing beaches, the movement of armies and the sites of battles are not usually high on the list of landscape historians' priorities. Such events tend to be left to military historians, as normally they have a minimum long-term impact on the landscape. In this respect, apart from the abbey and place name of Battle, the Norman invasion was no different, but as the story of the Battle of Hastings and Duke William's victory over King Harold are deeply embedded in the British national psyche, it is relevant to examine the narrative of the Conquest against the environment in which it occurred.

The conventional story of the invasion and the first phase of the conquest of England goes as follows. On the evening of 27 September 1066, Duke William sailed from Saint-Valéry-sur-Somme in Flanders, landing with an army the next morning at Pevensey on the southern coast of England. Soon after, William moved his army to Hastings, where it remained until 14 October when it met and defeated the English forces under King Harold at Battle, 10km to the north-west. After the Norman victory, William waited in vain for several days for the surviving English leaders to surrender, before travelling along the south coast to Dover and then on to London. After an inconclusive skirmish on London Bridge against an English force led by the royal pretender, Edgar the Aetheling, the Normans moved up the Thames Valley as far as Wallingford, where they crossed the River Thames. The army then travelled along the foot of the Chilterns and at Berkhamsted the Normans met with the English leaders, who surrendered to William. On Christmas Day 1066, Duke William of Normandy was crowned king of England in Westminster Abbey.

What was the geographical context in which these events occurred? One historical geographer has argued that 'medieval military historians have yet to demonstrate a complete understanding of the environment in which the 1066 campaign took place, and thus the event itself'.[1] The coastline of southern England that Duke William would have seen as he approached from Normandy at dawn on 28 September 1066 would have been very different from that of

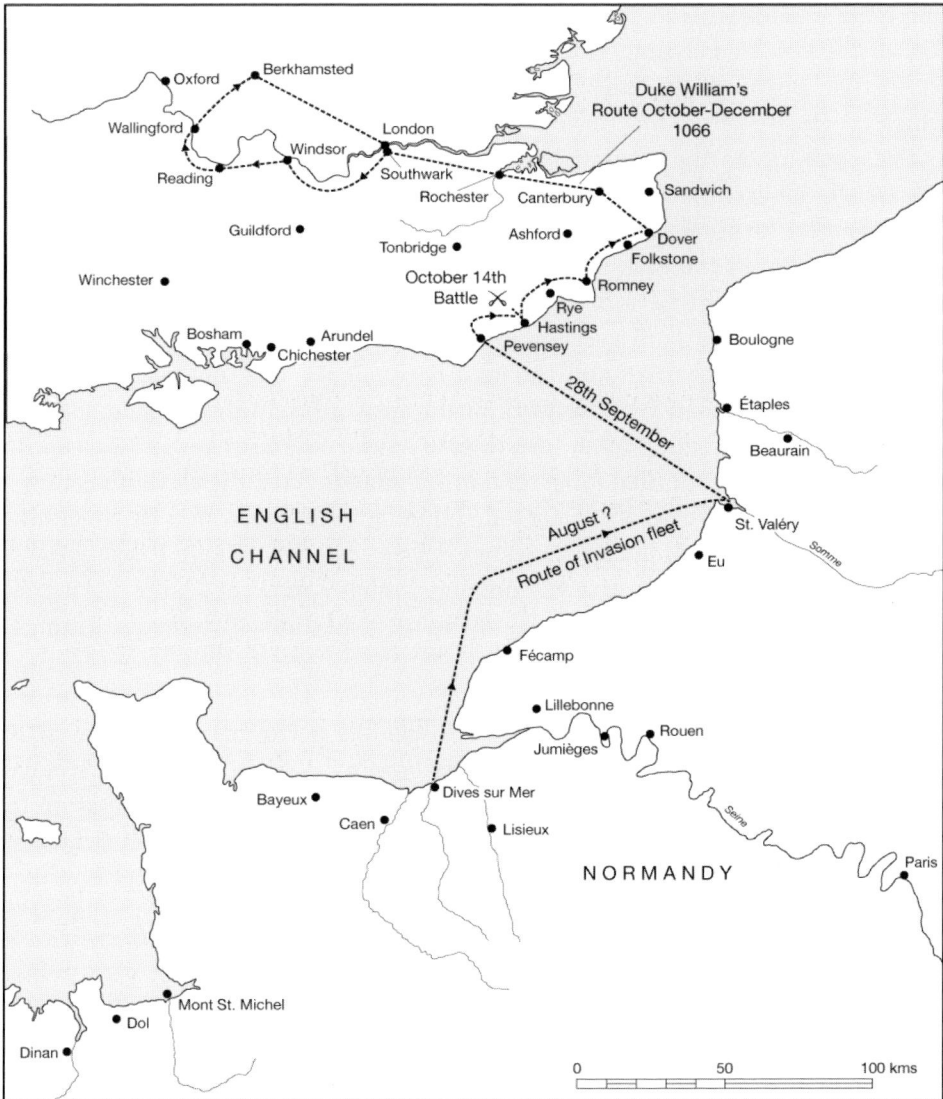

Map showing Duke William of Normandy's progress from August to 25 December 1066.

today, with rivers reaching the sea in tidal estuaries that penetrated several miles inland. Additionally, the Sussex coast was subject to constant change driven by longshore drift and the instability of offshore shingle barriers. Harbours could shift a considerable distance in a relatively short period of time. The sequence of easterly drift dictated the early development of Winchelsea and Hastings. Places such as Pevensey, Arundel, Steyning, Bramber and Old Romney were navigable seaports in the eleventh century and the area around Pevensey, where most of the Norman fleet is believed to have landed, was low-lying coastal marsh and open water, similar to the landscape around Rye to the east of Hastings today. Hastings itself had a complex history, and comprised a shingle harbour, with three additional landing places, one of which, at Bulverhythe, may have been an independent port at some stage.[2]

The openings to the shallow harbours that existed in 1066 were later fully or partially blocked by longshore drift. Later reclamation around the edges of marshland for farming, known as 'inning', led to a marked loss of water volume, and thus power, of the tidal scours that had kept the residual shallow harbours of Pevensey, Winchelsea and Rye navigable, and they gradually silted up. At Pevensey, silting and land reclamation have pushed the coastline southwards by about 1.5km since 1066 and the land between the fort and the sea is now flat marshland, drained by a network of ditches and field drains. The lagoon, which originally extended inland northwards as far as Hailsham and eastwards to Hooe, may have been tidal for several miles inland. From the eleventh century onwards, the eastwards drift of coastal shingle gradually isolated the inlet and salt marsh developed. However, a recent GIS survey of the region has suggested that even by 1066 Pevensey Bay was no longer open water, but a large salt marsh punctuated by loosely defined fluvial channels; a mixture of wetlands, saltings, mudflats and dunes.[3] (See Plate 2)

In contrast to this widespread silting, erosion has cut back the former sedimentary promontories along the Sussex coastline at a dramatic rate. The chalk and sandstone cliffs of the Hastings Beds have been calculated to have an average rate of erosion of 0.3m and 0.5m a year, with some stretches retreating at up to 1.25m per year. This has resulted in the loss of a number of medieval settlements, whose sites now lie up to a kilometre out to sea, notably, Isleham, near Climping; Cudlow; Charlton, near Bognor; Old Bracklesham; Kingston; and Balsdean, near Brighton.[4]

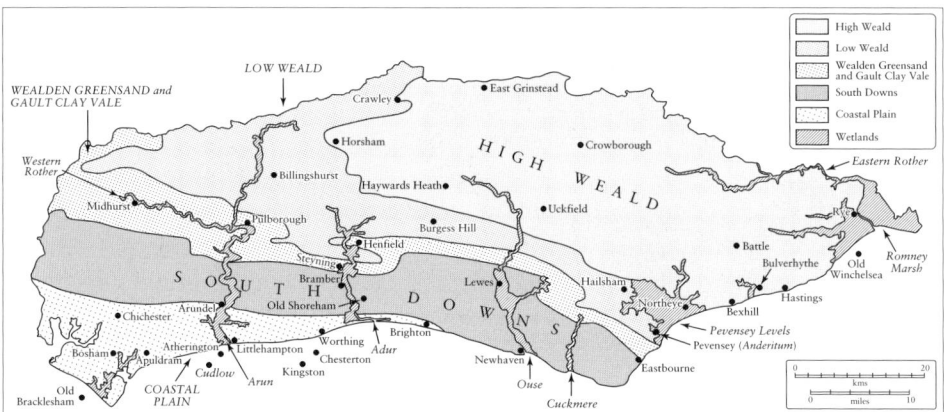

Map of the topography of Sussex, showing the location of settlements that have been lost through coastal erosion since the Conquest. (*From Leslie and Short, 1999: 7*)

Before the Battle

The *Anglo-Saxon Chronicle* records that during the summer of 1066, King Harold assembled a fleet at Sandwich in Kent and then sailed to the Isle of Wight, where he awaited the anticipated Norman invasion. There is little information about this phase and the *Anglo-Saxon Chronicle* mysteriously refers to a skirmish off the English coast some time before September, claiming that King Harold 'went out against Duke William with a raiding-ship army'. On 25 August, Harold disbanded his army in the belief that the Normans would not sail so late in the year. He returned overland to Westminster while his fleet sailed around the south-east coast and up the Thames estuary to London. News came to the king that an invasion army led by King Hardrada of Norway and his half-brother Tostig had sailed up the Humber towards York. Harold reconvened an army and moved northward at great speed and on 25 September decisively defeated the invaders at the Battle of Stamford Bridge. Duke William's intelligence must have kept him informed of the intended Scandinavian invasion and taking advantage of the situation on 27 September 1066, with a favourable wind behind it, William's armada set sail from Saint-Valéry, while the English army was still in York celebrating its victory over the Scandinavians.

William's ships were essentially Viking *langskips* (long, narrow, open war boats with drafts as shallow as 20cm) and *knörrs* (broader-beamed trading boats with deeper drafts), which could not sail easily into the wind and sidewinds could cause them to capsize. They used rising tides to enter harbour and falling tides to leave. Such ships were capable of entering shallow harbours and could sail or be punted

The Norman invasion fleet arriving at Pevensey, as depicted on the Bayeux Tapestry.

up rivers; they could also be beached, as depicted on the Bayeux Tapestry.[5] On the morning of 28 September, the fleet landed largely unopposed. John of Worcester reported that 'William, duke of the Normans had landed his fleet at a place called Pevensey with an innumerable multitude of mounted soldiers, slingers, archers and foot soldiers'.

The Normans already had close links with this region; the ducal abbey at Fécamp held several estates along the Sussex coast and it is reasonable to assume that William's agents knew the local topography. It is probable that the landings extended over a much wider area than Pevensey Bay to include Bulverhythe, Hastings and the shingle bar across the Rye Camber. At least two ships ended up as far east as Old Romney, 50km to the east of Pevensey, where their crews were killed by the townspeople, subsequently provoking William to devastate the town. Having landed, William's army began the process of ravaging the Sussex countryside – the intimidation of the English population then became the hallmark of the Conquest. Thus, the immediate impact of the arrival of the Norman army was to bring about considerable devastation to the Sussex landscape.

Pevensey

Pevensey in the eleventh century was still a substantial Roman fortification, defending a sizeable town and port (See Plate 2). It occupied a peninsula of sand and clay, about 10m above sea level, projecting into the south-western area of Pevensey Bay, which had served as a harbour for the Romans. This was the Roman *Anderitum*, which had originally been built *c.* AD 293–300 as a Saxon Shore fort – part of a network of military and naval fortifications built along England's south-eastern coast, possibly to protect against invasions by Germanic pirates. Along with Portchester, 115km to the west, it is the largest surviving fort of its date in Britain. The fort is oval, enclosing an area of about 3.67ha (10 acres) with walls standing to a height of up to 9m in places. Evidence of late Saxon occupation at Pevensey, in the form of cesspits, rubbish pits and ninth-century stratified coins, strengthens the argument that there was an Alfredian *burh* here, as discussed below.[6] Earl Godwin arrived here from Sandwich with a fleet of forty-two ships in 1049 and again in 1052, when returning with his fleet from exile. The Domesday evidence points to a flourishing port-town at Pevensey, recording that in 1066 it consisted of 110 households, 52 burgesses, tolls to the value of 20*s* and port dues of 35*s*. The civilian town, which appears to have largely been located within the fort, appears to have been removed after the Conquest. It was granted to William's half-brother Robert of Mortain, who garrisoned it, but then re-established a small borough outside the east gate.

William reinforced the defences of the Roman fortification by narrowing the former west gate with a wall in front of the guard chambers and cutting a curving ditch in front. The arch of the Roman east gate was also repaired

Pevensey Roman shore fort, *Anderitum* (fourth century), where the Norman fleet landed in September 1066. It was given to William's half-brother Robert of Mortain after the Conquest, along with the Rape of Pevensey. A mint and 110 burgesses were recorded here in the Domesday Book (1086), and these were probably located in a new borough at Westham, just outside the fort. Work on the stone castle was only started in the late twelfth century.

and fighting platforms were added to two other towers. The Norman works included the replacement of the collapsed southern part of the Roman walls, and herringbone brickwork in the defences may date from this time. A pit containing a wooden ladder, a cask, bowls and eleventh-century Norman pottery was found in the outer bailey, possibly relics from the invading force. Several sources relate that William built his first English castle here. William of Jumièges, for example, claimed that the Conqueror 'at once raised a strongly entrenched castle' at Pevensey. Excavations have shown that the ground surface in the south-eastern sector of the fort, in the vicinity of the later stone-built keep, was artificially raised sometime before 1200, indicating a motte, or more probably a ringwork castle, constructed by the duke. Within the inner bailey of this castle can be seen the footings of a simple church, which may predate the Conquest. When the stone keep was built here in the twelfth century, it incorporated one of the Roman fort's mural towers and its design was almost certainly inspired by the drum towers of the Roman walls.[7]

This church was replaced sometime after 1066 by St Nicolas parish church, located immediately outside the east gate of the fort. The significant size of this, mostly early thirteenth-century, building suggests that it was still serving an active seaport here. There is another church, located close to the west gate, dedicated to St Mary; this is the parish church of Westham, a small hamlet set out along the road leading westwards from the fort. The south wall of the nave and the transept contain eleventh-century herringbone flintwork and there are signs that there was a cloister to the south, suggesting that this was once the church of Holy Cross Hospital.

The Liberty of Pevensey was a medieval hundred, containing the parishes of Westham and Pevensey, regarded as forming part of the port of Hastings. Consequently, it was entitled to the privileges and immunities enjoyed by the Cinque Ports and was outside the jurisdiction of the county of Sussex until the nineteenth century. The history and topography of the settlements to the east and west of Pevensey fort would repay further investigation, which could hopefully provide clues to the role played by the site in the Conquest.

The Hastings Enigma

Why does the most famous battle in English history carry the name of Hastings? No one seriously suggests that it was fought in or even near to the settlement that now carries that name. In the Middle Ages, fifteen places in the south Sussex area were called Hastings, presumably a legacy of the '*Haestingas*', a group of seventh-century Saxons who remained isolated from the rest of Sussex, settling mainly along the coastal margins, particularly at the heads of river valleys, to the south of Battle Ridge. The name 'Hastings' appears three times on the Bayeux Tapestry, which dates from within a decade or so of the battle. This assertion of the place name in association with the graphic pictorial narrative of the conflict might be why it was transferred to the battle site from an early date.[8]

Given the importance of Hastings in the narrative of the Conquest, it is particularly frustrating that the archaeological record for the town and its hinterland is so sparse and confusing. The absence of datable structures, together with significant changes to the local topography as a result of longshore drift, silting and coastal erosion, has created an almost indecipherable puzzle concerning the area's late Saxon and immediate post-Conquest topography. The town of Hastings is located on the southern slopes and subsidiary spurs of the coastal end of Battle Ridge, which is part of the High Weald. The cliffs at Hastings are made up of friable Cretaceous Ashdown and Wadhurst Formations. These deposits consist of poorly cemented sandstones, silts, mudstones, pebble layers and clays, which are highly susceptible to erosion. In the early eleventh century there were landing places at the mouths of the Priory and Bourne valleys and Bulverhythe; the mercantile and fishing fleets of Hastings have always been beach-based.

The story told by the chroniclers, and apparently confirmed by the Bayeux Tapestry, is that soon after landing at Pevensey, William moved his fleet and troops eastwards to Hastings, where he built a second castle. According to the *Anglo-Saxon Chronicle*: 'As soon as they [William's army] were fit, made a castle at Hastings market town.' Hastings (*Haestingacaestre*) is recorded as a *burh* in a document known as the Burghal Hidage, compiled *c*.919. *Burhs* were fortified towns established in the late ninth or early tenth century as part of a defensive scheme against Viking raids, normally located on river crossings or coastal sites. It has been suggested that Hastings's *burh*, whose site has yet to be authenticated, was on East Hill, on the cliffs immediately to the east of Old Hastings town, where there are the fragmentary earthworks of a prehistoric promontory fort. There are other candidates for the location of the *burh*, including West Hill and Bulverhythe; it has also been claimed that the site has been completely eroded away. In an attempt to circumnavigate these confusions, it has been persuasively argued that the site of the Saxon *burh* of Hastings was actually at Pevensey.[9] The place name *Haestingacaestre* may have been applied to the Roman fort at *Anderitum*. In 1995, Combes and Lyne published an article in the *Sussex Archaeological Collection* (vol. 133) suggesting that the Saxon *burh* was not at Hastings at all and that it was at Pevensey. After all, Pevensey had a redoubtable stone and brick fortress, much more like other Alfredian *burhs*. In the tenth-century Burghal Hidage, both Portchester and *Haestingacaestre* are assessed at 500 hides; Portchester fort (3.6ha, 9 acres) and Pevensey fort (3.7ha, 9.1 acres) are actually the same size. The Saxon *burh* of *Haestingacaestre* could well have been at Pevensey.

Hastings, along with Dover, Hythe, Sandwich and Romney, was part of a confederation of coastal towns in south-east England established by Edward the Confessor as a means of securing the use of ships by the Crown. After the Conquest the group became known as the Cinque Ports. In return for significant trading and legal rights, the Cinque Ports provided ships and sailors to the king for a stipulated number of days. Hastings, for instance, provided twenty-one ships for fifteen days a year. Hastings is not recorded in the Domesday Book, apart from three references to contributory burgesses, but the other Cinque Ports appear as substantial settlements. For instance, Romney, which is described as a borough and a port, was attributed with 156 burgesses, while Dover had 420 households with a guildhall for its burgesses. By the early thirteenth century, each of the ports is recorded as having a number of settlements linked to them in a loose association, known as 'limbs'. Some twenty-three such settlements are specifically

Hastings Castle in the process of being constructed, as shown in the Bayeux Tapestry.

mentioned in the Magna Carta (1215). The 'limbs' attached to Hastings covered a similar area to that of the distribution of 'Hastings' place names, extending as far as Eastbourne to the west and Rye to the east.

The remains of a much-reduced castle, including some standing walls, sits at the south end of West Hill overlooking modern Hastings. The chronicler Wace suggested that Hastings Castle had been transported from Normandy in a prefabricated form, but no other source mentions this and there is no archaeological evidence to support his claim.[10] Originally the castle occupied a promontory overlooking the coast, similar to that at Dover, but in 1287 months of heavy storms brought part of the castle down along with much of the promontory. More of the remaining castle was destroyed in the late sixteenth century, when Edmond Saunders, a fisherman, recorded 'that yn his tyme the mayne sea did break upon the cliffe, whereby parte of the castell was fallen and decayed'.[11] Most of the standing remains on the clifftop relate to the church of St Mary in the Castle, which was founded by Robert of Eu, c.1075, with a college of secular canons. The church plan was similar to that of another early Norman eleventh-century chapel at Richmond Castle in Yorkshire. In the 1820s, Thomas Pelham, 1st Earl of Chichester, developed the land at the foot of the cliff to create Pelham Crescent; during the process, part of the cliff and more of the castle bailey were destroyed. William II d'Eu founded another St Mary's church in the late eleventh century, at the western end of a sandbank by the Glyne Gap, between Bulverhythe and Bexhill.

On the face of it, there would have been little strategic sense in moving the Norman army from the safety of *Anderitum* and Pevensey Bay until such time that was absolutely necessary, unless Pevensey harbour was inadequate to house the Norman fleet. There was no coastal road from Pevensey to Hastings and

Aerial view of Hastings Castle sitting on a cliff promontory above Pelham Crescent. (*Barbara van Cleve*)

The remains of St Mary's Chapel, Bulverhythe, originally built by William II d'Eu in the late eleventh century. It now sits in the middle of a housing estate. (*Trevor Rowley*)

William's army would have been required to circumnavigate the Pevensey Levels, a distance of approximately 25km (15.5 miles), or to have re-embarked and made the journey by sea. It has been argued that William did not move to Hastings at all, but stayed at Pevensey, but the weight of evidence suggests that such a move was indeed made.

Nevertheless, given the difficulty of pinpointing the location of the *burh*, the harbour or the original castle at Hastings, indeed any of the features associated with the Conquest, the Pevensey theory remains attractive. An alternative, suggested by some scholars, is that the functions of Hastings were dispersed among several small settlements along the coast, which would complement the idea that the place name covered the whole of the coastal area between Hastings and Pevensey. Was Pevensey the main centre with the *burh* and mint up until the Conquest, and did the substantive move to Hastings only occur after the Saxon borough at Pevensey had been dispersed after the Conquest? Jeremy Haslam has proposed another neat explanation, in which he argues that the *burh* of Hastings was at Pevensey, but that the name was transferred to the present castle site when King Aethelred built a fortified naval base in response to a new wave of Viking incursions in the late tenth century.[12] If this was the case, it would explain the attraction of Hastings to Duke William and the speed with which he transferred his forces there after the initial landing. Another possible motive was that the port of Hastings was probably already in the hands of Fécamp Abbey.

Norman Destruction before the Battle

No sooner had the Normans landed than they began plundering the Sussex countryside.[13] By ravaging the heartland of Harold Godwinson's estates, William was provoking the English king into returning south from York, in order to engage him in battle at the earliest opportunity. The *Song of the Battle of Hastings* describes a report sent to Harold saying that William's forces were taking captive boys, girls and widows as well as cattle. The enslavement and violation of women was a recognized method of intimidating the population as a whole. The Bayeux Tapestry shows cavalrymen racing off as soon as the invasion ships have beached, in order to support a foraging party depicted in the following scene, where a sheep and an ox are about to be butchered. In a later episode a woman and child are shown fleeing, hand in hand, perhaps for their lives, from a two–storey building that is being deliberately set on fire by Norman soldiers.

Ravage and plunder were a recognized means of carrying warfare to an opponent; the late Roman writer Vegetius could have been describing the Norman conquest of England when he observed that: 'The main and principal point of war is to secure plenty of provisions and to destroy the enemy by fire.'[14] An important source of information about the post-Hastings devastation by the Norman army is through the recording of 'waste' in the Domesday Book. The rape of Hastings records that it lost 75 per cent of its value after 1066 and that three coastal

Normans burning a house from which a mother and child are escaping on the Bayeux Tapestry. Such actions were part of regular military practice, employed partly to intimidate and reduce the enemy's capacity to respond.

hundreds, where the army may have been based, lost 80 per cent. Conventionally, historians have tended to interpret 'waste' in a literal sense – land that has been deliberately devastated. However, the Domesday Book term 'waste' has a variety of meanings: it covers land that is untenanted, where information is not available, land dedicated to hunting, or that is simply vacant. It ranges from holdings from which it is not possible to raise rent or tax, from uncultivated but grazed land, to land and settlements that have been deliberately and violently destroyed.[15] The extensive record of 'waste' in Sussex seems to represent evidence of genuine destructive activity. Where the Domesday survey provides three values for manors – 1066, c.1070 and 1086 – historians have used these figures to calculate the loss of value between 1066 and 1070 to show the damage inflicted by the Norman army as it moved across England.[16] In Netherfield hundred, in which the battle took place, values fell by 90 per cent.

Both the English and the Norman armies lived off the land through which they passed, resulting in the slaughter of livestock and the emptying of barns of grain, sometimes accompanied by gratuitous violence. Such damage was a universal feature of eleventh-century warfare, its severity depending to some extent upon the level of co-operation between the local lords, their tenants and the military. The second form of damage occurred when an attacking army deliberately destroyed the resources necessary for survival in the enemy's homeland. According to Robert Wace, Rollo, the first leader of Normandy, ravaged all the countryside around Bayeux in order to force the city's submission; while in England, the Danes had deliberately ravaged Yorkshire during Aethelred's reign. In 1041, King

Harthacanute sent a large force to burn Worcester and ravage the surrounding district after two tax collectors had been murdered in the city. Neither were the English averse to adopting a scorched-earth policy; according to William of Poitiers, on hearing of William's landing and activities in the south, King Harold's brother Gyrth recommended that the English should lay waste all the countryside between London and the south coast so that, even if the Normans won the initial battle, they would be starved into submission as winter arrived.

Undoubtedly, the fortnight the Normans spent before the battle was a destructive one during which they wrought significant damage in the Pevensey/ Hastings region. We do not know if any of this activity caused permanent change to the landscape; if, for instance, any of the communities that were sacked were then abandoned permanently or moved location. William of Poitiers reported that 'the furious king [Harold] was hastening his march all the more because he had heard that the lands near to the Norman camp were being laid waste'. Harold would not only have been aggrieved at the material damage to his home estates but would also have been painfully aware that one of his roles as king was to protect his subjects.

The Site of the Battle of Hastings

The site of the battle lies in the High Weald of Sussex, which the Romans called the Forest of Andred after *Anderitum* (Pevensey), from which the Saxons developed the name *Andredsweald*. In 892 the *Anglo-Saxon Chronicle* declared that the Wealden woodland was 'a hundred and twenty miles long or longer from east to west, and thirty miles broad'. The Weald was mainly used as common wood pasture by settlements around its edge; it had a small population located in scattered farms and hamlets and was still in the process of being settled in the eleventh century.[17] (See Plate 3)

In the eleventh century, most battles were fought on open flat or undulating ground, often close to a river crossing. The site of the Battle of Hastings is different and an intrinsically improbable one. It is located in the High Weald near the centre of Battle Ridge, which extends south-eastwards from Hadlow Down (3km to the north-east of Uckfield) to meet the coast, where it forms dramatic cliffs at Fairlight (5km east of Hastings). It is an area of poor, acidic soils developed over a succession of sandstones, siltstones and mudstones of the Hastings Beds (Lower Cretaceous). The landscape is heavily wooded, primarily with oak, with patches of poorly drained bog resulting from the sluggish flow of a complex network of Wealden streams. At lower elevations it has a rolling appearance, but can rise up to 240m. Battle Abbey church, where the English army was deployed, sits at 80m above sea level. The twelfth-century *Battle Abbey Chronicle* claimed that the site of the battle lay 'in a desert surrounded by swampy valleys and by forest out of which only a few homesteads had yet been carved'.[18]

It is unlikely that either army, given the choice, would have wanted to fight in this environment. A remote, wooded and marshy location with appalling communications gave an advantage to neither side. William would surely have chosen a more open, firmer landscape in which his cavalry and archers could operate freely and Harold would have wished for a more secure site on which to plant his shield wall. One can imagine two armies struggling to locate each other in the woodland of the Weald and eventually having to make the best of a bad job. The *Anglo-Saxon Chronicle* hints as much; it records that the English had a large army it at the 'hoary apple tree', and that William came upon it by surprise, before it was properly ordered. One of the reasons that the battle lasted so long, much longer than the few hours usual for a conflict at the time, was that neither side had been able to choose a site that gave them dominance.

Some early chroniclers called the site of the battle Senlac, a name probably derived from the Old English word *sandache*, meaning 'a sandy place', while others termed the battlefield 'the plain of Hastings'. The isolated location of the area meant that reaching it from either direction would have been difficult, but Harold's route from the north would have been the most problematic. There are several routes that the English army could have taken to Battle. These include the line of a possible Roman road from Rochester to the north of Hastings, used for the transport of Wealden iron, which has for long been favoured by local historians. There was another Roman road leading from London to Lewes, which Harold may have taken, but which would have involved marching on local tracks for the last few miles. The whole area is traversed with a network of trackways that served as livestock drove roads during the Middle Ages. It is unclear how these tracks originated as they appear to predate the Roman road system, but their deeply sunken and often muddy nature meant that they would not have provided comfortable passage for either army.

Several alternative locations for the site of the battle have been proposed, including Crowhurst, about 5km south of Battle, and steep-sided Caldbec Hill, about 1.5km to the north. One version of the *Anglo-Saxon Chronicle* records that 'King Harold was informed of this [William's invasion] and he assembled a large army and came against him at the hoary [grey] apple tree'. The conventional understanding is that this tree was on the summit of Caldbec Hill, where three administrative hundreds met. A recent analysis of the *Chronicle*'s text has indicated that *apuldran*, which conventionally has been translated as 'apple tree', could equally mean 'round tree' or 'veteran pollard'. A veteran tree at such a hundredal meeting place would have had a status more appropriate for a meeting of elite Anglo-Saxon warriors than a common fruit tree.[19]

The strongest argument for the traditional site is the siting of Battle Abbey and William's vow to found a monastery where he had defeated the English and where the usurper, Harold, had died. The place name Battle first appears in the *Anglo-Saxon Chronicle* c.1094, when it reported that William 'set up a famous monastery in the same place that God permitted him to conquer England'. The abbey was called St Martin de Bello Loco – St Martin of the place of the battle. The original monks who came from the ancient Benedictine abbey at Marmoutier-en-Loire to form the nucleus of the new community were faced with a major problem. The narrow ridge on which the Saxon army had been slaughtered posed serious construction difficulties, and the porous sandstone bedrock lacked a water supply. Reputedly, the monks started work on another, more favourable site to the west, but were forced to stop when William heard about it. He commanded them to obey his original instructions and promised that 'if God spare my life, I will so amply provide for this place that wine shall be more abundant here than water is at any other great abbey'.[20] It was necessary to undertake extensive terracing and the construction of a massive undercroft to accommodate some of the abbey buildings.

The sloping ground immediately to the south-west of the Battle Abbey ruins has for long been the area favoured by many scholars and now forms part of the English Heritage site at Battle. Topographically, it fits the description of a ridge, on which the abbey remains now sit, leading down to a stream, on the other side of which the ground rises. A recent digital survey concludes that 'the general shape and slope of the battlefield has remained the same since the battle'.[21]

The assumption has been that the English occupied the ridge, between Caldbec Hill to the north and Telham Hill to the south, while the Normans and their allies were lined up on the opposite slope. An examination of the area by Channel 4's Time Team using LIDAR geophysics in 2013 indicated that the area conventionally believed to be the site of the battle would have been too marshy for the repeated cavalry charges of the Normans. Their survey suggested that the ground to the east of Battle, along the A2100 road, was firmer and that it was on this slope, leading to the town of Battle, that the battle was fought. On the face of it, the argument is a strong one and would simply involve moving the site by 90 degrees from its present assumed location.[22] Gillingham has argued that the conventional interpretation of the battle as a conflict largely between the Norman cavalry and archers and the English shield wall, located along Battle Ridge, is an oversimplification; that it is likely a battle that lasted a whole day was more fluid and action would have taken place over a much wider area adjacent to the ridge.[23] A GIS analysis of the Battle region concluded that the battle could have taken place either on Battle Ridge or on Caldbec Hill.[24]

There is a quasi–legendary episode, an version of which is found in several of the histories, which seems to confirm the treacherous nature of the terrain on which the fighting took place. The Malfosse incident occurred when a large number of Norman and some English soldiers fell and were trampled to death after encountering a ditch or obscured structure. The timing of this event varies between accounts; it occurred either during a feigned retreat by the Normans, or during a Norman advance late in the day, or during the confusion and breaking of

A view of Battle Abbey showing the area conventionally believed to have been the field of battle in 1066.

The Bayeux Tapestry showing Normans attacking English troops, who are occupying what appears to be a representation of the ridge at Battle, on which the English shield wall was based.

ranks following King Harold's death, when the Normans were pursuing fleeing English combatants. All accounts agree that there was a considerable loss of life involving a ditch or pit, while William of Poitiers talks of 'a broken rampart and a labyrinth of ditches'. Most of the chroniclers imply that the Malfosse was a natural feature, but William of Malmesbury (1120s) argued that the English knew the route through the terrain and largely avoided the ditch, while Henry of Huntingdon (1140s) improbably claimed that 'a certain large pit' had been 'craftily covered' by the English and they lured the Normans into it.[25]

There are references to a great ditch called the 'Maufosse' in thirteenth-century charters, which disappear after the monks later turned the area into cattle pasture. What is known is that there are a number of pools and areas of treacherous, hidden

The marshy area below Battle Abbey, which may have been where the Malfosse incident occurred, when a significant number of Normans were killed.

Norman cavalrymen and horses falling into a watery area, in what could be a reference to the Malfosse incident, on the Bayeux Tapestry.

marsh in the Aspen Valley, to the south of the ridge on which the English army was based. It is therefore more than possible that a troop of cavalry in pursuit of their quarry could have accidentally stumbled into one of these features. In the Bayeux Tapestry there is a dramatic scene, not long before the death of Harold, graphically portraying a group of fallen Norman horses at the foot of the hill occupied by the English troops. Under the horses, a short stretch of water, which seems to be pierced by reeds or possibly spikes, is depicted. It is tempting to see this as one of the pools or marshes in the area, which just possibly had been engineered into a trap by the English.

After the Battle

Although the English had been roundly defeated and King Harold killed at Hastings, William's position was far from secure. He held only a small corner of England and the majority of the surviving English leaders had not capitulated; indeed, there were active attempts to place Edgar the Aetheling on the vacant throne. According to the Normans, legitimate war continued right up to William's coronation at the end of December; consequently, Normans who killed during this period still had to perform penance, but this was mitigated as it was viewed as an act of permissible warfare. The duke's main aim in the first instance was to secure the ceremonial, ecclesiastic and commercial capitals of the realm (Winchester, Canterbury and London). He managed to achieve this aim by the end of 1066 using a combination of brute force and diplomacy.

The conventional narrative of these last months of 1066 tells of William's army moving first to London and then in a loop, incorporating the Middle Thames

Valley and the Chilterns, to Berkhamsted. In reality, the story would have been far more complex, with separate contingents of the army taking different routes, securing important centres. Reinforcements would have arrived from the Continent by way of Southampton, Fareham, Pevensey and Dover to add to the Norman pressure on south-east England. During this period there would have been constant ravaging of the countryside as well as the forced collection of tributes. Fortifications were hurriedly erected in towns as they were taken and smaller, outpost castles may have been built at strategic points along the army's route. For instance, a small, but prominent, motte and bailey castle was built on the upper ridge of the South Downs at Edburton Hill, overlooking an important west–east routeway.

Our knowledge of events between the Battle of Hastings and William's coronation on Christmas Day 1066 comes primarily from the chroniclers and the Domesday Book, which provides evidence of depreciated land values in the wake of the invasion. Devalued estates can be identified in eastern Kent between Dover and Sandwich; within 5 miles of Dover, vills lost over 70 per cent of their value.[26] Lines of devalued manors can be traced, identifying the movement of different

Edburton motte and bailey castle, on the edge of the South Downs in Sussex. It has views over the coast and the Weald and is believed to have been built soon after the Battle of Hastings. (*Paul R. Davis*)

Norman forces and foraging bands. There is a clear line of such vills between Steyning (Sussex) and Winchester (Hampshire), perhaps marking the movement of a detachment of troops sent to 'negotiate' with the capital of Saxon England. There also seems to have been intense activity in the Thames Valley around Windsor, where there was a Saxon royal palace.

After the Battle of Hastings, the *Anglo-Saxon Chronicle* recorded that 'William harried that part of the country through which he advanced until he came to Berkhamsted'. The chroniclers tell of how, in response to attacks upon his troops, the duke sacked Romney. According to William of Poitiers, William 'inflicted such punishment as he thought fit for the slaughter of his men who landed there [Romney] by mistake'. In response to this brutality, the town of Dover submitted without resistance, but still did not escape mass eviction and arson. According to William of Poitiers, the duke 'ordered the English to evacuate their houses' in order to build the castle and William 'spent eight days adding fortifications' to existing Iron Age defences. The bank and ditch he constructed cut through the cemetery of the Anglo-Saxon church of St Mary in Castro. William's army also started a major fire in the town, apparently as a consequence of looting.

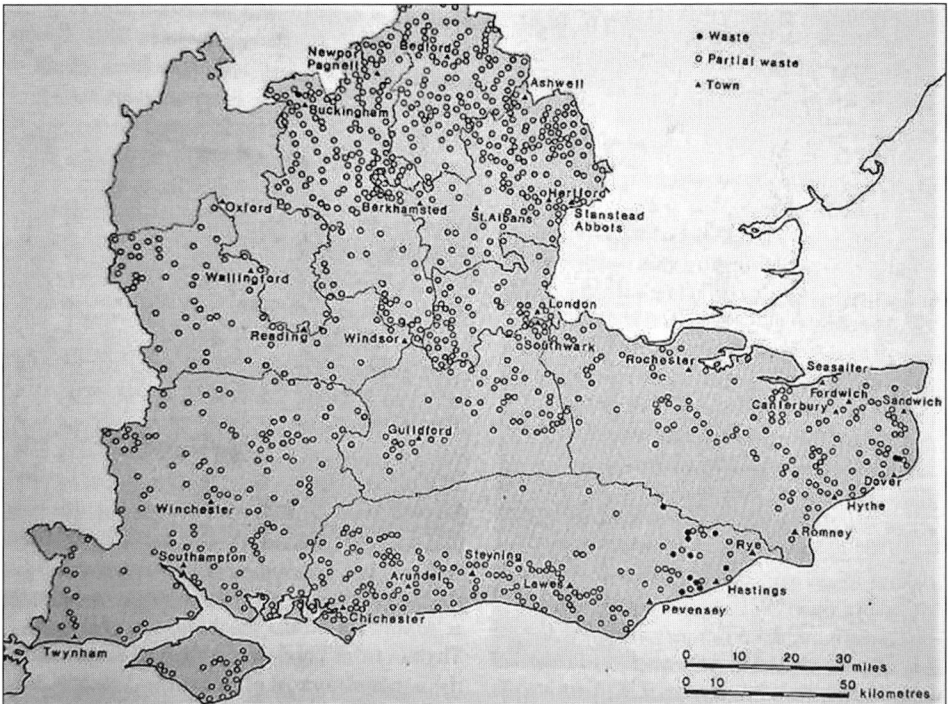

Waste and partly waste vills in south-east England, recorded in the Domesday Book in 1086, reflecting the movement of Norman armies immediately after the Battle of Hastings and subsequently in the transfer of land from English to French owners. (*After Darby, 1977: 244-5*)

Norman cavalrymen foraging and looting a village before the Battle of Hastings. Their commander is Wadard, a vassal of Bishop Odo of Bayeux, William the Conqueror's half-brother.

The Iron Age, Roman and Saxon fortifications at Dover, which were occupied and strengthened by the Normans after the Battle of Hastings while on their way to London. The formidable castle keep was built in the twelfth century. (*Kenphotopics*)

The bulk of the Norman army then moved north-westwards along Watling Street, taking the metropolitan capital of Canterbury and then Rochester. When he reached Southwark, William engaged in an inconclusive skirmish on London Bridge with an English contingent led by the *de facto* English king, Edgar the Aetheling. William decided against attacking London across the river from the south. He undertook a long, circuitous journey back to London, the aim of which must have been in part to weaken the resolve of the capital. As he progressed, the duke continued to receive submissions from the English aristocracy, both lay and ecclesiastic.

After sacking Southwark, William moved westwards up the Thames Valley through Windsor as far as Wallingford, where the army crossed the river, apparently

Berkhamsted Castle, Hertfordshire, where the English leaders surrendered before William the Conqueror's coronation. (*Historic England*)

without incident. Subsequently, the Normans travelled north-eastwards, following the Icknield Way along the foot of the Chilterns, before moving towards London and camping at Berkhamsted. Here, the remaining English nobles and clergy submitted and the 'men of London' agreed to surrender the city. The *Anglo-Saxon Chronicle* chided that they should have capitulated much earlier in order to spare the kingdom from William's ravaging. While at Berkhamsted, William built another castle, which passed into the hands of his half-brother Robert of Mortain.

Throughout the late autumnal march to London the Normans continued to devastate the areas through which they passed, sending out forays into adjacent districts to occupy strategic sites, gather provisions and terrorize the native English. John of Worcester (*c*.1100) reported that the Normans 'laid waste Sussex, Kent, Hampshire, Middlesex and Hertfordshire, and did not cease from burning townships and slaying men'. The final event of this tumultuous year of the three kings (four if you include Edgar the Aetheling, the *de facto* king between the Battle of Hastings and William's coronation) was William's coronation in the newly built Westminster Abbey, on Christmas Day. The coronation ceremony was a hybrid of Saxon and French rites, read in English by the Bishop of York and French by the Bishop of Coutances. It combined the rite of Dunstan, which had been created for the coronation of King Edgar at Bath in 973, with a rite used by the kings of France – the anointing with oil. The occasion was appropriately marked by further violence as the troops guarding the abbey mistook the acclamation during the service as signs of an uprising, and burnt houses in the vicinity.

Chapter 3

Rebellion and Retribution

The King stopped at nothing to hunt his enemies. He cut down many people and destroyed homes and land. Nowhere else has he shown such cruelty.

(Orderic Vitalis)

The Battle of Hastings and William the Conqueror's coronation at the end of 1066 only marked the start of the longer process of the Norman Conquest. The two decades that followed the coronation were among the most tumultuous in the whole of English history. Revolts against the Normans were followed by brutal reprisals against the English population and eventually by the wholesale transfer of land from English to French tenants. The pattern of landownership established then was to influence the shaping of the English landscape for the rest of the millennium.

King William was anxious to demonstrate his authenticity as the rightful successor to Edward the Confessor. He argued that his coronation represented an orthodox, traditional transfer of legitimate power. Many of the trappings of English monarchy, such as the coronation, crown-wearing ceremonies and design of coins, remained basically unaltered. Just as the king claimed to be the rightful successor to the Confessor, so his tenants were to hold land with all the rights and obligations of the Confessor's thegns. It was in this context that the new king claimed that he intended to maintain the status quo, to respect ancient laws, to keep existing secular and ecclesiastic institutions, perhaps together with many of the senior Anglo-Saxon officers that served them. This conventional view of William's early tolerant intentions has been questioned by Bates, who argues that the ruthless imposition of Normans into pivotal roles of government began immediately after the Battle of Hastings.[1]

Nevertheless, William may have intended to rule like that earlier eleventh-century conqueror King Cnut and allow some English landholders to retain their estates, perhaps even some of the largest Saxon magnates. In some respects, Cnut's takeover had been more violent than William's; potential opponents were killed and the surviving members of the Anglo-Saxon monarchy were sent into exile. At the same time, Cnut was a conciliator and gave gifts to English churches and monasteries to atone for the damage perpetrated by his father, Sweyn Forkbeard, and previous Danish kings. Within a decade of his accession Cnut was heavily reliant on English administrators and ecclesiastical advisors, and although many of his Danish followers were rewarded with estates, he did not transfer the land of England into Scandinavian hands.

If he had intended emulating Cnut, two factors gravitated against William fulfilling his ambition. First, he had many obligations, not only to those who had fought at Hastings but also to those supporters in Normandy and beyond who had given material, moral and spiritual support to the invasion. These included cathedrals, abbeys and churches who had been promised rewards in the event of William's success. Second, the rebellions of the late 1060s persuaded the king that he was unable to trust the English aristocracy or even the clergy and nothing short of their complete emasculation would be enough to remove them as a threat to his throne. These revolts, in turn, resulted in more great estates becoming available for redistribution. Henry of Huntingdon, writing in the 1130s, commented that: 'In the twenty-first year [1087] of King William's reign there was hardly a nobleman of English descent left in England, but all were reduced to servitude and mourning, so that it was a disgrace to be called an Englishman.' Much as the king might have wanted 'business as usual', there were pressing practical reasons for the Normans to transfer power and land to the victors. There were debts to be repaid, obligations to be met and a subject people to be controlled.

Superficially, the immediate impact of the Conquest made little difference to the everyday lives of the majority of English people; in reality, everyone, whatever their station in society, was affected. There were administrative, legal, linguistic and cultural changes, many of them subtle but also far-reaching. The power of the Crown and its officers increased greatly in many spheres; William claimed that the whole of the land of England was his and his alone. The removal of English tenants-in-chief, undertenants, bishops and abbots in itself would not have impacted many, apart from those immediately involved. However, the process of enacting such changes may have been accompanied by violence, during which there would have been collateral victims. In the Church, in law, in administration and even in commerce there were changes in personnel and changes in culture. The higher rates of taxation William introduced almost immediately he became king had an impact on almost everyone in the country. In 1067, William demanded a high geld off all his tenants, Norman and English, who in turn put pressure on rents and services to maintain high levels of profit from their manors. Some English thegns, who initially managed to hang on to their land, were thus forced out by higher taxation, and by 1086 numerous former sokemen and freemen had moved down the social order and been reclassified as villeins and bordars. For example, at Frostenden (Suffolk) in 1066 there had been eight English freemen; twenty years later there were just three, while the number of bordars had increased from fourteen to twenty.[2]

Townspeople in particular suffered during the early years of Norman rule; not only were properties destroyed for the building of castles and cathedrals, but numerous soldiers and workmen would have been forcibly billeted on to urban communities. In some cases, Englishmen were impressed to labour on building castles. Difficulties of communication would have exacerbated minor problems and Norman privileges would have excited envy and anger. 'Although it was sporadic, local and relatively ephemeral … repeated devastation was an ingredient of no mean importance in the life of medieval England.'[3] The archaeological and landscape record of these events appears to be mostly absent, but perhaps there are as yet undetected clues reflecting the thousands of small tragedies experienced during this early phase of the Conquest. In any case, they were but a prelude to a far darker chapter of Norman tyranny.

English Revolts and Norman Reprisals

Initially, it appears that William felt that he had done enough to subdue the English, and for a short while he seems to have been right. The king felt confident enough to leave for a triumphal tour of Normandy in March 1067, taking with him English leaders as 'hostages'; these included Archbishop Stigand and Edgar the Aetheling. This was done partly to deprive the population of potential resistance figureheads but also to demonstrate William's total control of his new realm to his Norman kinsmen. One consequence of this hubris was to create a well of hostility among the English leaders, virtually all of whom later rebelled against the Norman king. Added to which, he left behind as viceregents his half-brother Bishop Odo and trusted ally William fitz Osbern, who, according to Orderic Vitalis, 'oppressed all the native inhabitants of high and low degree and heaped shameful burdens on them'. One final insult was the expropriation of huge amounts of cash and Church treasures, which were shipped back to Normandy, starting as early as January 1067. The *Anglo-Saxon Chronicle*, commenting on William's reign in 1087, stated: 'The king and his chief men loved gain much and overmuch – gold and silver – and did not care how sinfully it was obtained.' In one episode in 1069, Archbishop Ealdred of York reproached King William personally after the Sheriff of York had plundered the archbishop's goods in order to feed the castle garrison.

These cumulative indignities, together with the wholesale transfer of land, created an atmosphere of resentment in the conquered English which quickly translated into mutiny. Orderic wrote in terms which have resonated down the centuries to the detriment of the Norman reputation: 'And so, the English groaned aloud for their lost liberty and plotted ceaselessly to find some way of shaking off a yoke that was so intolerable and unaccustomed.' William returned to England towards the end of 1067 after a minor rising at Dover, led by a disillusioned veteran of Hastings, Eustace of Boulogne, was easily suppressed. By the time of the Christmas court of that year the process of redistributing English lands to Normans was already well under way; the *Anglo-Saxon Chronicle* cryptically reported that William gave away every man's land. In February of 1068 there was trouble in Exeter, where William took exception to the citizens of Exeter attempting to negotiate with him over the terms of their formal submission. There were also the stirrings of a more widespread rebellion in the south-west, which prompted the king to respond rapidly and move down to the region with an army. King Harold's mother, Gytha, had retired to her western estates and was resident in the city at the time and may have played a role in the uprising. Exeter was well defended with its refurbished Roman walls, and following William's arrival in the south-west there was an eighteen-day siege, after which the city capitulated. Soon after, Rougemont Castle was built on a volcanic outcrop, in the northern corner of the Roman city.

On this occasion, the king showed clemency to the rebels and Gytha escaped before the siege was lifted. According to the *Anglo-Saxon Chronicle*, she took refuge on Flat Holm, a small barren island in the Severn estuary, together with 'many distinguished men's wives'. (See Plate 4). The men may have fled with Harold's sons to Ireland, from whence two unsuccessful raids were subsequently launched, one on Bristol and Somerset in the summer of 1068 and the other on Devon a year later. The damage caused by these raids was probably more extensive than the casual historical references imply. The Exeter Domesday record of nine manors in the extreme south of Devon that were laid waste by 'Irish raiders' is probably a consequence of the Devon raid. Only two of the manors had recovered their pre-Conquest values by 1086, and several were worth significantly less. There was damage further west, in the Lizard Peninsula, where out of the twenty-three manors recorded in Domesday, twelve had no plough teams and six had no inhabitants in 1086.[4]

Rougemont Castle, Exeter. Built into the northern corner of the Roman city walls in or soon after the city's rebellion against William the Conqueror in 1068. It incorporates Saxon upper windows and has been compared to a Saxon *burh-geat*, the fortified residence or gatehouse of a Saxon thegn. (*Juan J. Martinez*)

The king spent Easter 1068 in Winchester for the first of his great crown-wearing ceremonies. He was using pageantry to demonstrate his legitimacy, at the same time as he was having to suppress simmering discontent in various parts of his new realm. William was joined by his wife, Matilda, and on Whit Sunday she was crowned Queen of England at Westminster. It was a grand symbolic occasion attended by nobility and senior clerics from England and France. It was an affirmation of kingship on a Carolingian scale and confirmed that total power had been transferred from an Anglo-Saxon to a Frank.

After that, for the next few years the smooth Norman takeover of their newly won kingdom was punctuated by internal uprisings led by those who had been humiliated by William. The figureheads of these rebellions were the pretender to the throne, Edgar the Aetheling, and the surviving leading English aristocrats – the earls Edwin and Morcar; Roger, Earl of Hereford; the Anglo-Breton Ralph, Earl of East Anglia; and Waltheof, Earl of the East Midlands and Bamburgh – but also involving lesser thegns and outsiders. Edgar's sister Margaret married King Malcolm III of Scotland, creating a potentially dangerous alliance. The risings are normally portrayed as separate, independent events, but they were linked by common grievances and reflected the growing reaction to the Norman takeover. Effectively, there was guerrilla warfare in England from late 1067 onwards.

Serious resistance to the conquerors began in the Welsh Marches. The *Anglo-Saxon Chronicle* records that: 'Eadric Cild and the Welsh became hostile, and fought against the garrison of the castle at Hereford, and inflicted many injuries upon them.' In 1069, Edric besieged Shrewsbury Castle and burnt the town, but late that year an alliance together with two Welsh kings, Blein and his brother Rhiwallon, was decisively defeated by William at the Battle of Stafford. The extent of the damage in the Welsh borderland indicates that the impact of uprisings and reprisals was more widespread than generally thought and can be summarized by the Domesday Book's terse comment on two Shropshire manors: 'waste, just as many other manors'. In 1070 about a quarter of all Shropshire vills were recorded as waste or partly waste and about half of those remained in the same condition in 1086.

As with many of the rebel leaders, there is relatively little known about Edric the Wild, also known as Wild Edric, Edric Savage or Edric Cild (or Child). He was a Saxon magnate with widespread estates in the Welsh Marches and further afield. He was also known as Edric Silvaticus (the Forester), which is a reference to the 'silvatici', a group of rebels who, according to Orderic Vitalis did not live in houses but inhabited woodland in order to toughen themselves for resistance against the Normans. Edric's story lacks the romance of some rebel heroes because after his defeat at Stafford, he appears to have accompanied the king in the invasion of Scotland in 1072, and possibly even fought for the Conqueror in Maine in 1075. Nevertheless, Edric, like other contemporary rebels, was soon absorbed into folklore and his memory was embedded in the Shropshire place names Eudon George (formerly Eudon Savage), Walton Savage and Neen Savage.[5] His abrupt disappearance from the record and his association with woodland rebels ensured that legends became associated with him and it has been suggested that he was an early incarnation of Robin Hood (along with many other candidates).[6]

Trouble broke out on several other fronts in 1068, including East Anglia and the north of England, where Norman control had not yet been established. To some extent the risings represented a delayed reaction to the Norman political takeover of the country, but much of the unrest was undoubtedly provoked by the heavy-handed actions of the conquerors. An episode in Somerset, characteristic of the new Norman rulers' approach, resulted in a considerable backlash but may also have been part of the wider uprising in the south-west. In 1068, Robert of Mortain began to construct a castle and park at a place called *hogworesbeorh*. This occupied an isolated, conical hill, later called St Michael's, which was scarped to form a large oval-shaped motte with an outer terrace on three sides and a bailey on the south-east slopes and was called *Mons Acutus* (sharp hill) or Montacute by the Normans. The site had a symbolic significance for the English because it was here that a fragment of what was believed to be the True Cross had been found in 1035. The relic had been taken to Waltham in Essex, where Harold had endowed the Holy Cross monastery, but a chapel had been built on the site where the relic had been found. 'Holy Cross' had been the battle cry of the English army at Stamford Bridge and Hastings, and Robert could well have chosen the site deliberately to insult the English. In 1069 the castle was besieged and became the focus of an uprising, which was brutally suppressed by Bishop Geoffrey of Coutances, whose extensive lands in the region were also under threat. Ironically, there were English mercenaries among those who fought for the Normans to relieve the castle.[7] Subsequently, Robert made Montacute Castle the *caput* of his estates in the south-west of England.

St Michael's Hill, Montacute, Somerset. According to tradition, a relic of the True Cross was housed in a chapel on the summit in the eleventh century. The decision of Robert of Mortain to build a castle here in 1068 provoked a Saxon uprising against the Normans, which was ruthlessly put down by Geoffrey, Bishop of Coutances. (*Roy and Leslie Adkins*)

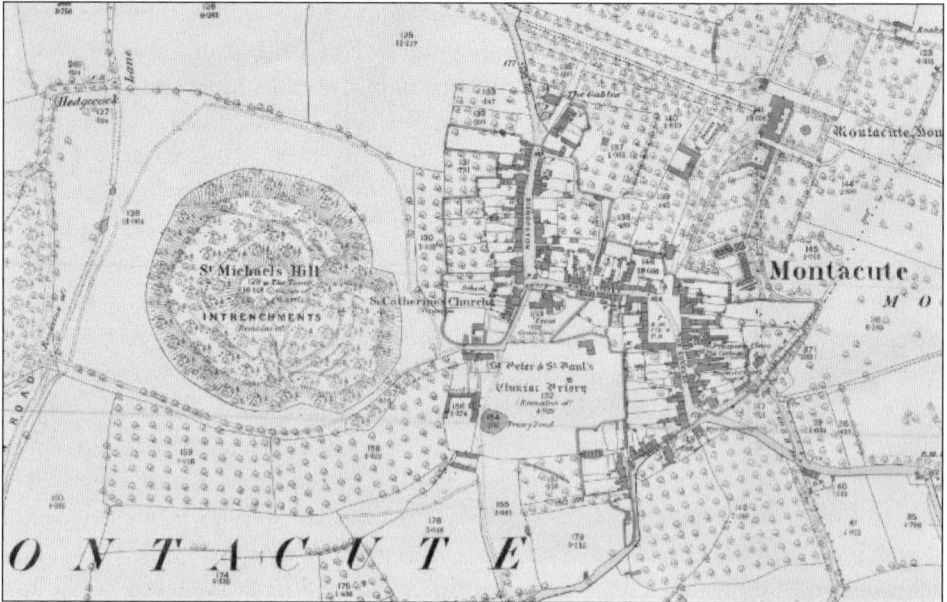

Map showing the relationship of St Michael's Hill to a Cluniac priory founded in the later eleventh century by William of Mortain. To the north of the priory lies the planned settlement of Bishopston, to the east the late eleventh-century borough of Montacute.

A coin hoard recently uncovered in the Chew Valley, to the south of Bristol, seems to confirm troubled conditions in the region at about this time. Some 2,578 coins were found in 2019; 1,236 were minted in Harold's reign and 1,310 dated from immediately after William's coronation. Most of the Harold coins were minted in Sussex and the south–east, which might indicate that the English king was making financial preparations in that region to resist the Norman invasion. The hoard appears to have been buried late in 1067

The largest hoard of late Saxon and early Norman coins ever found, from the Chew Valley, in the Mendip Hills about 15 km to the south of Bristol. They may have been buried in response to the troubled conditions in the south-west in the late 1060s. (*Pippa Pearce, British Museum*)

or early in 1068. Some of the coins are 'mules', that is, they have a design from different coin types on either side, a device used by moneyers to avoid tax. Although the hoard may have been buried in response to the Montacute uprising in the south-west, it could equally have been deposited at the time Harold's sons in 1068 raided around the mouth of the River Avon, close to the Chew Valley.[8]

The Harrying of the North

The most serious trouble the Normans encountered in the wake of the Conquest was a series of uprisings in northern England in 1069–70; these resulted in the infamous 'Harrying of the North'. The north of England was always going to pose a problem for the incoming Normans. The kingdom of Northumbria was culturally Anglo-Scandinavian in character and, although technically part of a united England since the mid-tenth century, still operated as a semi-autonomous region. Not only was the north culturally separate, but it provided the traditional gateway through which Scandinavian (and Scottish) invasions arrived. Many previous attacks on England had started here and in 1069 a Danish force under King Sweyn II threatened the region at the same time that there was a major native uprising. The Danish king probably did not have serious designs upon the kingdom and was more interested in obtaining large quantities of booty, but William was unwilling to allow him to run wild.

William had left the suppression of most of the unrest in the wake of the Battle of Hastings to his lieutenants, but the king himself quashed this, the most serious rebellion. The 'Harrying of the North' was a series of campaigns to subjugate northern England conducted in the winter of 1069–70. The capital of the north, York, was a Viking city, with Viking culture, and earlier kings of England had been content to leave the region and its capital largely to their own devices. William, aware of the danger of such laissez-faire, was determined to bring York and the north to heel. After the Norman invasion 'the north was seething with discontent' according to Orderic Vitalis, not helped by William laying waste one of York's seven 'shires' to build his first castle there.

In January 1069, Robert de Comines, the new Earl of Northumbria, was slaughtered along with a contingent of his men. The rebels then turned their attention to York where they besieged the castle, killing the constable and a number of soldiers. In response, William arrived in the city and killed the besiegers, but was unable to engage with Edgar the Aetheling's rebel army. Edgar had attempted to join forces with King Sweyn's invading army, but William was able to negotiate a payment of sufficient tribute to persuade the Danes to return home without a fight. Edgar, who had found sanctuary in Scotland on previous occasions, fled across the border once more.

As William was unable to tempt the rebel army into a pitched battle, he deprived them of food and support. John of Worcester described how the king, 'hastening with an angry heart into Northumbria, ceased not, during the whole winter, to lay waste the land, to murder the inhabitants and to inflict numerous injuries'. Apparently, the king's plan was to make it impossible for the north to revolt again after he departed. Leaving detachments to look after any further trouble and to repair damaged castles, he sent groups of soldiers throughout the Vale of York and the major river valleys with orders to ravage the land. The chroniclers report that some peasants were massacred outright, but the large numbers of refugees created were subject to harassment and to famine; there were even reports of cannibalism. Villages were burnt along with the grain from the last harvest, ploughs were destroyed and livestock slaughtered.

William, surrounded by the trappings of kingship, celebrated what must have been a bizarre and uncomfortable Christmas in the ruins of York. Early in 1070 he moved north with the intention of harrying Durham; his army was divided into smaller units, which were sent out to intimidate, loot and burn. The Normans marched in two groups through eastern and central Durham to the River Tyne, where they destroyed Jarrow. Bishop Aethelwine of Durham and his community fled in advance, 'fearing lest the king's sword should include equally the innocent and the guilty in indiscriminate slaughter'.[9] The Normans then devastated the Tyne Valley and Northumberland as far west as Hexham, but the region was sparsely populated and the scale of damage was less severe than that perpetrated in Yorkshire.

Afterwards, the king moved south to York again and in February 1070 crossed the Pennines in order to harry Cheshire, Staffordshire and Shropshire. The Pennine crossing in the snow proved to be so arduous that, according to Orderic Vitalis, it invoked a near-mutiny among the non-Norman troops, who complained that 'they could not obey a lord … who commanded them to do the impossible'. Nevertheless, William had at least partially solved the 'Northern problem' by 'pacifying' native society in Yorkshire and undermining Durham and counties further south. Scotland remained a challenge for the Norman kings and the threat of invasion from Scandinavia had not disappeared entirely. Despite the subsequent wholesale redistribution of land among Norman barons, the situation remained insecure.

According to William of Poitiers, William the Conqueror was a Christian hero who 'especially prohibited slaughter, fire and pillage', but the severity of the king's reaction has led some scholars to describe his strategy in the winter of 1069–70 as 'an act of genocide'.[10] Other contemporary chroniclers recorded the brutality of the campaign; several reported large-scale destruction, famine, burning and slaughter and many condemned William's actions. For example, the *Anglo-Saxon Chronicle* for 1069 recorded that William 'utterly ravaged and laid waste that shire [Yorkshire]', while the near-contemporary *Evesham Abbey Chronicle* tells of refugees from the Harrying being forced to move as far south as Worcestershire. Half a century later, Orderic Vitalis wrote:

To his shame, William made no effort to control his fury, punishing the innocent with the guilty. He ordered that crops and herds, tools and food be burnt to ashes. More than 100,000 people perished of starvation.

Land recovers fairly quickly from deliberate devastation, but people and the animals required to cultivate it do not. Sixteen years later, in 1086, Yorkshire still had a huge deficit of people and oxen. Oxen, if they can be bred in sufficient numbers, are unruly animals that take around five years to grow and to be trained to pull a plough. They are also crucial to the provision of manure. William appears to have systematically destroyed the long-term livelihoods of a generation of Yorkshire farmers.

Writing about 1100, Symeon of Durham claimed:

> So great a famine prevailed that these men, compelled by hunger, devoured human flesh, that of horses, dogs and cats … It was horrific to behold human corpses decaying in the houses, the streets, and the roads … For no one was left to bury them … the land thus being deprived of anyone to cultivate it for nine years … There was no village inhabited between York and Durham.

While William of Malmesbury, *c*.1125, observed that:

> Thus, the resources of a province, once flourishing … were cut off by fire, slaughter and … devastation; the ground, for more than sixty miles, totally uncultivated and unproductive to the present day. As for the cities once famous, the towers whose tops once threatened the sky, the fields rich in pasture and watered by rivers, if anyone sees them now he sighs as if he is a stranger, and if he is a native surviving from the past, he does not recognize them.

The roles of brigandage and revolt are sometimes conflated in contemporary accounts, as in the *Evesham Chronicle*, which attributed the harrying of northern Mercia to the king's wish to extirpate the 'outlaws and thieves who infested the woods in those areas'. In the aftermath of the Harrying, outlaws (or guerrillas perhaps) were an enduring problem and it was several decades before a degree of stability was restored to the remoter parts of northern England. William of Jumièges reported that defeated rebels took to raiding and amassing wealth by 'piratical theft', while Symeon of Durham claimed that deserted villages 'became lurking-places for wild beasts and robbers and were a great dread to travellers'. The *Abingdon Chronicle* reported that many plots were hatched by the English and that some hid in woods and some on islands, plundering and attacking those who came their way. It is alleged that the founder of Selby Abbey, Benedict, a monk from Saint-Germain of Auxerre, and his followers were routinely attacked by an outlaw called Swein. Another outlaw, Gillemichael, operated to the north of the Tyne and attacked the monks of Durham as they fled to Lindisfarne and 'inflicted many injuries upon the fugitives'.[11] A frequently repeated anecdote concerns Hugh fitz Baldric, Sheriff of Yorkshire (and Nottinghamshire), who used to travel with an armed guard by water whenever possible to avoid outlaws.

William felt it necessary to reintroduce the *murdrum* fine as a means of protecting the unpopular Normans in England. It was originally introduced by the Danes for the killing of an unknown man, who was presumed to be Danish. Under this legislation, all Frenchmen who settled in England after Hastings were specifically protected by the king and stringent fines were imposed on communities as a whole. The law forced Anglo-Saxon villagers to prove that any corpse found near their village was not a Norman. If the victim turned out to be Norman, the whole village was responsible for finding the culprit and had to pay a fine after the murderer had been executed.

Throughout his reign, William was to apply scorched-earth tactics in his campaigns, and, ironically, his own demise occurred within the context of such an episode in France. In the late summer of 1087, William was fighting the French king at Mantes in the Seine Valley, where, according to the *Anglo-Saxon Chronicle*, he had 'burned down the town … and all the minsters which were inside the town'. The chroniclers reported that the 'king who was very corpulent, fell ill from exhaustion and heat' and fell from his horse into the burning embers of the town he had just destroyed. Six weeks later he was dead.

Even allowing for the undoubted exaggeration of the chroniclers, there is a consistency in the reports, which suggests a degree of authenticity. More can be deduced from the Domesday Book evidence, which has been used by historians since the nineteenth century to calculate the scale of the damage inflicted by the Normans.[12] In 1086 there were still large areas of territory in Yorkshire and the North Riding recorded as 'waste'. Vill after vill is recorded as *wasteas est* (it is waste) or *hoc est vast* (it is wasted). Something like 60 per cent of all holdings were waste and numerous estates were sharply devalued; even the prosperous area of the county had lost 60 per cent of its value compared to 1066. It has been estimated that only 25 per cent of the pre-Conquest population and plough teams remained and that there was a loss of 80,000 oxen and 150,000 people.[13] Of the 199 manors held by Count Alan of Brittany in the castlery of Richmond, the Domesday Book specifically records that 108 were waste.

In the eastern parts of Cheshire and Shropshire, many wasted vills are recorded in 1070 that were not waste in 1066 and therefore must have been damaged as a consequence of Norman reprisals, either in response to local rebellion or to the more general northern revolt. In Cheshire, over half the county's estates were recorded as waste in 1070. The Domesday valuations of salt-working in Cheshire also provide an insight into the destructive impact of the Conquest. Salt pans in Northwich, Middlewich and Nantwich, valued at £8, £8 and £21 respectively in 1066, were all recorded as waste in 1070; and while Nantwich at £10 had partly recovered its former value by 1086, Northwich at 35 shillings and Middlewich at 25 shillings were still sharply devalued.[14] Clearly, whatever was responsible for this depreciation had occurred after the Battle of Hastings, and it seems probable that they were devastated by Norman troops in the wake of the native uprisings.

Orderic Vitalis believed that William's strategy had been successful and that by the mid-1070s 'peace reigned over England; and a degree of security returned to its inhabitants now that the brigands had been driven off'. Nevertheless, such was the apparent scale of devastation that it has led some scholars to argue that the Harrying of the North had a permanent and radical impact on the economic balance of England as a whole:

> Yet it would probably not be an overstatement to interpret the widespread reprisals in northern England as events which tilted the balance of economic activity for the long-term in favour of the south and east of England.[15]

This view has become increasingly unfashionable in recent decades. Several historians have questioned the reliability of the evidence from the chroniclers and the interpretation of the Domesday evidence. They argue that William would not have had the necessary military resources to wreak havoc over such a large area on such a scale in such a short time. It has been suggested that some of the destruction was caused by raiding Danes or Scots. Alternatively, it is argued that the Domesday evidence has been misinterpreted and that the term 'waste' in this context marked some form of manorial reorganization, or even a 'tax break', or merely reflected ignorance on the part of the Domesday commissioners, when unable to determine details of population and other manorial resources.[16]

Although Orderic Vitalis speaks of despoliation being carried out into 'forests and remote mountainous places', there is another interpretation for the documentary evidence favoured by some historical geographers. This view argues that, as many of the recorded empty settlements lay on higher ground and many lowland sites appear to have been relatively unscathed, then upland populations could have moved to valley settlements, which had in their turn been depopulated by the Normans.[17] Although this provides an elegant explanation for an anomaly, there is no corroborative evidence to support it. Similarly, the idea that many northern settlements were redesigned as planned villages subsequent to the Harrying cannot archaeologically be proved. There is, however, some evidence to suggest that new monastic granges were set up in 'waste' territory a few decades after the Harrying. Donkin has shown that 44 per cent of all known twelfth-century granges (mainly Cistercian) were built on land that was completely or largely 'waste' in 1086.[18]

Precise dating from archaeological evidence, which might confirm the extent of the Harrying, is difficult to pin down. It does appear that some of York's wealthier inhabitants must have fled to avoid robbery or death as there are an exceptional number of contemporary coin hoards ending with issues of c.1069–70, four of

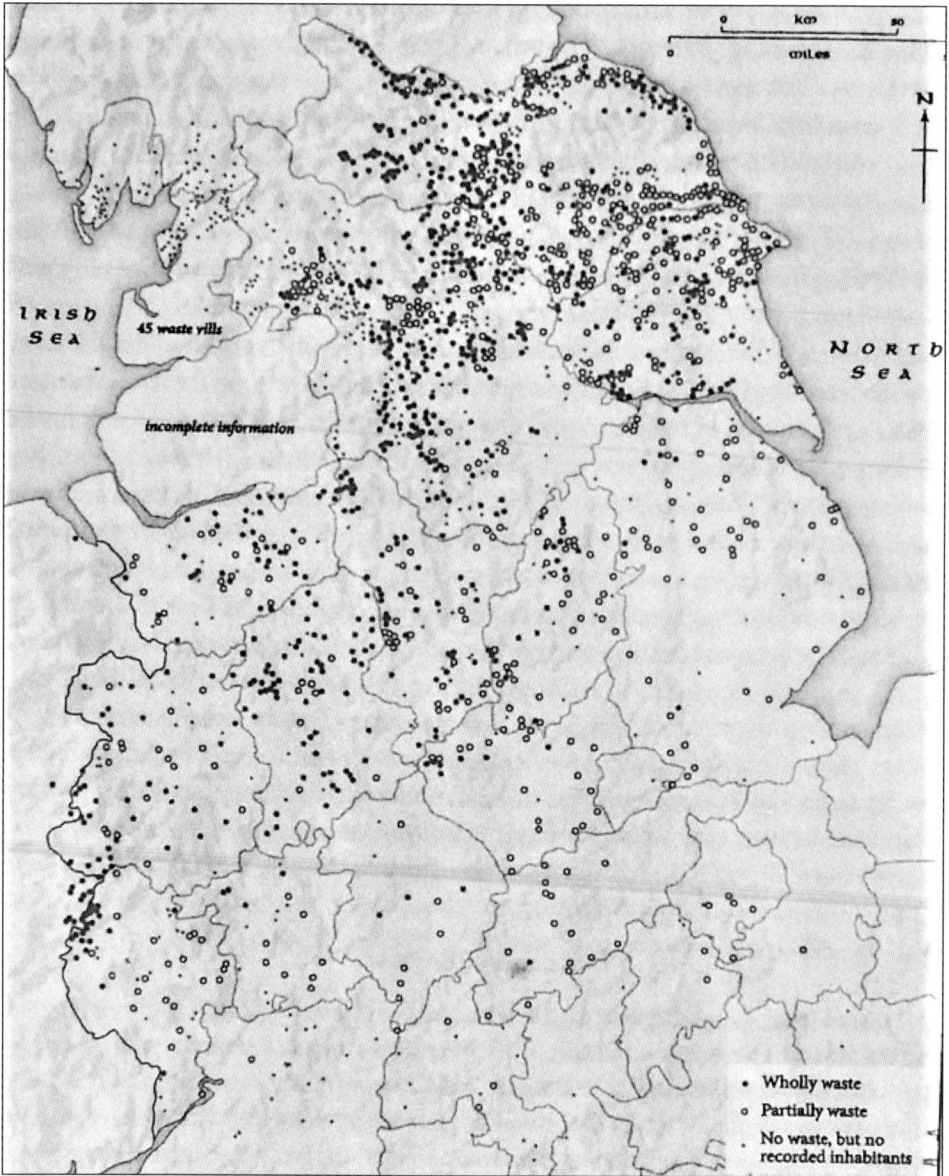

The distribution of waste vills in the north of England from the Domesday record of 1086. There is some dispute whether they are a result of King William's suppression of rebellion, the Harrying of the North.

them found within the city of York itself.[19] The decline in the number of moneyers minting coins in York from eleven in 1066–8 to just one in the early 1070s certainly points to a high degree of damage to the city, and York's commercial decline following the northern rebellion appears to be confirmed from its absence from the lists of high-ranking mints between 1068 and c.1120.[20] There is also some suggestion of decline in the abandonment of an earlier, thriving line of Coppergate frontage in York, but it is not possible to determine if this occurs before or after the Conquest.[21] However, pollen samples taken from northern locations such as Rookhope Burn (Co. Durham) and Hulleter Moss (Cumbria) do indicate a short-term decline in arable, accompanied by an increase in woodland at the time of the Harrying.[22]

The Domesday coverage of the north does demonstrate that when the land was eventually redistributed it was given in blocks to families such as the Percys and the Tisons. This was in contrast to much of the rest of England where barons' holdings tended to be deliberately scattered across the countryside.

Planned Villages

There are large numbers of regular planned villages in Yorkshire, Durham and Cumbria, many of which appear to have originated in or around the twelfth century. Where dating evidence is available, such planned villages appear to date from both before and after the Conquest. Some of these appear to have been as rigorously planned as contemporary new towns. Frequently, two rows of dwellings and tofts would face each other across the road or green, as at Huby, but usually there would just be one row, as at Gate Helmsley. Sometimes there were three rows, arranged around a triangular green, as at Nun Monkton. Some scholars have interpreted this phenomenon as representing a radical restructuring of rural settlement after the Harrying of the North.[23] It is argued that as a result of the Harrying, much of Northumbria remained sparsely populated for the last decades of the eleventh century and that it was not until Henry I began to distribute lands to a new aristocracy in relatively peaceful conditions that a degree of prosperity returned to the region. The new Norman lords built castles around which agricultural activity was concentrated, involving the reorganization of estate units. The communities that farmed these estates were often based in new, planned villages. Indeed, as many as 66 per cent of villages in Durham have regular plans, pointing to a massive programme of village creation and redesign, a programme that other scholars believe could have been well under way by the time of the Conquest.

The village of Wheldrake, just outside York, appears to have been laid out between 1066 and 1086, and was associated with woodland clearance. It consisted of sixteen crofts, eight on each side of the village street. Other regulated villages can be shown to have replaced an earlier arrangement of scattered hamlets; for instance, Appleton-le-Moors replaced two earlier settlements. Appleton has a distinctive regular plan with a wide central street lined with similar-sized plots and back gardens or garths, all of the same length, extending to two back lanes. Regular garths of about 330ft at Appleton were laid out in the twelfth century over ploughland that belonged to the lords of the manor, the Savarys. The process dates from the time of Abbot Savary of St Mary's Abbey, York

(1147–61), who established his kin in Appleton-le-Moors. Charters show that at this time the lost Domesday vill of *Baschebi* was amalgamated with Appleton, resulting in the addition of a third open field, the North Field, to the two that had previously existed.[24] The nearby villages of Levisham and Lockton share the same two-row plan and along with many other regular villages in this part of the Pennines probably originated in the century after the Norman devastation.

Planned villages were commonly located on the estates of high-status landowners such as the Archbishop of York. On the lands of the Bishop of Durham, for example, most regular plans are to be found associated with those villages directly under his control.[25] It has been suggested that such powerful men sought to stimulate recovery by attracting tenants to devastated areas, offering to accept rent payments rather than more onerous obligations of bondage and service.

The dating of these planned rural settlements remains a matter of debate and some historians point out the lack of specific documentary and archaeological

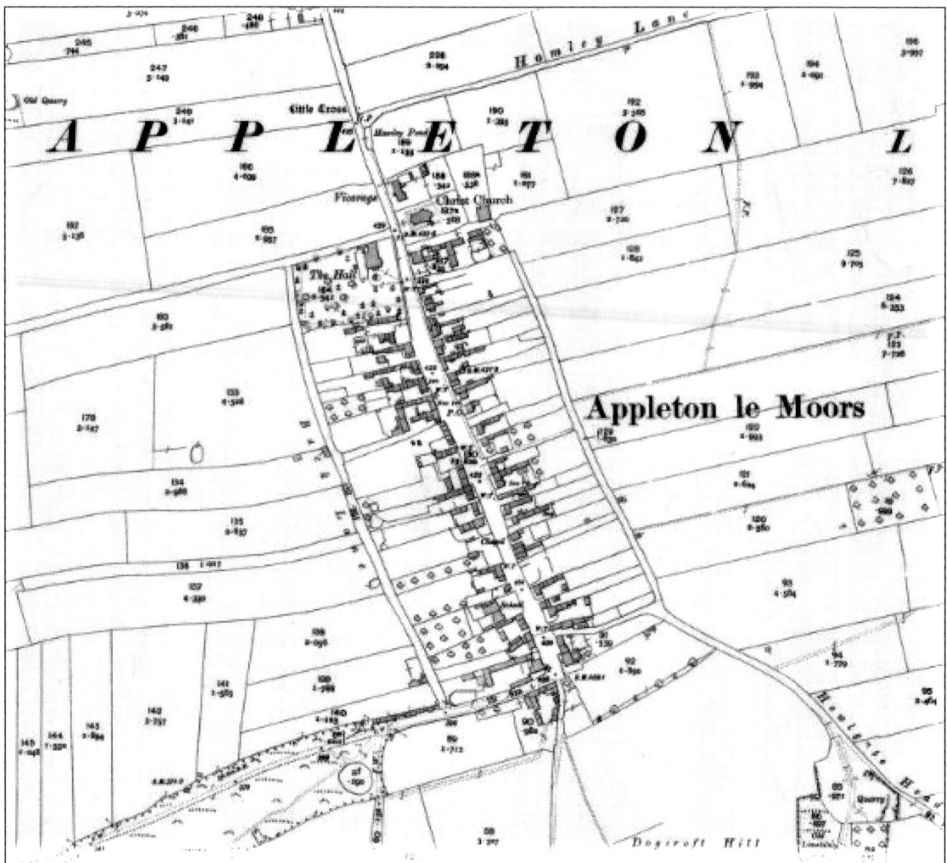

Map of the planned village of Appleton-le-Moors, North Yorkshire. It was laid out in the twelfth century by St Mary's Abbey, York, possibly over existing agricultural land.

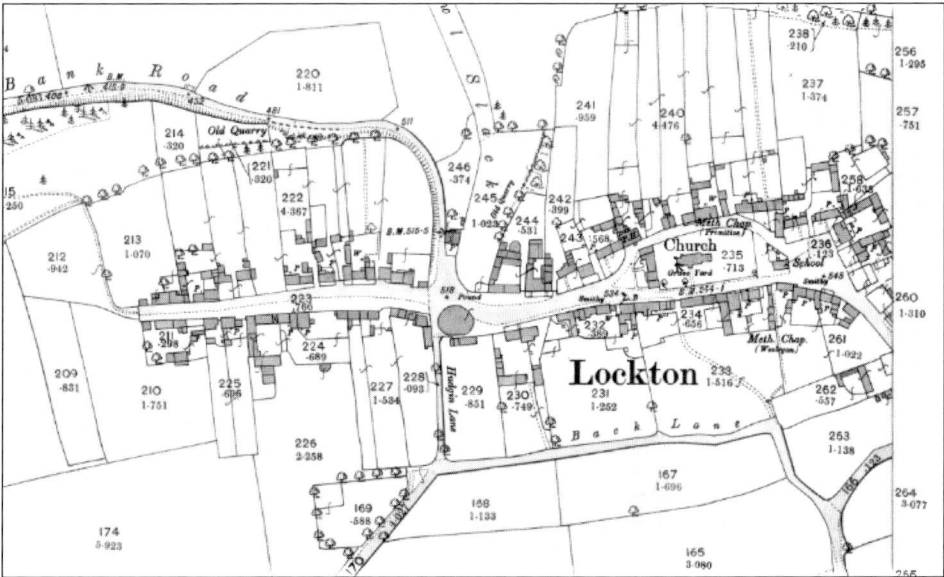

Map of the planned village of Lockton, North Yorkshire.

evidence to link the two events, suggesting that village creation could occur at any time between 900 and 1300.[26] Palliser has argued that the few regular plans that have been closely studied show no consistent relationship to the presence of waste in 1086. Perhaps Roberts's assessment that 'devastation by fire and sword offered opportunity for settlement planning, but not the certainty of this taking place' provides the safest interpretation.[27]

The Fenland Revolt

The risings of 1070 and 1071 were the result of resented appropriations at all levels of society, crises heightened by Danish involvement. A Danish army, which arrived in England in 1069 to support the northern rebellion, spent the winter in the Humber estuary and was reinforced by a second Danish fleet in 1070. The Danes then sailed to East Anglia where they raided the countryside. The *Anglo-Saxon Chronicle* stresses the serious nature of these events, twice reporting that the people expected the Danes would conquer the country.

The focus of unrest of this, one of the last major uprisings, was in the Fens, around the great abbeys of Peterborough and Ely. The chronology of events is hard to reconstruct since the sources are so imprecise. The leader of the English rebels, Hereward, held land of the abbey of Crowland and had earlier been exiled. Later sources suggest that he was a kinsman of Abbot Brand of Peterborough, by whom he was said to have been knighted. Brand had declared for Edgar Aetheling in 1066 and the abbey was long to continue as a stronghold of English culture.

The *Anglo-Saxon Chronicle* refers to Hereward and his followers as the 'men of the abbey'. His career as a monastic thegn was similar to that of Edric the Wild. The abbot's death in November 1069 seems to have triggered the revolt, when Brand was replaced by a Norman, Turold, who had a reputation as an unsympathetic abbot at Malmesbury, from whence he was transferred.

The Isle of Ely provided a safe haven for rebellious Englishmen. It was large enough to be self-sufficient and said to be able to resist a siege with ample supplies of crops, fruit, livestock, fish and wildfowl. The island measured 20 km by 16 km with only one reliable access point. A catastrophic raid on Peterborough was launched from Ely by the Danes and Hereward. However, after the Danes made an agreement with William they returned with their loot to Scandinavia. Turold entered the abbey, but Hereward and the English rebels stayed at Ely, which remained sympathetic to their cause. In 1071 the rebels were reinforced by the arrival of fresh forces, including Earl Morcar and Bishop Aethelwine of Durham. Hereward's last stand soon entered legend, but the essential elements of the story indicate that, after a siege, King William gained the surrender of the Isle of Ely. Aethelwine was sent into the custody of the abbot of Abingdon; Morcar was captured and imprisoned; while Hereward apparently made his peace, realizing that without Scandinavian support he could not succeed. At the same time Edric the Wild seems to have surrendered, also recognizing that without the Danes the cause was hopeless; both Edric and Hereward appear to have come to terms with the new regime.[28]

As with most of the revolts, the long-term impact of the Fenland revolt on the landscape was probably minimal, although it may have prompted William to build at least one causeway to the Isle of Ely. The Aldreth causeway is normally associated with William's campaign against Hereward, and it is likely that he also reinforced the shorter Stuntney causeway. Reputedly, he built siege castles at each end of the causeway. The remains of a substantial ringwork at Belsar's Hill, Willingham, known as Alrehede or Belassise Castle, a Norman name, lie at the southern end of the Aldreth causeway and are bisected by a driftway. Hereward's Castle, a large motte close to the cathedral, has traditionally been believed to have been built by William in 1070, but there is no archaeological evidence to confirm this claim.

There was one more abortive rebellion in 1075, again featuring East Anglia, which was really an attempt at an aristocratic coup. The earls of Hereford, Northumberland and East Anglia, according to the *Anglo-Saxon Chronicle*, 'planned to drive their royal lord out of his kingdom', but in the event it fizzled out as soon as it began. Roger de Breteuil, Earl of Hereford, was imprisoned for life; Ralph, Earl of East Anglia, fled to Brittany with his army of 'Breton dung', according to Lanfranc; and Waltheof, Earl of Northumberland, was executed the following year. Waltheof was only one of a small number of English aristocrats to be executed; most rebel leaders were treated with clemency. Edgar the Aetheling, who had been the leader of a series of uprisings since 1069 and still thought of himself as a contender for the throne, was actually received at William's court in 1075.

The Aldreth Causeway, an ancient road running from Cambridge to Ely across the Fens. It has traditionally been associated with Hereward's rebellion and was believed to have been built by the Normans in an attempt to take the Isle of Ely. Its origins are almost certainly older than that, but it may have played a role in William's campaign of 1071. It has also been argued that the ringwork called Belsar's Hill was built or adapted by the Normans as a temporary fort, as part of the same campaign. The name 'Belsar', or 'Belassise', is from the Old French for 'beautiful seat'. (*Jonathan C.K. Webb*)

The Aldreth Causeway, the putative route of the Norman attack on Ely from Belsar's Hill in 1071.

Chapter 4

The Kingdom Changes Hands

William ... the Conqueror ... dispossessed almost the entire English aristocracy, replacing them with French families: perhaps the most complete destruction of a ruling class there has ever been in Europe, up to 1917.[1]

About 95 per cent of England appears to have changed hands between 1066 and 1086. Something in the order of 4,000 to 5,000 English thegns were replaced by no more than 180 Norman barons. The transfer of land and the tenurial system that King William adopted had two major consequences. They created a new ruling class and tethered power to the possession of land; the new elite held their social status not through lineage but because of their estates. In the first instance, land was given directly by the king to tenants-in-chief. This land was then passed to their knights as tenants, who in turn often sublet it to undertenants.

King William doubled the Crown's share of land while the king's half-brothers, Odo and Robert, held estates of similar size to the former Saxon earls, and most of the rest was distributed between French nobles. Many of these brought the names of their French estates with them, using what are known as toponymic names. The great Norman families that settled in England and became the new aristocracy came from Aubigny, Beaumont, Bully, Grandmesnil, Mandeville, Montfort, Montgomery, Montbrai, Tosny and Warenne. Among the lesser nobility who carried toponymic names were families that came from Drincourt, Planches, Granville, Le Mesnil, Vernon, Aunou, Limesy and Louvetot.

The most thorough dispossession took place immediately after the Battle of Hastings, when the property of all those who had fought against William was confiscated. These estates were largely in the south-eastern shires and the West Saxon heartlands. There were further dispossessions after the uprisings of 1069–70 and later rebellions, and from those who later fell foul of the king for one reason or another. The confiscated land was redistributed to his supporters and to honour those pledges he had made to men and institutions in France. It was a massive undertaking; the former English landowners were often not recorded, and when they were it was simply to confirm the validity of the transfer of their land to the newcomers.[2]

Before his departure for Normandy in March 1067, King William had started to redistribute 'rich fiefs' to those of his followers who chose to take up land in England, although William of Poitiers claimed that 'no Frenchman was given anything unjustly taken from an Englishman'. He also claimed that Englishmen as well as Normans benefited from the king's largesse, but he appears to have been talking about those Frenchmen who were already established in England before the invasion, such as Humphrey de Tilleul and his son Robert of Rhuddlan, who had been in King Edward's service.

A new structure of Norman estates was established in the form of baronies, palatinates, castleries, honours and manors, introducing a new feudal vocabulary into English. William the Conqueror established his favoured followers as barons by installing them as tenants-in-chief with great estates to be held *per baroniam*, a largely standard feudal contract of tenure, common to all his barons. This process was known as enfeoffment, according to which knights pledged their service to the king or greater lord in exchange for freehold property or land. Lands forming a barony were often dispersed over several different counties, taking the name of the chief manor within it, known as the *caput* (Latin for 'head'). Thus, the barony of Turstin fitz Rolf was called the barony of North Cadbury, Somerset. If the estate-in-land held by a barony contained a significant castle as its *caput baroniae* and consisted of more than about twenty knight's fees (each loosely equivalent to a manor), then it was termed an 'honour'.

William's barons were not necessarily chosen from the Norman nobility but were selected often on account of their personal abilities and usefulness. Thus Turstin, a relatively humble and obscure knight, who had stepped in at the last minute to accept the position of Duke William's standard-bearer at the Battle of Hastings, was granted a barony which comprised well over twenty manors. Turstin was also involved with colonization in the region of Caerleon in south-east Wales. Dodgson memorably summed up the character of the 'new landholding aristocracy which was Norman or French or Breton or Flemish or whatever other breed or nationality of chivalrous but unscrupulous adventurer, desperate ne'er-do-well, or noble and dutiful vassal had been recruited to the Norman duke's ominous enterprise of England'.[3]

There were several methods by which land was transferred from its pre-Conquest owner to its new custodian, and although undoubtedly some land was seized illegally by powerful local lords, the story of a free-for-all land grab has almost certainly been exaggerated.[4] The largest area of land changed hands through a process known as *antecession*, whereby a Norman tenant-in-chief was granted the estates of a single English owner (predecessor or *antecessor*). For example, Geoffrey de Mandeville (d.1100) was given the 'inheritance' of Esger the Staller. Reputedly, Esger had been the wealthiest thegn in Saxon England with estates totalling over 300 hides extending over nine counties. Esger had not been present at Hastings and retained his estates for almost a decade after the battle, but around 1075 he fell foul of William. He was imprisoned, stripped of his land and removed from his various offices, which included Governor and Portreeve of London, and died a prisoner in Normandy around 1085. Geoffrey de Mandeville was one of that group of minor Norman landholders whose fortune was made at the Battle

Map showing the distribution of baronies in the early twelfth century.

of Hastings. Not only did he become immensely rich, but he also inherited some of Esger's roles including Sheriff of London, Essex, Middlesex and Hertfordshire and Constable of the Tower of London.

Another method of transferring land into French hands was through intermarriage between conquerors and conquered. Orderic Vitalis claims that by the early twelfth century marriage between the incoming French and native residents was common in English towns. Women whose husbands had died at Hastings could maintain an interest in their family land by marrying a Norman or Frenchman. King William himself seems to have been responsible for forcing some aristocratic English women to marry Frenchmen. Robert d'Oilly, from Calvados in Normandy, the first Norman Sheriff of Oxfordshire, gained estates as a result of marriage to Edith, daughter of Wigod of Wallingford. Wigod appears to have collaborated with William and possibly helped the Norman army to cross the river at Wallingford on its march towards London in the late autumn of 1066. On Wigod's death, Robert inherited his estates and his office as lord of Wallingford, building castles at Wallingford and Oxford. Other matches were less harmonious, and Englishwomen are known to have taken refuge in nunneries 'not for love of the religious life but from fear of the French', according to Archbishop Lanfranc, who suggested that force was used on occasion to establish connubial relationships. Lanfranc explains in his letters: 'Noble maidens were exposed to the insults of low-born soldiers and lamented their dishonouring by the scum of the earth.'[5] The enforced marriage of widows had also been a source of complaint after Cnut's conquest.[6]

Some Frenchmen were awarded a round number of manors verbally by the king, with the implementation left to the sheriff or other royal official. This responsibility of reallocating tens of thousands of hides in the aftermath of Hastings must have been a temptation to the enablers, and it is hardly surprising that royal officers were guilty of retaining the occasional half-hide of land for themselves. The sheer volume of transactions alone inevitably led to omissions and mistakes. Perhaps unsurprisingly, most of the disputes about redistribution were not between Saxon and Norman but between the victors themselves.

Those English landholders who survived held considerably smaller estates than their French counterparts and have been described as 'the flotsam and jetsam of an aristocracy wrecked in the storms of the Conquest'.[7] Many English landholders survived as subtenants, and in some areas, such as Shropshire, 'Englishmen were not so much dispossessed as depressed in tenurial status', some surviving as holders of a portion of their ancestral estates.[8] Nevertheless, only a small minority held fragments of their former estates directly from the king; normally they appear as tenants of the incoming Continental magnates. For example, in 1086, Aelfwine, son of Edwin, was a modest subtenant of Walter de Lacy with two manors in Herefordshire. Another well-known example is Ailric, who in 1086 continued to hold his land at Marsh Gibbon in Buckinghamshire but now as a tenant of William fitz Ansculf, 'heavily and wretchedly' according to the Domesday Book. However, perhaps he was not as badly affected as the majority of dispossessed English. According to one historian, the very mention of his name in the Domesday Book indicates that he remained of high status: 'To put Ailric's dilemma in modern terms, he had probably had to sell the Porsche and his wife's Renault and rely on the four-wheel drive, but I doubt if he was actually on the breadline.'[9]

Occasionally, the Domesday survey reveals the identity of a third layer of undertenant, and these are often English. At Rollington (Dorset) in 1066, nine thegns are recorded as holding land; in 1086 they were still holding land but as tenants of a Norman subtenant. It is probable that a large number of unrecorded English tenants continued to farm the land that they had owned before the Conquest, but from one or two rungs lower down the social scale. The increase in taxation imposed by King William on barons, lords and freemen eventually found its way down to impact rural villeins and cottagers. Serfs eventually disappeared, but villeins and cottars were tied more firmly to the land and their obligations more rigorously enforced than previously. Consequently, everyone's place in rural society would have been more firmly delineated than before 1066.

The Domesday lists of tenants-in-chief and their tenants reveal the overwhelming dominance of non-English names. The scale of the transference is illustrated by examining a list of the new landholders in the county of Oxfordshire in 1086. Out of the fifty-nine named landholders in the county, the first authentic Englishman, Thorkell of Warwick, who seems to have survived by ingratiating himself with the Norman lords of Warwickshire, appears at number fifty-seven, holding five hides in Drayton. Thorkell was unusual in that he was one of only thirteen natives to survive as a tenant-in-chief; with a total holding of 132 hides, he ranked as the third largest English landholder in that category in the country.[10]

Another surviving English tenant-in-chief was Colswein of Lincoln, who was rewarded with extensive estates in Lincolnshire for unspecified services to the king. It is possible that he was the town reeve of Lincoln. The lands granted by William included an estate on the edge of Lincoln, where Colswein built thirty-six houses and two churches, one of which was St Peter Ad Fontem.[11] Both Thorkell and Colswein benefited from the acquisition of the estates of dispossessed fellow Englishmen. Ironically, the highest rate of survival of native landholders was in the north of England, which was the region that resisted Norman rule longest. Several English sheriffs remained in place until the late 1060s and early 1070s, but by 1086 only three shires were in the hands of Englishmen. King William's own court was overwhelmingly French in character. Charters written in the 1080s rarely contain an English name. For example, a charter confirming grants to St Peter's, Gloucester, issued in 1085 has eleven witnesses, all of whom came from Normandy or northern France apart from Archbishop Lanfranc, who was Italian.[12]

Castleries

An important method of land transfer was to grant land on a geographical basis regardless of pre-Conquest tenure. A castlery, sometimes called a territory, was a substantial block of land attached to a castle or within its jurisdiction. There are fourteen recorded in the Domesday Book, most of which contained in excess of one hundred manors. In critical frontier and coastal districts, blocks of territory were granted to single individuals. Best known are the Scottish and Welsh border areas and the Sussex rapes. Thus, in those areas, which William believed to be vulnerable, he created castleries such as those found in Normandy; for example, to strengthen his borders in Normandy, William had taken Ponthieu to the north and Bellême to the south as client counties under his vassalage.

The frontier zone against Wales (the Marches) was split into three Marcher earldoms – Chester, Shrewsbury and Hereford – which were themselves divided into powerful lordships based on castles, such as Oswestry, Caus, Clun and Wigmore.

Initially, the Welsh Marcher counties formed palatinate territories, where the earls were all-powerful; the king granted them virtual independence in what amounted to petty kingdoms. Marcher lords could build castles, administer laws, wage wars, establish new towns and were in possession of all the royal perquisites – salvage, treasure trove, plunder and royal fish. They were enabled to move into Welsh-held territories and keep the land they conquered or negotiated.

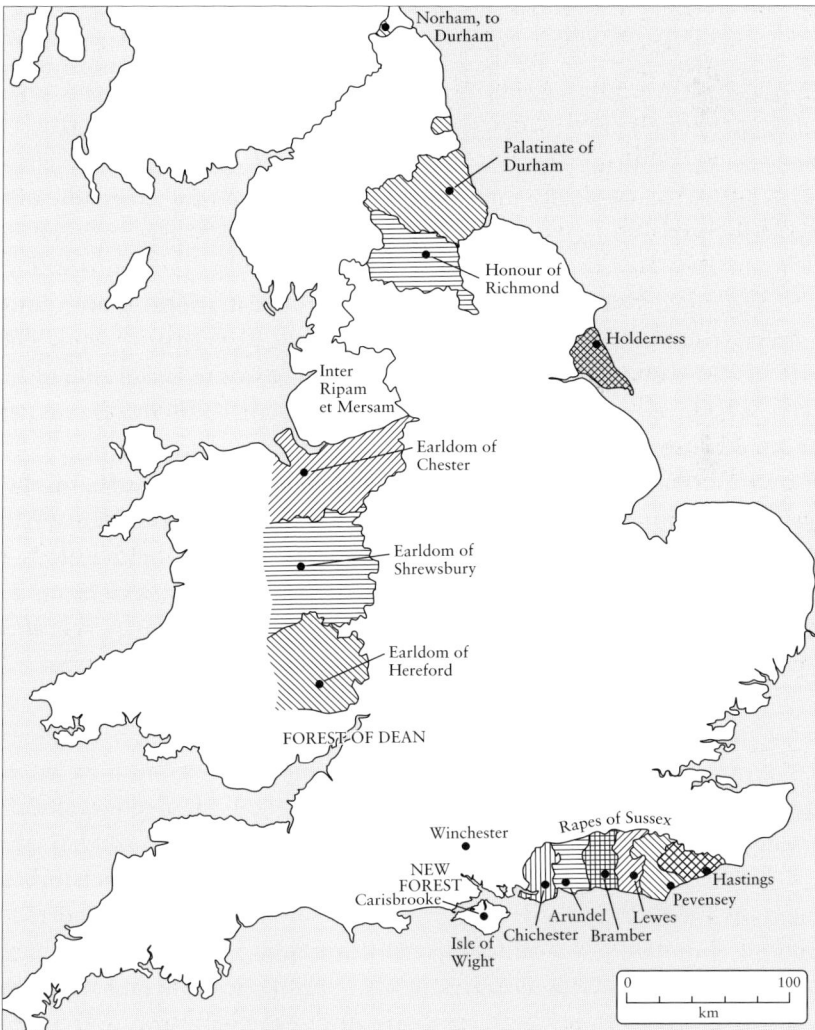

Map showing earldoms and palatinates in border regions after the Conquest.

Clun Castle in southern Shropshire, which was originally built as a large motte and bailey castle by Picot de Say soon after 1066. By the thirteenth century, it controlled a semi-autonomous Marcher Barony, known as the Honour of Clun. In 1199 the Honour was joined with that of Oswestry, under William Fitz Alan. The Fitz Alans, later Earls of Arundel, controlled a large Marcher Barony here until the end of the Middle Ages. The stone keep on the side of the motte was built as a grand hunting lodge, in a consciously antique Norman style in the thirteenth century (*Rowley, 2022*).

The Sussex rapes were formed soon after the Conquest, probably after the king's return from Normandy in December 1067. The rapes were large regional divisions designed to withstand an attack from the south, the route that William himself had taken. These responsible positions were entrusted to kin and trusted friends of the king: Robert, Count of Eu, a relative of the king's who had provided ships for the invasion fleet, received Hastings in May 1070; Pevensey was given to his half-brother, Robert of Mortain; Roger de Montgomery, another of King William's distant relatives, received Arundel and the Warenne family held Lewes. There were only four rapes up until 1073, plus the Banlieu of Battle, which was a Royal Peculiar, responsible directly to the Crown. The fifth rape, Bramber, was added by taking part of Arundel and part of Lewes. The most westerly of the rapes was that of Chichester, under the control of Roger de Montgomery as part of the rape of Arundel. Chichester does not appear as a separate rape until the fourteenth century, although it may have existed as an administrative unit even before the Conquest.

These castleries covered zones that controlled inlets, harbours, estuarine routes and landing beaches, giving access to the littoral zone of Sussex; they also had extensive hinterlands, allowing defence in depth and also some control of east–west movement. At the heart of these territories were powerful castles, supported in the surrounding countryside by subsidiary fortifications. Such administrative units were new to England and cut across traditional Saxon governmental arrangements. Castles such as those at Bramber, Portchester and Lewes had large, open enclosures in addition to mottes and stone keeps and would have been used to hold cavalry

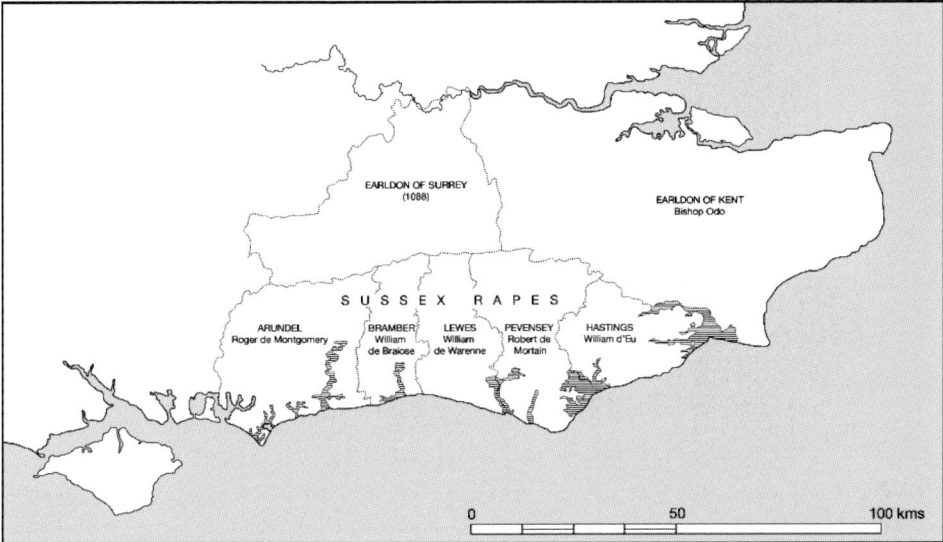

The Norman administrative divisions of rapes in south-east England, designed to protect the region from coastal attack. The New Forest may have formed part of this scheme. Each of the Rapes was based on a castle located close to the coast.

during the early years of the Conquest. Their role would have been not only to keep the peace but also to facilitate the confiscation and transfer of landholdings. In the first instance they were bases from which land transfer could be orchestrated, with contingents of Normans riding out into the countryside around to enforce the exchange of lands and then returning to the safety of the fortified cavalry barracks.

The Isle of Wight was held by William fitz Osbern, and after 1075 the king resumed direct overlordship. Further west there were groups of manors granted

Bramber Castle, close to the town of Steyning, overlooking the River Adur. It was originally built by William de Braose as the *caput* of the Barony and Rape of Bramber. The ruins of the castle are dominated by the remains of a substantial twelfth-century gatehouse.

to Robert de Mortain around Portland, protecting Dorset, Poole harbour and the River Frome. There were smaller honours around Exeter and Totnes, although William retained much direct overlordship in this area. In Kent, to the east, Bishop Odo (Earl of Kent) held Dover and extensive areas around Sandwich, Folkestone and north Kent, and there was a smaller coastal zone around Hythe – the 'divisio' of Hugh of Montfort with a castle at Saltwood.

The Lands of Bishop Odo of Bayeux

The acquisition of English estates after the Conquest raised many men of humble origins to great heights; it also enriched men of standing to even greater heights. One such was Bishop Odo of Bayeux, who became the wealthiest tenant-in-chief in England after the Conquest. Odo became Earl of Kent soon after the Battle of

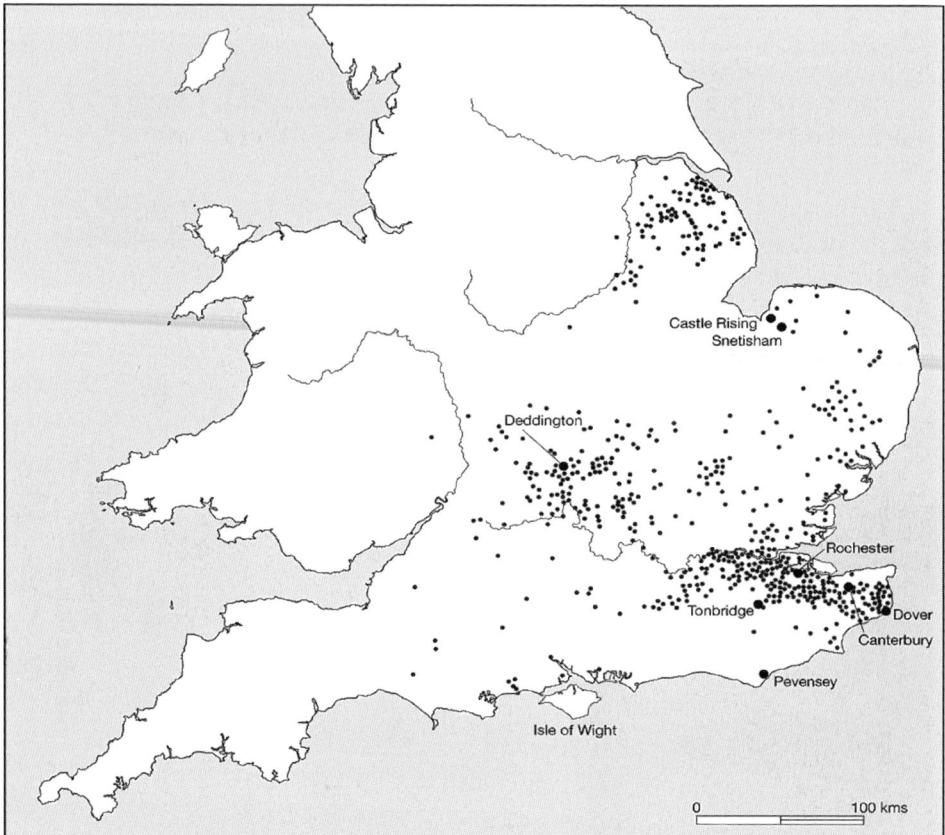

Map showing the distribution of the estates of Bishop Odo of Bayeux, William the Conqueror's half-brother, in the Domesday Book. After the king, Odo was the wealthiest landholder in England, although by this stage he had been imprisoned by William. The estates were concentrated in the south-east, the south Midlands, East Anglia and Lincolnshire. (*After Ivens, 1984*)

Hastings and was co-regent of England in 1067. William may have intended to treat Kent as a castlery, like those in Sussex, with the bishop as tenant-in-chief. In the Domesday Book, Odo is credited with estates valued at over £3,000, chiefly in the south-east. His lands far exceeded those of any other French baron's holdings, with something in the region of 456 manors spread over 22 counties. The bishop was also an enabler, involved in land transfer, and clearly some of it was transferred into his own hands.

Odo appears to have acquired the bulk of his land in the five years after Hastings, but he continued to accumulate assets right up to his fall from William's favour in 1082. The largest concentration of his lands was in Kent, acquired soon after 1066, with its *caput* at Rochester, and in terms of value he held almost half the land of Kent, more than that of the Archbishop of Canterbury.[13] He then acquired his estates in Buckinghamshire, Bedfordshire, Oxfordshire, Surrey, Hertfordshire and Essex, areas where he was actively transferring land in the post-Conquest period. In Oxfordshire, Odo took over a large group of manors to the west of the River Cherwell, lying in Wootton hundred; in all they comprised 161 hides, 79 of which were in demesne.

Odo's estates were never fully organized into baronies as the bishop fell from the king's favour before this could be achieved. Wootton appears to be a

Deddington, Oxfordshire. The oval enclosure to the right of the village represents the earthworks of Bishop Odo's castle here, probably the *caput* of his south Midland estates. Several early castles were in the form of large fortified enclosures, which could have been used as bases for the transfer of land from Saxon to Norman.

proto-barony based on the manor of Deddington.[14] A third, much looser, spread of manors was in the east, some in East Anglia and some in Lincolnshire, which he acquired after his role in subduing a rebellion in that region in 1075. It is possible that Snettisham or nearby Castle Rising was intended as the *caput* for this group. All three locations appear to have had large, fortified enclosures, with the capacity to house Norman cavalry.

Most of Odo's supporters did not belong to the Norman higher aristocracy, and men of relatively humble origins became the bishop's English barons. Lords such as Ilbert de Lacy, Hugh de Port and Roger Bigod had held modest estates in Normandy, yet were handsomely rewarded after Hastings and went on to found important Anglo-Norman dynasties. Other major English tenants, such as Wadard, Herbert fitz Ivo and Ralph de Courbépine, are not recorded as holding land in Normandy at all. Wadard is one of those rare knights actually named on the Bayeux Tapestry, where he is shown leading the foraging party soon after the Normans landed in 1066. Odo launched a number of his followers on to prestigious careers. For instance, Adam fitz Hubert was appointed a Domesday commissioner and, ironically, Hugh de Port was one of those responsible for proscribing Odo after he rebelled against William Rufus in 1088.[15]

Extract from the Bayeux Tapestry showing Wadard, one of Bishop Odo's vassals, leading a foraging party before the Battle of Hastings.

The French Connection

Edward the Confessor had already introduced a number of Normans to England on becoming king, although the scale of the Normanization of Edward's court has been questioned. They were nonetheless perceived by some as being a significant influence in the kingdom.[16] During the Godwin purge of Normans in 1052, the *Anglo-Saxon Chronicle* reported that 'all Frenchmen', except for a few selected by the king, were outlawed in the peace settlement because 'they promoted bad law and gave bad judgement and bad counsel in this land'. Many left with the re-establishment of Godwin control, but a few survived until the Conquest.

The Norman Conquest of 1066 resulted in a largely Norman, socially dominant, French-speaking elite occupying the overwhelming majority of positions of power in England after 1066. In that respect the Conquest represented a classic case of colonization, but at no stage was it associated with mass migration. Neither was there much large-scale settlement, either to replace the resident English or to people previously unoccupied areas. There were some communities that maintained their French character, some of whom displaced native populations and, in several towns, separate French quarters were established.

Apart from those knights who fought at Hastings, it is not known precisely how many Frenchmen came across to England either as part of William's army or later as migrants. It is generally agreed that there were relatively few immigrants, but where they can be identified they seem to have made an impact. The Domesday Book records 259 Frenchmen (*Francigenae*) scattered throughout England as well as sixteen *Francigenae servientes*, four *Franci* and eight *Franci homines*. There were 145 Frenchmen in York, reflecting York's importance as the northern capital of England, and sixty-five Frenchmen in Southampton, linked to cross-Channel trade. A large concentration of Frenchmen (forty-eight) was associated with the estates of St Albans Abbey in Hertfordshire. It appears to have been the policy of the first Norman abbot, Paul of Caen (1077–93), to invite or encourage French settlers on to his manors; in 1086 there were four Frenchmen at Rickmansworth, four at Hemel Hempstead, four at St Albans, three at Cassiobury and one at another four of St Albans' vills.

In some cases, the Frenchmen appear to have lived in discrete communities attached to castles; for example, at West Bytham (Castle Bytham), Lincolnshire, seven *Francigenae* had two ploughs and three ironworks. The castle here was founded for Drogo de la Beuvrière, the Flemish lord of Holderness. The village street plan seems to incorporate the line of a semicircular enclosure, which includes a dependent unit of settlement and the church, attached to the seigneurial complex.

In Leicestershire, Frenchmen were located in four manors with earthwork motte castles, three of which, Gilmorton, Ingarsby and Kibworth Harcourt, have identical dimensions. It is possible that these sites were the seats of a group of colonist subtenants, introduced to cultivate the demesne of newly acquired estates.[17]

Castle Bytham, Lincolnshire, which was possibly originally one of Bishop Odo's castles. In 1086, when the lord was Drogo de la Beuvrière, a Flemish associate of King William, a community of seven Frenchmen lived here. (*Richard Carter*)

There was a particularly large concentration of Frenchmen in the Welsh Marches, some of whom had been there before the Conquest. In Hereford itself we know that a contingent of Frenchmen were involved in the defence of the city before the Conquest, and that before 1072, King William granted the town the Laws of Breteuil, a set of regulations that offered favourable privileges to French settlers. These laws were accompanied by the development of a suburb for French migrants, which became the new site for the town's marketplace and court meetings. The Breteuil laws, designed to attract French migrants to frontier areas, became the prototype of the charters granted by many Norman lords to their English and, particularly, Welsh boroughs. Among the Welsh border towns to adopt them was Shrewsbury, where the chronicler Orderic Vitalis had gone to school. Orderic, the eldest son of a migrant French priest, noted that in the 1070s, French merchants could be seen in villages as well as towns. In 1086 there were 43 French burgesses in Shrewsbury, whose privileges included exemption from geld payments as well as the right to acquire the burgage plots of resident Englishmen.

There were other 'French boroughs' at Pontefract, Norwich and Richmond (Yorkshire). At Carlisle, a French borough was not designated as such, but the different communities occupied different parts of the town; the French were in the south-west corner around French Street, while the English concentrated in the eastern part around English Street (later, renamed High Street). At Stafford, a small community of French settlers was founded at Monetville, adjacent to the baronial castle outside the town. Such was the initial success of the French settlement at Lynn in Norfolk that in 1135 a second 'French' town was laid out alongside the first on the riverbank.

Nottingham belongs to the first phase of Norman town design when William was intent upon establishing a dominant Norman presence with a castle and a borough. During his march to subdue the northern rebels the Conqueror planted castles in strategic towns, including that at Nottingham, which was founded in 1068 on a strong, naturally defended site west of the former Scandinavian *burh*, known as the English borough. The French borough, as it continued to be called, had its own defences, streets and church. Within the new circuit of defences, encompassing some 120 acres, the northern and western walls of the Scandinavian *burh* were abandoned and by 1086 the ditch had been built over, but the distinction survived throughout the Middle Ages, each borough having its own sheriff and bailiff. The inheritance practices prevailing in both parts were quite distinctive; that in the English *burh* still being 'borough English' rather than the usual primogeniture. Yet while legal distinctions remained between English and French communities at Nottingham, they were physically united within integrated town defences by the middle of the twelfth century. A deer park to the west completed a classic example of Norman town and country planning comprising castle, borough and hunting park.

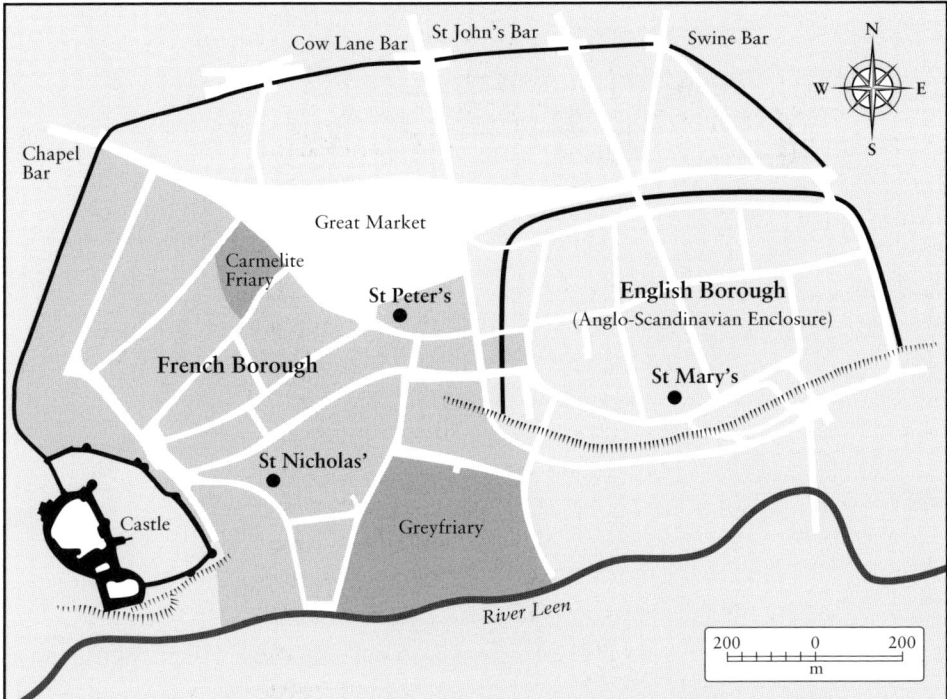

Plan of Nottingham showing the relationship between the castle and the French and English boroughs.

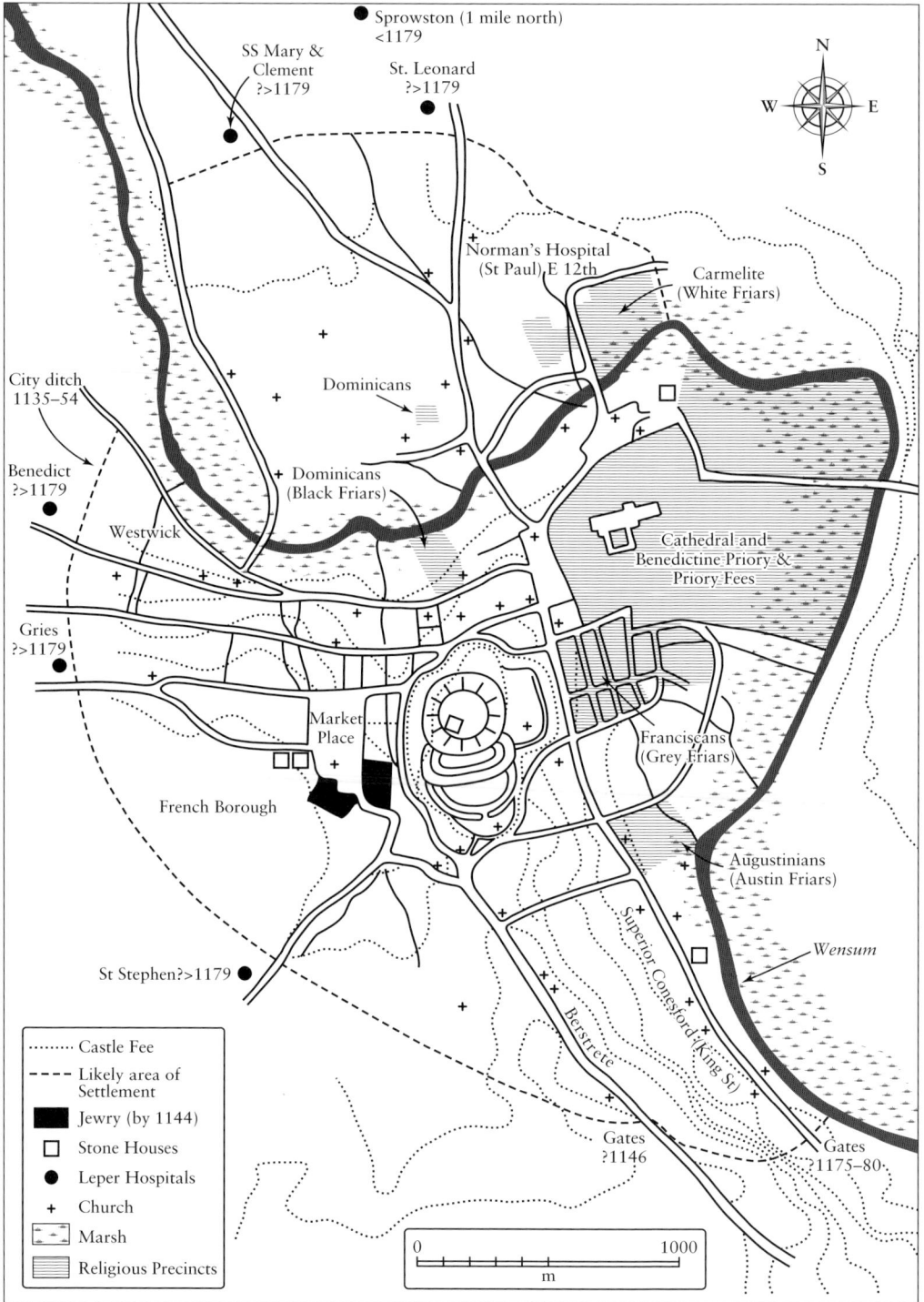

Plan of Norwich in the twelfth century, showing the location of the French borough in relation to the market, castle and cathedral. (See Plate 14 and p.157)

Elsewhere, differences between French and English sectors can be detected in other ways; at Southampton, for example, Domesday recorded 65 Frenchmen, who established a separate quarter around the castle in the north-west corner of the town. The church in the French quarter, dating from 1070, was dedicated to St Michael, the patron saint of Normandy, and there are also a number of standing stone buildings from the Norman period. Significant differences in pottery have also been identified; imported glazed ware is rare outside the French quarter. Other subtle changes in the pottery sequence point to different living standards and social customs between the French and English populations of Southampton.[18]

At Norwich, thirty-six Frenchmen at first shared their 'new town' with six English neighbours, but by 1086 the English had been replaced by more Frenchmen. An alternative marketplace had been established by Earl Ralph in the French quarter by 1086, on the west side of the castle, adjacent to the Great Cockey. This foundation was described as a 'new town' (*novus burgus*) in Domesday and had a 6:1 ratio of French to English residents. French settlers were found in other parts of Norwich too. Although the earl had taken the initiative in founding this partner town, he shared lordship of it with the king on the same basis as lordship of the older part of Norwich. The new town plantation was part of a broader Norman policy of deliberate colonization of important Anglo-Saxon town centres. The new town was later referred to as Newport, and still later as Man(nes)croft. Mancroft was more than an outer garrison for the castle; part of its purpose was to attract merchants and craftsmen to service the castle. Mancroft was made a borough in its own right, with customary dues pegged at 1*d*. a head to attract traders. It may well have had its own reeve and court. Its market, with a monopoly on castle business, gradually superseded Tombland and it became the focus of the city's commerce.[19] Some of the land in Mancroft was held by Norman soldiers, while houses in other parts of the town were held custom-free by men associated with the castle guard (e.g. crossbowmen and watchmen). By 1086, the number of French burgesses had increased from 36 to 125, while the Anglo-Saxon population had decreased.

Colonists from Outside Normandy

In addition to Normans, William's victorious army was recruited widely from various parts of northern and western France. The largest contingent were the Bretons, who made up just under 4 per cent and who, together with other French soldiers, formed the right wing of William's army at Hastings; Flemings 2.5 per cent; Picards 2 per cent; Poitevins 1 per cent; and soldiers from other regions of France 4 per cent.[20] Some of those who fought at Hastings, such as Amaury, *vicomte* of Thouars in Poitou, were paid off and returned to France, but many others settled on estates in England. In the decades after the Conquest, more migrants from these regions moved across the Channel; there were concentrations of settlers from different Continental areas in England, Wales and Scotland.

There were three main groups of Bretons. One was settled mainly in the north and east of England and held land directly or indirectly with the honour of Richmond. The lords of Richmond were brothers, Alan the Red and Alan the Black of Penthièvre. The second group was settled mainly in the south-west and was associated with Robert of Mortain. This group came from the north-east of Brittany and included Judhellus filius Aluredi, who became lord of Totnes and held 107 manors in Devon. After 1068, the third group was led by Ralph of Gaël, Earl of East Anglia and son of Ralph the Staller, a trusted baron with both Edward the Confessor and William the Conqueror. Although born in England with an English mother, he had estates in Brittany and formed the focus for a group of rebellious Bretons in 1075. After the uprising failed, he and many of his fellow Bretons returned to Brittany.

In 1092, William Rufus settled colonists around Carlisle after consolidating Norman control of Cumbria, Cumberland and Westmorland from the Scots. It has been suggested that many of the new settlers were Flemings and that the regular street villages of the region were built by them. In some cases, the uniformity of planning found in these settlements could have been due to the use of *drengs;* these were the northern English equivalent of *locatores* employed in mainland Europe and in areas of Anglo-Norman/Flemish colonization in Pembrokeshire.[21] Roberts argues that *drengs* operated as land agents, who could supervise the plantation of new villages on behalf of a lord. The *Anglo-Saxon Chronicle* suggests that military conquest accompanied by some element of devastation was followed by reorganization and pioneer peasant settlement. In 1092, William Rufus seized Cumbria, planted a castle at Carlisle and settled knights and peasants in the neighbourhood under Ranulf le Meschin, *vicomte* of Bayeux. According to the *Anglo-Saxon Chronicle*:

> In this year the king William [Rufus] travelled north to Carlisle with a very great army, and restored the town, and raised the castle, and drove out Dolfin who earlier ruled the land there, and set the castle with his men and afterwards returned south here, and sent very many peasants there with women and livestock to live there to till the land.

Roberts cites the example of planned Cumbrian villages Gamblesby and Glassonby that take their names directly from settlers (*drengs*) during the reign of Henry I.[22] Villages around Carlisle such as Aglionby, Harraby and Wiggonby also appear to have taken their names from William Rufus's new settlers.

There was also a concentration of Flemings in Holderness and south-east Lincolnshire, where a large number of individual Saxon estates were replaced by the single lordship of Drogo de la Beuvrière. A number of Drogo's subtenants had Flemish names and this may be reflected in land divisions. Long-furlong field systems are characteristic of this area and could represent Flemish influence as they reflect wetland reclamation in the Low Countries of the same date. It is also striking that Holderness was one of the few parts of lowland Yorkshire where there

Gamblesby, Cumbria, whose name incorporates the Flemish personal name 'Gamel', who was specifically recorded in the early twelfth century as a *dreng* in a writ of Henry I. It seems probable that the village was named after the colonist who created the settlement here. (*Roberts, 2008: 97*)

were hardly any vills described as 'waste' in 1086.[23] An alternative view is that after the Conquest, Flemish landholders were deliberately spread out across England in a broad zone stretching from Devon in the south-west to the East Riding of Yorkshire in the north-east.[24]

Wales

He governed the Welshmen,
Aethelred's son; ruled Britons and Scots,
Angles and Saxons, his eager soldiers.
All that the cold sea waves encompass
Young and loyal yielded allegiance
With all their heart to King Edward the noble.

Thus claimed Edward the Confessor's obituary, and it is true that the English Crown already did lay claim to overlordship in both Scotland and Wales. Bleddyn and Rhiwallon had been established as kings of all Wales under Edward's suzerainty (overlordship). King Malcolm III of Scotland (1058–93) in part owed his kingship to Edward and almost certainly recognized his overlordship.[25] On becoming king, William the Conqueror claimed an overlordship at least as extensive as that exercised by Edward the Confessor.

Soon after 1066 the Normans moved across the Welsh border and William fitz Osbern established bridgeheads in south-east Wales. William the Conqueror travelled to Wales in 1081, travelling as far as St David's in Pembrokeshire, ostensibly on pilgrimage. The king is said to have ordered a castle to be built at Cardiff, in the Welsh kingdom of Morgannwg, and the discovery of his coins there suggests that there may even have been an early Anglo-Norman colony, possibly with its own mint. The main conquest of Wales came in the reign of William II, spearheaded by Robert fitz Haimon. Robert had supported William during an abortive rising in 1088 and had been given estates in Gloucestershire, including the port of Bristol. He appears to have been invited to intervene in a dispute between two Welsh princes, and as commonly occurred in such circumstances, he began the process of colonization. He established the broad outlines of the later lordship of Glamorgan by distributing land to his followers and ordering castle-building at key points. He also gave Welsh churches and Church land to monasteries in England, particularly Gloucester and Tewkesbury.[26]

The very nature of Welsh kingship meant that there were pretenders in almost every kingdom and a constant succession of dynastic conflicts. This provided the Normans with the kind of opportunity that they were adept at seizing, as witnessed in south Italy and again, later, in Ireland. From the beginning the Norman border barons took every opportunity to involve themselves in Welsh affairs, whether by invitation, intervention or invasion. However, whenever they were involved, the Normans soon made it their objective to remove the Welsh kings and princes and to take over. Roger de Montgomery built a castle at Montgomery, to the west of Offa's Dyke, within a few years of the Conquest, to act as a forward base for launching attacks into central Wales. In 1074 the *Annales Cambriae* laconically record that the Normans pursued a scorched-earth policy along with diplomacy as they moved to the west of Offa's Dyke: 'From Montgomery Hugh [Roger's son] devastated Cardigan.'

The Norman barons took over the rights and obligations of the Welsh kings and the princes that they replaced, thus creating essentially Welsh principalities in Norman hands, and the extensive 'liberties' of the Marcher lords were secured by combining the prerogatives of a Welsh prince with the powers of a feudal lord. Conquest was followed by colonization. Once established on their Welsh lands, the Norman barons created tenancies for their vassals and knights there. In some places, notably in southern Pembroke and in Gower, French, English and Flemish freemen were settled on the land in large numbers. In each lordship there was an Englishry, usually consisting of castle, borough and manor, and often settled with people of non-Welsh origin, on the lower ground. The Welshry was usually on the higher land, where many ancient traditions survived; it was exploited indirectly by the conquerors,

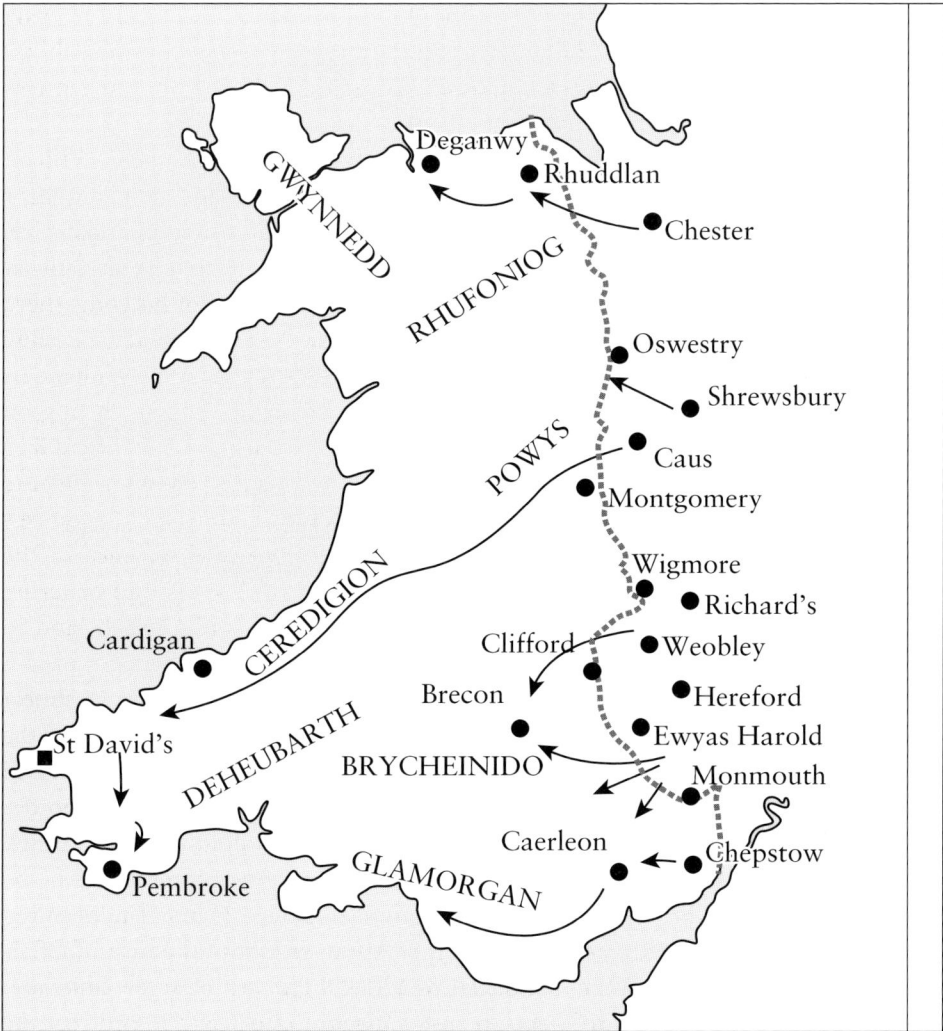

Map showing the early campaigns (eleventh century) of the Normans against the Welsh.

through tribute, though there are instances of Welsh nobles holding lands of Norman lords or of the king on much the same terms as the Normans held among themselves.

In Wales, the boroughs the Normans founded beside their castles represent the beginning of urban development in the country. There were only a few before 1135, but in Rhuddlan there were elements of industry and commerce already by 1086, and the burgesses had been given the 'Laws of Breteuil'. In these boroughs the Normans were basically providing for the needs of those who garrisoned their castles, but they also ensured that trade developed under their control. Pembroke is typical of the castle towns established by the Normans, with a castle founded in 1093 and a borough attached to it.

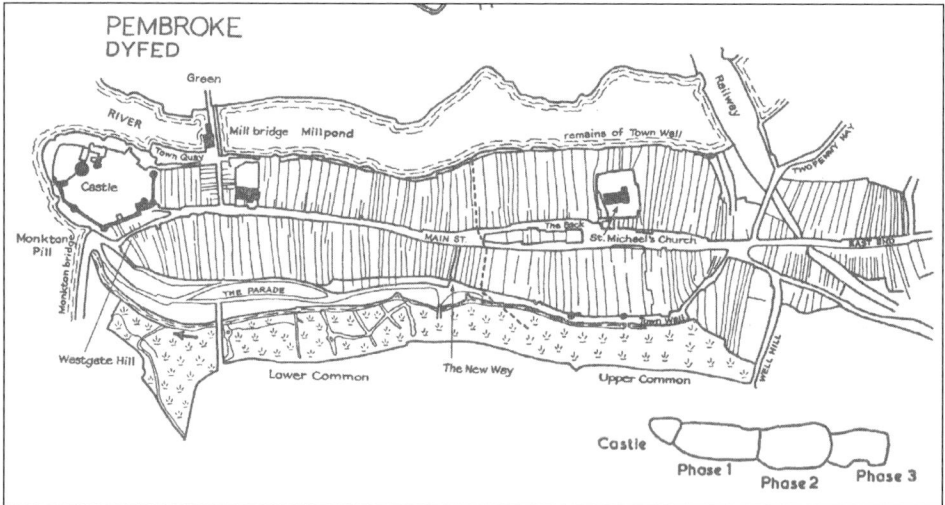

Plan of Pembroke showing the burgage tenements of the planned Norman town running at right angles on either side of Main Street. (See Plate 5) (*Aston and Bond, 1976: 82*)

As in England also, the process of colonization in Wales extended over a considerable period, and was still in progress at the end of Henry I's reign. By that time the greater part of the country south of a line from Aberystwyth to Montgomery was in Norman hands and the whole land was under the over-lordship of the Norman king. There was no move, however, to incorporate Wales into the kingdom of the English, and the Welsh kept their own laws. Nevertheless, much of the wealth of the country was falling into the hands of Anglo–Normans.

According to both Welsh and Anglo–Norman chroniclers, Henry I established Flemish colonies alongside earlier Norman plantations in Pembrokeshire. There is a clear cultural division between the north (Welsh) and the south (Anglo–Norman) in that county in terms of church design and dedication, field systems and village topography. Flemish place names, however, are spread much more evenly across the whole county.[27] William of Malmesbury and others claimed that settlers had left Flanders in the early twelfth century, following extensive flooding, and came as migrants to England. Subsequently, Henry 'removed all the Flemings in England into Wales' and 'the country was overburdened with them'. A second contingent of Flemings was sent to south-west Wales in 1113 according to Welsh sources. This may have been in response not so much to a Welsh uprising, but to a rebellious Montgomery faction of Norman barons who had created their own power base here. William of Malmesbury reported that Henry: 'As if he were pouring them into a common sink, he settled them with their goods and chattels in Ros, thus relieving the English and restraining the stupid ferocity of the Welsh.' While Caradoc of Llancarfan observed that the Flemings 'desired him to give them a void place to remain in, who being very liberal of that which was not his own, gave them the land of Rhos in Dyfed'. More charitably, in the 1180s, Gerald of Wales described the Flemish settlers of his native Pembrokeshire as 'strong and hardy people … who spared no labour and feared no danger by sea or by land in their search for profit; a people as well fitted to follow the plough as wield the sword'.[28]

It has been suggested that Henry was buttressing his royal lordship by bringing in colonists from Flanders to help build and garrison castles at strategic points such as Carew, Manorbier, Wiston and Haverfordwest. A number of communities in Rhos and Daugleddau appear to be planted settlements with castles, perhaps

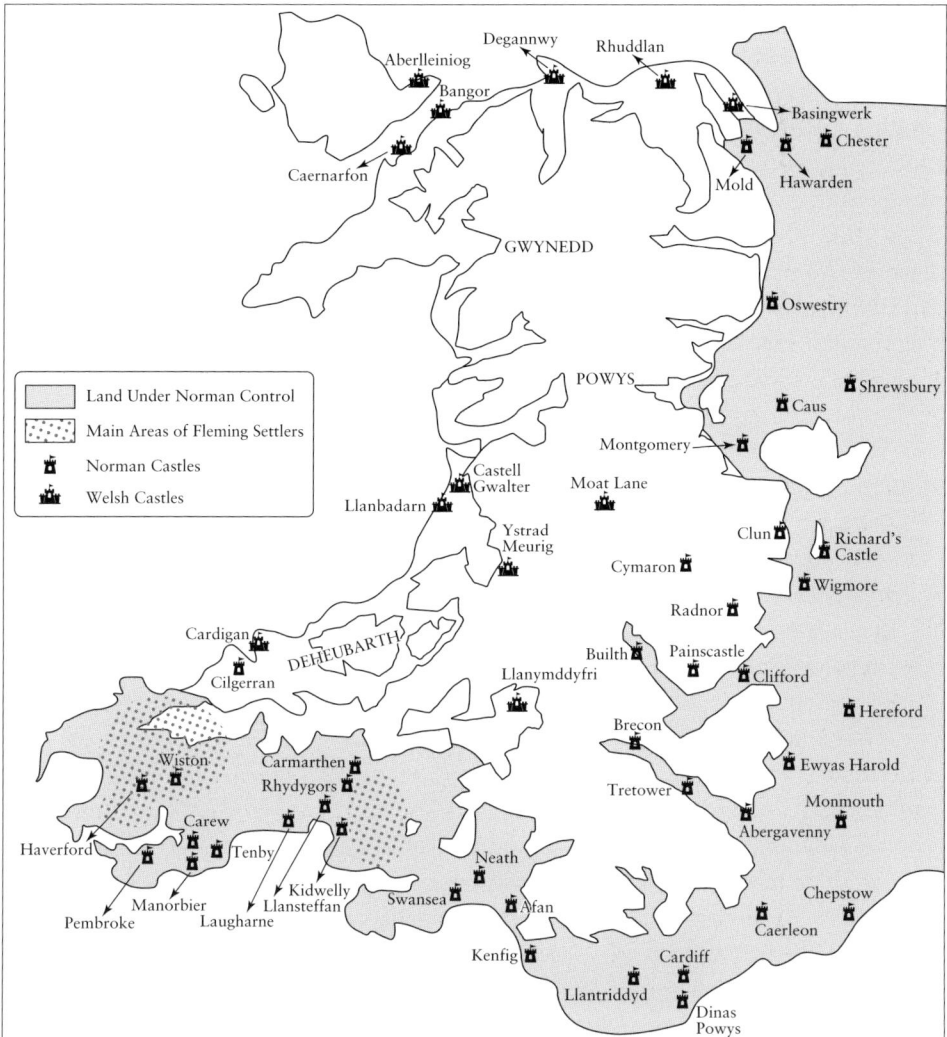

Map of Wales and the Welsh Marches showing land under Norman control in the first half of the twelfth century and areas of Flemish settlement.

representing Flemish colonization. There were a number of *locatores* or *drengs* who were responsible for planting new settlements and attracting colonists to populate them: Letard 'King of the Flemings' founded Letterston, Tancard founded Thankerton, while Wizo the Fleming is attributed with establishing a castle, church and borough at Wiston. The *Chronicle of the Princes* records that in 1193, Wizo's descendant Philip fitz Wizo and his family were captured by Hywel Sais, the son of Lord Rhys, but that there were sufficient Flemings in the area of Wiston and Llawhaden to retaliate and put the Welsh to flight.[29]

The motte and ringwork castle at Wiston is one of the largest and best preserved in Wales. The ringwork bailey originated as a large Iron Age rath – a large farmstead surrounded by a circular bank and ditch. The parish church of St Mary occupies a square enclosure to the south of the castle, probably representing a second bailey. The village straggles along a road that runs between castle and church, but the surrounding landscape is one of irregular fields.

Other Flemish settlements in Pembrokeshire, such as Letterston, Ambleston and Narberth South, are linear villages laid out along a street, perpendicular to which were a series of long, narrow tenements, contained within discrete blocks. They show all the signs of having been deliberately laid out, and at Letterston many of the plots to the north and south of the village measure a consistent 55m or 110m. In Holland, in contemporary colonies on the lands of the archbishops of Bremen and Hamburg, tenements were 30 *roeden* (110m) wide.[30]

Wiston Castle, Pembrokeshire, was founded by a Flemish settler called Wizo in the early twelfth century. It is one of the largest and best-preserved motte and bailey castles in Wales. (*Coflein Mapping*)

Locatores acted as middlemen between settlers and lords and in some cases shouldered the cost of the move, the maintenance of the settlers until the first harvest, and the provision of houses, church and mills. In return they received large plots of land and a proportion of the profits of the courts and other concessions. In other parts of Europe, *locatores* moved on to found colonies in other regions once they had completed their work. It has been suggested that Wizo and Tancard could have moved on to southern Scotland as regular villages incorporating their names are also found at Wiston and Thankerton in Lanarkshire.[31]

Scotland

Scotland was a major irritation to William, particularly during the early years of his reign, when King Malcolm III (1058–93) was actively involved in the northern uprisings and provided safe haven for rebel leaders. In 1072, Malcolm was obliged to recognize William as his overlord, although he had earlier strengthened his claim to participate in English affairs through his marriage to Edgar the Aetheling's sister, Margaret. In Scotland, as in Wales, the establishment of Norman overlordship was followed by a degree of Norman colonization, and initially it appeared as though the colonization of Scotland might take much the same form as in Wales. During the reign of Malcolm and his sons the Scottish Lowlands underwent a process of Normanization but within the framework of largely Scottish control.

Like the Welsh kings and princes, Scottish kings were often glad to make use of Norman troops in their own domestic warfare, but, unlike the Welsh, they never completely lost control of them. The Norman colonization of Scotland was eventually achieved in a quite different way from their colonization of Wales and was less extensive. All four of King Malcolm's sons had spent a considerable time at the court of the Norman king before they succeeded to the throne. Their experience had given them the opportunity to understand how the Normans organized their affairs. The Norman kings had a control of their aristocracy through homage and fealty and a military power through knights and castles, which the traditional social and political institutions of Scotland could not provide. It was therefore necessary to rationalize the Scottish government along Norman lines.

The best policy for the Scottish kings was to accept Norman suzerainty and to reorganize the government on the Anglo–Norman model, which included the settlement of Anglo-Norman barons on Scottish lands. Although limited in extent, it meant that families of French origin, with estates in England and sometimes in France as well, could now extend their fortunes into Scotland. The newcomers included the French and Flemish families of Oliphant, de Graham, Comyn, de Bailleul (Balliol) and de Brus (Bruce). Under King David I (1124–53) the rights of landownership were formalized, with the introduction of a bureaucracy and written title deeds. He established towns and regional markets and encouraged

Melrose was a Cistercian abbey founded in 1136 at the request of David I of Scotland. It was the chief house that order in Scotland and the burial place of several Scottish kings. (*Secret Scotland*)

the development of the textile industry and the wool trade with Flanders. A rationalized diocesan system was established and abbeys were founded by the reformed Benedictine orders in the Borders at Kelso (1128), Melrose (1136), Jedburgh (1138) and Dryburgh (1150).

Romanesque architecture was imported from England and elsewhere in Europe at an early date, and is found not only in monasteries and cathedrals, but also in the growing number of parish churches of the twelfth century. Immigrants who were encouraged into the Borders contributed to long-term changes in language and customs in the region.

By accepting the suzerainty of the Norman king and the Normanization of the Scottish monarchy and the Scottish Church, the Scottish kings of the early twelfth century were doing what the Norman dukes themselves had done in their duchy during the eleventh century. They were bringing in new men whose relationship to them would be that of vassal to lord and who would owe substantial advancement to them, and they were doing this to enlarge their own military and political strength and to increase the hold they had on their country.

Chapter 5

Castles in the Landscape

The King rode into all the remote parts of his kingdom and fortified strategic sites against enemy attack. For the fortifications called castles by the Normans were scarcely known in the English provinces so the English in spite of their courage and love of fighting could put up only a weak resistance to their enemies.

(Orderic Vitalis)

Castles were the hallmark of Norman England and the most obvious evidence of a military takeover. They also served as indicators of rank and prestige within the Norman world. The historian William of Newbury (1136–98) observed that castles 'were the bones of the kingdom' and it is estimated that as early as 1100 there were at least 500 castles in England and Wales. The castle was ideal for the Norman conquest of England, where a small number of Normans needed to dominate an overwhelmingly larger English population. Castles could be built quickly with conscripted native labour, providing a stronghold from which mounted soldiers could control newly conquered towns and countryside. William of Malmesbury observed that: 'There were many castles all over England each defending its own district or to be more truthful plundering it.' Castles were particularly valuable in holding on to disputed areas such as South Wales. During one Welsh uprising, against Henry I in 1116, the prince of Deheubarth, Gruffydd ap Rhys, complained that he found he could take the 'outer castles' of fortifications such as that at Swansea, but that 'the tower' was able to hold out.[1] Another important function of the castle for the Normans was its symbolism – a dominant physical representation of power, wealth and status. As such they were often built to impress and intimidate the English, Welsh or Scottish population among whom they were located, as well as the lord's own Norman peers.

In the century and a half following the Battle of Hastings, the nature and form of the Anglo-Norman castle was adapted to meet changing requirements. In addition to operating as strategic centres of conquest, castles became the seats of Norman administration and law. They acted as collection and distribution hubs for weapons and provisions. They also provided a defended home for the Norman king, baron or lord, together with his family and followers, and in this context the emphasis changed subtly from defence to the provision of improved living conditions, even within the short time span of Norman kingship.

The choice for the siting of individual castles appears mainly to have been a pragmatic one, as castle builders adapted to local geography, settlements, building resources, tenurial arrangements and routeways. Military considerations often seem to have been low on the list of priorities. After the initial phase of royal and baronial castles, the second and third waves of castle-building were led by the major tenants-in-chief and then by the undertenant knights on their new estates. Away from the south coast, the Welsh Marches and the Scottish borders, it was the disposition of such estates that determined the siting of many of these castles as much as anything else.

The location of a castle was sometimes used to emphasise continuity by the incoming Normans by siting their strongholds in existing centres of power or status, in prehistoric hill forts as at Old Sarum, Roman forts as at Pevensey or Saxon *burhs* as at Wallingford. Many more were located in previously unfortified places, close to that other symbol of lordly power, the church, and designed to command an estate, settlement or routeway. In a number of cases a Roman or prehistoric site was chosen, both for strategic and symbolic reasons. Some eighty-four English castles have been recognized as occupying earlier sites, but there are probably many more as yet unidentified.[2] At Marlborough, Wiltshire, recent investigation has shown that the huge castle motte had been largely constructed in the late Neolithic period, about the same time as the great mound at Silbury Hill, not far away. In this case the builder, Roger, Bishop of Salisbury, may have been combining the pragmatic use of an existing earthwork with the appropriation of its associated mystique.[3]

In recent years, castle studies have highlighted the importance of the location of castles in relation to features such as visibility, vistas, monastic houses, lakes and fishponds, and parks. From an early date castle sites seem to have been chosen or designed to provide special environs for the lord and his entourage, which in some cases could lead to a radical restructuring of the surrounding landscape. As with many monasteries, the establishment of a castle frequently led to the construction of extensive water works to service moats, mills and fishponds. Deer parks and dovecotes were also common adjuncts to castles from the twelfth century onwards[4].

Norman castles were built of earth and timber or of stone and often a combination of both. At the heart of each castle there was a stronghold in the form of a wooden or stone tower, often sitting on an earthen mound, the motte. Attached to the stronghold was a defended enclosure, the bailey, which would have contained standard features including a hall and kitchen, gatehouse, chapel, stables and other ancillary workshops and storerooms. By the mid-twelfth century many of these features were located within stone tower keeps. On some excavated sites, evidence of smithies, limekilns, and lead- and iron-working hearths has been found. Castles, like churches, were added to, replaced or abandoned over the centuries; consequently, few authentic, unaltered Norman castles have survived, but the cores of many extant fortifications date from the eleventh or twelfth century. The earthwork remains of motte and bailey castles are particularly numerous in former border areas but are found scattered throughout the land: 'Next to the Briton the Norman has left the most enduring, the most numerous and the most impressive marks upon our soil.'[5]

Castles required a cohort of craftsmen, labourers, tradesmen and agricultural workers, some of whom were housed within the fortification, while others lived in adjacent settlements. Such communities were frequently created to service the castle's many needs, and their topography was frequently shaped by the proximity of the castle in what is known as a 'plan-unit'. Examples of this phenomenon can be seen at Pleshey (Essex), where the settlement is in the form of an extended semicircular bailey, or at New Buckenham (Norfolk), where a small market borough was laid out on a grid plan to the north of William de Albini's castle.[6] Benedictine and Cluniac priories were frequently established alongside castles, as at Castle Acre (Norfolk), creating formidable evidence of Norman power.

Creighton distinguishes between examples where castles were built within an existing village and cases where a secondary village grew up adjacent to a primary castle.[7] In the first instance, the castle may well have disrupted the existing village

Aerial view of Castle Acre showing the massive earthworks of William de Warenne's castle in the foreground. Beyond that there is an extended outer bailey, in which the original settlement lay. At the top of the photograph are the remains of Castle Acre Priory, founded by William's son, c.1090. (*Historic England*)

Eaton Socon Castle, Cambridgeshire, lying within a bend of the Great Ouse. Excavations in the 1960s found evidence that a Saxon vill, including a church and graveyard, was destroyed to make way for the Norman stronghold, possibly during the twelfth century-Anarchy. (*Cambridge HER 00374*)

Oswestry, Shropshire, where only the motte of an important Marcher castle survives. The outline of the bailey can still be seen in the road pattern in the town centre. (*Shropshire HER*)

Oswestry, Shropshire depicted as a castle and church on a seventeenth-century map. (*NLW. Aston Hall Deeds, File 2777*)

layout, as at Burwell (Cambridgeshire), where a castle built by King Stephen during the Anarchy clearly impinged on the pre-castle village properties as well as a Romano-British temple.[8] While at Eaton Socon (Cambridgeshire), a castle was built which sealed a late Saxon church and cemetery together with other village buildings.

Even where castles were later destroyed, their imprint had a lasting impact on town and village. Coventry Castle, which lay at the heart of the medieval town, was abandoned by the earls of Chester in the second half of the twelfth century. The vacated area was rapidly redeveloped as the castle ditches were backfilled and most of its buildings demolished. Nevertheless, the footprint of the castle remained in the street alignment and the outline of the castle precinct can still be traced in Bayley Lane. The footprints of the boundaries of former castles are commonly found in English townscapes, for example at Oswestry and Pontefract.

Private Fortifications in France Before 1066

Private fortifications had developed in France following the breakdown of central Carolingian control resulting in local lords waging war against each other. Prominent among these was Fulk Nerra, Count of Anjou (987–1040), who was responsible for building a chain of fortresses in western France and demonstrating the value of the castle as a means of conquest – an example that was quickly copied by the Norman dukes. One of the earliest known references to a stone castle in France is to Doué-la-Fontaine (Maine-et-Loire), built by the Count of

Blois, where a ground-floor hall that had been built here *c*.900 was converted into a fortified first-floor hall *c*.950. The entrance was on the first floor and in the eleventh century an earthen mound was heaped up around its base. Another early example was built by the Count of Anjou in the form of a two-storey hall tower at Langeais in Touraine about 990. References to such fortresses, often known as 'towers', became common in the later tenth century, when some communal fortifications were equipped with a strongpoint for the local lord. To begin with, the strongpoint and the lord's residence remained separate, as the lord and his retinue continued to live in a nearby manor house or palace. In due course, strongpoint and residence merged into one and the castle-keep was born. This process has been demonstrated by excavations at Fécamp in Normandy, where in the early eleventh century there was a significant replanning of the defences, as Duke Richard II converted what had been a communal fortification into a castle. The ducal palace was surrounded by an oval, fortified enclosure and divided internally into a palace zone and a separate, monastic focus.

From 1035, when William became duke at the age of 7, Normandy had been disrupted by periodic civil war with a number of ruling families jockeying for supremacy. Duke William was eventually able to quell this unrest by the imposition of centralized control; among the measures he used was a programme of ducal castle-building, linked to the demotion or exile of rebellious families. New landowners supportive of William moved in to replace disaffected nobles, and many of those knights that fought at Hastings had acquired their estates only

The surviving remnants of the ducal palace at Fécamp, Normandy, the coastal base for the dukes of Normandy from the tenth century. (*Renoux, 1991*)

in the three decades before 1066. Just as Normandy created a new Church in the eleventh century, so too it created a new nobility, with immigrant families such as the Beaumonts, Bohuns and Warennes assuming a central role. These 'new' Franks brought military methods to Normandy based on cavalry and castles, which tied to social changes created a feudal structure that was to prove particularly potent in Britain. At least three large stone tower castles (donjons) were built in Normandy by members of the ducal family, at Rouen, Ivry-la-Bataille (Eure) and Avranches (Manche). Duke Richard I's stone fortress known as the Great Tower at Rouen, which features on the Bayeux Tapestry but has long since disappeared, may have provided the model for the great tower keeps of England. The Château d'Ivry-la-Bataille was built *c*.1000 by Rodulf, Count of Ivry, who was regent of Normandy during Duke Richard II's minority.

At first only the major landowners, counts, bishops and officers of state fortified their homes, but when central authority weakened, the practice spread downwards to the lower members of the feudal nobility. Throughout West Francia, fortified estate centres developed in the later tenth and eleventh centuries at a lower level of society. These were characterized by earthen ringworks, mottes or moats, providing their occupants with a base from which they were able to move around

The castle at Ivry-la Bataille, Eure, was constructed *c*.1000 by Count Rodulf of Ivry. It has been suggested that it was a model for a number of later keep castles in Normandy and England, notably Avranches and the White Tower at the Tower of London. (*Tristan Nino*)

The 'Tower' at Rouen depicted on the Bayeux Tapestry.

the landscape rapidly on horseback. These were normally not large aristocratic centres and were often on poor agricultural land. They reflect the emergence of a *milites* class from the ranks of the richer free peasants who have been called 'chevaliers-paysans'.[9] Despite references to at least forty castles in pre-Conquest Normandy, authentic examples of pre-1066 mottes are rare, although earth and timber castles are known from places such as Rubercy, Gravenchon, Olivet-à-Grimbosq and Plessis-Grimoult. The motte and bailey castle became the most common form of private fortification in Normandy immediately after the conquest of England.

Defence in England Before the Conquest

Before 1066, defences in England were primarily built for communal protection, as found in the town fortifications of *burhs*, but there were already some smaller private defensive enclosures in existence. Modest pre-Conquest private fortifications on rural sites at Sulgrave (Northamptonshire) and Goltho/Bullington (Lincolnshire) have been known since the 1970s, and several other sites have been identified since then. The excavations at Goltho demonstrated the difference between a late Saxon thegn's defended house and its Norman equivalent.

There has been much discussion about the role of the late Saxon gatehouse, *burh-geat*, in the context of late Saxon defences. In the early eleventh century, Archbishop Wulfstan of York listed the attributes required to become a thegn:

And if a ceorl prospered so that he had fully five hides of his own land, a church and a kitchen, bell-house and *burh-geat;* seat and special office in the king's hall, then was he henceforward entitled to the rank of thegn.[10]

The gatehouse is here being used as shorthand for the manor house, which suggests that it was a prominent feature of the establishment. The existence of a gatehouse implies a boundary fence or hedge, indicative of some form of barrier or defence. Several eleventh-century documents mention the obligation to establish hedges or dig ditches associated with a manor house.[11] The gate tower of Rougemont Castle, Exeter, built *c.*1070, may represent the continuation of the Saxon *burh-geat* tradition in stone. The tower, which has a number of Saxon architectural features, was built into the northern corner of the Roman city walls soon after the rebellion against the Normans in 1068.[12]

Blair has argued that examples of English circular or oval defensive earthwork enclosures can be found at places such as Fowlmere (Cambridgeshire) and Pontefract (Yorkshire), and undoubtedly there were many more. Although they represented a form of private defence for the gentry class, they did not dominate the landscape in the same way as those built after 1066, but in some cases they did provide the basis for post-Conquest castles, often by the addition of a motte to a pre-existing Saxon enclosure. Blair suggests that there could have been an integrated system of defence in mid-eleventh-century England: 'Fortified residences … sited at strategic nodes in the landscape … earls and lesser ministerial figures … built them by royal command and in accordance with a national defence scheme.' Blair cites standardized coinage and seal matrices as evidence of the Crown's ability to design and implement such a scheme.[13]

We know of a few castles which were built in England by Normans who had accompanied Edward the Confessor from France in 1041. Edward had appointed his cousin Ralph of Mantes as Earl of Hereford and Warwickshire.[14] Ralph came from the Vexin region in the east of Normandy, where the duchy bordered French Crown territory, and he was therefore familiar with border strategy and may have been charged with protecting the Wye Valley and the southern Welsh border. One of Earl Ralph's vassals, Osbern Pentecost, constructed a castle at Ewyas Harold in the south-west of Herefordshire as early as 1048. This was located above the valley of the Dulas Brook, a tributary of the River Dore, which runs through the Golden Valley. The valley, which lies immediately to the east of the Black Mountains in Wales, housed a line of earthwork castles after the Conquest. There are well-defined earthworks of a fine motte and bailey castle at Ewyas, which may have been a later construct of William fitz Osbern, *c.*1068. The castle is mentioned in the Domesday Book and an alien priory was built in the outer bailey about 1100. Another Norman, Richard Scrob, King Edward's housecarl and probably Sheriff of Worcester, built a castle just to the south of Ludlow at Richard's Castle before 1052. This formidable earthwork castle is hidden in the hilly woodland of northern Herefordshire; a ditch separates the steep-sided motte from the bailey, which incorporates the parish church with its detached bell tower, which presumably was originally the castle chapel. To the east of the castle and church are further earthworks contained within an extended, rectangular outer bailey, representing a later failed medieval town.

An outlier of these pre-Conquest castles in Herefordshire was built at Clavering in Essex by Robert fitz Wimarc, a kinsman of both Edward the Confessor and William the Conqueror, who despite his French roots also survived the 1052 purge of Normans. Little is known of Clavering Castle, which consists of a pronounced oblong, earthen enclosure surrounded by a moat to the north of the parish church, within a bend of the River Stort. These earthworks could well incorporate pre-Conquest elements as, soon after the Conquest, Robert's son Swein built a substantial motte and bailey

The motte and bailey at Ewyas Harold, Herefordshire. It is possible that there was a pre-Conquest castle on the site, possibly the work of Osbern Pentecost, who had accompanied Edward the Confessor upon his return from exile in 1041. It is argued that this castle was destroyed in 1052 and replaced by one built by William Fitz Osbern, soon after 1066. In 1100 a priory was founded within the castle precincts. (*Paul R. Davis*)

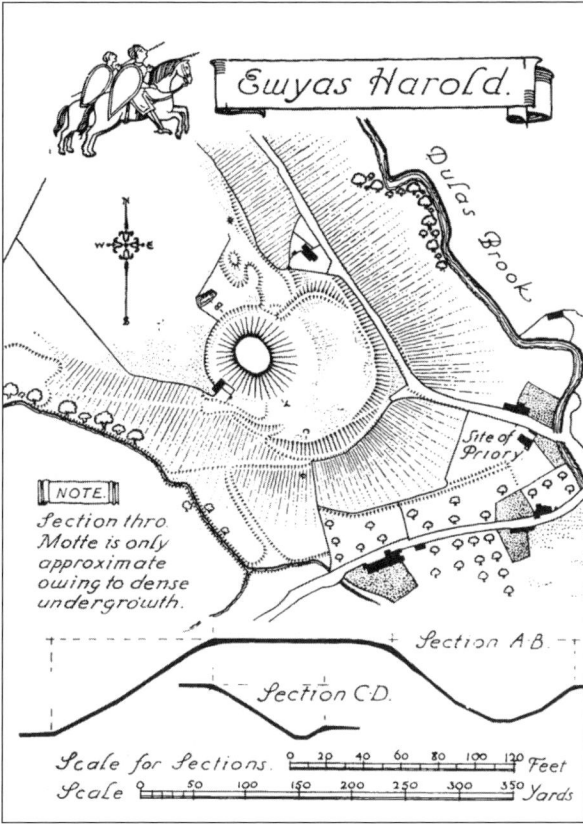

Left: Survey of Ewyas Harold Castle showing the site of the priory. (*RCHME, 1931: 62-64*)

Below: The earthwork plan of Richard's Castle in north Herefordshire. Richard 'Scrob' built a pre-Conquest fortification on the site. It is probable that this was replaced by the present motte and bailey after 1066. A borough, which was subsequently added to the castle, failed in the later Middle Ages and traces of former burgage plots can be seen as earthworks.

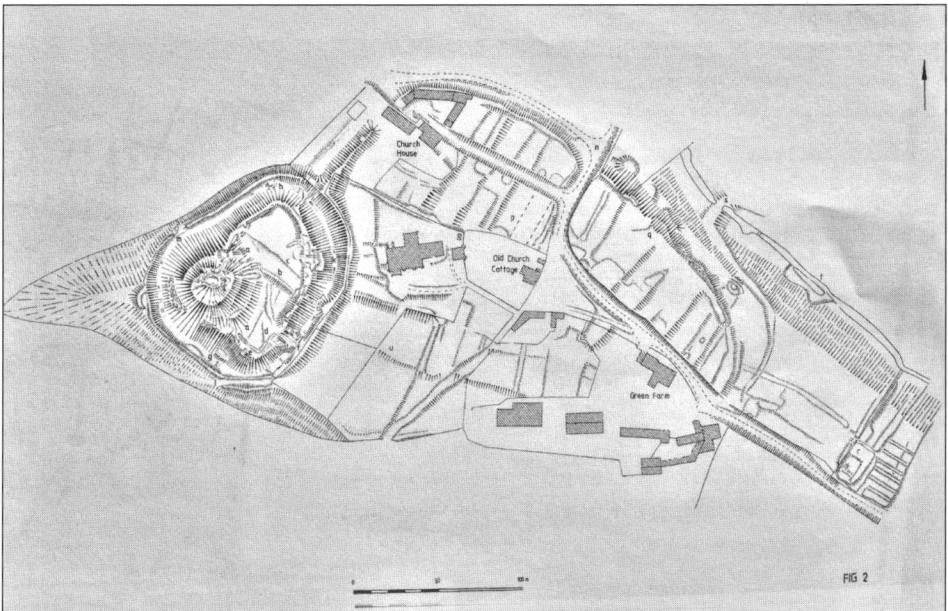

castle at Rayleigh, Essex, close to the Thames estuary. Rayleigh replaced Clavering as the *caput* of the Wimarc estates in eastern England.

One particular pre-Conquest structure deserves attention – St George's Tower in Oxford Castle, which seems to have been built before 1066. Archaeological and architectural evidence proves that the tower, long thought to have been part of the original Norman castle, predates the Conquest. It is the earliest of the great stone tower keeps that became symbolic of Norman power in England. The tower at Oxford sits immediately to the south-east of the later castle motte and was for long believed to have been part of a circuit of towers built around the Norman castle bailey. Its construction and alignment do not fit with what we know of the original Norman castle, and it now appears to have been built as a watch tower, associated with the west gate on the perimeter of the Saxon town. It probably contained a chapel, because of its post-Conquest housing of St George's Chapel. The construction of the Oxford tower has been attributed to Earl Ralph of Hereford in the 1050s. When Robert d'Oilly built the castle *c*.1071 the tower was probably used as a keep before a motte with its own tower superseded it.[15]

The surviving earthworks of 'Robert's Castle' mentioned in the Domesday Book at Clavering, Essex. The original castle was built by Robert FitzWimarc before 1066, but it was almost certainly rebuilt after the Conquest. (*Libby norman*)

Early Castles of the Conquest

Almost as soon as he landed in England, William began erecting castles, first at Pevensey, then at Hastings, and work on others such as Wallingford, Berkhamsted and possibly Winchester had started before he reached London. William's initial strategy was to build a castle on the acquisition of each county town and strategic centre that he conquered. By 1100, almost every major English town was furnished with a royal or baronial castle and a garrison. Norman sheriffs were installed in all the county towns, charged with raising taxes and administering justice, with the county castle serving as the sheriff's accommodation and administrative centre, repository and gaol. In the countryside, hundreds of ringworks and motte castles were attached to villages as fortified manor houses. Such castles were both a physical demonstration of conquest as well as providing the Normans with the footholds from which they could subdue and govern their newly won kingdom.

Although it is the large stone keep castles that are normally associated with the Norman Conquest, it was earth and timber enclosures that characterized the first phase of the Norman takeover in the countryside. Most of the castles to be built in England immediately after the Conquest took the form either of a motte and bailey or simple earthen ringwork or enclosure. These would have been relatively easy to build during the first phase of the Conquest, using material to hand, namely, wood and earth. It was these early, unpretentious castles that established the framework of the Conquest, rather than the more spectacular examples of the twelfth century. Such early castles, which were capable of withstanding a siege as well as delaying or blocking an enemy's progress, played a decisive role in consolidating the Norman Conquest. Some of the earliest fortifications built by William's barons were large, defended enclosures, often covering several hectares, which provided the space to house a large body of troops.

Such castles were almost certainly involved in the process of the transfer of land from Saxon thegn to Norman lord. Bishop Odo, Earl of Kent, was an enabler, responsible for the redistribution of land after the Conquest. Two of his early castles, at Rochester (Kent) and Deddington (Oxfordshire), were in the form of large, fortified enclosures, located on sites suitable for monitoring and controlling the region around them. Rochester Castle was sited between the River Medway and the Saxon cathedral on a slight hill, guarding the Saxon bridge over the river. The first castle was in the form of a large earth and timber enclosure, which lay in the south-west corner of the Roman town of *Durobrivae*. The fortification at Rochester covered an area of around 1.7ha, contained within a massive rampart, incorporating a section of Roman wall and a 2m-deep ditch. Nothing is known of the internal plan of Odo's castle, but it would have had a timber hall, chapel, numerous ancillary structures and probably a wooden tower.[16] It would have been from this earth and timber castle that Odo organized the transfer of land throughout Kent. It was also here that the bishop and the rebellious barons held

Rochester, Kent, showing the cathedral and castle in close juxtaposition. The classic Norman stone keep dates from the twelfth century, but the large enclosure in which it sits formed part of the original immediate post-Conquest castle. (*Clem Rutter*)

out against William Rufus in 1088, in what was to be the troublesome prelate's last stand against the Norman monarchy.[17]

Deddington Castle, which has the appearance of an Iron Age hill fort, lies on a limestone ridge in north Oxfordshire, about 100m to the east of the later church and marketplace.[18] The castle predated the separate unit of marketplace and church, which form the core of a later planned borough.[19] The earthworks consist of impressive banks and ditches forming a sub-rectangular enclosure of about 3.5ha with an inner enclosure of about 0.4ha at the eastern end. Deddington would have been Odo's south Midland *caput* where he assembled his forces. The earliest identified structure, dating to the eleventh century, is an earthen ringwork at the east end of the large enclosure, inside which a small L-shaped stone hall was built, with a garderobe pit at its west end, all of which appear to be contemporary with Odo.[20]

The Motte and Bailey and Ringwork Castles

The Normans required a form of castle that could be defended by a small number of troops against a large number of opponents and yet could be constructed with speed, and for these purposes the ringwork and motte and bailey were ideal. Ringworks were simply fortified, banked enclosures, often with a wooden gate tower. The great advantage of such fortifications was that they could be constructed using materials to hand and if destroyed could be rebuilt quickly. There were no problems in finding quarries or masons or arranging for the transport of stone; all that was required was a team of carpenters and a force of labourers. Mottes were normally conical in shape, ranging in height from 3m (10ft) to 30m (100ft), and were surrounded by a ditch from which the material making up the mound was extracted. The success of the practice of piling earth round the base of a wooden gatehouse or tower located within an earthen enclosure (ringwork) to prevent it being burnt down easily may well be the reason why the motte became one of the principal features of Norman castles in England. There was a wooden bridge leading from the castle enclosure or bailey to the motte; the latter was normally capped by a tower, which in the early stages was almost always built of timber. The bailey was surrounded by a rampart on top of which a palisade was built and defended by a ditch or ditches. Inside the bailey there were a variety of structures; for example, at Hen Domen (Powys), built *c*.1070, excavations uncovered evidence of about fifty wooden buildings contained within the bailey, which was encircled by a double bank and ditch.

An early-twelfth-century description of a motte at Merchem, near Dixmude in Flanders, provides a revealing description of this form of castle:

Castle Bryn Amlwyg, which sits just on the Shropshire side of the Welsh border. Little is known of its history, but it was originally a ringwork to which a round stone keep was later added. It was strategically placed at the western extremity of the Honour of Clun. (*Shropshire HER 01187*)

Bishop John [of Thérouanne, d.1130] used to stay frequently at Merchem ... near the churchyard was an exceedingly high fortification, which might be called a castle or *municipium*, built according to the fashion of that country ... many years before. It is the custom of the nobles of that region, who spend their time for the most part in private war, in order to defend themselves from their enemies to make a hill of earth, as high as they can, and encircle it with a ditch as broad and deep as possible. They surround the upper edge of this hill with a very strong wall of hewn logs, placing towers on the circuit, according to their means. Inside this wall they plant their house (*domus*), or keep (*arcem*), which overlooks the whole thing. The entrance of this fortress is only by a bridge, which rises from the counterscarp of the ditch, supported on double or even triple columns, till it reaches the upper edge of the motte (*agger*).[21]

Wooden towers on the top of mottes have been perceived as ephemeral, but it is estimated that as they would normally be built of oak that they could have survived for several generations. Motte towers shared the same construction techniques as wooden church towers and, in some cases, may have presented quite substantial structures, which carried the same social prestige as stone keeps. The elaborate motte towers depicted on the Bayeux Tapestry have been generally dismissed as fanciful, but perhaps they are more realistic than has been believed up to now. The majority of motte towers would have been 9-12 m in height, with that at South Mimms projected at a lofty 30 m. They would have acted as impressive visual statements of power within the Anglo-Norman landscape.[22]

It remains an open question whether there were mottes in England before 1066, as excavation has so far failed to reveal the existence of any mottes in late Saxon England. Mottes at the two known pre-Conquest Herefordshire castles, at Richard's Castle and Ewyas Harold, appear to have been built after the Conquest. There are several mottes depicted on the Bayeux Tapestry, an embroidery believed to have been created within a decade or so of 1066 – four in France (Dol, Dinan, Rennes and Bayeux) and one in England (Hastings). All of these, apart from Hastings, are portrayed as mounds capped with elaborate timber towers. The Tapestry designer and embroiderers, probably working at St Augustine's, Canterbury, in the early 1070s, may have been able to look outside the abbey and see such a castle motte, known as Dane John, just inside the circuit of the town defences. It is clear that whatever form these early castles took, they made an impression on the English, as the *Anglo-Saxon Chronicle* for 1051 records that 'the foreigners then had built a castle in Herefordshire in earl Swein's province and had inflicted every possible injury and insult on the king's men in those parts'.

The greatest density of earthwork castles was in troubled border areas such as the Welsh Marches and South Wales. These ringworks and mottes were built in a

The motte castle at Dol in Brittany on the Bayeux Tapestry. The tapestry uses castles as a means of depicting towns. The elaborate wooden tower on top of the motte is on fire and Count Conan is shown escaping by way of an improbably rigid rope.

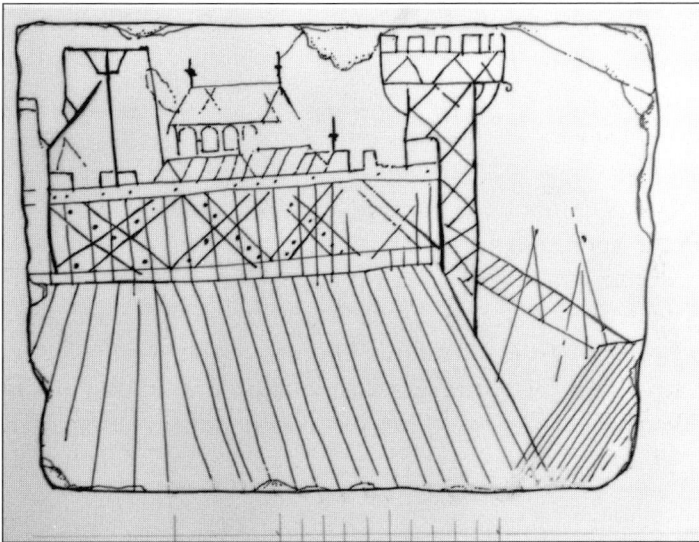

Outline sketch of a motte castle graffito on a stone from Caen Castle, early thirteenth century. (*Impey, 2020*)

wide variety of forms by local lords, anxious both to preserve the estates they had recently obtained and to demonstrate their new status both to the native English (and Welsh) and to neighbouring Norman lords. Some of these early castles enjoyed only a short lifespan and were abandoned when they had outlived their use and were replaced by more comfortable dwellings as soon as expedient. There are several regional varieties of motte. In East Anglia, for example, they tend to be tall and steep-sided as at Clare (Suffolk) and at Thetford (Norfolk), built within an Iron Age hill fort; whereas in the Welsh borders many of the numerous mottes are relatively small. For example, a group of timber castles dating from the end of the eleventh century, lying to the east of Offa's Dyke, in the Vale of Montgomery, are characterized by shallow mottes with small tops. The area, which was held by the Corbet family under Earl Roger de Montgomery, was recorded as 'waste' after the Conquest and this homogeneous group of castles may have been established as part of a resettlement plan.

The motte and bailey castle remains the most tangible and distinct Norman contribution to the English landscape. Their sheer size has ensured that many mottes have survived in earthwork form as they are not easily demolished. A few motte and bailey castles have been destroyed and can be identified only through the medium of aerial photography or excavation, as at Repton (Derbyshire),

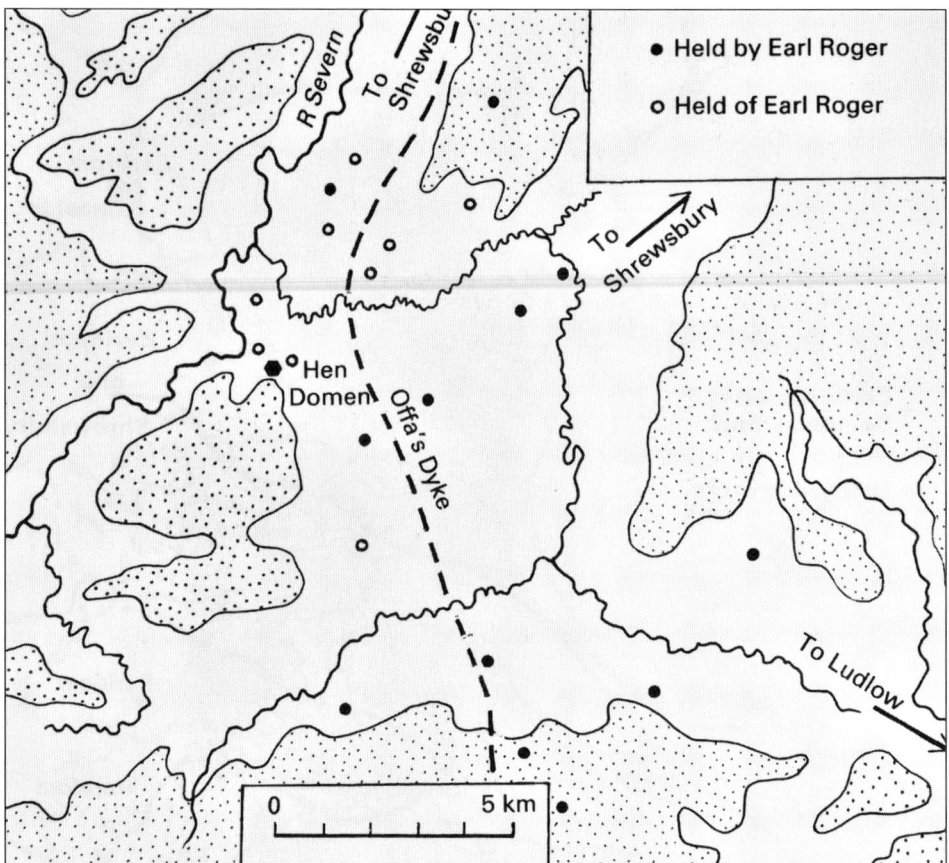

Plan of Roger de Montgomery's early castles on either side of Offa's Dyke in the Upper Severn Valley around Montgomery. (See Plate 6) (*Higham* and *Barkes*, 1992).

for example, where a motte and bailey castle was destroyed to make way for an Augustinian priory. The motte at Hereford was demolished along with much of the rest of the castle after the Civil War; according to John Leland, the early-sixteenth-century antiquary, Hereford Castle was 'one of the fairest and strongest in all England' and 'nearly as large as that of Windsor'.[23] Mottes of all shapes and sizes survive today and are now prized and protected for their historical importance. The great age of the motte and bailey was in the century after 1066, when many hundreds were built in Britain, Normandy, Brittany and elsewhere in Europe.

Distribution of motte and bailey castles throughout Britain, showing an extraordinary concentration in the Welsh borders and south-west Wales.

Ploughed out
motte and bailey
near Bishop's
Castle, Shropshire.
(*C. Musson*).

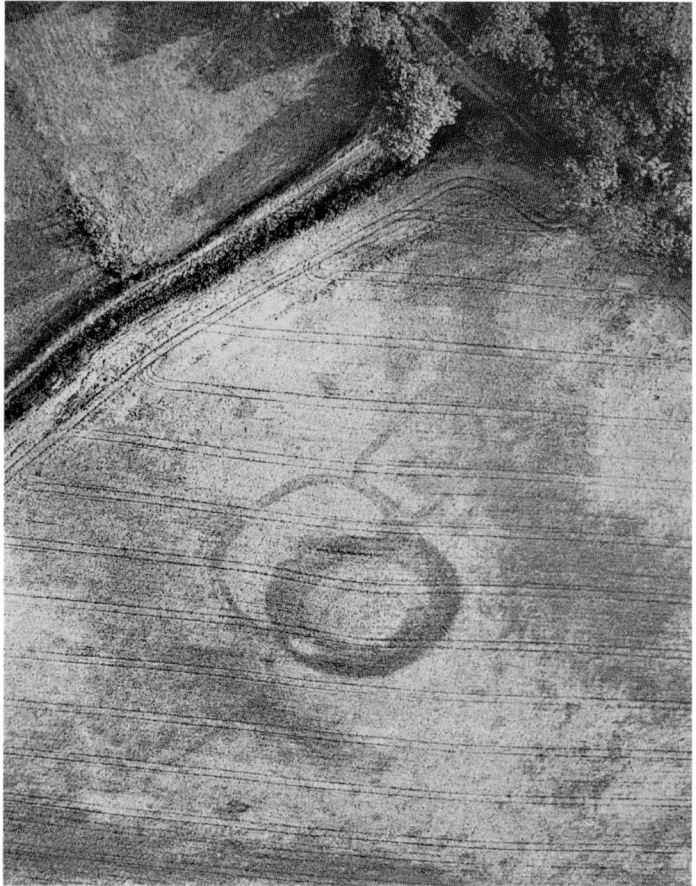

Donjon and Keep

The most imposing buildings of the Norman era were the great stone keeps; in France, such stone towers were known as *donjons* (Latin *dominium*, 'lordship'). The advantages of the stone keep over the earthen motte were obvious in terms of their durability and defensive capacity. Their disadvantages were that they were expensive to build and maintain and they took far longer to construct. Initially, keeps were relatively simple stone towers, designed basically to impress, intimidate and to withstand a siege. The White Tower at the Tower of London was the earliest stone keep to be constructed by the Normans in England and one of the largest, standing at 90ft (27.5m) high, with foundations up to 26ft (7.9m) wide. The symbolic significance of locating the White Tower within the corner of London's Roman walls on the Thames would have been self-evident. Although this was the obvious strategic location for the capital's premier castle, its size dominating the former city defences would have sent a clear and powerful message to London's population. Work probably started on the building at about the time of William's coronation, as according to William of Poitiers: 'Certain fortifications were completed in the city to protect the king against the fickleness of the vast and fierce populace for he [William] realized that it was of the first importance to overawe the Londoners.'

Above the basement vaults, the rooms of the castle were on two floors. On the lower floor there was a large guard room, a chamber and a crypt below St John's Chapel (for the use of the garrison). Above, there was a two-storeyed hall, a great chamber and the chapel, with a gallery running round all three. South of the keep lay the bailey with its service buildings, at first defended on the city side by a ditch, but by 1097, when the Tower was approaching completion, the *Anglo-Saxon Chronicle* reported that 'men from many shires in fulfilling their labour service to the city of London were oppressed in building the wall around the Tower'. The Tower was largely built of Kentish ragstone and local mudstone, with Caen stone imported to provide detail for the facings. The English citizens of London must have regarded it with fear and astonishment, visibly dominating their city and controlling the access to the Thames estuary and the sea. It remains, with limited later changes, both as an outstanding example of innovative Norman architecture and as the most complete survival of a late-eleventh-century fortress-palace in Europe[24]

The designer of the White Tower, Gundulph, Bishop of Rochester, was responsible for another great contemporary castle, at Colchester. The great fortress-palace at Colchester was an atypical urban castle in many respects. It was the largest Norman keep in England and occupied a central position within an *insula* of the former Roman town, while the extension of the bailey defences caused the high street to be diverted. The decision to build on this site, just to the east of the centre point of the town, hemmed in by town houses, makes little military sense and it has been argued that the castle was located here for symbolic and propaganda reasons. The castle keep, located on the podium of a classical temple to the Divine Claudius Caesar, was larger than the White Tower.

Large keep castles were later constructed at Rochester (1126–39) and Dover (1180–90). Both these great Kentish keeps are notable for the large buildings over the entrance stairs, each of which incorporated a chapel as at Castle Rising. Rochester, which has four storeys, is the tallest of the stone keeps in Britain, rising to a height of almost 40m (130ft). Many other great Norman rectangular keeps survive, and among the most notable are Bamburgh (Northumberland), Norham (Northumberland), Bowes (Co. Durham), Canterbury (Kent), Corfe (Dorset), Kenilworth (Warwickshire), Middleham (Yorkshire) and Hedingham (Essex). (See Plate 7).

Over time keep castles were built in various different forms as their functions changed along with techniques of warfare. By the middle of the twelfth century, most major English castles had either been rebuilt in stone or had stone structures added to them. The keep was used for housing stores, armaments and other equipment and providing accommodation on a series of floor levels, within a

Colchester Castle, Essex. The ground plan of the building is one and a half times larger than the White Tower, making it the largest area of any medieval tower in Europe. It was built symbolically on the foundations of the Roman Temple of Claudius. (*Colchester and Ipswich Museum*)

Kenilworth Castle, Warwickshire, was founded in the early 1120s by Geoffrey de Clinton, Lord Chamberlain to Henry I. (*Trevor Rowley*)

Ludlow Castle, Shropshire. The keep, which was built in *c*.1075 by Walter de Lacy, a vassal of William Fitz Osbern, was one of the earliest masonry castles in England. It was originally a gatehouse and the profile of the infilled entrance at ground level can be seen clearly. (*Trevor Rowley*)

large square or rectangular stone tower. The difference between earth and timber castles and their stone equivalents was simply the building material used. Both forms performed the same functions and tended to contain the same facilities, such as stronghold, hall and chapel. Although most early Norman castles were built of earth and timber, a few occupying strategically imperative sites were constructed of stone from the outset. London and Winchester were the prime examples, but some Welsh border castles, such as Chepstow and Ludlow, and Richmond in the north fall into this category.

A remarkable early example of a stone keep is Richmond (Yorkshire), originally built as a fortified gatehouse, which was then blocked, entry being made at the first-floor level from the rampart walk of the surrounding curtain wall. There was a similar transformation from stone gatehouse to keep at Ludlow. Henry I's keep at Portchester is somewhat larger with an elaborate forebuilding to the east and is preserved in part to the top of the battlements on one side. The castle was built in the north-east corner of the Roman fort, located in a similar position to that at Pevensey.

Richmond Castle, North Yorkshire, was started in 1071 by Alan Rufus, a Breton companion of William the Conqueror, following the suppression of the northern rebellion. The Honour of Richmond was one of the largest Norman estates in England. The upper part of the keep was added during the second half of the twelfth century. (*Historic England*)

The curtain wall of Richmond Castle is one of the longest stretches of surviving eleventh-century fortification. 'It is probably the best-preserved castle of this scale and age in the country.' (*Goodall, 2011: 87*)

If the castle was the instrument with which the Conqueror consolidated his grip on England, he was helped in this task by the use of the horse. A large number of horses were brought from Normandy to participate in the conquest of England – most importantly, a heavier fighting horse known as the 'destrier' was used. The Normans took considerable care to breed and train fighting horses, sometimes in specially designated parks, importing thoroughbreds from Muslim Spain. The horse that Duke William rode at Hastings was said to have been brought from Spain. Several of the greater Norman abbeys founded in forest regions were actively involved in horse-breeding, and after the Conquest, several English monasteries had horse-breeding programmes for palfreys and draught animals. Horse studs were often established in deer parks in England.

The horse transformed the castle from a means of passive defence into an instrument for controlling the surrounding countryside. A mounted garrison based on a castle could dominate a large area, and thus castles formed secure bases from which territory could be controlled. During the Anarchy, John of Worcester recorded that the men of Malmesbury Castle 'exhausted the whole neighbourhood by their ravages'. William of Malmesbury also noted that: 'There were many castles all over England each defending its own district or to be more truthful plundering it.'

Royal and Episcopal Palaces

Before the Conquest, the English kings owned palaces in towns such as Winchester, Westminster and Gloucester. They also held rural palaces, for instance at Woodstock, Calne and Windsor.

The design of these structures was essentially a development from the early Saxon hall, as excavated at Yeavering (Northumberland). The difference between a palace and a castle is often difficult to discern; for instance, in 1138 the Bishop of Winchester 'built a palatial house and a strong tower at Winchester [the Wolvesey]; and castles at Merdon, Farnham, Waltham, Downton and Taunton'.[25] Many other major palaces, such as the palace at Westminster, which lay adjacent to the abbey, were virtually undefended apart from a perimeter wall. When Edward the Confessor's palace was rebuilt by William II in the 1090s, it became the largest in England, and possibly in Europe, measuring 240ft (80m) long and 67ft 6in (22m) wide. The king famously thought it 'too big for a chamber and not big enough for a hall'.[26] The rebuilding by Richard II in 1394–1402, which produced the present hall, heightened and remodelled the walls, but much of the original Norman structure survives.

The Normans established Westminster as the centre of royal law and ceremony as well as the Crown's primary residence in London. As the king's court grew into various departments of medieval administration, so the facilities available at Westminster were correspondingly enlarged and adapted. During the twelfth century the treasury was moved here from Winchester, and eventually there was

Woodstock Palace in 1714 before its destruction and replacement by Blenheim Palace. A hunting lodge with a menagerie was built here by Henry I, and it was later developed into a palace by Henry II.

Westminster Hall was erected in 1097 by William II. The hammerbeam roof, originally supported by pillars, was replaced by Richard II in *c*.1390. Much of the fabric of the walls belongs to the original Norman building. (*Tristan Surtel*)

a great complex of buildings containing virtually every department of English government. There were also a number of other unfortified royal palaces outside London at Woodstock, Kingsholm, Clarendon and Cheddar. Such palaces were often located close to royal forests or hunting parks, and served as bases for the royal court and council, which were constantly on the move.

In the eleventh century there were great ceremonial occasions centred on the major palaces, the most important of which was 'crown-wearing' in the old Carolingian tradition. The *Anglo-Saxon Chronicle* records that William the Conqueror 'kept great state. He wore his royal crown three times a year as often as he was in England: at Easter at Winchester, at Whitsuntide at Westminster, at Christmas at Gloucester. On these occasions all the great men of England were assembled about him: archbishops, bishops, abbots, earls, thegns and knights.' In 1069–70, William extended the Saxon palace at Winchester to perhaps twice its former size. It has been suggested that the balcony on the west front of Winchester Cathedral, although fourteenth-century in date, is the successor of an earlier, Norman balcony, where king and queen would have appeared wearing crowns. There are indications that such ceremonies were in decline by the mid-twelfth century, and this is reflected by the gradual abandonment of the palaces at Kingsholm and Old Windsor and even the great royal palace at Winchester.

During the twelfth century it was not so much the Crown but the Church, through its prelates, that was responsible for building palaces. Some of these buildings were virtually indistinguishable from castles in the scale of their fortification. William Giffard, Lord Chancellor of England (1093–1101) and Bishop of Winchester (1100–29), provides a prime example of someone who combined palace-building with cathedral-building in his diocesan capital. Giffard re-established the great complex at Wolvesey, the former island site that has been the principal residence of the bishops of Winchester for a thousand years. Giffard's work at Wolvesey was taken over by his successor, Henry of Blois, grandson of William I and brother of King Stephen. In the east range there was a great hall with a gallery: 'A true hall, a place of gathering, not merely for feeding and sleeping large numbers of retainers, but for meeting and ceremonial. It measured 28m by 9m (88ft by 29ft).'[27] Giffard also created Winchester Palace at Southwark, and the idea of establishing a London residence was subsequently emulated by every other bishop in the land and by many nobles as well. The bishops of Winchester had several palaces elsewhere within the diocese and beyond, and by the end of the twelfth century they had at least ten residences in addition to the Wolvesey. Excavations at Witney (Oxfordshire) have shown that the fortified palace there dates from Giffard's time. Bishop Henry of Blois built the castle-palace at Taunton (Somerset), which formed the centrepiece of an impressive seigneurial complex including a new town and a priory.

The episcopal palaces, like their lay equivalents, were frequently accompanied by a hunting park, extensive fishponds, dovecotes and ample wine cellars to entertain

Wolvesey Palace, Winchester, was originally built by the bishop of Winchester in the late tenth century. The surviving building was largely the work of the Prince-Bishop Henry of Blois, King Stephen's brother, who fortified it during the Anarchy. (*Historic England*)

Winchester Palace, Southwark, from a print of 1830. Founded by Bishop Henry de Blois in the twelfth century as the London base for the Bishops of Winchester, it was mostly destroyed by fire in 1814. (*W. Capon*)

the bishop and his guests. Thus, the palaces of the Norman prince-bishops were often as imposing as any of those of their lay contemporaries. This reflected their central and sometimes divisive role in twelfth-century England, where the strength that William had invested in the Church eventually rebounded to challenge the authority of the Crown.

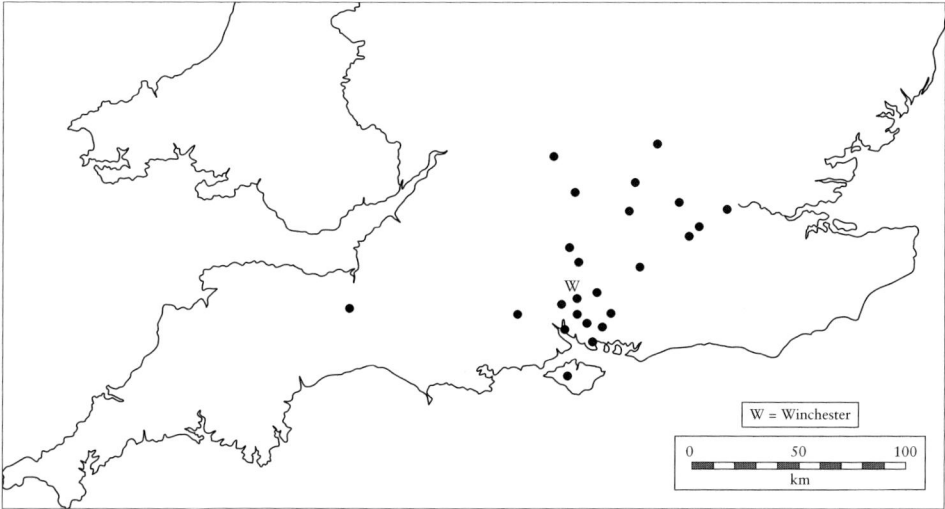

Map showing the distribution of the Bishop of Winchester's medieval palaces in southern England. Although concentrated in Hampshire, there were several in the Thames Valley and at least three to the north of the Thames, outside the Diocese of Winchester.

Castle Towns

'The widespread presence of a new model of urban form, the castle town, seemingly brought across by the Norman magnates with the Conquest, and deployed across England and Wales, is a very clear manifestation of a new stage in English urban development.'[28] The castle borough was a specific form of new town; dozens of such towns were created after the Conquest. The classic castle–market–church arrangement was already present in Normandy in places such as Damville, Lyons-la-Forêt and Le Neubourg (Eure). The Normans used urbanization as a tool of colonization and it is possible to link both the governance of towns and their form to the work of specific individuals, such as William's close associate William fitz Osbern, who was given a castle at Breteuil-sur-Iton (Eure) c.1060, where soon after he added a new town. The Statutes of Breteuil were imported to English and Welsh towns after the Conquest, where they gave a distinct economic advantages to Norman settlers.

Castle boroughs were a particular feature of frontier districts; in Wales, the Welsh Marches and the Scottish borders they were the dominant urban form. Such boroughs were part of the process of colonization, bringing Norman control and trade to regions where there had previously been little town life. Town and castle complemented each other with the castle providing a stronghold, while the town with its market and burgages encouraged new settlers to take up residence there. Castle towns were normally arranged on an axis, with the town's main street being aligned on the castle gates, often with a church at the other end of the street. The main street is frequently widened to create a market space.

Breteuil-sur-Iton (Eure), whose trade regulations were adopted by many medieval English and Welsh towns, appears to have been planned by William Fitz Osbern, *c*.1050. (*Collection jfm.fr*)

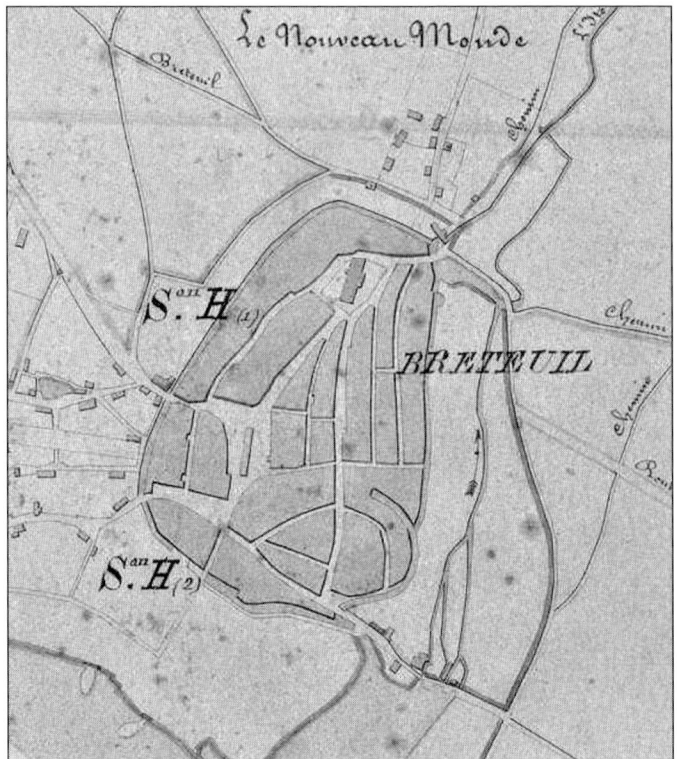

An eighteenth-century plan of Breteuil-sur-Iton showing the oval-shaped site of the castle at the bottom of the Medieval walled area. The church of St Sulpice is at the top and in between are the parallel streets of the Norman planned town. (*Archives d'Eure-et-Loire*)

Since St John Hope's perceptive paper on the 'Ancient Topography of the Town of Ludlow' was published early in the twentieth century, Ludlow has been recognized as a classic example of Norman castle town plantation.[29] The town, which occupies one of the finest defensive sites in the Welsh Marches, is encircled on two sides by the River Teme. This natural defence is reinforced by a sandstone ridge that presents a precipitous cliff face of almost 30m to the north and west. To the south and south-east, the land falls gently into the Teme Valley and it was on these slopes that the streets of the medieval planned settlement were laid out.

Ludlow Castle, which dominated the town, was the greatest of the Norman castles in the Welsh border country and the key to the understanding of the town's creation and development. Between 1085 and 1095 the semicircular inner bailey and the great gatehouse keep were constructed, forming a stone version of a ringwork. The keep originally served as the gatehouse, with a decorated entrance at the base of the building, as at Richborough. This was eventually blocked and replaced by a causeway and entrance to the east of the tower, which was then converted into a regular keep. With its circular plan and grand entrance tower, the early castle has been compared to pre-Conquest *burh-geat* structures.[30] The sandstone for the building of the castle came from the bedrock on which it stands, and much of the material for the castle would have been quarried in the making of the moat that was dug into the split rock alongside and evidence of the

Ludlow, Shropshire, was a de Lacy creation and has long been recognized as a classic planned castle borough, although there is still some dispute about the phases of its development. (*Trevor Rowley*)

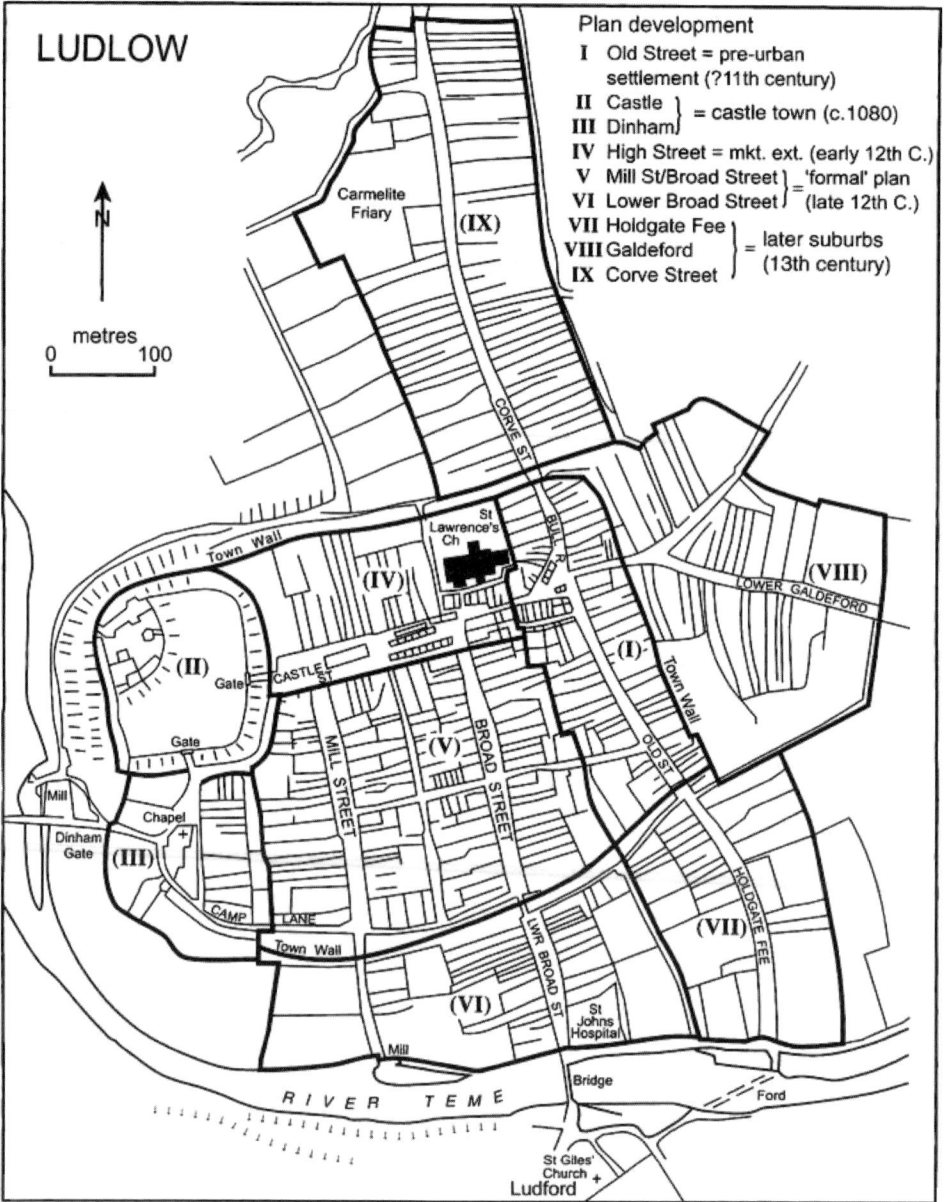

LUDLOW

Plan development

I Old Street = pre-urban
   settlement (?11th century)
II Castle } = castle town (c.1080)
III Dinham }
IV High Street = mkt. ext. (early 12th C.)
V Mill St/Broad Street } = 'formal' plan
VI Lower Broad Street }   (late 12th C.)
VII Holdgate Fee   } = later suburbs
VIII Galdeford   }   (13th century)
IX Corve Street   }

Plan of Medieval Ludlow with suggested units of development. (*Lilley, 2002: 143*)

medieval quarries can be seen on the slopes beneath the castle. Gilbert de Lacy built the castle chapel of St Mary Magdalen in the inner bailey *c.*1150; with its circular nave it resembles the Church of the Holy Sepulchre in Jerusalem. About 1158, Gilbert surrendered his Marcher estates to his son Robert and became a member of the Knights Templar. He was a precentor of the Templars in the Crusader County of Tripoli, where he almost certainly died. Gilbert's son Hugh de Lacy probably built the outer bailey and as a result extended the area of the castle fourfold.

The first of the town streets were probably laid out in the decade of castle-building between 1085 and 1095. Although subsequently encroached upon, the key element in Ludlow's plan is the broad High Street that runs from west to east along the ridge top from the castle gate to the Bull Ring. The second part of Ludlow's medieval plan consisted of three broad streets, Old Street, Broad Street and Mill Street, which lead off from the High Street at right angles down the gently sloping plateau towards the Teme. Time has changed this central axis of Ludlow. At the eastern end, closely packed buildings had been built on narrow islands in the former wide street by the close of the fifteenth century. Until the 1980s, an incongruous, Victorian red-brick market hall occupied much of the original Norman High Street. Its destruction has enabled the scale of the original medieval market area to be fully appreciated. The east end of the market has been intensively encroached on over the centuries, reducing it to a narrow, winding street.

The plan was completed with a gridiron pattern of narrow lanes that divide the slopes south of the High Street into a pattern of rectangles. In turn, these rectangles were subdivided into the long, narrow plots owned by the burgesses of the medieval town, with a house or shop on the street front, and sheds, workshops and gardens behind. One of the greatest modifications to the town plan resulted from the extension of the castle towards the end of the twelfth century. The huge curtain wall that encloses the outer bailey was built on the south side, encroaching

Encroachment on to the market area in Ludlow has resulted in an infill of buildings divided by narrow alleys. (*Trevor Rowley*)

on the western part of Ludlow so that part of the High Street disappeared under the new outer bailey. This development involved the destruction of a street called Bell Lane that once ran down to the Teme. Across the rectangle of land between Mill Street and the castle, now largely taken up with gardens, Bell Lane continued towards the little twelfth-century chapel of St Thomas of Canterbury.

Bridgnorth, another Shropshire castle borough, was developed in a series of stages. In the late eleventh century, Robert de Bellême transferred the small Domesday town of Quatford, on the River Severn in Shropshire, to a new site to the north, which enjoyed a more commanding location overlooking the river and the bridge that gave its name to the town. There had been a motte castle at Quatford with a small accompanying borough, which is recorded in Domesday, but Bellême built a new stone tower keep on the sandstone promontory. Attached to the castle was a small, regular town with a marketplace, occupying the equivalent of a northern castle bailey. The regular property boundaries running off West and East Castle streets at right angles formed the core of this early town. Early in the twelfth century, after Henry I had seized the town from Bellême, a second, larger unit was added, based on a new, broad market street. This extended northwards from the gates of the original castle town. The properties in this extension were larger than those in Bellême's town. A third area of planned burgages was added later in the twelfth or early in the thirteenth century, whose alignment was at right angles to the phase two development. It consisted of a denser arrangement

Bridgnorth, Shropshire, a post-Conquest planned town based on the castle perched on a sandstone ridge above the River Severn. (*Shropshire County Council*)

of plots and streets.[31] When town walls were built in the thirteenth century, they followed the natural geography of the promontory and appear to cut off part of the last phase of the plantation.

A few kilometres to the south-west of Ludlow, close to the Welsh border, Clun provides another good example of a Marcher castle town. The earliest part of Clun is represented by the church, isolated from the rest of the town and surrounded

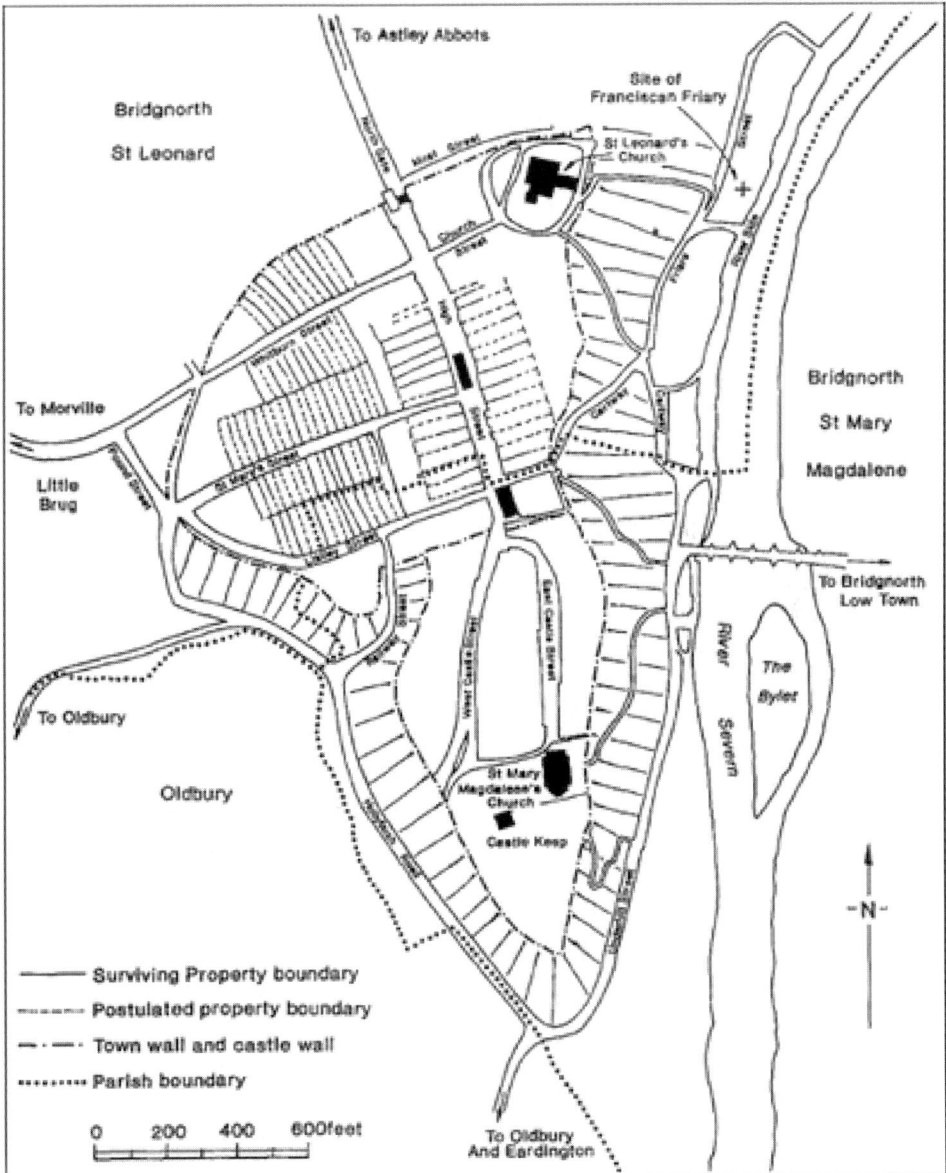

Plan of Bridgnorth showing suggested units of development. (*Lilley, 2002: 142*)

by a deep ditch on the south bank of the River Clun. Clun had formed part of the extensive estates of Edric the Wild in 1066 but had passed to Picot de Say, one of Earl Roger de Montgomery's chief vassals, after the Conquest. The castle became the centre of one of the great Marcher lordships, the barony of Clun, with territory stretching for over 35km from the upper valley of the Teme towards the southern end of the Long Mynd. Picot de Say and his successors as lords of Clun were responsible for the building of the castle and the laying out of the streets of the little borough on the north bank of the river. No documents survive that allow one to date with any precision these events and it is only by the beginning of the thirteenth century that we hear of a borough and a flourishing market centre at the gate of the castle when Clun acted as a meeting place for English and Welsh traders.

Like many castle settlements, Weobley (Herefordshire) did not grow significantly beyond its original size, although it has the plan of a classic castle town but without defensive walls. At the south end of the village are the earthworks of what was a substantial castle, founded by the de Lacy family in the eleventh century, while at the other end of the settlement is the large parish church of St Peter. Between the two runs Broad Street, which has been widened at the castle end to create a triangular marketplace. The remains of former burgage plots can be clearly detected on either side of Broad Street. The market's location emphasizes the importance of the close relationship between the castle and the market, reflecting the desire of the Norman lord, and his retinue, to be in a place that allowed direct view on to – and surveillance of – the activities taking place in the street below, including not just trading activities but other social gatherings that could threaten the lord's authority.

Swansea, in the Gower Marcher lordship, was established on an elevated site overlooking the River Tawe. The town sat at the mouth of the River Tawe, adjacent to a large bay at the western end of the Bristol Channel. A castle was built by the river about 1100 by Henry de Beaumont, 1st Earl of Warwick and lord of Gower. The Norman castle in Swansea was located at the northern end of Wind Street, looking down upon and along the town's main street. Wind Street functioned as the town's main marketplace in the late eleventh century. The broadening of Wind Street, towards its northern end, accommodated the market stalls in the street. Archaeological investigation of properties in and around Wind Street revealed a range of trade and servicing activities, involving craftspeople, artisans, merchants and others. The built-up area of Wind Street had a defensive circuit dating to c.1100, linked to, but distinct from, the castle defences. On the east side of Wind Street, the river provided a defence. At this stage the town does not seem to have had its own church, and the townspeople probably worshipped at a castle chapel, which was associated with the Knights Hospitaller.

Carmarthen is sited some 20 miles (30km) north-west of Swansea in a similar strategic location, an elevated site above the River Towy. Carmarthen had Roman

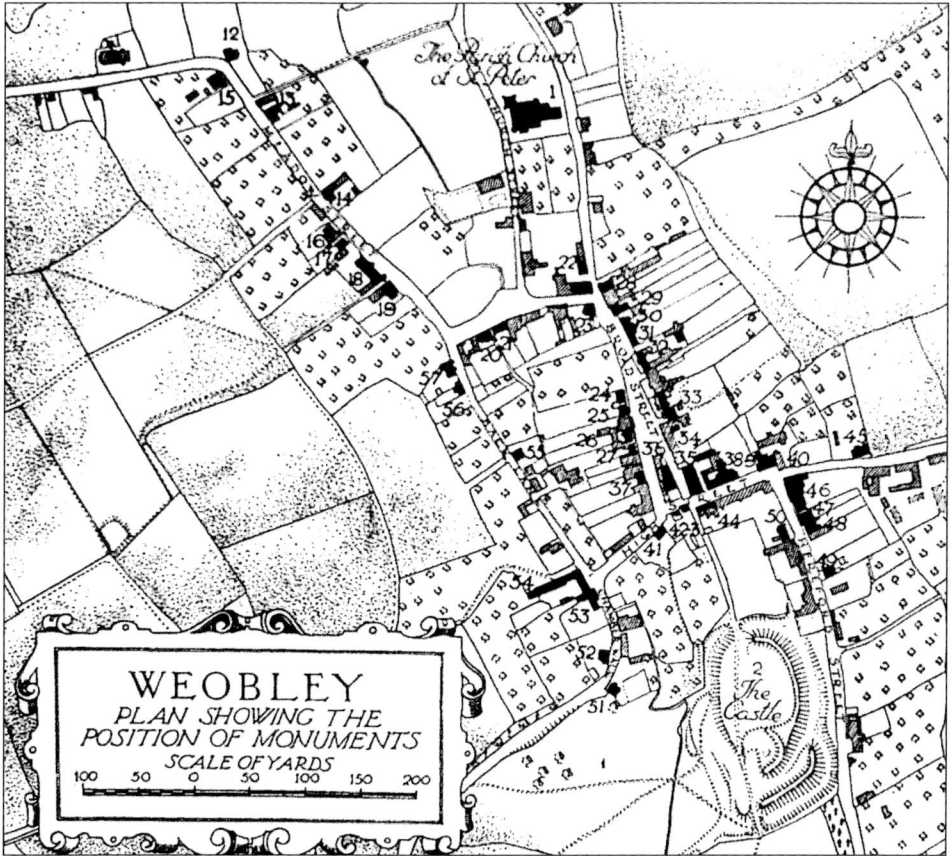

Weobley, Herefordshire, is not an obvious castle town, but it has all the topographical ingredients. The castle was the base for the de Lacy Marcher lordship and has a typical linear shape leading from the castle through the market to the church, while burgage plots run off Broad Street at right-angles. There is no obvious evidence for the defensive circuit mentioned, c.1200. (*RCHM, 1934: 192-203*)

origins (*Moridunum*), unlike Swansea, and the Roman defensive circuit was adapted by the Normans. The castle was established on the king's instruction by William fitz Baldwin in 1094 and is situated immediately above and overlooking the bridge across the river. The castle gate faces north-west on to the town's marketplace, which is a broad street aligned with the entrance to the castle.

Between the castle town and the area of Roman Carmarthen there is a pair of streets, running almost in parallel, connecting the castle town with the church of St Peter, which sits just inside the former Roman defences and may represent the site of an earlier church of St Teulyddog. The pattern here is reminiscent of that at Swansea, where High Street and Back Lane connect the castle town with the early church of St John's. At Carmarthen, the parallel streets and the area

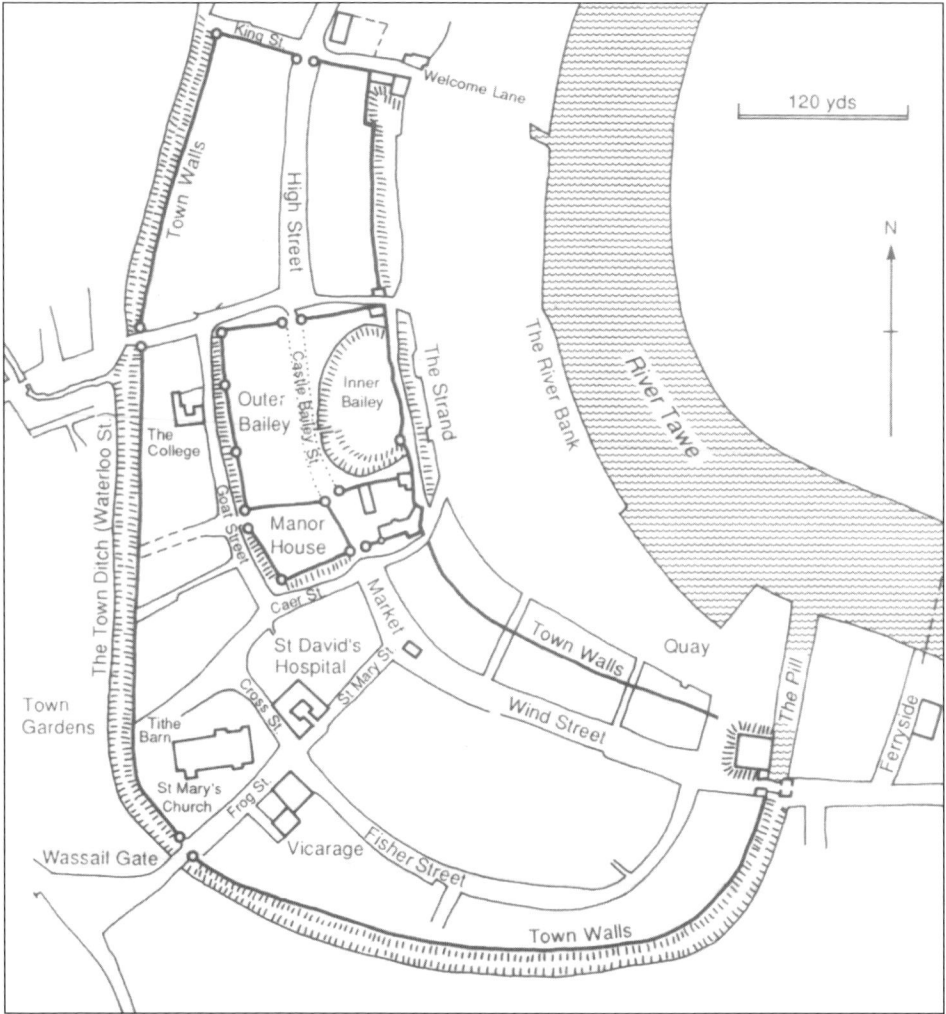

Map of Swansea, West Glamorgan. The town was created within the shadow of a castle after the Conquest. The shape of the castle and old town reflects that of the River Tawe to the north. (*medievalswansea.ac.uk*)

around them probably represent an early expansion of the castle town, infilling ground between the castle and church, perhaps after the town was burned by the Welsh in 1116.

A series of strategic castles, with attached settlements, was established in northern England in the second half of the twelfth century to consolidate Henry II's repossession of Northumberland in 1157. At places such as Alnwick, Warkworth, Barnard Castle, Bamburgh, Newcastle and Norham, there were markets, important for the sale of produce from the lord's estate and for exacting tolls, adjacent to the castle gates. Norham Castle was built on a promontory, overlooking the River Tweed, by Ranulf Flambard, Bishop of Durham, *c*.1121, and was intended 'to inhibit the raids of brigands and the incursions of the Scots' according to Simeon of Durham. There may well have been an earlier fortification on the site, which overlooks an ancient ford, but the majestic red sandstone keep towering over the Tweed was the work of Henry II, *c*.1170. The village of Norham, which is separated from the castle by a stream – the Mill Burn – displays all the elements of a castle town and was granted a borough charter in 1160.

The town of Warkworth (Northumberland) occupies a pronounced loop in the River Coquet, 2km inland from its estuary; a site similar to that of Durham. The town's medieval history reflects the complex border politics of the area. Prince Henry of Scotland reputedly built a motte and bailey here, after becoming Earl of Northumberland in 1139, but it is more likely that the castle dates from Henry II's repossession of the region in 1157. The present stone castle appears to be the work of Robert fitz Roger, *c*.1200, following an attack on the town by the Scots, in which the population was slaughtered. The castle occupies the neck of the river loop, with the main street running northwards towards the twelfth-century church of St Lawrence and the medieval fortified bridge. It has been suggested that given the disturbed character of the region the church may have been defensible, or at least have provided a refuge in times of trouble. It seems probable that the town, with its regular burgage plots running down to the river on either side, together with a triangular marketplace, dates from the early thirteenth century.[32]

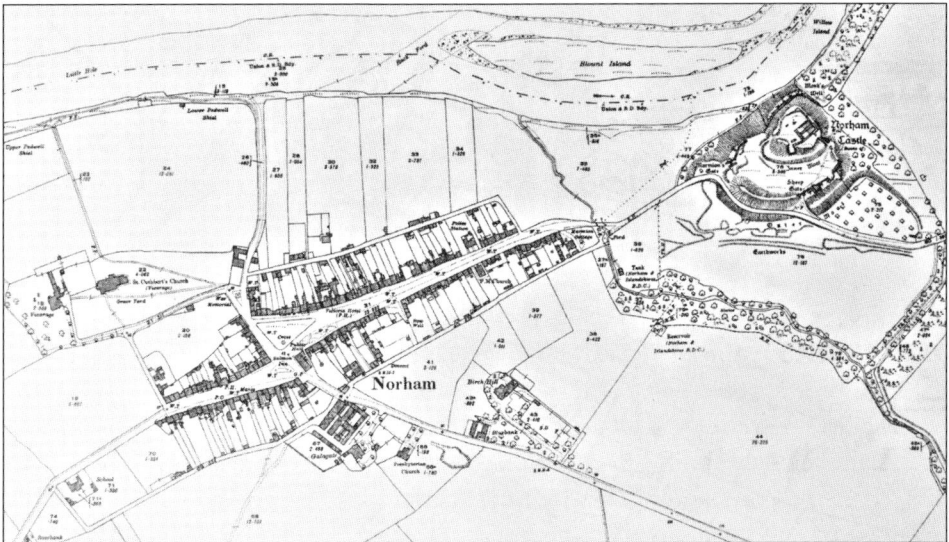

Norham Castle and 'town' lie on the South bank of the River Tweed, which here forms the border between England and Scotland. (See Plate 7)

Warkworth, Northumberland. A border castle and borough contained within a narrow meander of the River Coquet, providing a strong defensive site. Unusually, the borough does not lie at the main castle gateway. (*Russel Wills*)

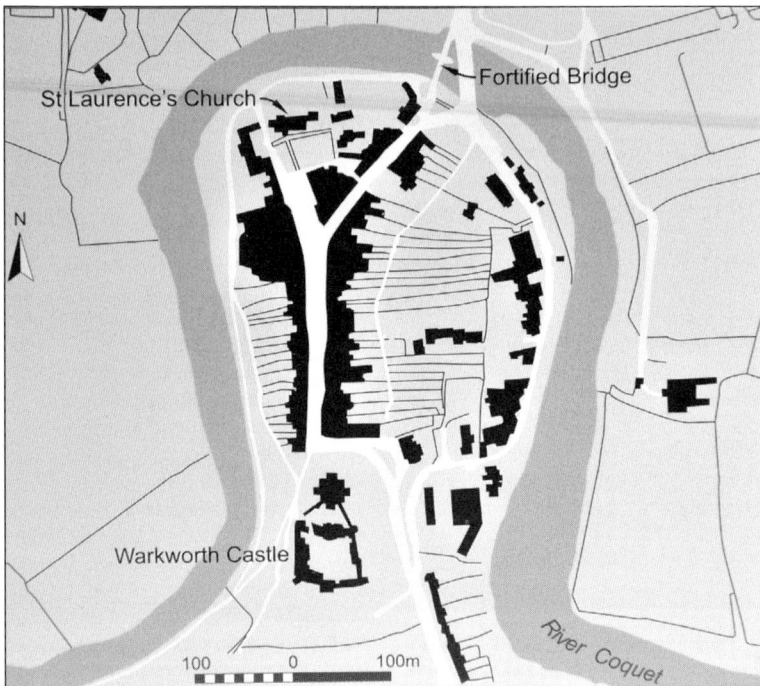

Plan of Warkworth. (*Aalen. 2006: 63*)

There is another category of castle town, where the castle has effectively been overtaken by its markets. Bishop Roger of Salisbury built a castle at Devizes (Wiltshire) *c*.1120 and a market with burgage plots, reflecting the shape of the outer bailey, was established to the east of the castle. Subsequently, a second market was inserted within the outer bailey. To the west of the castle there was a large oval-shaped deer park, reflecting the shape of the castle form. The whole twelfth-century town plan was thus dictated by the shape of the castle, but the importance of the castle, which originally dominated the settlement, has been diminished by the later development around the market areas.

In addition to castle towns of various shapes and sizes, the topography of many smaller rural settlements was fashioned by the presence of a castle.

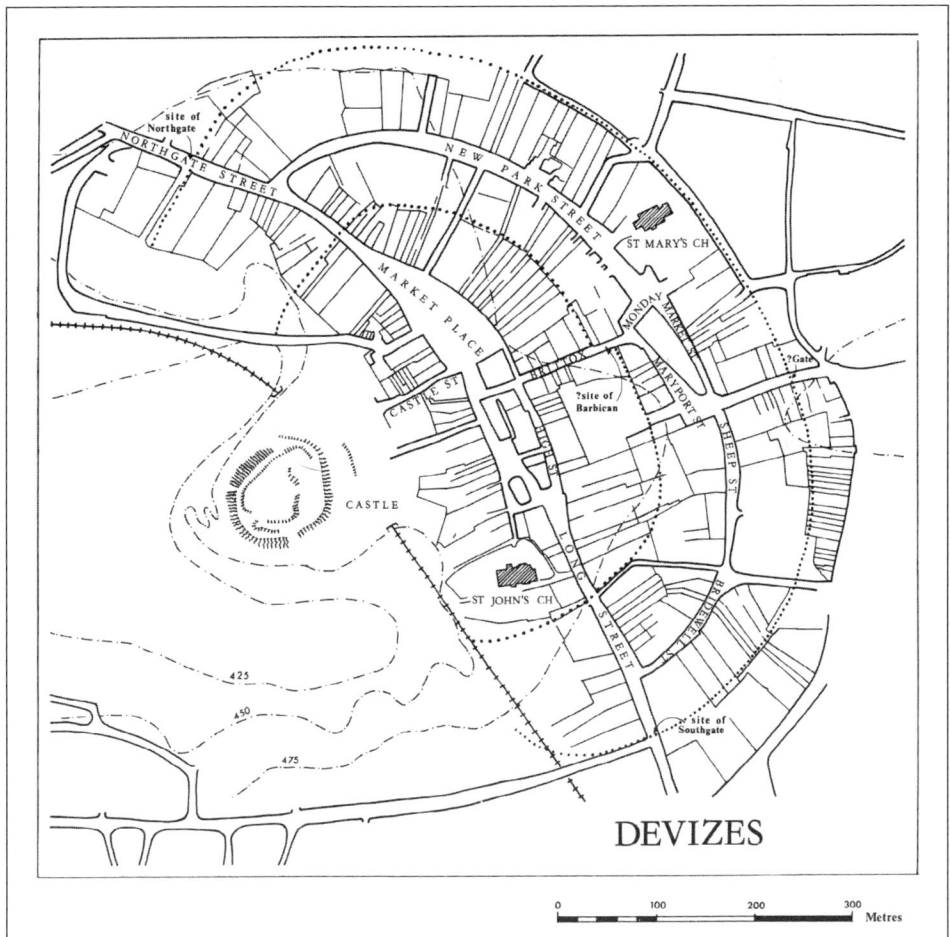

A plan of the classic castle town of Devizes, Wiltshire, which was the work of Bishop Roger of Salisbury, *c*.1120. The town lies to the east of the castle in two extended baileys, with a large deer park to the west. (*Royal Archaeological Institute*)

Aerial view of Devizes, showing the close relationship between the castle, borough, and former park. The name Devizes is post-Conquest, coming from *burgus de devisis*, the borough at the boundary of two manors, Bishop's Canning and Potterne. (*Beresford, 1967, 504*)

Pleshey, Essex, is one of the best-known examples. Another is at Kilpeck, Herefordshire, renowned for its remarkable twelfth-century church. Kilpeck Castle appears to have been built towards the end of the eleventh century as *caput* of Archenfield, when it was in the hands of the royal forester of Haywood, William son of Norman. There is a small bailey to the north-east of a large earthen motte, capped with the remnants of a stone shell-keep, beyond which lies the church and the earthworks of a deserted settlement, clearly demarcated by a rectangular boundary bank and ditch. Traces of houses with attached plots can be clearly seen within the enclosure.

Kilpeck Castle was the caput of Archenfield, a region that was descended from the Welsh kingdom of Ergyng, where Welsh custom and language survived throughout the Middle Ages. In 1134 there was a 'chapel of St Mary of the castle' in addition to the adjacent, remarkable Norman parish church (see p.292). (*Allen Brown, 1989: 136-7*). (*Paul R. Davis*)

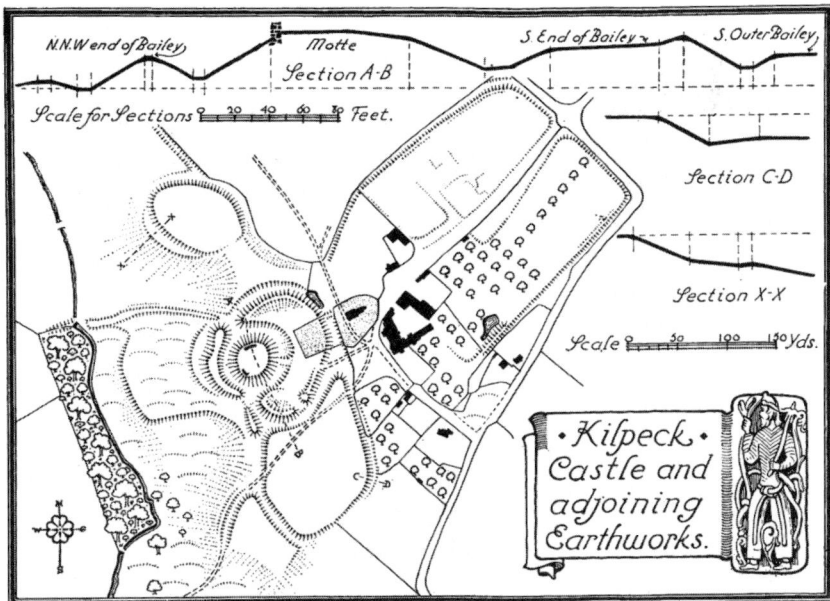

Plan of Kilpeck Castle and adjoining earthworks showing a secondary bailey to the south of the motte. A large rectangular enclosure to the north–east of the castle represents the boundary of a former castle settlement here.

Chapter 6

The Impact of the Conquest on Towns

'To glance at the urban landscape of Norwich, Durham or Lincoln is to be forcibly reminded of the impact of the Norman invasion'.[1] (See Plate 8)

During the Middle Ages, towns were best defined by their function, rather than by their size or legal status. They would normally possess one or more of the following features – a mint, administrators, defences, markets, craftsmen, industrial workers and traders. In England, many Roman towns such as Winchester, Chichester and Colchester, whose fortifications largely remained intact, had been refitted for use during the Viking era, while new defended towns, such as Oxford and Wallingford, had been built on greenfield sites. These were Saxon *burhs*, designed to restrict the movement of Viking armies and to provide refuge in times of war. They acted as focal points for trade and services and helped the revitalization of urban life in England. There were equivalent Scandinavian fortified boroughs in the Danelaw region, notably, Derby, Leicester, Lincoln, Nottingham and Stamford. There were also specifically Danish boroughs further south, in places such as Northampton. The establishment of a national system of shires in the tenth century required regional centres to administer them; several of these, such as Worcester, Gloucester and Leicester, had Roman origins, while others were based on new Saxon and Scandinavian *burhs*. Towns had developed or were developing as trading centres at crossroads, river crossings and coastal sites. Market traders and craftsmen settled at the gates of the revitalized monasteries of late Saxon England, leading to the growth of several towns at places such as Abingdon, Glastonbury and Bury St Edmunds. A small number of towns, such as the salt-producing centres in Cheshire and Worcestershire, might be classified as industrial.

The Domesday Book incorporates the first national survey of English towns, but its coverage of towns is unsystematic and incomplete. The survey's prime targets were rural estates and it found difficulty in interpreting the complexity of towns, which are variously described as *civitas*, *burgus* and *villa*. Domesday does reveal that many towns were intimately connected to their rural hinterland and that they contributed significantly to the Crown's finances, but it only identified 112 places as boroughs. In the top rank were London, York, Norwich, Lincoln and Winchester with populations in excess of 5,000. At the other end of the scale were tiny boroughs such as Langport and Axbridge (Somerset), attributed with

Oxford *c.*1150, showing the Norman castle superimposed on the western end of the Saxon town. Oxford was a shire capital established as an Alfredian *burh* on a crossing point of the River Thames in the ninth century, with an eastern extension added in the eleventh century. (*Crossley, 2021*)

fewer than 35 burgesses in 1086. Towns accounted for something in the region of 10 per cent of the population in 1086, but most of the urban centres were small, normally with a population of fewer than 2,000 people.

The impact of the Normans on the topography of English and Welsh towns was profound and of lasting significance. What might be seen as an experiment in the use of towns in Normandy prior to 1066 was applied on a grand scale in England and Wales. In Normandy before the Conquest, towns and castles had been developed as instruments of government, and they had been used successfully as a means of centralizing political and economic control. Rouen, along with the other Norman cathedral towns, had Roman origins but had developed as an important Viking port and later as the capital of the newly established duchy. William the Conqueror had nursed the development of Caen as his own ducal town, with a massive castle and a series of *bourgs* attached to it. To cement his hold on the town, he founded the Abbaye aux Hommes (Saint-Étienne) and the Abbaye aux Dames for his and Matilda's memorials. Before he became Archbishop of Canterbury, Lanfranc, then abbot of Saint-Étienne, had overseen the canalization of the River Odon, a tributary of the River Orne, in order to develop a port for Caen suitable

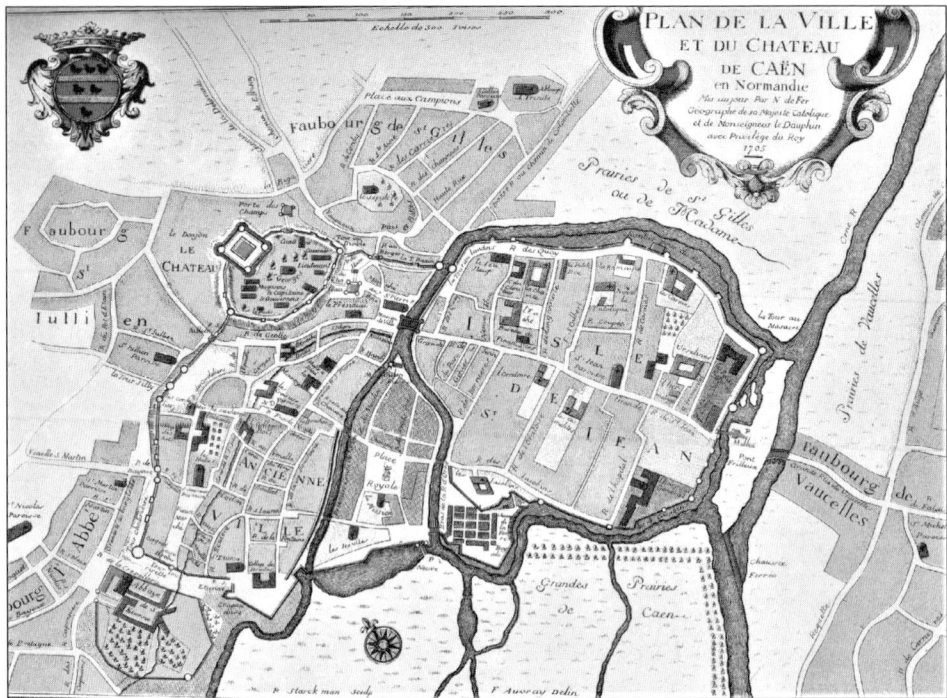

Plan of Caen in 1705 by the cartographer Nicolas de Fer. Duke William developed the town as his headquarters in western Normandy. At the core was a massive castle surrounded by a series of *bourgs*. To the north was Matilda's abbey of Sainte-Trinité and to the south William's abbey of Saint-Étienne.

for seagoing ships.[2] Subsequently, the sea crossing between Caen and Winchester, by way of Southampton or Portchester, became the axis on which the Norman monarchy ran its cross-Channel empire.

The immediate impact of the Conquest on many towns was in many cases little short of disastrous. The Domesday Book records that one of the seven wards at York was entirely destroyed; at Lincoln, 166 houses were destroyed, 113 at Norwich, 51 at Shrewsbury and 27 houses at Cambridge; all to accommodate the castles or to create a clear line of fire around them. Smaller-scale destruction is recorded at Canterbury, Gloucester, Huntingdon, Stamford, Wallingford and Warwick. These were mostly royal castles constructed during the first phase of the takeover of England. Yet within a century every county town and many other urban centres were furnished with castles, new cathedrals or abbey churches, new parish churches as well as some stone-built vernacular buildings. In the two and a half centuries following the Conquest, the urban geography of England and Wales was mapped out in a pattern that survived virtually unchanged until the Industrial Revolution; not only were hundreds of new towns created, but separate districts with castles, churches and markets transformed many existing towns.

London

In 1066, London was the most populous city in England and its commercial capital, although not yet its political or administrative centre. In 1066, the majority of Londoners still lived within the Roman walled city, although during the tenth and eleventh centuries there were already developments along the Thames waterfront. Despite its importance, the overall layout of much of London remained unchanged after 1066. In part this was because Edward the Confessor had decided to build the new regal centre at Westminster on the River Thames, a kilometre or so to the south-west of the walled city. Thus, the royal abbey of Westminster and its associated palace were not sited in the heart of the old city, but on an island at the confluence of the River Tyburn with the Thames.

The 3.2km-length of the Roman city wall of *Londinium* was still standing with six of the original gateways in place. The Normans rebuilt and reinforced decayed parts of the wall and established fortresses in the west and in the east, the most important of these being the emblematic great stone keep Tower of London. The Tower was sited within the south-east corner of the Roman wall circuit, close to where it met the Thames.

There were two smaller castles on the western edge of the city, Baynard's Castle and Montfitchet's Tower. Under this arrangement, the city was protected from attack both upstream and downstream, replicating the defensive arrangements at the ducal capital of Rouen.

There were many other secular structures in Norman London, including the first stone bridge over the Thames (1176–1209) and probably the earliest Guildhall, but little of this work survives. London Bridge, which replaced the

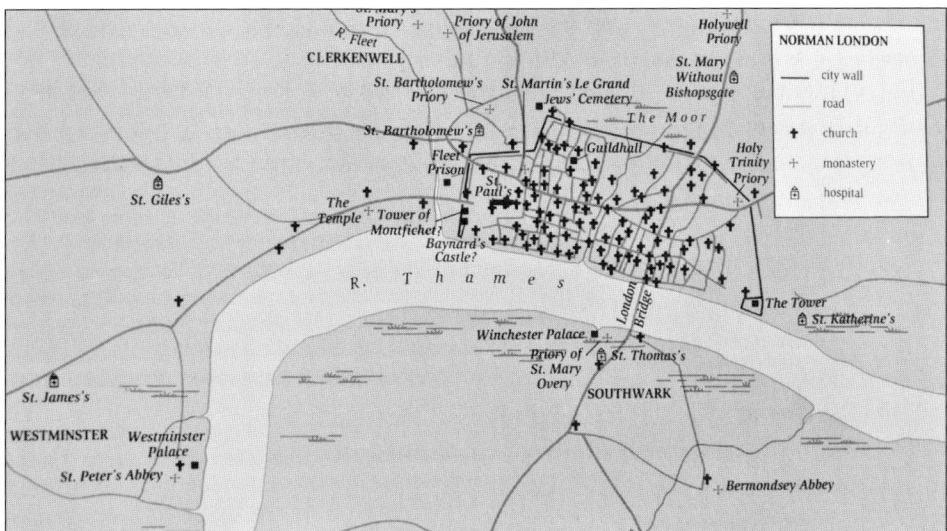

Plan of Norman London. (*Clout, 2007: 43*)

The Tower of London lying next to the River Thames, occupying the south-east corner of the Roman city. (*Duncan*)

earlier, wooden crossing, was started by Henry II, who created a monastic guild, the 'Brethren of the Bridge', to oversee all work on its maintenance. London Bridge was the only dry crossing point in the south-east and travellers moving south to north were therefore obliged to pass through the city. Added to which, the bridge formed a barrier to larger ships sailing upstream, meaning that they had to unload, leading to the construction of new wharves by the Norman riverside landowners. Repeated rebuilding and periodic fires mean that little Norman domestic architecture survives in the capital, and archaeological evidence shows that the vast majority of domestic buildings in the post-Conquest period were built of timber.[3] In order to restrict the danger of widespread fire, in 1077 the king issued a decree to the effect that all fires must be extinguished by 8 pm. This was described as a 'couvre feu', the origin of the English term 'curfew'. Among the wooden houses there were some grander stone houses from quite an early date. For example, in the early twelfth century:

> Abbot Reginald of Ramsey [sold] some … land on the Walbrooke … and also a house of stone and a cellar which he had built on that land with iron doors and windows upstairs and downstairs.[4]

The major Norman ecclesiastical contribution to London was St Paul's Cathedral. There had been a church dedicated to St Paul on Ludgate Hill in the west of

Old London Bridge in 1632 by the Dutch painter Claude de Jongh.

the walled city since the early seventh century, but along with much of Saxon London it was destroyed in 1087 when, according to the *Anglo-Saxon Chronicle*, 'the holy minster of St Paul, the cathedral church of London, was burnt down, and many other churches, and the largest and fairest part of the city'. Work on a new, much larger cathedral began almost immediately under Maurice, Bishop of London (1085–1107). This building was not completed until around 1190, when its eleven-bay nave formed the core of one of the longest churches in the medieval world. St Paul's cruciform plan placed it in the same league as other great twelfth-century pilgrimage churches at Saint-Martial, Limoges, Santiago de Compostela, Saint-Sernin, Toulouse and Pisa Cathedral.[5] The Norman nave survived until the Great Fire of London, though it was by then in a state of serious decay. Christopher Wren was dismissive of the Norman building, complaining that old St Paul's 'was both ill design'd and ill built from the Beginning'.

St Paul's was only one of many new religious buildings under construction in London and its suburbs during the late eleventh and early twelfth centuries. In the 1170s, William fitz Stephen counted 126 parish churches in London, many of which appeared after the Conquest. In Cheapside there was one remarkable new church, St Mary-le-Bow, which Archbishop Lanfranc (1070–89) built as part of Canterbury's administrative centre in the heart of the city. The restored crypt survives beneath a Wren church. To the south of the river, Cluniac monks from La Charité-sur-Loire (Nevers) founded Bermondsey Abbey, *c*.1089. Pilgrims, attracted by a relic of the Holy Cross housed in the abbey, according to the Domesday Book built a 'new and beautiful church' here. The site is now occupied by Bermondsey Square. Henry I's wife Matilda founded Holy Trinity Priory, Aldgate, in 1108, the largest of three Augustinian houses in London. Other Augustinian houses dedicated to St Bartholomew and St Mary Overie were founded outside the city walls; the latter eventually became Southwark Cathedral.

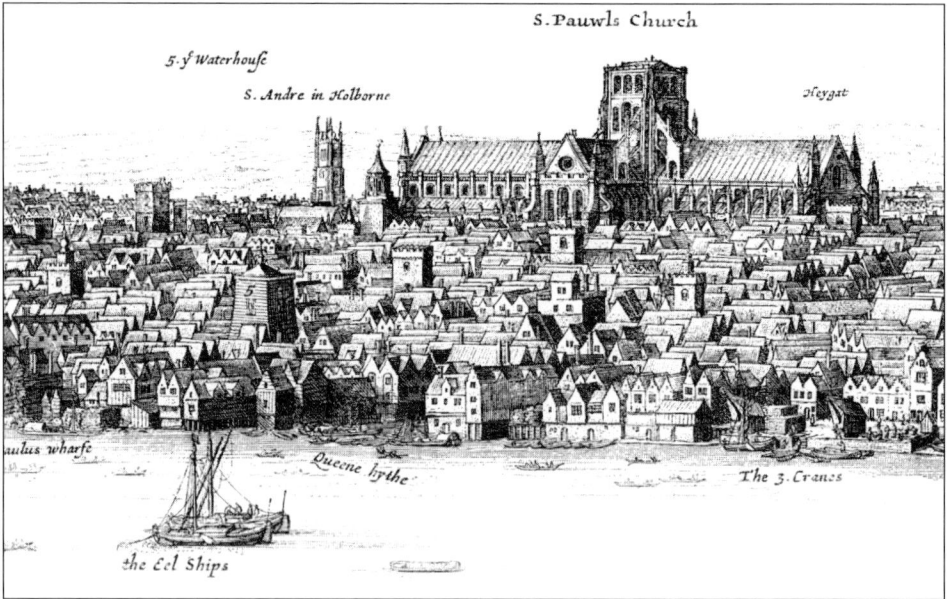

Old St Paul's Cathedral, before it was destroyed in the Fire of London (1666), seen from the Thames in a drawing by Wenceslaus Holler.

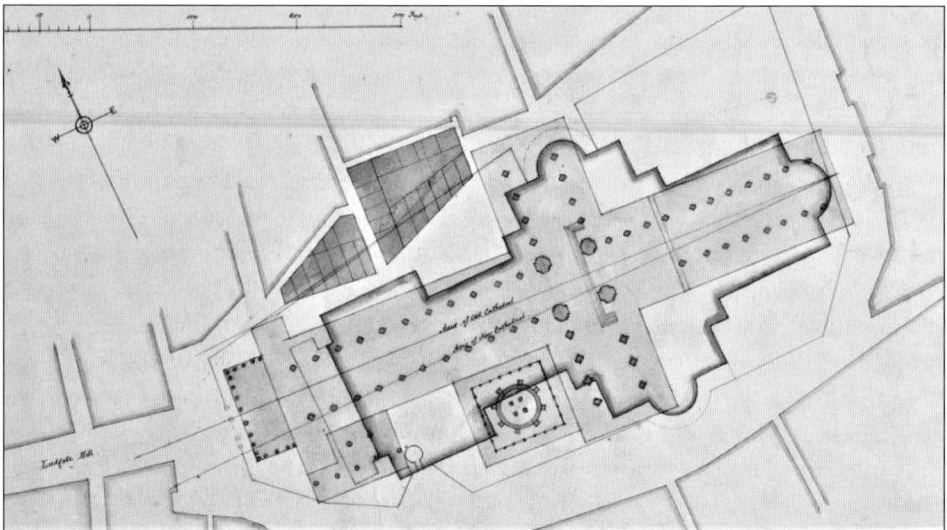

A comparative plan of 1872, showing New St Paul's superimposed on the outline of Old St Paul's.

By the latter part of the twelfth century, London was a major European city and port, dominated by the Tower in the south-east and the vast St Paul's in the west. While Westminster, still a separate community to the west of the city, was a major religious centre with a royal palace and England's largest ceremonial hall.

A reconstruction of Bermondsey Abbey, which was founded as a Cluniac priory in the 1080s in Southwark, to the south of the Thames. (*Alistair Douglas*)

Winchester

Winchester was a Roman city (*Venta Belgarum*), a Saxon *burh* and a diocesan seat since the seventh century. From the mid-tenth century it had also been the royal ceremonial capital of a united England; Saxon kings were crowned here and many, including Alfred the Great, were buried in the cathedral (Old Minster). In addition to the bishop's palace there was a royal palace, which housed the royal treasury. In the area around the cathedral and royal palace there were many moneyers working for the royal mint. By about 900 a rectilinear pattern of cobbled streets had been created. Despite an almost complete rebuilding of the city after the Conquest, the Anglo-Saxon street pattern remained largely intact.

William the Conqueror received the surrender of Winchester while he was at Wallingford on his circuitous route to London in the late autumn of 1066 and he may have started work on the castle here even before his coronation. Certainly, he would have seen the military, political and symbolic importance of securing the city with its treasury as soon as possible. The castle, together with the palace, remained the effective centre of government for almost a century. It occupied a salient in the highest part of the walled town, and sat on a large earthwork platform constructed over the Roman defences and part of the Saxon town, which involved the destruction of at least two streets, one inside the walls, the other on the outside. Henry II added a stone keep to house the royal treasury, but all that survives above ground is the magnificent thirteenth-century Great Hall.

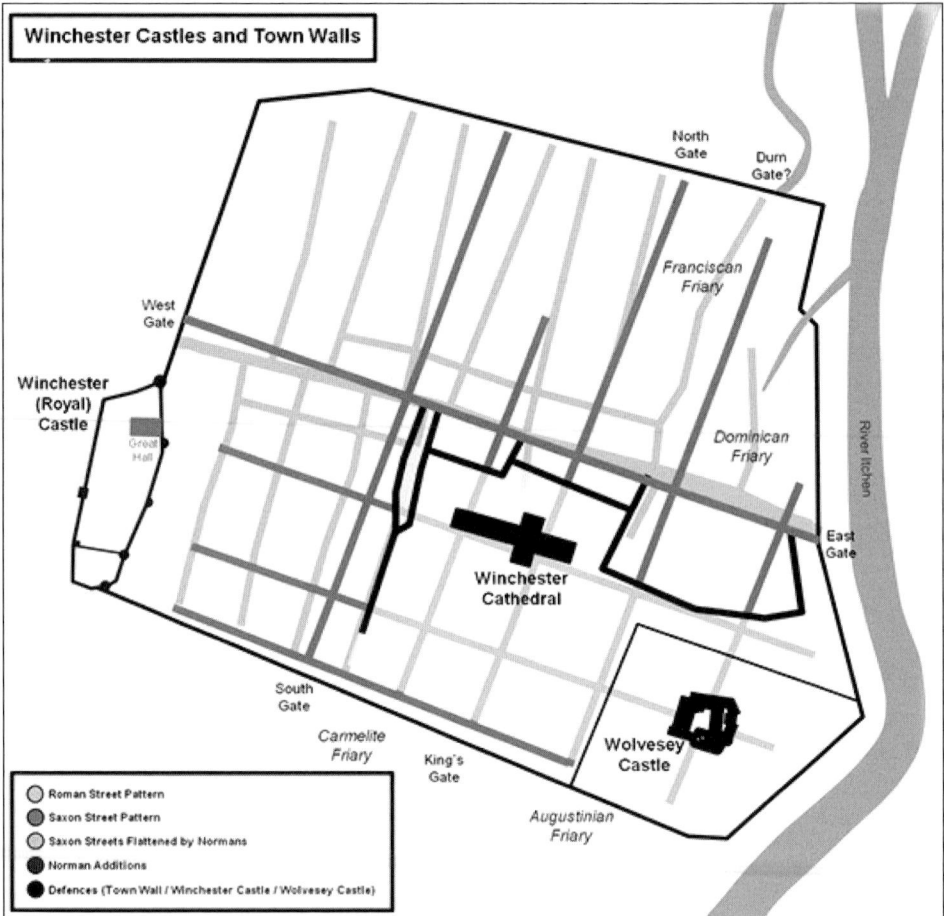

Winchester Castles and Town Walls

North Gate

Durn Gate?

Franciscan Friary

West Gate

Winchester (Royal) Castle

Great Hall

Dominican Friary

River Itchen

East Gate

Winchester Cathedral

South Gate

Carmelite Friary

King's Gate

Wolvesey Castle

Augustinian Friary

○ Roman Street Pattern
● Saxon Street Pattern
○ Saxon Streets Flattened by Normans
● Norman Additions
● Defences (Town Wall / Winchester Castle / Wolvesey Castle)

Plan of Roman and medieval Winchester showing the principal Norman additions. (*James Lancaster*)

About 1070, William rebuilt the Saxon royal palace on a larger scale by taking in the western part of the New Minster precinct and several buildings in the High Street, including five moneyers' workshops. At least one church, together with a graveyard, was destroyed in the process. The king also closed a street that led from the High Street to the old and new minsters in order to build the palace kitchen.[6] By around 1110 there were at least eighteen forges housed in the north-eastern corner of the extended palace, many of which would have been used by moneyers. During William's reign, Winchester maintained its position as England's premier mint; almost a quarter of all of his coins were produced here, twice the amount minted in London.[7] The palace was destroyed in 1141 by Matilda, during the Anarchy, and nothing remains of it apart from a pilaster in the wall of St Lawrence Church, which probably occupies the site of William's chapel. Its former significance may be reflected in a simple ceremony that still

Above: 1. The crowning of King Harold, from the Bayeux Tapestry. It is likely that the court had not dispersed following the consecration of Westminster Abbey on 28 December 1065 and the burial of King Edward on 5 or 6 January 1066.

Right: 2. Pevensey Bay with a 3m above datum flood, highlighting the historic location of Pevensey on a narrow peninsula, and the probable shape of the bay in the eleventh century. (*J. Haslam*)

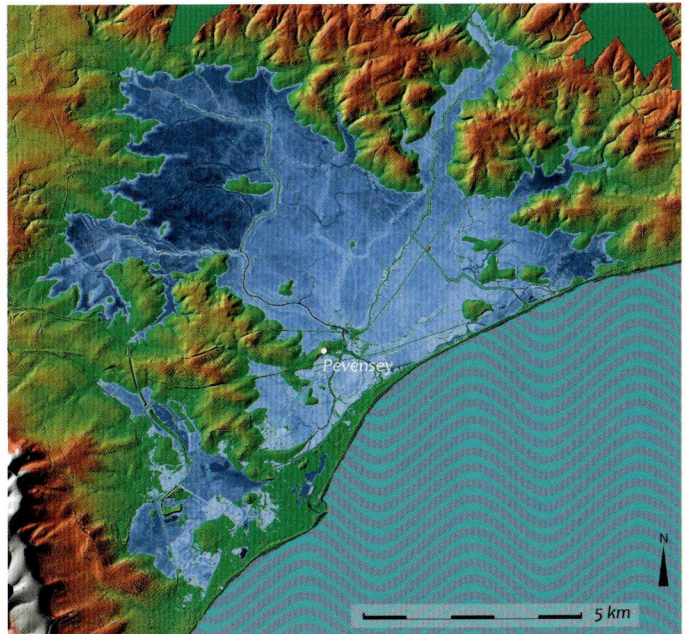

3. Aerial view of open woodland in the High Weald of Sussex, looking much the same as it would have been in 1066.

4. The small limestone island of Flat Holm in the Bristol Channel, which lies 6 km from the Welsh coast. The *Anglo-Saxon Chronicle* records that King Harold's mother, Gytha, took refuge here after the uprising in the south-west of England, accompanied by other aristocratic Saxon women fleeing the Normans. (*Visit Cardiff*)

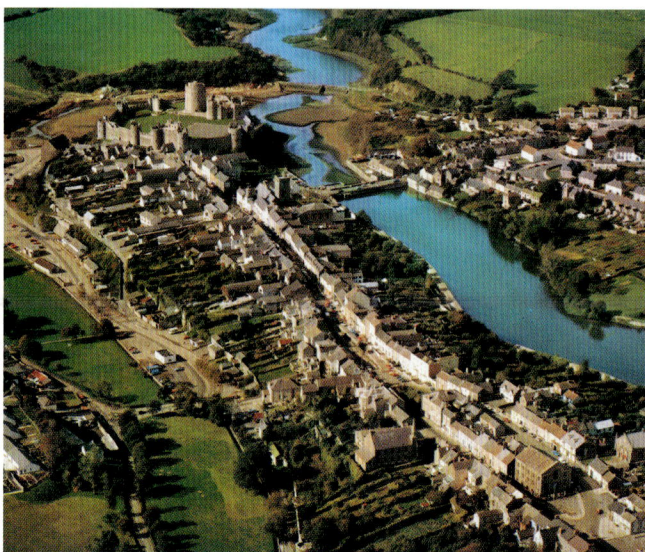

Left: 5. Pembroke, showing the planned town running along a ridge to the south-east of the castle, founded by Arnulf of Montgomery in 1093. (See plan of Pembroke, p.90)

Bottom: 6. The motte and bailey castle at Pulverbatch, Shropshire. The name derives from the Norman-French word *motte* meaning mound, and bailey refers to an attached enclosure. This castle is located on a ridge leading from the Welsh uplands, where it might have controlled the route leading from hill country to the Severn Valley, possibly levying a toll on traffic (Stillman, 1980: 18). Its distinctive flat top indicates that it might have formed part of a group of Upper Severn Valley castles, which acted as a foothold for the Normans to penetrate into Wales in the immediate post-Conquest period (see page 112). (*Paul R. Davis*)

Right: 7. The keep of Norham Castle, Northumberland. The castle was founded by Bishop Ranulf Flambard of Durham in the early twelfth century; the distinctive planned settlement was created soon after (see p.133).

Below: 8. Norwich from the air showing the relationship between the castle and the cathedral. The church of St John Maddermarket sits immediately to the left of the castle. (*Artelia Group*)

9. Old Sarum, Wiltshire, showing the castle and original Norman cathedral occupying a former prehistoric hill fort. The cathedral was abandoned in the early thirteenth century and replaced by a new cathedral at New Salisbury, in the valley of the River Avon, to the south. (*Mick Aston*)

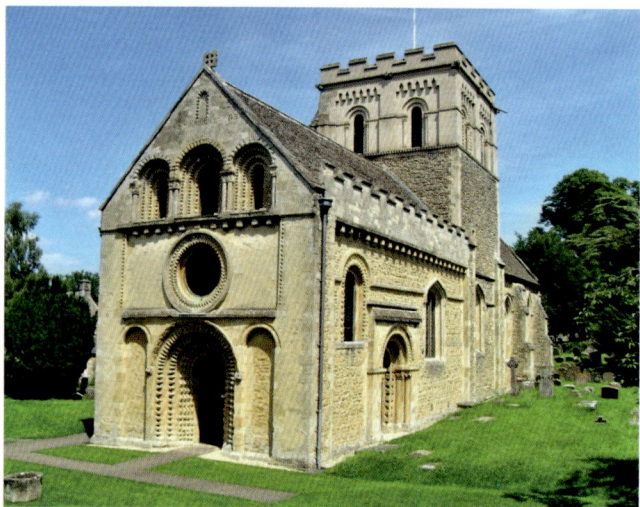

Above: 10. Alnmouth, Northumberland. Designed as a new port for the castle and abbey at Alnwick. (*Northumberland Aerial Views*)

Left: 11. The great inscribed drum columns in the nave of Durham Cathedral are regarded by many as the apotheosis of Norman Romanesque architecture in England. (*Michael D Beckwith*)

12. The fine Romanesque church at Iffley, Oxfordshire, was built *c.*1160 by either Robert of Saint-Rémy or his daughter Juliana. The elaborate decoration and material used, including Tournai marble shafts from Flanders, were intended to make a statement of wealth and prestige. For a while the church was in the hands of Kenilworth Priory, but it later passed through the hands of a number of families, who fortunately for us showed no interest in rebuilding it.

13. Reconstruction of the first Cluniac priory in England at Lewes, Sussex. The priory was founded 1078–1082 by William de Warenne and his wife, Gundrada. (*Andy Gammon*)

Above left: 14. The circular nave of the chapel of St Mary Magdalene in Ludlow Castle. The chapel was probably built *c*.1150 by Gilbert de Lacy, who in later life joined the Knights Templar. (*Trevor Rowley*)

Above right: 15. Gatehouse at Bury St Edmunds, which leads from the abbey precinct into the town. Built by Abbot Anselm (1120–48), it also served as a belltower for the adjacent church of St James. (*Elliot Brown*)

16. A Frankish youth in armour hunting stags, from the *Stuttgart Psalter*. (*Goldberg, 2020: 158*)

Above left: 17. A sixteenth-century map of a deer park at Canterbury, which originally belonged to St Augustine's Abbey. It shows the park pale as a wooden fence, a lodge, and a herd of deer. (*Canterbury Cathedral Archives Map/49*)

Above right: 18. The Norman King Roger II of Sicily receiving the crown from Christ, from a mosaic in the Martorana Church, Palermo. Roger, who is dressed in the robes of a Byzantine emperor, often referred to himself as Emperor. (*Mathias Suessen*)

19. The ruins of St Julian and St Botolph's Priory, Colchester, founded 1093-1100, showing the extensive reuse of Roman brick and tile. St Botolph's was one of the earliest Augustinian houses in England. (*John Armagh*)

20. The distinctive image of Rochester Cathedral from the south-west. The church lies parallel to the line of the Roman defences. (*Prioryman*)

21. Tewkesbury Abbey church was built as a Benedictine monastery during the first half of the twelfth century. It is larger than most English cathedrals and is one of the finest surviving examples of Norman Romanesque architecture in England. (*Jack Boskett*)

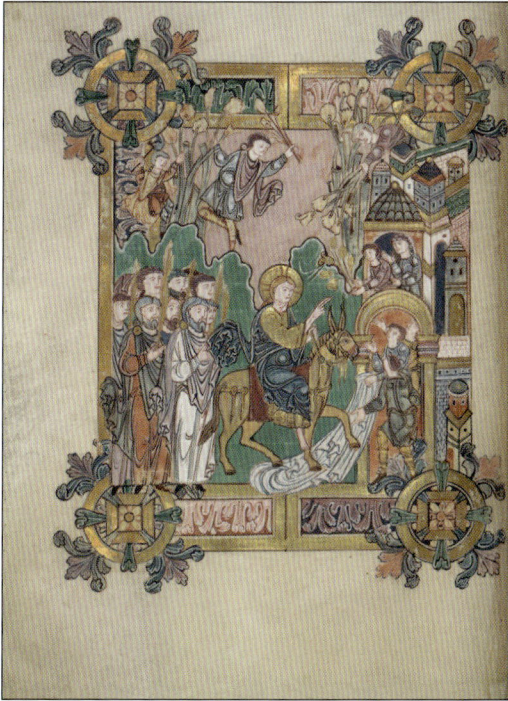

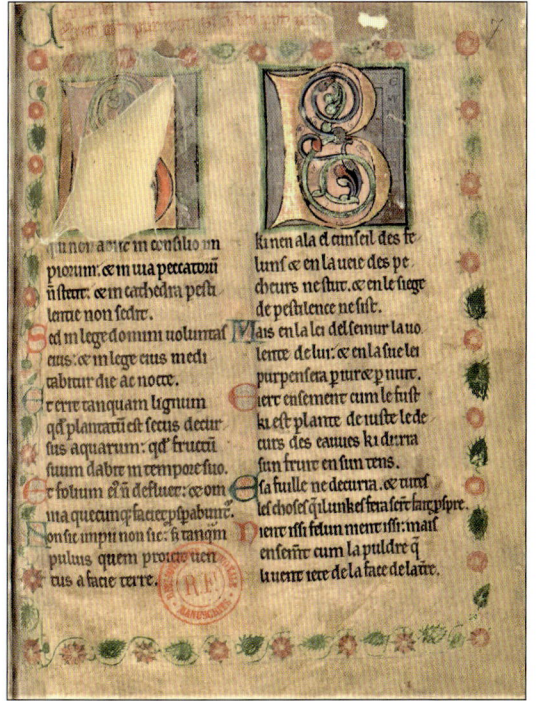

Above left: 22. Christ's entry into Jerusalem, from the *Benedictional of St Aethelwold* (971-984). A masterpiece of late Anglo-Saxon illumination from the Winchester School, the *Benedictional* remained in the Norman cathedral after the Conquest. (*BL. Add MS 49598 f.45v*)

Above right: 23. Extract of verse from an early-twelfth-century psalter, probably copied at Canterbury, written in Anglo-Norman and Latin. (*Bibliotheque nationale de France, NAL 1670*)

24. Perdigon, a medieval troubadour, playing his fiddle. In the Anglo-Norman world, troubadours singing in French were known as *trouvères*. (*Bibliotheque national de France MS-854-fol 49*)

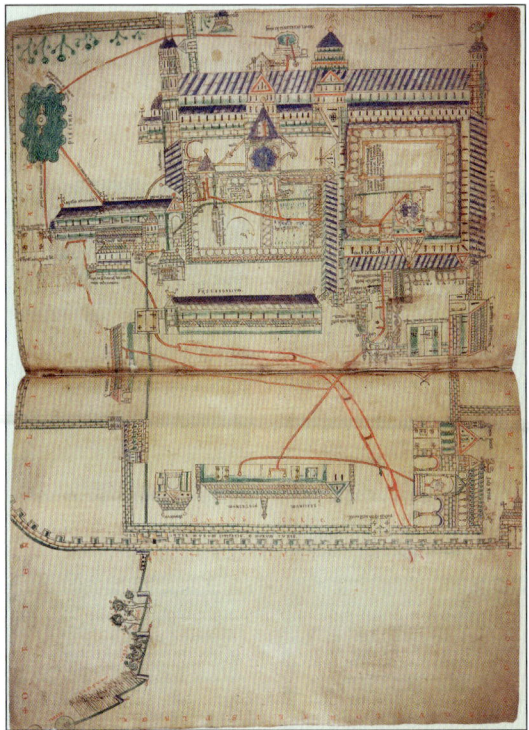

Above left: 25. Eadwine the scribe at work, from the *Eadwine Psalter* (*c.*1147). This lavishly illustrated psalter was produced at Christ Church, Canterbury, and was written in three languages: Latin, Old English and Anglo-Norman. Its design was influenced by the Carolingian *Utrecht Psalter*, which was in Canterbury for a time in the Middle Ages. (*Trinity College, Cambridge MS R.17.1, f.283 verso*)

Above right: 26. Illustration of the water systems of Christ Church, Canterbury, from the *Eadwine Psalter*. The piped and pressurised water and drainage systems were the work of Prior Wilbert (d.1167) and were probably the first systems to be installed in Britain since Roman times. (*Trinity College, Cambridge MS R.17.1, f.284v-285r*) precedes the enthronement of every new bishop. This minute church is where the prospective prelate comes to pray and be gowned before moving on to the cathedral for the inauguration.

In 1070, King William's chaplain, Walkelin, became Bishop of Winchester and began work on a completely new cathedral church in 1079. According to the *Winchester Annals*, the new building was consecrated on 8 April 1093:

> In the presence of almost all the bishops and abbots of England, the monks came with the highest exultation and glory from the old minster to the new one: on the Feast of St Swithun, they went in procession from the new minster to the old one and brought thence St Swithun's shrine and placed it with honour in the new buildings; and on the following day Walkelin's men first began to pull down the old minster.[8]

A substantial amount of the fabric of Walkelin's building, including the crypt, transepts and the basic structure of the nave, survives, providing a superb example

The north transept of Bishop Walkelin's cathedral at Winchester. Dating from the late eleventh century, it incorporates some of the finest early Norman architecture in Britain.

of early, plain Norman church architecture. The original crossing tower, however, collapsed in 1107, an accident blamed by the cathedral's medieval chroniclers on the fact that in 1100 the 'dissolute' William Rufus had been buried beneath it. The nave of Walkelin's cathedral was replaced in the fourteenth century, but it occupies the footprint of the original Norman building. The outline of the Old Minster, which was excavated in the 1960s, is laid out in the churchyard adjacent to the cathedral. The massive scale of the Norman cathedral in comparison with its Saxon predecessor is graphically illustrated by this exercise. It remains one of the largest cathedrals and the length of its nave is unsurpassed in Europe (see p.291).

Just to the north-east of the cathedral lay St Mary's Abbey, founded in 1108 on the site of the Nunnaminster, a nunnery originally established by Alfred the Great's wife, Ealhswith, in the early tenth century. The nunnery church at St Mary's, one of the four largest in Norman England, was destroyed along with much of Winchester in 1141, during fighting between Matilda and Stephen. Hyde Abbey, a Benedictine house located outside the North Gate, c.1110, replaced the New Minster which had been built alongside, almost touching the Old Minster, c.901–3. The remains of King Alfred and Queen Ealhswith, their son Edward the Elder and

The Cathedral Church of the Holy Trinity, St Peter, St Paul and St Swithun is over 150 metres long, making it one of the longest churches in Europe. Its length is due to the marshy ground on which it was built, which restricted the height of the church. William the Conqueror built a royal palace to the north-west of the cathedral, which was destroyed in the mid-twelfth century.

two of his sons, and of King Eadwig were moved here from the New Minster and reburied before the high altar of the vast new Romanesque church. The abbey was dissolved in 1539 and almost immediately completely destroyed. By 1200 there were fifty-seven churches and chapels, the majority of which appeared after 1066 and included four chapels located over the city's gates. To the south of King's Gate there was a hospital attached to the cathedral, later known as Sustren Spital.

The original bishop's palace was built *c*.970 on an area known as Wulf's Island, which lay in the south-east corner of the Roman and Saxon defences of Winchester. The second Norman bishop, William Giffard, constructed a new hall to the south-west of the Saxon palace *c*.1110, and his successor, Henry of Blois, younger brother of King Stephen, added a second hall to the west (1135–8). The *Winchester Annals* record that Henry 'built a house like a palace'.[9] In 1141, Henry linked the two Norman halls with a curtain wall, which obliterated the remaining parts of the Saxon palace. This structure became known as Wolvesey Castle.

Henry of Blois was also responsible for the construction of the Hospital of St Cross *c*.1132 – the largest and most impressive medieval almshouse in England. The hospital sits on the River Itchen, about 1.5km to the south of the cathedral, to which it bears a striking resemblance. Henry refounded the leper hospital of St Mary Magdalen on the hill 2.5km (1.5 miles) to the east of the city. Excavations here have produced evidence of a pre-Conquest leper hospital on the site, the first of this date to be identified in England.

Henry was a prodigious builder and he contributed to Glastonbury Abbey, where he built a bell tower, chapter house, lavatory, refectory, dormitory, infirmary,

Reconstruction of the twelfth-century bishop's Wolvesey Palace at Winchester. (*Liam Wales*)

The Hospital of St Cross, Winchester, was founded by Henry de Blois in 1136, close to the River Itchen. Bishop Henry de Blois' great twelfth-century church resembles a cathedral rather than an institutional church.

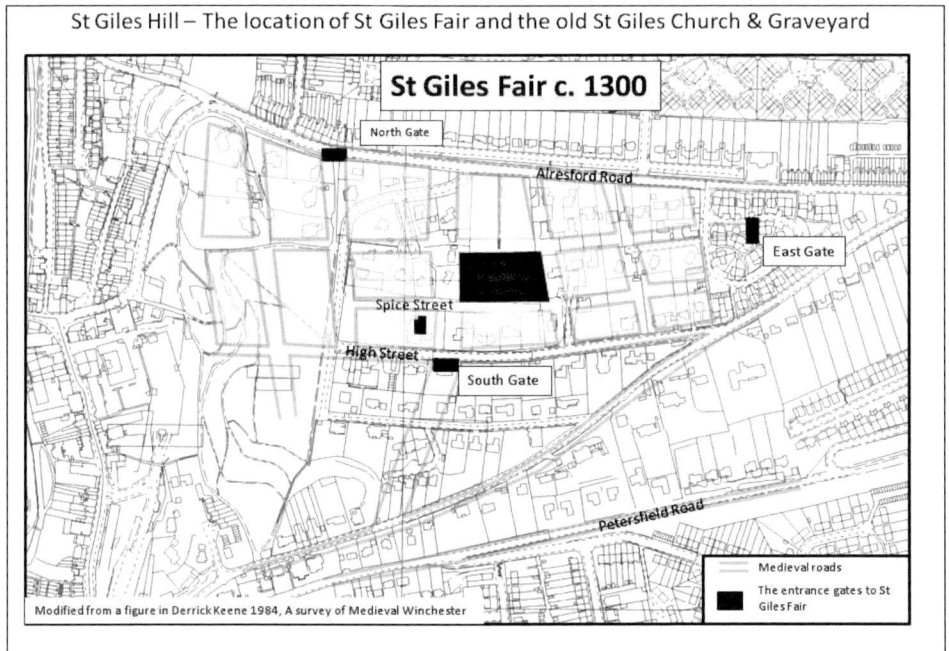

St Giles Hill – The location of St Giles Fair and the old St Giles Church & Graveyard

St Giles Fair c. 1300

North Gate

Alresford Road

East Gate

Spice Street

High Street

South Gate

Petersfield Road

Medieval roads

The entrance gates to St Giles Fair

Modified from a figure in Derrick Keene 1984, A survey of Medieval Winchester

The site of the international St Giles Fair, to the east of Winchester. It was founded by Bishop Walkelin at the end of the eleventh century. (*Derek Keene*)

the '*castellum*', an outer gate, a brewery and stables. During the Anarchy, Henry was also responsible for building six castles/palaces, including those at Bishop's Waltham, Farnham, Merdon and Taunton.

Although Winchester lost its role as capital of England during the later twelfth century, it remained an important royal and ecclesiastical centre. It was also a major commercial hub for the region, with an international annual fair. St Giles Fair was held annually on the summit of St Giles Hill, immediately to the east of the city. It was probably already well established by 1096 when William Rufus granted three days of the fair to the Bishop of Winchester. During the twelfth century it was extended to over two weeks in length and attracted traders from throughout Europe. During the fair the site functioned as an extramural town, with some permanent buildings and a street grid centred on St Giles Church and the bishop's courthouse laid out in the twelfth century. The lines of some of these streets may have been preserved in nineteenth-century field boundaries on St Giles Hill.

York

Under the Norman kings, York became the royal capital of the north and its skyline was transformed after the Conquest; the north of the city was dominated by the Norman minster, while York Castle towered over the south. York sits at the confluence of the rivers Ouse and Foss, which cut through the ancient city. The main part of the Anglo-Viking settlement was located on or close to the old Roman fortress, sited on higher ground between the two rivers. Some of the internal Roman street plan survived, but most of the Roman walls had been dismantled. Much of the Danish settlement was outside the fort and the walls of the city had been extended to enclose the land between the two rivers. Just as at London, Winchester and Lincoln, most of the post-Conquest development took place within the framework of the former Roman fortified area.

According to Orderic Vitalis, after 1066 the city 'was seething with discontent' and by 1086 had lost approximately 30 per cent of its inhabited housing. Hugh the Chanter reported that when Thomas of Bayeux became Archbishop of York in 1070, 'he found everything deserted and waste ... the burnt city and ruined church ... the rest were dead or driven away'. Thomas began repairing the cathedral church, but it was destroyed once more by Danes in 1079. The construction of the castles led to the destruction of one of the city's seven wards, which was, according to Domesday, 'laid waste for the castles'. There was a significant influx of French migrants into York after the Conquest, which would have added to the unrest. Nineteen 'Frenchmen' were listed in Domesday, holding 145 messuages, and King William's half-brother Robert of Mortain held a central block around the Pavement and the Shambles.

Aerial view of York showing the relationship between the Minster cathedral and the Roman and medieval city walls. (*DACP*)

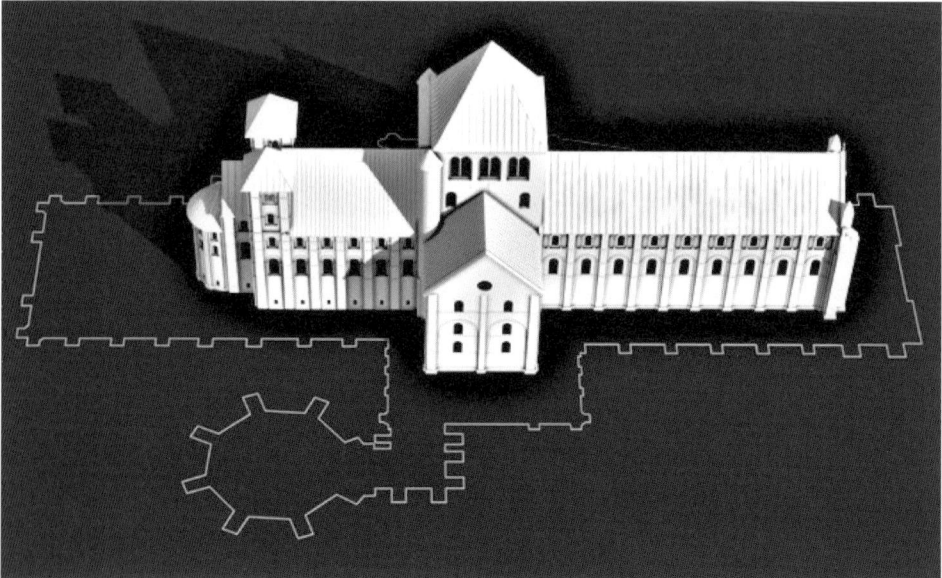

Reconstruction of the Norman minster at York in relation to the church today. (*Tony Elms*)

York was the only city, apart from London, with two Norman castles; both were built in 1068 according to the *Anglo-Saxon Chronicle* and would have dominated the Anglo–Viking city when first constructed. They lay in the south-west on either side of the River Ouse, which bisects the walled city. Both were destroyed in the rising of September 1069 but were rebuilt by the end of that year. York Castle lay to the north of the main river but was contained within a loop of a tributary, the River Foss, which was used to form part of the castle's defensive moat and a lake. This work caused a further flooding a little way upriver, where a second, much larger pool was formed. The Domesday Book of 1086 recorded that 'the King's pool destroyed two new mills worth twenty shillings and of arable land and meadows and gardens fully one carucate' (about 150 acres). The dam also blocked

Speed's map of York (1606). York Castle is in the south, occupying the fork of the junction between the rivers Ouse and Foss. Baile Hill Castle was on the western side of the Foss. The Minster is at the north of the plan; its location within the Roman walls may have been symbolic.

the Foss to navigation, confining the city's wharves to the Ouse waterfront. The second castle was a motte and bailey called Baile Hill. It was built first of timber but reconstructed in stone by Henry III in 1245–70. All that now remains is the motte and Clifford's Tower and part of the bailey wall; the moats have been backfilled and are now occupied by roads and car parks.

At York, a vast new cathedral was built in the 1070s and would have been much larger than anything then existing in either England or Normandy. It should be seen within the context of the rivalry for pre-eminence between York and Canterbury. It would have dwarfed the remains of the pre-1066 cathedral, which had been severely damaged by William the Conqueror's attack on the city in 1068. The new cathedral was built on a new site away from the Saxon minster, whose precise location is unknown. This building, which was itself largely destroyed by fire in 1137, appears to have been different from most contemporary cathedrals built in England. It was longer (365ft), with no aisles in the nave, and had a rectangular ring crypt, a style that was outdated by 1075. The minster

Detail of an inscribed Norman column from the crypt of York Minster.

appears to have been built directly on top of the *principia* of the Roman fort with its imperial associations. The new cathedral was completed within twenty years and built on a raft of timber filled with rubble and mortar; the current cathedral still stands on these Norman foundations. The new archbishop's palace appears to have been built in the north-eastern corner of the old minster precinct.

St Mary's Abbey was founded on the site of the church of St Olave in Marygate, immediately to the north-west of the Roman town walls. Its establishment had the Conqueror's support, so that religion should be encouraged in that city 'in which more blood had been shed than in the other cities of the English'.[10] There were eight parish churches recorded in 1086, but this was an underestimate. One of these, Christ Church, was described as being 'a ruined and poverty-stricken church'. It was rebuilt and established as Holy Trinity, a Benedictine priory, in 1098 by Ralph Paynel. Before 1100, the church of All Saints, Fishergate, was granted to Whitby Abbey and refounded as a Benedictine cell.

The surviving tower of the twelfth-century church of Old St Lawrence, York. (*Guillaume Tell*)

Norwich

The Norman impact on Norwich was as great as on any other town in the kingdom; the conquerors stamped their authority upon the city with such thoroughness that the topography of the centre is still fundamentally Anglo-Norman. The physical appearance of the town altered too, increasing in size by about a third and with the prolific usage of stone, both local and imported.[11] The city resembled those large Continental towns that were made up of several separate units or *burgs*, with discrete Norman zones consisting of the castle quarter, the cathedral close and the English and French boroughs. When the Normans arrived Norwich was a shire town, which they transformed into a regional capital. Within a generation after 1066 the topography of the city had been altered on a scale that would not be repeated until the twentieth century. (See Plate 8 and plan on p.84)

In 1066 there was already a thriving urban centre at the East Anglian capital of Norwich, which lay on either side of the River Wensum, with defences, a mint and the river providing an important trading link to the east coast. Norwich was the third most important east coast port after London and York during the eleventh century and was regularly described as the Port of Norwich. The precise topography of the late Saxon town is not entirely clear, but it appears that there was a defended enclosure to the north of the river, which housed the mint. To the south of the river was a larger, occupied area, which contained markets and a number of churches.

In 1066, 1,320 burgesses were recorded, but by 1086 this number had fallen to 655. Twenty-two burgesses had fled to Beccles in Suffolk and the Domesday Book acknowledges that 'those fleeing and others remaining have been utterly devastated'.[12] There were also '480 *bordarii* who, because of their poverty, pay no customary dues'; probably these *bordarii* had fallen from the ranks of Norwich's burgesses through the devastation of their homes. This decline was a consequence of castle-building and was exacerbated by the response to the Saxon rebellion of 1075 and by increased Crown taxation.

At Norwich, the castle was enormous; in addition to a great motte, on which a palatial stone keep was later added (1120–30), there were a series of four heavily defended baileys. The eastern bailey was called Castle Meadow and it may have provided grazing for the livestock of the sheriff and other royal officials. It has been observed that the castle enclosed as much ground as a small Roman town – its size a reflection of its role as the only royal castle in the two East Anglian counties of Norfolk and Suffolk.[13] The castle was located in the south-west of the Saxon town, between the Great Cockey river and the main north–south through road that led to the principal crossing point of the River Wensum at Fye Bridge. Work started on the castle soon after the Conquest and involved the destruction of up to 113 houses and two churches. Beneath the castle, evidence of a thriving pre-Conquest economy has been found in the form of metal-working, textile manufacture, and bone and antler-working. The castle became the dominant feature of the Norwich townscape and was virtually autonomous. The 'castle fee', the area within the jurisdiction of the castle, did not become part of the borough in a legal and administrative sense until the middle of the fourteenth century.

Further disruption occurred in 1096 when the East Anglian episcopal see was transferred to Norwich (a plan delayed by the rebellion) and the construction of a cathedral began, enough of which had been completed by 1100–01 for it to be consecrated. Much of the stone for the cathedral came from Caen, and a channel which ran from the Wensum to the cathedral close may have been built specially for stone to be transported almost to the building site. This channel was backfilled in the eighteenth century. Where the castle had been a case of disruption of

Norwich Castle keep was built between 1094 and 1121, although the castle was founded by William the Conqueror before 1075. Its palace-like appearance reflects the fact that it was the only major royal castle in East Anglia. (*Andrew Hurley*)

existing settlement through imposition, the building of the cathedral priory was a matter of piecemeal acquisition of land; but its construction also led to the demolition of entire streets of houses and two churches. The lands given by king and earl for the purpose covered much of the old borough centre in northern Conesford, stretching eastwards from Tombland to the marshy banks of the river. The area claimed for the cathedral priory was even larger than that occupied by the castle. The combined positioning of castle and cathedral served to cut off southern Conesford from the other sectors of the borough, and two major Anglo-Saxon buildings – St Michael's and the earl's palace – were pulled down. The disruption to the Saxon town at Norwich caused by the establishment of the large cathedral precinct prompted extensive suburban development along the major access routes.

It is possible that the first Bishop of Norwich, Herbert de Losinga (d.1119), was attempting to create an episcopal city in the Carolingian tradition. The cathedral is remarkable for its scale, with a nave of fourteen bays, and for its cosmopolitan sophistication. It was, in essence, an ancient Roman basilica, whose elaborate decoration differed from the simplicity of the first generation of Norman Romanesque. The later bishop's palace, which was added on the south side of the cathedral by 1119, was in the form of a miniature keep. De Losinga's ambitions were not restricted to Norwich; he made Lynn on the coast into an episcopal town and had considerable interests in Yarmouth. He established cathedral cells throughout East Anglia and gained Church control of much of Norwich's rural

Norwich Cathedral was begun in 1096 by Bishop Herbert de Losinga, after the diocesan see was moved here from Thetford. It was completed in 1145 and despite many later changes, it retains its largely Norman complexion.

hinterland.[14] With royal and ecclesiastical patronage, Norwich developed to the point that by 1200 it had become England's leading provincial city.[15]

Old Sarum

Old Sarum is a spectacular example of a failed Norman town, but it failed only in so far that the town was eventually transposed 3km to the south in the Avon Valley, where it flourished as New Salisbury (see Plate 9). Old Sarum was a prehistoric hill fort that, during the Roman period (*Sorviodunum*), was used as a military fort and later a temple, when it sat at the junction of a network of roads. There was a mint within the hill fort by 1003 and a probable settlement outside. William the Conqueror chose the site for a castle, thrown up in the centre of the hill fort soon after Hastings, almost certainly as part of a strategy to subdue central southern and south-western England. The hill fort would have provided a ready-made base for a large body of troops, serviced by an excellent communications system, during the early stages of the Conquest. Subsequently, the site was chosen as a new shire capital for Wiltshire and diocesan centre, transferred here from Sherborne. With its castle and Romanesque cathedral contained within a mighty fortification, by 1100 Old Sarum provided a symbol of Norman domination *par excellence*.

The raised, circular mound that formed the inner bailey of the Norman castle sits at the centre of the earthwork and is surrounded by a wide, deep ditch. Within the bailey the ground was levelled up with quantities of chalk from the enlarged ditch. All the structures that had formerly stood within the ramparts were covered, and it would appear that the whole of the outer bailey was regarded as part of the royal castle. Bishop Osmund built his new cathedral church in the north-west segment after the see of Sherborne was transferred to Salisbury in 1078; the cathedral was consecrated in 1092. There was also a substantial royal palace in the south-east quadrant of the outer bailey. Recent geophysical work at Old Sarum has in part resolved some of the outstanding questions concerning this remarkable site. The entire outer bailey was heavily built up in the early Middle Ages, containing a dense concentration of structures, representing elements of the Norman borough. One large rectangular structure has been interpreted as the royal palace. Outside the main earthworks, evidence of extensive exterior suburbs has also been identified.[16]

The site was clearly valued by William I, who was presented with the Domesday Book here in 1086, the same year that he held a council to which he summoned the prelates, nobles, sheriffs and knights of his dominions, who swore allegiance to him by the Oath of Salisbury. Old Sarum provided an ideal site for a demonstration of Norman power during the early phases of the Conquest, but it proved totally inadequate for a thriving commercial and cathedral town. In the early twelfth century, William of Malmesbury identified some of the problems that eventually led to the town moving to a better site: 'Sarum is more like a castle than a city, being

A geophysical survey showing traces of extensive buildings, including a possible royal palace, in the outer bailey at Old Sarum. (*Historic England*)

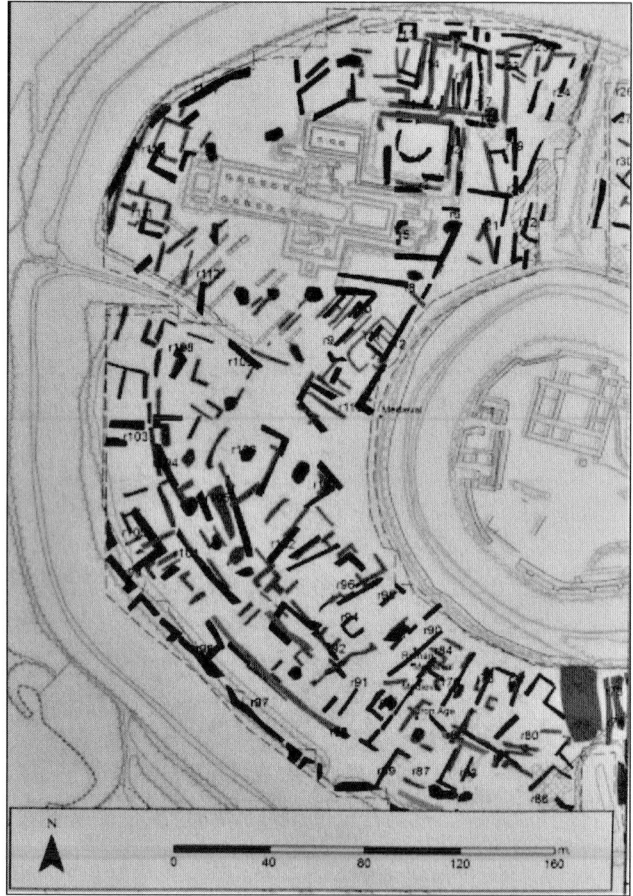

environed with a high wall ... such was the want of water that it sold at a great rate.' While later in the century, the historian Holinshed noted that the clerics attached to the cathedral brawled openly with the garrison troops from the adjacent castle. Henry II imprisoned his queen, Eleanor of Aquitaine, here during the 1180s, and arrangements were in hand to move the cathedral during Richard's reign. Eventually, the cathedral and town were moved to the present site of Salisbury during the 1220s.

New Towns

The steady growth in population throughout western Europe from the tenth century onwards was reflected in the growth in the number and size of towns. At least two hundred new towns were founded in England and Wales in the century and a half after 1066, more than doubling the number of towns, and at a faster rate of new town creation than in any other similar-length period in British history. Kings, bishops, abbots and lords all promoted the development of towns by allowing townsmen to hold their properties for rent, without the work obligations that were customary in the countryside. These towns had distinctive shapes, normally centred on a market area, with the provision of plots for the townsmen or burgesses. Some of the most successful towns became independent boroughs, where the burgesses paid for a royal charter. Many smaller new towns remained 'seigneurial boroughs', whose burgesses were able to claim some control over their affairs, often through a guild. In such cases the lord maintained certain powers through the manor court and claimed a percentage of market income and court fines.

It has been argued that the design of Bury St Edmunds, which is recorded in the process of being planned in the Domesday Book, belonged to a tradition of laying out towns developed in Normandy before the Conquest. In addition to Rouen, which was redesigned in the tenth century, there were pre-Conquest planned towns at places such Beuzeville (Eure), Aunay-sur-Odon (Calvados), and Broglie (Eure). These were characterised by large, open markets, normally triangular or boat-shaped, sometimes attached to a fortification as at Falaise (Calvados) or monastery as at Bec-Hellouin (Eure). Following on from Bury St Edmunds, numerous new settlements were laid out using a similar design. It would therefore appear that the impetus and inspiration for the medieval planned towns of England and Wales can be added to the contributions that the Normans made to the British landscape.[17]

Before 1100 a third of planned towns were royal foundations and some 80 per cent of the boroughs established were created close to castles, one of which, Newcastle, famously took its name from a castle built on the River Tyne. At Windsor, the site of the Saxon palace on the floodplain at Old Windsor was spurned and the castle was built on a chalk promontory which forms the only strongpoint in the Thames Valley between London and Wallingford. New Windsor (the site of the present town) was attached to the castle. At Marlborough (Wiltshire), William the Conqueror created a new borough on a royal estate close to the Forest of Savernake. Marlborough Castle was probably built during the first phase of the Conquest as part of the campaign to subdue the south-west. The castle, whose motte was based on a Neolithic mound, was a popular royal hunting centre and Henry I held an Easter court here in 1110. A broad market was laid out, running from the castle to St Mary's Church, in the 1070s or 1080s and the mint was moved here from nearby Great Bedwyn. The new town was provided with a church, whose small parish encompassed the new urban area, and by 1163 the town had its own merchant guild. The majority of new towns founded after the Anarchy (1135–53) were established without a castle, and where there was an earlier castle the new town plan was often divorced from it, as for example at Kendal, Beaconsfield, Chipping Norton and Penrith.

Marketplaces, which normally formed the foci of new towns, were laid out in square, rectangular, oval or triangular shapes in most cases, with regular-sized burgage plots running off at right angles. Access to the market was normally

Marlborough,
Wiltshire, from
the air, showing
the characteristic
features of a
planned town.
The broad high
street has regular
burgage plots
running off at right
angles. The church
sits in the middle
of the street, which
would have served
as a market.

controlled through narrow 'pinch points', which enabled the ready collection
of tolls. In many places the original plan has been well preserved, for example
at Ripon, where a new town centred on a large rectangular marketplace was
grafted on to the minster church. Here, as elsewhere, it is common to find that
the marketplace was encroached upon, when the stalls that were used just once a
week became permanent structures. Such encroachments characteristically have
no gardens or land attached, and have narrow alleyways separating the buildings.

Towns that were grafted on to an existing village normally left the ancient
parish church isolated from the new market centre, while in those towns which
were located on completely new sites the church would be integrated into the
overall plan. At Market Harborough, on the Leicestershire–Northamptonshire
border, a town planted on a greenfield site, the church sits in the heart of
the marketplace but without a churchyard, as for many centuries it was a
dependent chapelry within the parish of Great Bowden. In the ancient county
of Oxfordshire in 1086, Oxford was the only settlement that was identified as

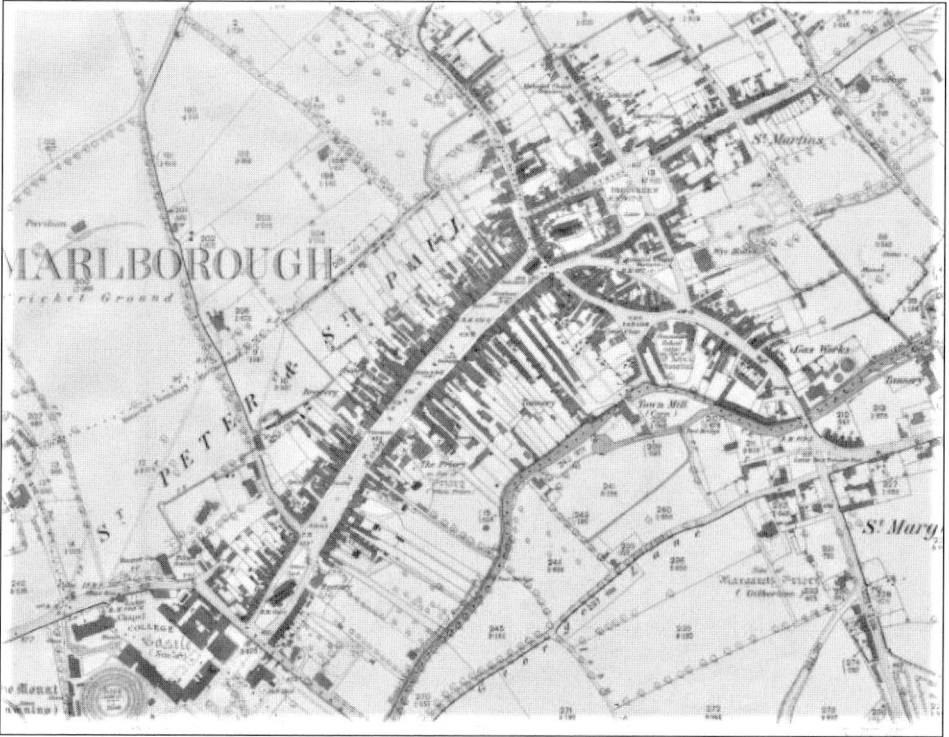

Above: Map extract showing the relationship of the planned town to the castle in the extreme south of the settlement, which was begun in 1067.

Left: Chipping Norton, Oxfordshire, from the air. The castle and church on the left mark the site of the original settlement. The planned town with its distinctive design was laid out quite separately. (*Historic England*)

www.britainfromabove.org.uk/image/EAW049010   © Historic England

Witney, Oxfordshire, a
planned medieval town
laid out by the Bishop of
Winchester. (*Mick Aston*)

urban, although there were other market centres in the county at places such as Bampton and Banbury. By 1200, Oxfordshire could boast a network of market centres, whose planned origins are clearly identifiable in their distinctive design. Eynsham, Deddington, Thame, Burford and Chipping Norton were all laid out around new markets, which lay adjacent to older Saxon villages, while Witney was a completely new settlement. The process of laying out these towns is rarely documented, but the similarity in the design of their core market areas means that they are post-Conquest.

Woodstock, the only Oxfordshire plantation that enjoyed royal patronage, was laid out by Henry II on the edge of an ancient hunting park. The original settlement at (Old) Woodstock lay to the north of the River Glyme in Wootton parish, while Henry's new town was to the south of the Glyme within Bladon parish. Bladon maintained some parochial rights over Woodstock until the mid-nineteenth century. Two of the towns that had the most distinctive plans were episcopalian foundations – Witney by the Bishop of Winchester and Thame

Plan of Witney, highlighting the planned new town with its classic design of a broad market place and burgage tenements. (*VCH Oxford, 14, 2004*).

by the Bishop of Lincoln. The small town of Eynsham was created by Eynsham Abbey, while Burford, Deddington and Chipping Norton were secular seigneurial creations. None of these new towns were initially granted formal borough charters, although some achieved charters at a later date. The manorial system of control was evident in all of them and was an important impetus for their development. The bishops, abbots and lords behind these ventures kept control of the markets in order to farm the tolls and collect the court fines. In the course of time, various municipal structures evolved at the expense of the power of the lord, but in the first instance all the new towns were owned by their creators.

Some Norman magnates established new ports, both coastal and inland. St Ives in Cambridgeshire was founded on the River Ouse by the abbots of Ramsey in the late eleventh century. An Easter fair was granted in 1110 and an elongated market street was laid out parallel to the river, and the road to the existing village of Slepe was diverted over a new causeway and bridge across the river. The new port prospered through its Continental trading links.

Another inland port on the east coast was established at Hedon (East Yorkshire) by Count Stephen of Aumale, *c*.1130. The town sits on a minor tributary of the River Humber and was probably designed to transport produce from Stephen's estates in Holderness to his lands in northern Normandy. It gained a mint soon after and in its charter of 1158 the burgesses were granted privileges equal to those enjoyed by the citizens of York and Lincoln. Further north, a new port at Alnmouth was established for the castle, abbey and borough at Alnwick (Northumberland). In 1152, William de Vesci was granted 120ha, taken from the common land of Lesbury, for a settlement at Alnmouth, close to the estuary of the little River Aln, and by 1207/8 the de Vescis had royal sanction for a port and Wednesday fish market.[18] (See Plate 10)

At Bawtry (Yorkshire), the Great North Road was diverted to run through the middle of a new medieval river port. The old parish church stands on the bank of the River Idle, hidden from the large rectangular marketplace and regular street pattern founded around 1200 by Robert de Vipont. In the south, because of its close proximity to Normandy, a number of new coastal ports were created, such as Newtown and Yarmouth on the Isle of Wight.

The most successful new towns were those established by 1250, but even among this cadre there were a number of failures. These were mainly towns that were badly sited or lost their original, often strategic, function. For example, an attempt by the Knights Templar to establish a commercial centre adjacent to their preceptory at Temple Bruer, on a heathy plateau to the south of Lincoln, was unsuccessful. Aerial photographs suggest an attempt was made to lay out planned tenements around a marketplace in the second half of the twelfth century. At Baschurch (Shropshire), Shrewsbury Abbey attempted to create a new town about 1200, close to the existing village. The settlement was laid out in a simple T shape, and decayed burgage plots can be traced on the ground in an area known as Newtown. A mile to the west, the Fitzalans (later, earls of Arundel) founded another town at New Ruyton (later, Ruyton-Eleven-Towns) at about the same time. The competition between them stunted both, although Ruyton eventually received a borough charter (1308).[19] There are at least a dozen failed castle boroughs in Wales and the Welsh Marches, towns that lost their original strategic function and that were eventually abandoned or severely shrunken. At Caus, Westbury (Shropshire), Roger fitz Corbet built a large motte and bailey castle on the Welsh border, at the eastern end of the Long Mountain,

St Ives, Cambridgeshire. The town was created by the abbot of Ramsey Abbey *c*.1110 and became the centre for a major international Easter fair on the edge of the Fens. (*John Fielding*)

where it overlooked the strategic route from Shrewsbury to Montgomery. The castle was built within the south-eastern sector of an Iron Age hill fort and at some stage in the twelfth century a borough was planted alongside the castle by the Corbets. The borough failed during the later Middle Ages and the castle was demolished after the Civil War.

In his pioneer work *New Towns of the Middle Ages* (1967), Maurice Beresford identified 172 medieval new towns in England with a further 84 in Wales.[20] Almost as soon as Beresford's work was published, it was clear that he had underestimated the number of market centres that had originated or were extended in this way. The features he had pointed out as typical of planned medieval urban settlements — market 'square', burgage plots, back lanes, controlled points of access and egress — were to be found throughout England and Wales, and indeed most pre-Industrial Revolution market towns were started or were significantly modified at this time. The very universality of these features has led to their being discounted in many instances. Furthermore, there are many smaller settlements, thought of as villages, which display similar characteristics, some of which represent failed attempts at urbanization. The process of new town creation extended well after any direct Norman involvement can be claimed. However, it was during the Norman era that town creation received an impetus that persisted into the fourteenth century and that has left an imprint on hundreds of English and Welsh settlements.

Above: The earthworks of the abandoned castle-borough of Caus, Shropshire. Hidden in the wood is a massive motte and bailey castle built by the Corbets, who were important Marcher lords. (*Shropshire County Council*)

Right: Earthwork plan of Caus castle and borough. (*Fradley and Carey, 2016*)

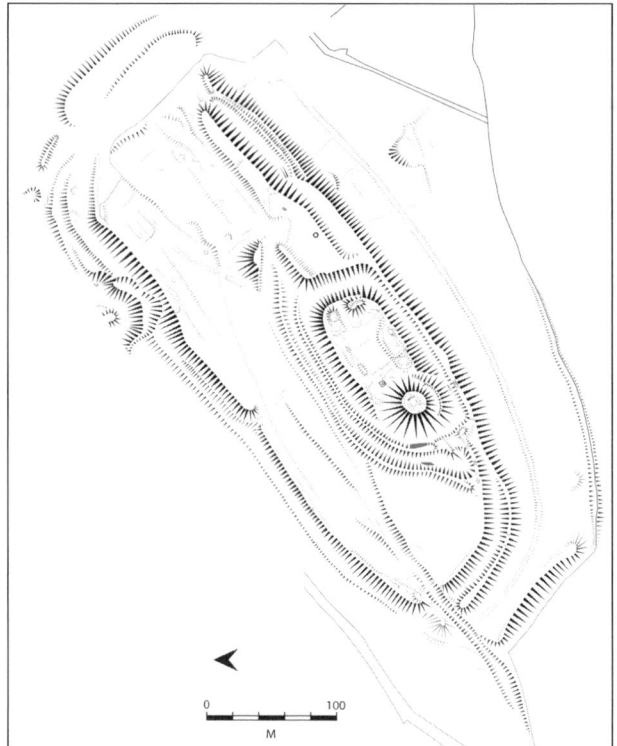

Chapter 7

The Impact of the Conquest on the Church

It is surely one of the stranger among historical paradoxes that a settlement of parasitical, heathen pirates in the first half of the tenth century should have produced, in the second half of the eleventh, a remarkably centralized political community and a notably successful Church.[1]

Although the Church had played an important role in late Saxon society, between 1066 and 1200 the English ecclesiastical landscape was transformed. In the eleventh century, building a church could be as powerful a statement of might as building a castle. Secular and ecclesiastical realms were twin hemispheres and God was the judge of righteous war. The Conquest heralded a dramatic expansion in virtually every aspect of Church activity; in particular, the physical presence of religion became far more prominent through an unprecedented increase in the number and size of church buildings. The Norman era saw 'one of the most astonishing building explosions in recorded history';[2] not only were churches rebuilt in the new Romanesque style, but after 1070, they were built on an unprecedented scale. English monasteries were reformed along Norman lines and eventually hundreds of new abbeys and priories were founded. Cathedrals were constructed close to castles at places such as Norwich, Lincoln and Durham, establishing powerful colonial complexes. 'Anyone surveying the English landscape even within twenty years of the Conquest would have noticed a difference, as great new churches were under construction at Lincoln (1072), St Albans (1077), Winchester (1079), Ely (1081) and Worcester (1084).'[3] These buildings were constructed on a scale unknown since the Roman occupation.

After the Conquest the Church in England became an important arm of government, patronage and control. The Norman kings and their barons developed a strong sense of proprietorship; for example, John of Worcester recorded that William the Conqueror had deposed a number of English abbots at the Council of Winchester in 1070, in order 'to confirm his power in a kingdom which he had but newly acquired'. William Rufus expressed the Crown's attitude to the Church in extreme terms when asked by Archbishop Anselm to make appointments to vacant abbeys. According to the chronicler Eadmer, the king replied, 'What concern is that of yours? Aren't the abbeys mine? … can't I do what I like with my abbeys?'[4]

Nevertheless, Norman leaders, whose ancestors only a hundred and fifty years earlier had been pagans, had become enthusiastic patrons of the Church by

1066. They had initially been destroyers of Church buildings and stolen Church land and treasures, but during the eleventh century a thriving Norman Church developed. By the time of the Conquest, several cathedrals in Normandy were in the process of being rebuilt and the number of monastic institutions had increased from just five in 1000 to over thirty by 1066. The Norman Church had gained a European-wide reputation for learning and spiritual excellence, attracting scholars and clerics from many countries. The new foundations centred on Le Bec-Hellouin became wealthy and prestigious institutions, exploiting their direct links with the great monasteries of Germany, Burgundy, northern Italy and Rome. Duke William, with the aid of capable clerical lieutenants such as Lanfranc (d.1089), strengthened the Church and forged it as a major tool of government.

Even before the Conquest, the Crown's links to Normandy meant that several Norman abbeys had acquired estates in southern England. For instance, c.1017, Cnut granted the manors of Brede and 'Rameslie' with its ports at Rye (and probably Hastings) to the monks of Fécamp. Fécamp's southern English estates were enlarged under Edward the Confessor in the form of gifts given in gratitude to his Norman protectors during his exile. Edward added the royal minster church at Steyning and its port on the River Adur, plus the church at Eastbourne; Lamport, a tithing of Eastbourne hundred; and a saltern called Horse Eye together with twelve houses at *Caestra* (Pevensey). Steyning had passed into Earl Harold's hands by 1053, but Fécamp had provided ships for William's invasion fleet and Steyning was restored to the abbey after 1066. Both before and after the Conquest, the abbots of Fécamp took a close interest in their southern English estates, partly as the result of a series of disputes, one of which, involving hunting rights in Steyning, prompted Abbot William (1080–1107) to come to England in 1103. Elaborate carving on some of the capitals, similar to that found at Fécamp, dates from about this time.

Edward's other gifts to Norman monasteries were also largely located on or near the coast. For instance, Saint-Ouen in Rouen was given East Mersea on the Essex coast.[5] Edward had bequeathed estates to abbeys outside Normandy, including the ancient minster at Deerhurst (Gloucestershire), which was granted to Saint-Denis, the traditional burial site for French kings.

The Norman Church and the support of Rome provided William with a potent weapon in his conquest of England, not only giving him moral and fiscal support but also after the Battle of Hastings helping him achieve English clerical compliance. Duke William received political and strategic support for the invasion of England from a number of European rulers, including the Holy Roman Emperor; critically, he also acquired the papal seal of approval. William's cause was pleaded in Rome by the Archdeacon of Lisieux, on the grounds of Harold's alleged perjury, and a conclave was held where Harold was declared a usurper and William the lawful successor to Edward the Confessor. Pope Alexander II (1061–73), who, it was for long believed, had been educated at the Abbey of Our

St Andrew and St Cuthman, Steyning, Sussex. The north aisle (*c*.1165) and part of the chancel arch, which is the oldest part of a once cruciform church, were begun *c*.1080. Steyning was the centre of Fécamp Abbey's estates in England and the church would have been built under the auspices of the abbot.

Lady of Bec in Normandy, bestowed his blessing on the expedition, sending William a consecrated banner as a sign of St Peter's approval. In return, William committed to reform the 'irregularities' of the Anglo-Saxon Church and return it to the Roman path; after his victory the new king repaid the pope with the defeated Harold's banner. Papal support for the Conquest enabled William to turn the invasion expedition into a crusade. The concept of a holy war was not a new departure in Norman history and had already been used as a pretext for territorial expansion in Spain and southern Italy as well as the Levant, albeit Norman forces from time to time were pitted against those of the papacy.

After 1066 the English Church came under the new management of French clerics, who introduced major organizational changes. Norman ecclesiastical nominees, supporters of the Crown, dominated the English Church during the last decades of the eleventh century and well beyond. Just as the Norman kings ensured that their political and military system was operated by loyal supporters after the Conquest, King William and his magnates used the Church in England as an instrument of government. By the end of the Conqueror's reign, the episcopate had been almost totally Normanized, as had the leadership of most English monasteries.

Selby Abbey, North Yorkshire, was founded in 1069 by Benedict of Auxerre and is one of the earliest post-Conquest abbeys in the north of England. Significant sections of the original Norman church survive today.

Only a handful of new monasteries were established in the years immediately after 1066, but abbeys such as those at Selby (1069), Battle (*c*.1070), Lewes (*c*.1078) and Shrewsbury (*c*.1085) were all built on a scale to impress.

By 1100 at least fifteen monastic cathedrals and major abbey churches had been built or were under construction, either on the sites of previous churches or grafted on to existing towns. Not only were the Saxon buildings removed, but there was a cultural revolution – the Church was Normanized. Worcester, Exeter, Peterborough and a few other monasteries remained centres of Anglo-Saxon learning well into the twelfth century, but even these eventually succumbed to Latin and French conventions.

Norman conquest and colonization affected the Church in Wales perhaps even more profoundly than its impact on the Church in England. The Normans completely reorganized the old quasi-monastic and tribal institutions into a Church with territorial dioceses, archdeaconries, rural deaneries and parishes, firmly under the metropolitan jurisdiction of Canterbury and subservience to Rome. Progressively, the colonization of the Church spread across the country, although there were far fewer French bishops and archdeacons than in England.

Norman exploitation showed itself more clearly in the seizure of the property of the Welsh Church. Some of this was restored to the new or renewed foundations; some went to the priories that the Normans often founded beside their castles and

St David's Cathedral, Pembrokeshire, with the Bishop's Palace in the background. The core of the church is late Norman in design. (*British Pilgrimage Trust*)

that were usually dependent upon their 'family' monasteries in France or upon the Normanized monasteries in England; and some was lost to the Church for ever. Changes to the Welsh diocesan structure took longer to emerge and were the result of a fusion of native and Anglo-Norman ecclesiastical practice. By the early 1140s, four territorial bishoprics had been created or recreated: St David's and Llandaff in south Wales, and Bangor and St Asaph in north Wales. The ancient *clas* churches were mostly reduced to parochial status and lost the greater part of their endowments; dedications were often changed from Celtic to the conventional saints of western Christendom. It is true that the Welsh clergy were not transformed overnight and were not generally replaced by 'Frenchmen'. Many ancient usages (the quasi-hereditary succession to some ecclesiastical offices, for example) persisted for some time; but the new order, besides profoundly changing the Church in Wales and giving the opportunity of territorial and spiritual gain to Norman barons, provided the Norman and, later, Angevin kings of England with a powerful weapon of political control in Wales.

Norman Attitudes to the Anglo-Saxon Church

William the Conqueror claimed that the degeneracy of the English Church was one of the justifications for launching his invasion. William of Malmesbury attributed the revival of the rule of religion in England, 'which had there grown lifeless', to the Normans; while Knowles observed that before the Conquest: 'The [Saxon] Church in England was reduced to little more than a performance, by an ill-educated, ill-found clergy, of the essential liturgical and sacramental services in the village churches and halls of the landowners.'[6] Other historians have strongly disputed this and point to the wealth of learning and cultural achievements of the late Saxon Church. Monastic reform by St Dunstan (*c*.909–88) and others in the second half of the tenth century had resulted in a revival of literary, musical and artistic achievements within the English Church. Contacts with France had been an important element in this revival and in order to ensure 'correct practices', English Church leaders had turned to French houses for assistance. Monks from Abingdon had been sent to Fleury Abbey on the Loire, where the relics of St Benedict were held, in order to learn the implementation of monastic rule and the proper singing of chant. Books were sent from Fleury to Winchester and one abbot of Fleury spent two years instructing the monks of the newly founded abbey of Ramsey (986–8). After the millennium, the reform movement in England had stalled, just at the time that the Church in Normandy was being energetically rejuvenated. The contrast between the two establishments, both physically and spiritually, must have seemed stark to the incomers.[7]

Initially, the Conquest was accompanied by the deliberate plundering of England's cultural heritage, which was primarily located in churches. The loss of art was on a scale unparalleled since the early Viking era. Although the Normans tried to legitimize their looting behind a Christian facade, like the Vikings ultimately they relied on the sword. The Waltham Chronicler complained bitterly that the pillage was like amputating the limbs of God's Son in one country in order to offer them to the same God in another.[8]

The Peterborough version of the *Anglo-Saxon Chronicle* recorded that the monks of Peterborough Abbey came to meet the Normans to request peace:

> But they [the Normans] did not care about anything, went into the minster, climbed up to the holy rood, took the crown off our Lord's head … all of pure gold … then took the rest which was underneath his feet … that was all of red gold … climbed up to the steeple, brought down the altar-frontal that was hidden there … it was all of gold and of silver. They took there two golden shrines, and nine silver, and they took fifteen great roods, both of gold and of silver. They took there so much gold and silver and so many treasures in money and in clothing and in books that no man can tell another.

William of Poitiers was overwhelmed by the wealth to be found in English churches and monasteries:

> Treasures remarkable for their number and kind and workmanship had been amassed there, either to be kept for the empty enjoyment of avarice, or to

be squandered shamefully in English luxury. Of these he [William] liberally gave a part to those who had helped him win the battle, and distributed most, and the most valuable, to the needy and to the monasteries of various provinces.

Poitiers was at pains to explain that the king only gave from his own property and compensation was given when objects were removed from English churches. The *Anglo-Saxon Chronicle* for 1070 tells a rather different story and records that once the countryside had been subjugated, 'in the following spring the king allowed all the minsters which were in England to be raided'.

Poitiers also boasts of the amount of art that went overseas. Much of the ecclesiastical art looted from English churches went to enrich those of Rome and France, especially William's duchy of Normandy. While in Normandy, William is said to have lavished his church of Saint-Étienne, Caen, with gifts including embroideries and other richly worked objects from England:

In a thousand churches of France, Aquitaine, and Burgundy, and also Auvergne and other regions, the memory of King William will be celebrated forever … Some churches received very large golden crosses, wonderfully jewelled; many others pounds of gold, or vessels made of the same metal; quite a few vestments or something else of value.

Poitiers talks of crucifixes, chalices, censers, ewers, copes, chasubles and treasures, which would take too long to enumerate, let alone describe. When William returned to Normandy in the spring of 1067 with his English hostages, a collection of looted treasures was conspicuously displayed during his 'imperial' triumphal progress around the duchy. These included garments heavily embroidered with gold, and gold and silver vessels. Additionally, Poitiers recounted that William paraded the youth of the defeated country, 'with its long hair and comely features'.

The plunder did not stop with the Conqueror; in 1096, William's son William Rufus had art treasures melted down in order to raise the money to pay for the mortgage of Normandy from his brother Robert, in order that the duke could take a Norman contingent on the First Crusade. William of Malmesbury claimed that the levy 'completely beggared the whole kingdom sparing no ecclesiastical ornaments, no sacred altar vessels, nor reliquaries, no gospel books bound in gold and silver'. In order to meet its contribution, Malmesbury Abbey was obliged to strip down eight shrines, eight crucifixes and twelve bindings of gold and silver.[9]

There is some limited evidence to indicate that the Normans deliberately destroyed Anglo-Saxon stone crosses and burial slabs. On the other hand, there is also evidence to show that they consciously incorporated these items into new churches, perhaps in order to indicate a form of local continuity.[10] In the longer term there were enormous losses associated with the destruction and rebuilding

Malmesbury Abbey, Wiltshire, was one of the Saxon foundations that lost many of its treasures immediately after the Conquest. (*hobbiesphotographic*)

of every cathedral and abbey in the new Romanesque style. Historically, such architectural replacement schemes are not unusual, but this one was carried out with the ruthless efficiency which only a colonial conqueror could harness.

Although many Norman clerics distrusted aspects of the English Church, they respected its wealth and required its support. They disliked its archaic Roman liturgy, its buildings, constructed in what they regarded as an outmoded style, and its incomprehensible learning. Initially, the Normans viewed some Anglo-Saxon saints with suspicion, particularly those with only a local following. David Knowles argued that the Norman abbots and bishops did not respect the old English saints; a view that was widely held until Susan Reynolds countered by claiming that the new Norman churchmen celebrated their inherited tradition and saints, using them to establish their authority, to integrate themselves and to guard their communities' land and possessions.[11]

Pre-Conquest churches that became Augustinian priories after 1066 were able to retain their Saxon saint dedications; for example, Cuthbert at Durham, Aetheldreda at Ely and Frideswide at Oxford. In some cases, after the Conquest the Saxon saint was coupled with St Peter or the Virgin Mary, as at Evesham Abbey, which was dedicated to St Mary and St Egwin. There are, however, some well-rehearsed examples of Norman disdain for the communion of Saxon saints. At Canterbury, for example, Archbishop Lanfranc removed many local saints from the cathedral calendar and dislodged their relics from the building. Lanfranc seems to have demoted the Saxon saints Dunstan, Aelfheah and Wilfred, whose shrines at Canterbury were hidden from prominence. He observed:

> These Englishmen among whom we are living have set up for themselves certain saints whom they revere. But sometimes when I turn over in my mind their own accounts of whom they were, I cannot help having doubts about the quality of their sanctity.[12]

With less circumspection, Lanfranc's kinsman Abbot Paul broke up the tombs of the former abbots of St Albans, whom he referred to as 'uncultured idiots'. The new abbot of Abingdon tried to completely obliterate the memory of St Aethelwold, whom he called 'an English rustic'. While at Evesham, Abbot Walter (1077–1104) put the saints' relics to the test by fire – only those that survived were deemed to be genuine. The abbot had previously witnessed a similar episode as a monk at Cerisy-la-Forêt in Normandy, where a relic of St Vigor, a sixth-century bishop of Bayeux, had been tested by fire.[13] One English saint bucked the trend, St Cuthman of Steyning, whose relics were moved to the mother house at Fécamp in the early twelfth century. Eventually, many of the English saints were rehabilitated, but by the mid-twelfth century there was clearly a desire for saints with whom the Anglo–Norman population as a whole could associate. The martyrdom of Thomas Becket in 1170 met that need admirably.

A number of the incoming bishops and abbots, such as Turold of Fécamp, the first Norman abbot of Peterborough, regarded their new institutions as sources of wealth for themselves and their followers. Turold, who was imprisoned briefly during Hereward's uprising, seized half of the abbey's possessions for himself and his associates, which had been valued at £1,050 on his arrival in 1070 and scarcely £500 on his departure in 1098.

Church Dedications

The Normans were not hostile to the point of multiple destruction of cults; for instance, in Winchester there was discrimination between different pre-Conquest saints. Aethelwold's cult had enjoyed the same status as that of St Swithun before 1066, but under the first Norman bishop of Winchester, Walkelin (1070–98), the cult of Swithun was encouraged, while that of Aethelwold was suppressed. In April 1093, when the monks were removed from the Old Minster into the partially built, new cathedral, the high altar was dedicated to St Swithun, with no reference to Aethelwold. The following year, the relics of St Swithun and some other Saxon saints were moved to the new cathedral; Aethelwold was again ignored. The motive for this discriminatory treatment was political as Aethelwold had been a reforming bishop of Winchester (963–84) who was greatly admired by the monastic community, to whom he was known as 'the father of the monks'.

He had been responsible for strengthening the monastic community at Winchester and they prayed to him for assistance against Walkelin, who was trying to disband them. In the event he failed to do so, but the Norman bishop's relegation of Aethelwold was probably the reason that he was never formally canonized.

At Ely, Aethelthryth, a popular Saxon saint, received rather more sympathetic treatment by the Normans. She was a seventh-century East Anglian princess and foundress and abbess of Ely. During the Fenland uprising she was called upon by the English rebels for help, and it was believed that she played a role in the early success in defending the abbey against the Normans. Subsequently, she does not seem to have suffered as a result of her association with the rebellion and, when the new Norman abbey at Ely was consecrated in 1107, her relics were duly translated from the Saxon abbey. Her shrine remained an important centre of pilgrimage throughout the Middle Ages, although the Normans revenged themselves on the institution as a whole by confiscating three-quarters of the abbey's estates.[14]

Any hostility to the English saints did not survive the first generation of Norman clerics. The writings of contemporary chroniclers did much to re-establish the reputations of the most famous saints and the Church increasingly appreciated the financial importance of their relics in attracting pilgrims. Furthermore, the

St Aethelwold, Bishop of Winchester (963–984). A saint who was particularly popular with the English after the Norman Conquest. (*Abingdon Town Council*)

new Church aristocracy needed to win the trust of the English and adopting their traditional saints was a relatively painless way of doing so. There was even a modest reverse movement, with English saints being revered in France. For example, St Edmund became very popular in Normandy after the Conquest, gaining a reputation for protecting those at danger at sea. Edmund was commemorated at Le Bec, Jumièges and Saint-Evroult, and the monastery at Bury was rewarded with property in France.[15]

Some pre-Conquest Celtic and English dedications were replaced in the two centuries following the Conquest by saints who were popular in Normandy, such as St Michael and St Stephen. There was also a tendency to apply dedications that were internationally popular, such as the Virgin Mary or the Holy Trinity. At Nevern, Pembrokeshire, the church was rededicated to St Mary, while the annual fair retained its allegiance to the original Celtic saint. There was no attempt to systematically introduce popular Norman saints into England, although occasional examples can be found; there are, for example, dedications to St Vigor at Fulbourn, Cambridgeshire, and Stratton-on-the-Fosse, Somerset. On the other hand, there were very few new dedications to Anglo-Saxon saints after the Conquest; the dedication of Hereford Cathedral to the eighth-century Saxon king Aethelbert in the early twelfth century being an exception. In the long run, established Saxon saints such as Cuthbert, Birinus, Guthlac and Swithun continued to be honoured along with the more recent reformers Dunstan and Aelphege.

The New Norman Church

After 1066, links between England and the French Church were immediately strengthened; the Conqueror paid his debt to Valéry, the Picard saint, for the favourable breeze that blew him to England before the Battle of Hastings by granting the manor of Takeley in Essex to the Saint-Valéry priory.[16] The following year, Hayling Island was granted to the monks of Jumièges to celebrate the consecration of their church and in 1069 the abbot of Sainte-Trinité-du-Mont, Rouen, came to Winchester to petition William fitz Osbern. It was on this occasion that reputedly the king 'playfully' pretended to stab the abbot's hand with a knife as he gave him the manor of Harmondsworth (Middlesex). This apparently was a well-established Carolingian tradition to demonstrate how firmly the grant would stick![17]

The conquest of England must have seemed to offer an almost providential source of monastic endowment to the many Norman foundations that had been created in the decades leading up to 1066. Altogether, nearly thirty Norman monasteries received gifts of manors, estates, churches and tithes in England during the decade subsequent to the Conquest. By the time of King William's death in 1087, the ducal abbeys of Caen, Jumièges, Saint-Wandrille, Fécamp,

Mont-Saint-Michel, an ancient monastery on the border between Normandy and Brittany, which later benefitted from the theft of treasures from English churches after the Conquest. (*Bretagne*)

Bernay, Montvilliers and Mont-Saint-Michel had all acquired English parishes. Initially, the new Norman barons also preferred to make an offering of their newly found wealth, both in lands and in churches, to monasteries with which they had some connection in France, rather than establish new houses in England.

Political considerations were a major element in the Norman treatment of the Church. William required bishops whom he could trust and who could serve as vice-regents in his newly won kingdom. Partly prompted by involvement of English clerics in the northern risings, he instigated a radical restaffing of the English Church and set about the systematic replacement of the upper sections of the Anglo-Saxon Church hierarchy. It was not until 1069 that Archbishop Stigand, whom the Normans regarded as a usurper, was removed as Archbishop of Canterbury and replaced by William's friend and confidant Lanfranc. Over the next decade, all but one of the Saxon bishops were replaced by Norman, French or Flemish men. So complete was the eventual foreign 'takeover' that William of Malmesbury, *c*.1125, claimed that: 'England has become a residence for foreigners and the property of aliens. At the present time there is no English earl, nor bishop nor abbot; strangers all, they prey upon the riches and vitals of England.'

Lanfranc, unlike several of his contemporaries in Normandy, apart from being a resourceful politician was also a dedicated churchman and enthusiastic ecclesiastical reformer. The archbishop introduced a set of reforms at Canterbury designed to spread and improve monastic life; in particular, he brought the English liturgy into line with Continental practice. He brought with him to England a group of pupils and associates from Bec and Caen, most of whom were destined for promotion. These included his nephew, Paul, who became abbot of St Albans and started work on the abbey church in 1077, Gundulf, who became bishop of Rochester (1077) and surveyor of the king's works at the Tower of London, and Gilbert Crispin, who became abbot of Westminster (*c*.1085). Within ten years of the Conquest, all the English sees with the exception of Worcester, which was still held by the Saxon Wulfstan, were under the stewardship of foreigners.

King William and Archbishop Lanfranc believed in a sharp hierarchical Church structure and insisted that Canterbury had primacy not only over England but over the whole British Isles – a view enforced by Church councils held at Winchester and Windsor in 1072. A council at London, held in 1075, decreed that each rural see should be moved to a major town in its diocese. This was not only to concentrate secular and ecclesiastical power in the same centre, but because all these towns had Roman origins, there was also a symbolic value of returning Christianity to its roots. This manoeuvre had many implications, particularly as the ancient centres were associated with the relics of revered Saxon saints. William of Malmesbury attributed the English custom of siting their cathedrals in the country to the influence of Irish missionaries who 'preferred to bury themselves ingloriously in marshes than to dwell in lofty cities', but in reality, their locations reflected the geography of former Anglo-Saxon kingdoms. The see at Dorchester-on-Thames was transferred to Lincoln; Sherborne to Old Sarum; Selsey to Chichester; Elmham to Norwich by way of Thetford and the silted-up port of Dunwich; Wells to Bath; and Lichfield to Chester. Although there were subsequent readjustments – Henry I created a new diocese in each province, Ely in Canterbury and Carlisle in York – these changes established the diocesan framework in England, which survived until the Reformation. Only ten Saxon cathedrals out of seventeen retained their rank. The centres of the new Norman dioceses were in cities, and eight of them were located in wealthy Saxon monasteries that had been founded during the tenth-century monastic revival. One immediate result of this reorganization was that the now well-endowed cathedrals could build on the same scale as the great Benedictine monasteries.

The bishops were able to compete with the great monastic churches in their architectural ambitions for their cathedrals, as the estates of the churches were divided – one part for the support of the bishop, the other being allocated to the monastic chapter.

Whereas Roman administrative centres served in Normandy up until the French Revolution, in England and Wales it was the Normans who created the basic ecclesiastical administrative infrastructure. Lanfranc introduced regular national synods to England and he replaced Anglo-Saxon monastic rule – the *Regularis Concordia* – in many churches with his own *Monastic Constitutions*. Bishops were ordered to appoint qualified ecclesiastical officials; the dioceses were divided into archdeaconries and eventually these were subdivided into rural deaneries, thus establishing the pattern of ecclesiastical territories until the Reformation and beyond. William also strengthened the Church's legal power and separated ecclesiastical from lay jurisdiction, thereby creating problems for future monarchs.[18]

In one other respect the Conquest saw a major change in the relationship between the Church and the Crown. After the Conquest, King William imposed knight quotas on twenty-four of the largest English monasteries. The concept of the warrior bishop is personified on the Bayeux Tapestry, where Odo of Bayeux is shown on a horse, wielding a baton, in the midst of the Norman army during the Battle of Hastings. It seems unlikely that Norman prelates actually fought in England, as they were forbidden to spill blood personally, but Odo, Wulfstan of Worcester and Geoffrey of Coutances all led forces to suppress English rebellions. William of Poitiers confirms that bishops were non-combatants when observing that Bishop Odo 'struck fear into the hearts of warriors, for he helped in war with valuable counsel when necessity required, in so far as he could while keeping his religion intact'.

In 1095, Archbishop Anselm of Canterbury records that the king placed him in charge of knights and foot soldiers to guard Canterbury and the coast. However, it was not the individual bishops and abbots that were required to fight; it was the ability of their institutions to raise knights for the king. In 1072, William issued a writ to Aethelwig, abbot of Evesham, to bring 'those five knights you owe me from your abbey' to 'Clarendon a week after Whitsun'.[19] Peterborough was required to supply sixty knights, Glastonbury and Bury St Edmunds forty each, Abingdon thirty and Coventry just ten. Each establishment had its own solution to meet this obligation, normally by allotting parts of their estates to knights as military tenants. In the late eleventh century, the Bishop of Bath granted two hides of land to Hubert Hose 'on condition that he provide military service, with arms and horse'.[20] Castle mounds are sometimes an indication of these estates; for instance, Tout Hill in the garden of the dean at Peterborough.

In addition to replacing English bishops with French prelates, all of the English cathedrals were rebuilt in the Romanesque style of architecture that accompanied the Normans from the Continent. This great rebuilding, which began a few years after 1066 and continued beyond the twelfth century, was characterized by

Bishop Odo of Bayeux featured as a warrior on the Bayeux Tapestry. Although it is unlikely he actually fought at the Battle of Hastings, he was involved in quelling English uprisings in the 1070s.

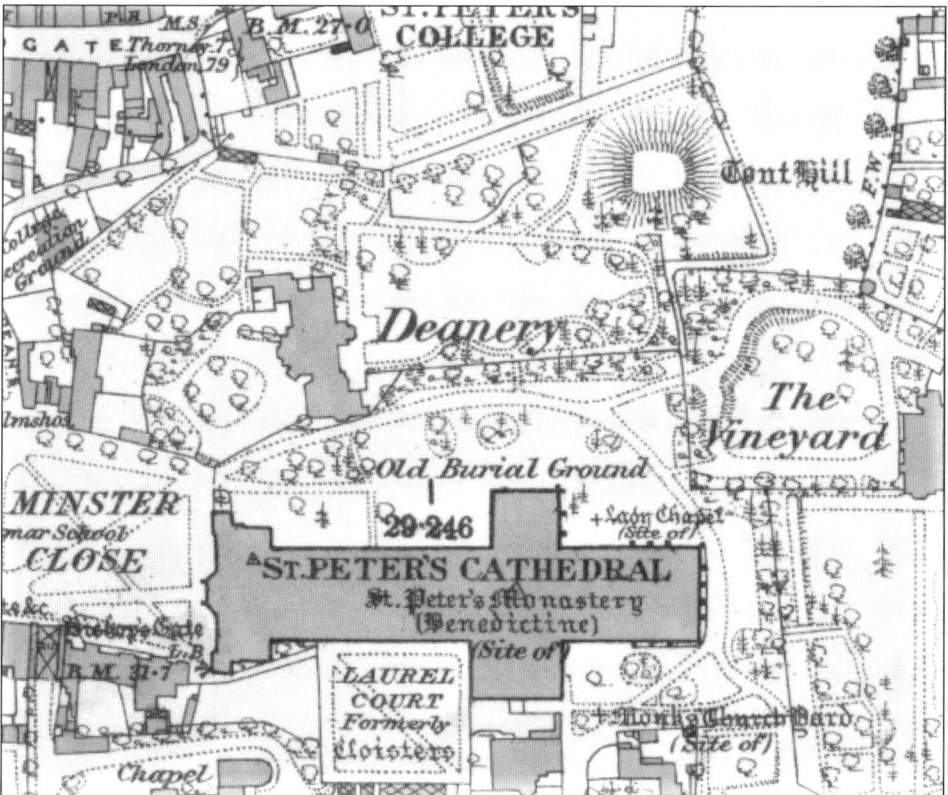

Peterborough Cathedral. The site of Tout Hill castle mound, which lies to the north of the church in the Dean's Garden, is believed to have been built by Abbot Thorold in the eleventh century. It may have performed a role in the provision of the sixty knights the abbot was obliged to find for the king.

abbeys and cathedrals of immense size, much larger than anything that had been seen before in England. The premier Saxon cathedral abbey at Canterbury was damaged and partly destroyed by fire in 1067. Archbishop Lanfranc built a new one on the site of the old between 1071 and 1077, leading William of Malmesbury to remark: 'You do not know which to admire more, the beauty or the speed.' The design was based upon that of Saint-Étienne, Caen: both had elaborate western facades, and a spacious nave to match the intended function of the church – to accommodate crowds on the great festivals as well as to demonstrate the prestige of the community.

Work on the cathedral at Lincoln was begun by Bishop Remigius of Fécamp in 1072–3 and it was consecrated in 1092. Lincoln was unlike any other English cathedral, with its 'fortified' west end, and described by Henry of Huntingdon as 'invincible to all enemies'. Bishop Hermann started the cathedral at Old Sarum, which also had martial overtones, between 1075 and 1078. The original Salisbury Cathedral was built within the fortifications of an Iron Age hill fort and lay in the shadow of a massive royal (later bishop's) castle. Rochester Cathedral was started by Bishop Gundulf shortly after his consecration in 1077 and completed within a few years. Durham, often seen as the archetypal Norman cathedral monastery, was not started until 1093.

Above left: The west façade of Saint-Étienne, Caen. The two western towers became a standard feature of Anglo-Norman churches.

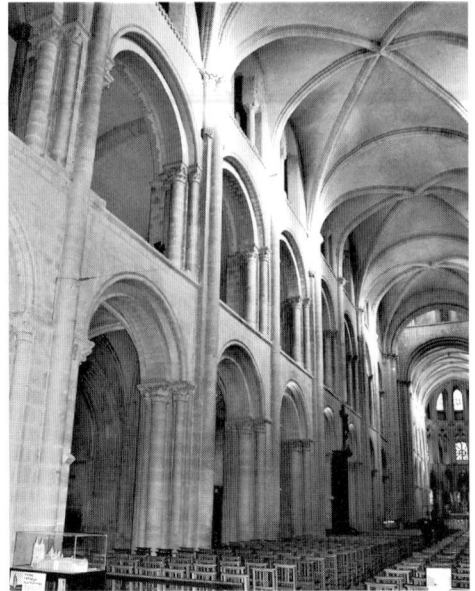

Above right: The interior of Saint-Étienne. The church was founded by William the Conqueror in 1063 for his burial, and its design was influential at Canterbury Cathedral.

The crossing and apse at Canterbury Cathedral, whose design appears to have been influenced by King William's abbey church at Saint-Étienne, Caen.

Durham Cathedral

Durham Cathedral (see Plate 11) is one of the most dramatic church sites in Britain, perched on a promontory, overlooking a hairpin bend in the River Wear. In 995 the site was chosen for a strongly fortified refuge to house the relics of St Cuthbert, but after the Conquest it became a symbol of Norman dominance. In 1083, William of Calais, the first Prince-Bishop of Durham, founded the Benedictine priory of St Cuthbert to replace the Saxon cathedral. He ejected the secular canons, and their families, who had been in charge of the shrine of St Cuthbert, replacing them with monks from Jarrow and Monkwearmouth monasteries. In 1093, William ordered the construction of a new cathedral monastery 'on a nobler and grander scale' than its predecessor. The building of the new cathedral was witnessed by Symeon of Durham, who recorded his observations in *The Little Book on the Origins and Progress of this Church, That Is of Durham*. The digging of the foundations began after prayers on 29 June 1093, and the foundation stone was laid on 11 August the same year; it was completed in 1133. Symeon mentions that while the monastic buildings were paid for by money raised by the monks, the cathedral was financed by the bishop and chapter (senior clergy). The details of the financing are not recorded, but it was normal for money to be raised from pilgrims and the congregations within the diocese. The Prince-Bishop of Durham was a member of the inner circle of the royal

Durham Cathedral was begun in 1093 and was a bold statement of Norman power in northern England. (*UGC TNE*)

household and it has been plausibly argued that he was the mastermind behind the Domesday Book. He would have been a wealthy man in his own right and his own contribution towards the new cathedral must have been significant.[21]

Worcester Cathedral

At Worcester, the English prelate, Bishop Wulfstan, had been appointed in 1062, but it was not until 1084 that he began work on a new cathedral church when the old building proved inadequate for the enlarged community. A charter issued by the bishop in 1089 explains:

> I Wulfstan, by the grace of God, pontiff of the church of Worcester, desiring to enlarge the monastery of the holy Mother of God, Mary, built in the episcopal see by my predecessor of pious memory, that is by blessed Oswald – to enlarge it with greater honour and dignity, not only in the building and adorning of the church, but indeed also of the monks serving God there, I have sought to enrich it by an augmentation of property ... For since few more than twelve brethren were found by me, up to fifty have been gathered by me there in the same monastery, given up to the service of God. ... I have acquired – with great labour and with money from the gift of King William the Elder – a certain estate of 15 hides, which is called

Alfestun by the locals; and having acquired it have given it for the food of those brethren, serving God in the same monastery.[22]

By May of 1089 the new building was sufficiently far advanced for the monks to move in, indicating that within a space of only five years from the start of the works, the liturgical choir together with the presbytery was virtually complete. William of Malmesbury claimed that: 'When the work of the main church, which he had begun from the foundations, had advanced to that stage of growth that now the monks might move into it, the old church which blessed Oswald had built was ordered to be unroofed and destroyed.' Wulfstan was not entirely happy with this demolition:

We miserable people have destroyed the work of saints, that we may provide praise for ourselves. The age of that most happy man did not know how to build pompous buildings, but knew how to offer themselves to God under any sort of roof, and to attract to their examples their subordinates. We on the contrary strive that, neglecting our souls, we may pile up stones.

Nevertheless, William goes on to record that Wulfstan 'completed the new church, and you could not easily find the ornament that did not decorate it, so marvellous was it in single details and singular in all parts'.

The multi-columned crypt with its cushion capitals at Worcester Cathedral is the earliest part of the building remaining from the church begun by St Wulfstan of Worcester in 1084. (*Dean and Chapter of Worcester Cathedral*)

Parish Churches

Although local churches were never as physically imposing or aesthetically impressive as cathedrals or abbeys, their ubiquity, prominence and accessibility ensured that they played a major role in the lives of all strata of society. They served as the site of day-to-day religious activity, a focal point for the display of secular wealth and authority, the arena in which the major milestones of life were marked and a hub for formal and informal contact with other members of the community. The establishment of a parish church often had landscape consequences beyond the location and architecture of the church building. If the church was established adjacent to an existing manor house, little change to the existing rights of way would have been required for access. If, however, a new church was built at a distance from the manor, perhaps on open ground away from any settlement, then new routes and rights of way would have been needed. Thus, the location of a church could have a significant impact on the parochial system of communications. There would have been similar readjustment of routeways associated with the creation of monastic granges and field chapels.[23] At Asheldham (Essex), the Saxon church lay alongside and was aligned on a Roman road. The construction of the Norman church was accompanied by the expansion of the burial ground, which encroached on the road, causing its diversion.

St Lawrence's Church, Asheldham, Essex. (Clive Nason)

By 1066, progress towards a parochial structure was well advanced in parts of the country, involving the subdivision of large *parochiae*, which had been based on Saxon minster churches. The process of partition was also well advanced by the time of the Conquest, by which time the minster churches had already lost their predominance and had been reduced in number and some were transformed into communities of monks or canons. Only in the north of England did enormous parishes survive into the late Middle Ages and beyond. Most early parish churches were created by Saxon lords largely for their own use, the boundaries of whose secular estates often corresponded with those of the parish. The thegns appointed and paid the priests. The lay ownership of tithes and the appointment of priests by laymen were condemned by Pope Nicholas II in 1059, and the pressure to devote tithes to ecclesiastical purposes would have been a factor in what is known as the 'great rebuilding' of parish churches from 1050 onwards.

By 1200, much of England had a network of parishes, many of them with their own parish church and dependent chapelries. The minster church of Morville

St Andrew's Church, South Lopham, Norfolk. The central tower, dating from *c*.1120, represents one of the finest Norman examples of its type in East Anglia. (*Trevor Rowley*)

(Shropshire) provides us with an insight into parochial development. In 1066 the church of St Gregory, Morville, was served by eight canons, but by 1086, when it had passed into the hands of the newly founded abbey at Shrewsbury, there were only three priests here. In the following century, eight new chapels were built in the parish, one of which, at Aston Eyre, contains a remarkable tympanum showing Christ's entry into Jerusalem, dating to *c*.1140. Subsequently, six of these became parish churches. In many other large parishes, there was a similar burst of activity. St Mary's Church at Shawbury (Shropshire), founded chapels at Acton Reynald, Moreton Corbet, Grinshill and Great Wytheford. A certificate of Bishop Roger de Clinton, dated 1140, tells of the time when these manors were without chapels and that he himself had consecrated three of them. This pattern of chapel foundation was repeated throughout the region. In the south-west of Shropshire there were extremely large parishes containing only scattered settlements; chapels tended to be planted in hamlets along the river valleys. A line of such chapels, later to become parish churches, follows the county boundary with Herefordshire along the Teme Valley at Bedstone, Bucknell, Stowe and Llanfair Waterdine. In the foothills of Brown Clee in south Shropshire it is possible to trace the evolution of the parish system through the activities of Wenlock Abbey. The abbey held extensive estates in the area and established minster churches, including one at Stoke St Milborough, where there is a well dedicated to St Milburga, the abbey's seventh-century first abbess. The large parish was divided into chapelries; that at Heath, with its remarkably preserved early-twelfth-century chapel, is the best known.[24]

The expansion of towns in the late Saxon era led to a proliferation of urban churches, many of which started life as private chapels, which extended their pastoral care to the surrounding community. By 1066, towns could be ranked by the number of churches they had; London had more than 100, Norwich and Winchester had more than fifty, York and Lincoln more than forty and Exeter

The twelfth-century tympanum of the church at Aston Eyre, Shropshire, shows Christ's entry into Jerusalem. (*Trevor Rowley*)

The remarkable isolated Norman chapel at Heath, Shropshire, dates from the first half of the twelfth century. Heath was originally the chapelry of a mother church at Stoke St Milborough, which itself was an early dependent foundation of Wenlock Abbey. (*Trevor Rowley*)

The excavated footings of St Mary's, a Norman church at Tanner Street, Winchester. (*Hampshire Chronicle*)

about twenty. Most urban churches were out of necessity small, but some that were located in markets were larger as they had more space to expand.

For the most part, a parish church would be endowed by a local lord, and frequently it was this endowment that would pay for building the church, although the lord may have paid for part or all of that as well. The responsibility for maintaining the building and its upkeep lay with the rector, who would be appointed by the lord, using the revenue from tithes and glebe land with which the parish had been endowed. In some cases, having endowed a church, the lord would pass it directly into the care of a monastery, which would then act as the rector. The monastery would normally hire a parson to administer to the parish but would retain up to two-thirds of the endowment for its own use. By 1200, something like a quarter of parish churches, together with their glebe and tithes, were in the hands of religious houses. For example, around 1090 a local lord, Wulfgar, paid for the construction of a church at Milford on Sea (Hampshire). Additionally, he gave an endowment of a half-virgate of land to the minster church of Christchurch in order to provide a parish priest. When, about 1160, Christchurch became a house of Augustinian canons, Milford church was given to them in its entirety. Monastic financial involvement contributed to the great church rebuilding of the twelfth century, but in some instances, particularly in the case where French monasteries were involved, such an arrangement could lead to the church and parish being starved of resources.

Parish churches in the new 'Norman' style were built throughout the land, many of them stone buildings replacing wooden predecessors. Excavations at the redundant parish church of St Lawrence, Asheldham (Essex), revealed just such a sequence, where a late Saxon two-cell timber church was replaced by a tripartite apsidal stone church soon after the Conquest. Unusually, this church had a tower over the chancel.[25] At Chale (Isle of Wight), a new church was founded in 1114 by the lord, Hugh Gernon, who paid for its construction; at Shalfleet, also on the Isle of Wight, a fortified church tower was built by Gocelin fitz Azur before the end of the eleventh century.

At Clopton (Northamptonshire), William Clopton replaced his timber chapel with a stone building at the end of the twelfth century, when it became an independent parish church. For good measure, he installed his younger brother, Reginald, as the first rector.[26] Almost without exception, such churches would have been the largest and most imposing building in Anglo-Norman rural communities. Some Normans who died on campaign wanted their bodies to rest in churches that they had founded or patronized, and as they did not build ostentatious tombs, entire churches acted as their memorials. Through their endowed parish churches these new men were demonstrating their dominant position in local society, at the same time taking out an insurance policy on their souls. Norman lords built for God, their peers and their tenants but not necessarily in that order. One scholar summarized this Norman mix of pride and

Shalfleet church, Isle of Wight, has a fortified west tower that was built *c*.1070. (*Rupert Willoughby*)

St Margaret's, Hales, Norfolk. The apsidal chancel was typical of many early Norman Romanesque churches in England. The tower, which predates the rest of the church, is also eleventh century. (*roundtowers.org*)

piety as follows: 'The Norman baronage of the late eleventh century was cruel, greedy, proud, domineering, oppressive, class-conscious, usually race-conscious, extraordinarily self-confident – except on their death beds.'[27]

The size and form of these churches varied enormously according to the resources of the patron and wealth of the community, but very few Norman churches have remained unaltered. Where they have survived intact it is normally because they have for various reasons been deprived of resources over the following centuries. (See Plate 12)

Hospitals

Another element of the medieval Church was the charitable founding of hospitals. Some hospitals were built for the use of pilgrims and other travellers; others were essentially almshouses, intended for the poor and elderly. Nevertheless, some provided accommodation for the sick and even forms of rudimentary treatment for common ailments. Hundreds of hospitals were established after 1066, but there were a few in existence before the Conquest, for example at York and Worcester. After the First Crusade, pilgrimage in Europe to Jerusalem, Rome and Santiago de Compostela in north-west Spain became increasingly important and hospitals, which acted as hospice, almshouse and clinic, sprang up along the network of routes. Some were attached to existing institutions while others were specifically created by larger monasteries and other benefactors. A number of European routes began in England, notably from Reading Abbey, which was closely associated with the cult of St James at Santiago de Compostela, and hospitals were established in London and along routes leading to the ports. In the late twelfth century, the shrine of St Thomas of Canterbury became a particularly important goal for pious wayfarers, and hospitals at Canterbury and Southwark, bearing the martyr's name, were amongst the earliest. Within a very few years they proliferated and by the mid-thirteenth century there were almost 1,000 hospitals in England.

One form of institution that until recently had been thought to be a post-Conquest introduction was the leprosy hospital (*leprosarium*), but there is some evidence for leprosy in later Anglo-Saxon England and a leprosy hospital has been uncovered at Winchester. After the Conquest they became common and Lanfranc was responsible for founding a leprosy hospital of St Nicholas at Harbledown, outside Canterbury, c.1084. He had already established a regular hospital dedicated to St John outside the city's Northgate. This hospital comprised a huge cruciform building with a north–south dormitory range over 60m long with a chapel and masonry reredorter. This foundation appears to have been inspired by Italian hospitals, rather than Norman.

About the same time other *leprosaria* were established at Chatham and Rochester by Bishop Gundulf, who, like Lanfranc, had been a monk at Bec, and at

The Leper Chapel of St Mary Magdalene, Cambridge, built *c*.1125. The chapel was the beneficiary of the annual Stourbridge Fair, which developed into the largest fair in Europe.

Lewes (*c*.1080), York (post-1088) and the Winchester hospital refounded (*c*.1090). Relatively little is known of these early institutions, but Roffey has argued that they may not have resembled the quasi-monastic hospitals of the later Middle Ages, but were more like village communities made up largely of wooden buildings.[28] They were usually built on the edge of towns or in rural areas near crossroads on major communication routes. The lepers needed to stay in contact with society to beg alms, trade items and offer services such as praying for the souls of benefactors. The leper chapel at Cambridge dates from about 1125, but in 1199 King John gave it the right to hold an annual three-day fair to raise income for the patients.

Chapter 8

The Spread of Monasticism

Successive orders like successive tribes and nations crossed the frontiers as if they were impelled by those behind who had come from a greater distance.[1]

One important aspect of the late Saxon ecclesiastical reforming movement to survive the Conquest was the monastic cathedral, a largely English phenomenon. In the tenth century, monastic cathedrals were established at Canterbury, Winchester, Worcester and Ely. These were Benedictine priories,

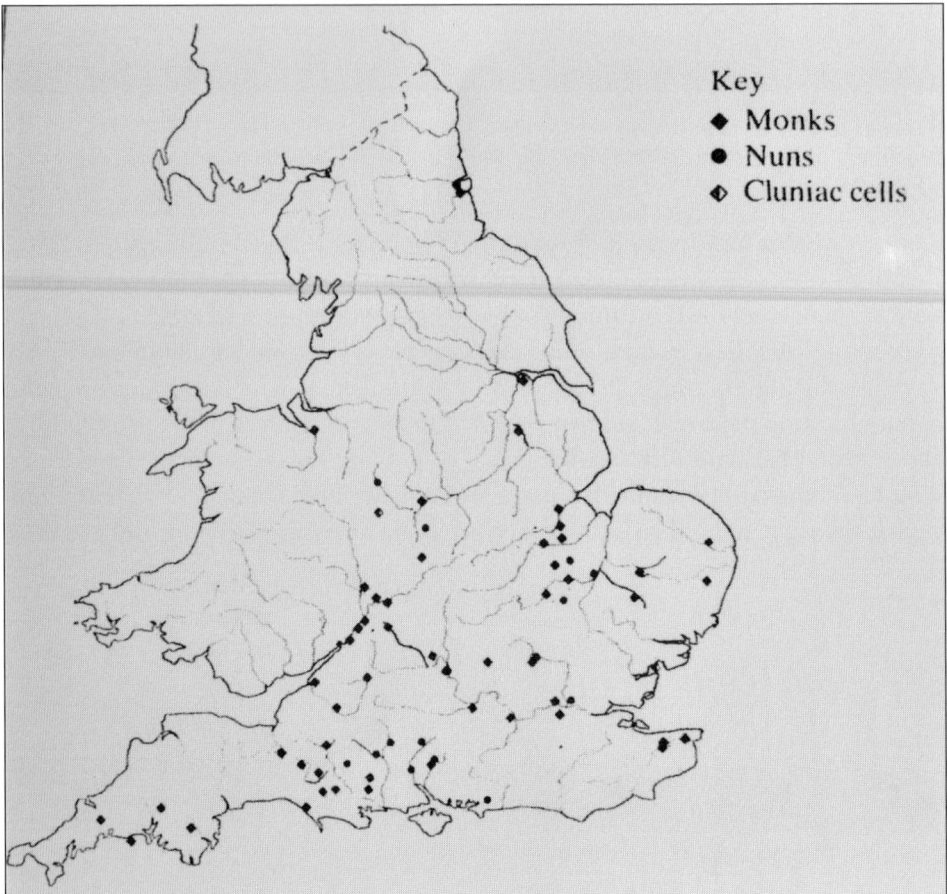

Key
◆ Monks
● Nuns
◇ Cluniac cells

Monasteries in 1066.

where the bishop was the titular head, with a prior in charge of the monastery. Benedictine monks either replaced or supplemented the secular canons who had previously serviced the cathedral. Unlike secular cathedrals these institutions housed large numbers of monks and laymen and tended to attract much larger endowments. Although the Normans were initially suspicious about this arrangement, they soon adopted the practice themselves and between 1080 and 1100 founded monastic cathedrals at Rochester, Durham, Norwich and Bath, with Coventry following in 1102 and Carlisle in 1133.

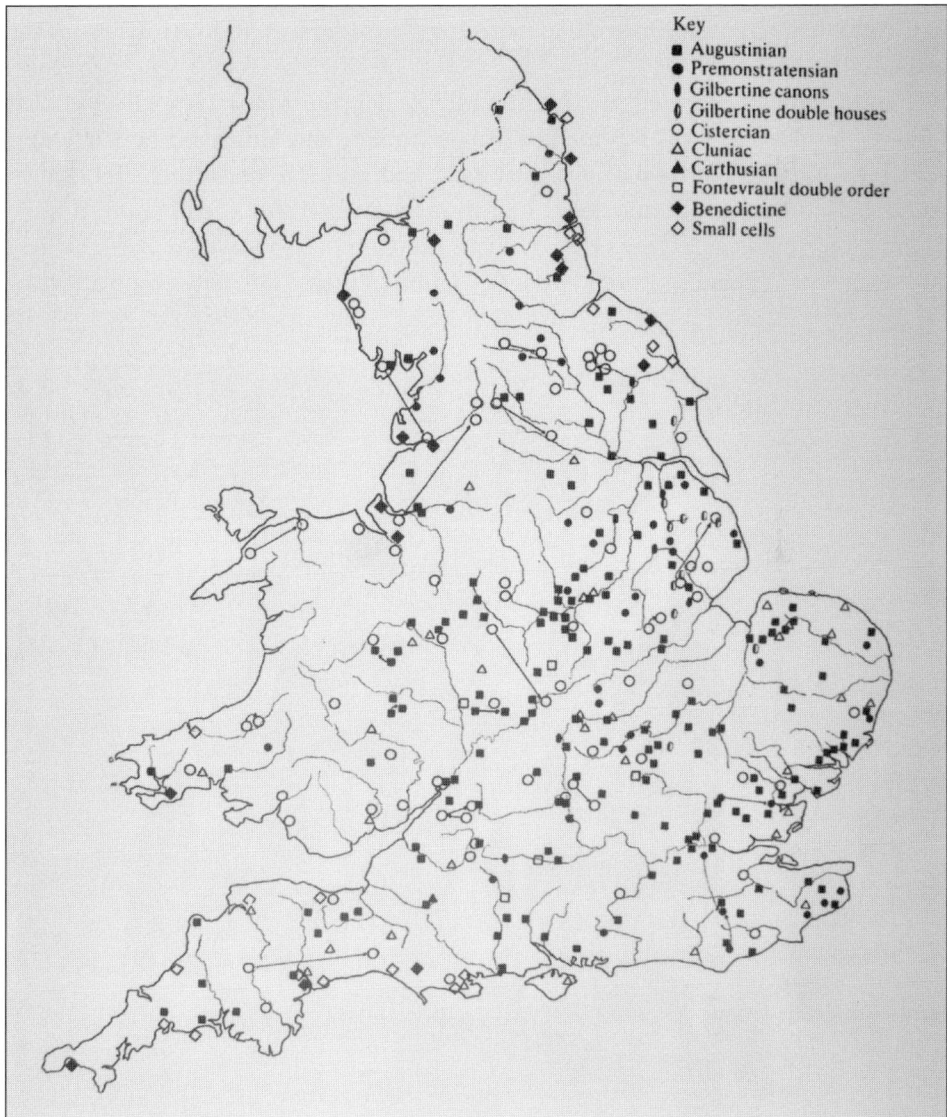

Key
■ Augustinian
● Premonstratensian
⦙ Gilbertine canons
◗ Gilbertine double houses
○ Cistercian
△ Cluniac
▲ Carthusian
□ Fontevrault double order
◆ Benedictine
◇ Small cells

Monasteries in 1200.

In 1066 there were some fifty-two well-endowed, but unevenly distributed, Benedictine monastic institutions in England. Most were located in Wessex, the Fens and the Severn basin, and there were none to the north of the Humber. These were autonomous houses with few dependent priories or cells, whose institutions were essentially English in their origin but who drew some of their customs and observances from Cluniac and Lotharingian sources. Their buildings were relatively modest in scale, although some were elaborately decorated. Unlike those monasteries built after 1066, they did not follow a standard plan and such was the rigour of the Norman rebuilding programme that little above-ground evidence of the pre-Conquest houses survives. By 1200 there were about 600 houses of various sizes belonging to a dozen or so orders, including nine monastic cathedrals.

The Conquest provided all the ingredients for the monastic explosion that followed in the late eleventh and twelfth centuries and which brought about a transformation of the monastic topographic and cultural landscape. The Crown and a cadre of powerful new lords had the resources to build and support such foundations on their large estates. William the Conqueror founded Battle Abbey and several of William's senior supporters founded monastic houses soon after the

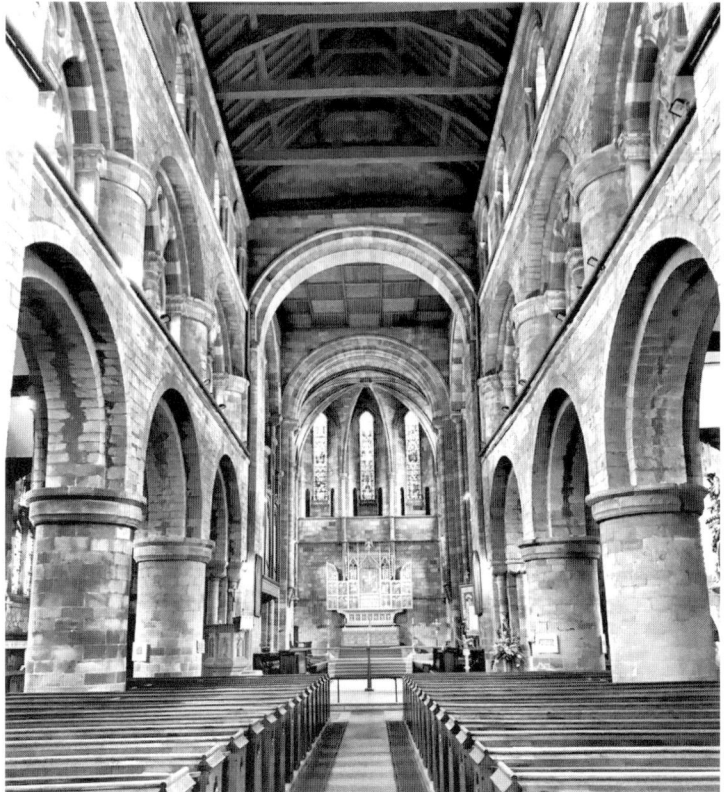

Interior of the Abbey Church of St Peter and St Paul, Shrewsbury. It was founded as a Benedictine monastery in 1083 by Roger de Montgomery. The Anglo-Norman historian Orderic Vitalis was sent to school at the church on the site which preceded the abbey.

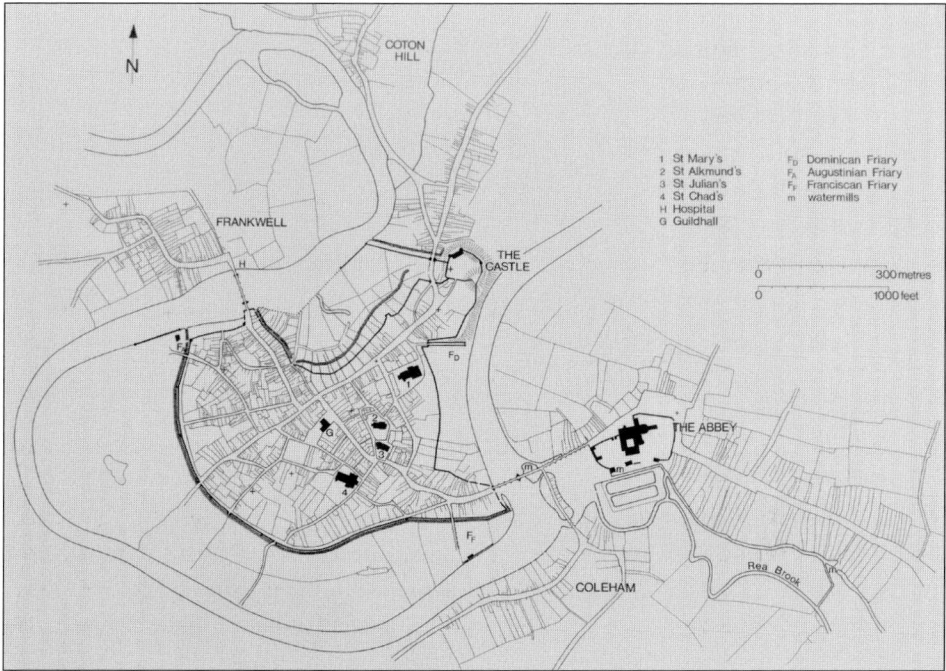

Plan of Shrewsbury showing the relationship of the abbey to the town and Roger de Montgomery's castle.

Conquest. William de Warenne founded Lewes Priory (*c*.1077) and his son, Castle Acre Priory (1089). Robert, son of William Malet, founded Eye Priory (*c*.1080), Roger de Montgomery refounded Wenlock Priory (1080) and founded Shrewsbury Abbey (1083), Henry de Ferrers founded Tutbury Priory before 1086 and Juhel de Totnes founded Totnes Priory (*c*.1087). Many of these early post-Conquest foundations were located close to seigneurial castles in strategically sensitive areas. The early abbeys, almost as much as castles, were statements of power.

Early Norman Monasteries

After the Conquest, the great monastic invasion began slowly as many Normans were reluctant to found or support new houses in England rather than in their native Normandy, but once started it soon picked up pace and continued for two and a half centuries. The first to arrive were Benedictine monks from the Conqueror's duchy; many of them were men who combined native energy and organizational ability with the zeal of a new and fervent religious movement. Some of them were carefully chosen to govern the existing monasteries, while others came to colonize the new foundations such as Shrewsbury, from Saint-Martin-de-Séez (Orne). Some came to reinforce existing communities and their daughter houses at Canterbury, Rochester and Colchester, or to man the small priories and

Lanfranc was the most influential churchman in early Norman England and Archbishop of Canterbury, 1070-1089. (*Bodleian Library, MS Bodley S69 folio 1r*)

cells that sprang up throughout the great Norman fiefs, where lesser lords, unable to found an abbey, set up small priories in their castle or near their hall. To begin with, the abbeys of Bec and Jumièges in Normandy were the most influential. It has been estimated that between 1066 and 1130 about forty abbots or priors of monasteries were recruited directly from one or other of the twenty-six Norman abbeys, and that fifteen of these came from Jumièges. It would be impossible to exaggerate the regenerative power of the great Benedictine Norman abbots and priors of the first and second generation.

One of the first and most important of the early foundations was a privileged royal church, which also served as a victory memorial – Battle Abbey. The abbey chronicle reports that William wanted the abbey to be built at the scene of the fiercest fighting, with its high altar on the site where Harold had been killed. The *Battle Abbey Chronicle* specifies that this is where the defeated king's standard was toppled and William of Malmesbury (*c*.1095–*c*.1143) notes that the high altar stood where Harold's corpse was found. Although the abbey has generally been thought of as a war memorial for the victors, it may equally have been founded as an act of penance. The loss of life at the Battle of Hastings had been particularly high and in 1070, a papal legation led by Bishop Ermenfrid of Sion issued a Penitential on those that had fought in the battle. This established a sliding scale of penance in relation to sins committed in battle and it has been argued that King William's contribution was a new abbey.[2]

Although the eastern arm of Battle Abbey church was sufficiently complete to allow for its consecration in 1076, it was not until 1094 that the finished church was finally consecrated. The Conqueror bequeathed to the community at Battle his royal cloak, a collection of relics and a portable altar used during his military campaigns. He had also endowed the abbey with extensive estates, including all the land within a radius of a mile and a half (2.5km) of the high altar (known as the Banlieu). Within this specified area around the abbey, the abbot enjoyed a unique jurisdiction over land and men. William's gift promoted Battle to the rank of fifteenth wealthiest religious house in England. Much of the abbey fabric, including the church, was destroyed at the Dissolution in 1538, but in 1903 a memorial marking the location of Harold's death was placed on the site of where it was believed the high altar had been. In 2016 the memorial stone was moved 6m to the east of its original location as a result of a reinterpretation of the precise siting of high altars in Romanesque great churches.

The earliest of the new monasteries in the north of England were refoundations of ancient Saxon institutions, such as that at Whitby, sited dramatically on a coastal headland overlooking the estuary of the River Esk. Whitby Abbey had originally been founded in the mid-seventh century, but had been abandoned following Danish raids in the ninth century. A new Benedictine community was founded on the site by Reinfrid, a knight who may have participated in the Harrying of the North and was reputedly inspired by the ruins of the old abbey

The site of the high altar at Battle Abbey, where King Harold was slain during the Battle of Hastings.

The altar stone was moved a few metres to the east in 2016 because of a recalibration of the location of such altars in mid-eleventh-century churches. (*The Times*)

when he was a serving soldier. After leaving the army he became a monk and in 1078–9, Reinfrid established a community, endowed by William de Percy, where the emphasis was upon solitude and individual life. St Mary's, York, founded by Alan I of Richmond before 1086, occupied the site of a church dedicated to

Tynemouth Castle and Abbey, Northumberland. There was a monastery on the site in the eighth century, but it was constantly under attack and eventually destroyed during the Viking era. It was refounded in the late eleventh century and fortified during the twelfth century.

St Olave of Norway in 1055. Its early years were troubled by a dispute with the clerics of York Minster, but it went on to become the richest abbey in the north of England. The ancient monastery at Jarrow was refounded, initially as a subsidiary of Durham, in 1074, and in 1083, Turchil, a Jarrow monk, founded Tynemouth Priory on a promontory. In 1090, Robert de Mowbray, Earl of Northumbria, granted his Tynemouth lands, including the headland, to St Albans Abbey. In 1095, Robert rebelled against William Rufus and took refuge in the 'stronghold' at Tynemouth, an indication that the site was already fortified.

A Great Wave of Monasticism

Benedictine monks were soon followed to England by a sequence of reformed orders. Foremost among these were the Cluniacs, who had already introduced a network of dependent houses in mainland Europe. The Cluniacs had been established in the tenth century in an attempt to restore traditional Benedictine practices of dedication, encouragement of the arts and caring for the poor. In England, the first Cluniac house was at Lewes (Sussex), founded by William de Warenne and his wife, Gundred, who c.1076 visited Cluny Abbey in Burgundy as part of an abortive pilgrimage to Rome. They were so impressed with the order and its buildings that they determined to establish a Cluniac priory in England

and *c*.1081 began work on the site of a Saxon church dedicated to St Pancras. The new priory was housed with a prior and monks brought directly from Cluny and laid out as a replica of Cluny. The Cluniacs chose their sites with particular care and Lewes established the topographical pattern for several other of the order's priories. It was located by a stream, on the site of an existing shrine, close to a castle and town with good communication links to the Continent (see Plate 13). The Cluniacs branched rapidly out into a family of houses that were dependent upon the great Burgundian mother house. Although there were thirty-six Cluniac foundations by 1160, they did not flourish in a similar manner as the Cistercians, who followed from France later. Among the most impressive and successful were Wenlock Priory, founded by Roger de Montgomery on the site of a seventh-century monastery (*c*.1080), Thetford Priory, established by Roger Bigod, 1st Earl of Norfolk, in 1103 and Castle Acre Priory, founded by William de Warenne's son in 1089.

Following the Cluniac monks came the Regular Canons, notably the Austin or 'Black' Canons who adopted the Rule of St Augustine. The Austin Canons, whose first English house was St Botolph's at Colchester in 1100, were mendicants dependent on alms and accordingly tended to locate their foundations in well-populated towns. Typical of this generation of priories were two Augustinian foundations in Oxford. St Frideswide's had been one of the earliest churches in the city, located close to the southern gate within the defensive walls. There are several

Castle Acre castle, and the ruins of the priory on the extreme left, are a perfect example of Norman power imprinted on the landscape of north Norfolk. The castle was built soon after 1066 by William de Warenne, a close associate of William the Conqueror, and the Cluniac priory was added between 1081 and 1085. A small, planned settlement was built between the two.

St Milburga's Priory, Much Wenlock, Shropshire. Roger de Montgomery refounded Wenlock Priory as a Cluniac house *c*.1080, bringing monks from La Charité-sur-Loire to house it. (*Shropshire County Council*)

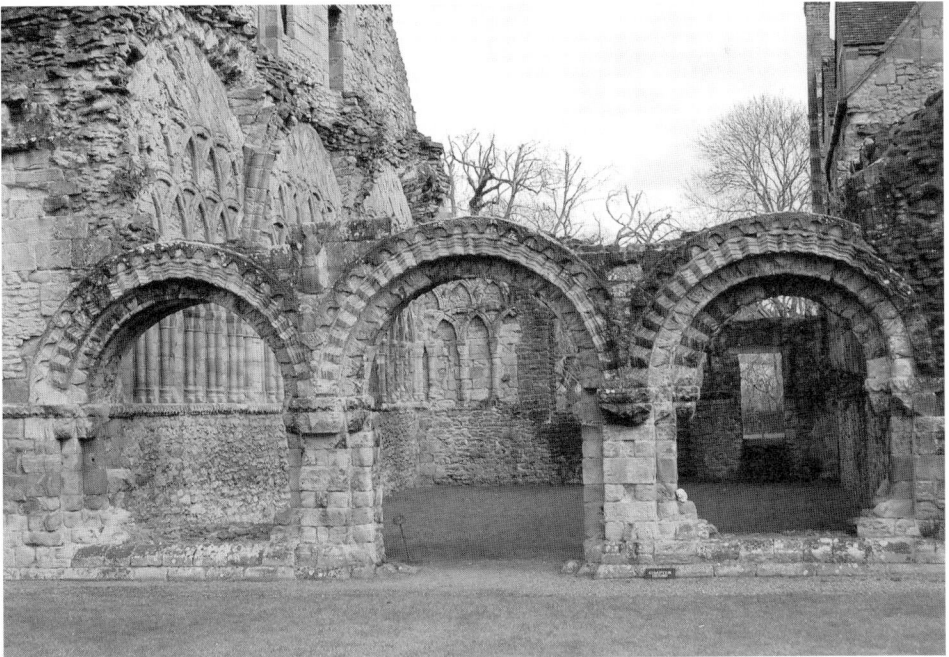

The three-arched entrance to the remains of the splendid chapter house at Wenlock Priory, dated *c*.1140. (*Trevor Rowley*)

foundation stories associated with St Frideswide, who is traditionally depicted as a Mercian princess (*c.*700) who became patron saint of Oxford. The church was burnt down in 1002 when a Danish community here was massacred and subsequently a house of secular canons was established on the site. Henry I gave the church to Gwymund, a royal chaplain, who established an Augustinian priory here in 1122. St Frideswide's was the only monastery within the city walls and about 1136 the priory was given permission to extend its precinct to the north and south on condition that it maintained the city defences where they coincided with the precinct boundary. In common with many other monasteries, new accounts of St Frideswide's life and miracles were written or 'discovered' later in the twelfth century, coinciding with the translation of St Frideswide from her original resting place to the new priory church. This building was a Norman/Gothic transitional structure, larger than the size the St Frideswide community warranted, and the saint's shrine became an important pilgrimage centre for the Oxford region.

Osney was an Augustinian priory founded by Robert d'Oilly, son of the original Norman lord of Oxford, in 1129. It lay to the west of Oxford Castle on a floodplain island in the River Thames and flooding was a perennial problem. In

The reconstructed shrine of St Frideswide in Oxford Cathedral. St Frideswide, or Frithuswith, is the patron saint of Oxford. The remains of the saint were translated into the church, of what was then an Augustinian priory, in 1180. The shrine became an important regional pilgrimage centre. (*Trevor Rowley*)

1154 the priory was elevated to an abbey and it became the wealthiest monastic house in Oxfordshire and one of the great Augustinian Canon Regular houses in England. Osney was granted churches and property in more than 120 places, largely scattered across Midland England. It developed important sheep flocks concentrated in the Cherwell Valley and the Cotswolds. The abbey church, which would have dominated the western approach to Oxford, was the largest in the city. After the Dissolution of the Monasteries, it acted as the cathedral for the new diocese of Oxford for a few years before it was moved to St Frideswide's. Like so many medieval gems, it was subsequently destroyed and no above-ground evidence survives. The abbey precinct is now covered by the railway line leading into Oxford station, a cemetery, Victorian housing, the Oxford Canal and a boatyard.

Unlike the Benedictines and their reformed offshoots, the Augustinians became involved with the communities amongst whom they lived, establishing schools and hospitals. By the end of Henry I's reign in 1135, 43 Augustinian houses had been founded in England and Wales, and by 1200 there were 140, mostly in the Midlands and East Anglia. During the twelfth century they assumed

The ruins of Osney Abbey, Oxford in 1640. Founded by Robert D'Oilly the Younger as an Augustinian priory in 1129, it became an abbey c.1154 and was one of the wealthiest of all the monastic houses in Oxford. For a few years after the abbey was dissolved it served as Oxford's cathedral, but virtually nothing of it survives today.

responsibility for an increasing number of parish churches, as lay owners were pressured to divest themselves of such property by Church reformers.

The greatest monastic impact on the British landscape was made by the Cistercians, an austere order who aimed at following the Rule of St Benedict to the last letter (*ad apicem litterae*). St Bernard of Clairvaux (1090–1153) was a powerful advocate of the order, who reacted against the liturgical and architectural excesses of the early twelfth-century Church. In 1125, in response to the increasingly confident flamboyance of the Romanesque buildings, he pleaded: 'I say naught of the vast height of your churches, their immoderate length, their superfluous breadth, the costly polishings, the curious carvings and paintings which attract the worshipper's gaze and hinder his attention ... For God's sake, if men are not ashamed of these follies, why at least do they not shrink from the expense?' It was not long before Cistercian churches, like those at Fountains and Rievaulx, were themselves monumental buildings, dominating the rural landscape.

The first Cistercian plantations in England were at Waverley (Surrey) (1128) and Rievaulx (Yorkshire) (1132). Thenceforward, the movement spread with remarkable speed over England and Wales. The order created a labour force of cottars, bordars and small freeholders as lay brethren, and in doing so they opened the religious life to classes hitherto excluded from it. Conventionally, it has been asserted that Cistercian foundations were established on wasteland in remote and uncultivated districts, and were perceived in biblical terms as making desolate landscapes fruitful. Closely linked to this idea was that their physical exertion, in clearing wasteland for agriculture, thus spiritually transformed the wilderness. This was, in part, a myth and recent studies of Cistercian houses in Burgundy and in Britain indicate that their agricultural regime was often based on an existing settlement structure, adopting landscape management and animal husbandry practices already in place. The Cistercians had a much larger proportion of lay brothers than other orders. These were largely recruited as labourers, emphasizing 'the spiritual advantage of hard manual work, giving both dignity and holy profit to labour'.[3]

The Cistercians created a stronghold in Yorkshire, with eight houses founded between 1132 and 1150, from whence they established colonies throughout the land until 1152, when the Cistercian general chapter restricted any further foundations.[4] Possibly, nobles deliberately chose to found Cistercian houses to buttress their own power in the region, in a way that Benedictine houses could not, as the Cistercians were not tied to governmental structures of Church and state and were in practice free from episcopal interference. After 1152, donors changed their allegiance to another semi-autonomous order, the Premonstratensians.[5]

The premier Cistercian house in the north was Fountains Abbey, founded in 1132–3 after a dispute and riot at the Benedictine abbey of St Mary's in York. Several monks were expelled and resettled as Cistercians on land given by Archbishop Thurstan of York, in the valley of the River Skell, a tributary of the

Ure. It was an almost perfect site for an order seeking solitude and self-sufficiency, with water, woodland, building stone and pasture, but according to Serlo, a contemporary monk at Fountains, it was located at 'a place which had never been inhabited, overgrown with thorns, a hollow in the hills between projecting rocks; fitter, to all appearance, to be a home for wild beasts than a home for men'.[6] Fountains was at the head of a complex network of estates, where outlying granges were particularly important and 'the role of the lay brethren was crucial'.[7]

The Cistercian abbey at Rievaulx (1132) was established by Walter l'Espec, a prominent northern nobleman whose father had fought at Hastings. The first brethren were twelve monks from Clairvaux in Burgundy. The abbey was located to the west of Helmsley in North Yorkshire, in a secluded, wooded valley next

Fountains Abbey, North Yorkshire, was founded in 1132 and became the wealthiest of all the Cistercian houses in Britain, with a network of subsidiary granges across north-east England. (*Dave MacLeod*)

Tintern Abbey, Monmouthshire, was founded as a Cistercian monastery on the Welsh bank of the River Wye in 1131. (*Dougal*)

to the River Rye, but the subsequent economic and spiritual success of the monastery did not lie in its isolation. It actively harnessed the resources of the region, establishing a network of granges allowing it to develop major upland sheep-farming estates. By the mid-twelfth century there were 140 monks and 500 lay brothers at Rievaulx, 'so that the church swarmed with them like a hive of bees', and under its second abbot, Aelred of Rievaulx (d.1167), it founded five daughter houses in England and Scotland.[8] There was a second foundation in Ryedale: the Savigniac abbey at Byland (1143) on Roger de Mowbray's estates. It was alleged that the two houses were so close that 'at each hour of the day and night, both abbeys heard each other's bells'[9] and brethren working in the fields could not distinguish which bells were calling them. Thus, in 1147, Byland Abbey moved to a new site, on marshy land to the south of the Hambleton Hills; at the same time, all the Savigniac houses were absorbed by the Cistercians.

Although the Cistercians' reputation as pioneer colonists was not altogether deserved, they were instrumental in peopling sparsely populated areas in northern England. Donkin has shown that 44 per cent of all known twelfth-century granges (mainly Cistercian) were built on land that was completely or largely 'waste' in 1086.[10] Conversely, there are instances where monastic communities brought about the destruction or movement of settlements. For example, the monks of Rufford monastery (founded *c*.1145) destroyed two Nottinghamshire villages, one of which had ten villeins and the other, eleven villeins, and a church in 1086. At the southern end of the Lincolnshire Wolds, the foundation of Revesby

Rievaulx Abbey, North Yorkshire, the first Cistercian monastery in the north of England, was founded by monks from Clairvaux Abbey in 1132. (*Dave Hamster*)

Abbey in 1142 uprooted three villages, while in Warwickshire, the village of Upper Smite was swept away by the foundation of Combe Abbey in 1150. In most cases, a twelfth-century foundation in the more densely settled areas of central and southern England resulted in disturbing the local settlement pattern. During the twelfth century the new wave of monastic foundations would have impacted some rural settlements. In particular, the Cistercians gained a reputation for their ruthless removal of existing villages to create the isolation that they required for their new abbeys and granges. Although this notoriety may have been exaggerated, helped by the writing of Walter Map, who claimed that, where no solitude existed, the Cistercians would create one for themselves by razing churches and villages and evicting their inhabitants, nevertheless, the proximity of many Cistercian abbeys to deserted villages does lend some weight to these claims. Bordesley Abbey (Worcestershire) lay near the vanished Domesday vill of Osmerley and the earthworks of two deserted hamlets lie within a mile of the abbey precinct. At Hailes Abbey (Gloucestershire), the thirty-two families listed in the Domesday Book have left little trace of their settlement, apart from the parish church that lies close to the abbey gates.[11] Otherwise, new monastic houses were rarely founded in or adjacent to existing villages, apart from a few nunneries, as at Polesworth (Warwickshire), Malling (Kent) and Wherwell (Hampshire).

The Premonstratensians, also known as Norbertines or White Canons, originated as an apostolic preaching movement but developed into a semi-monastic

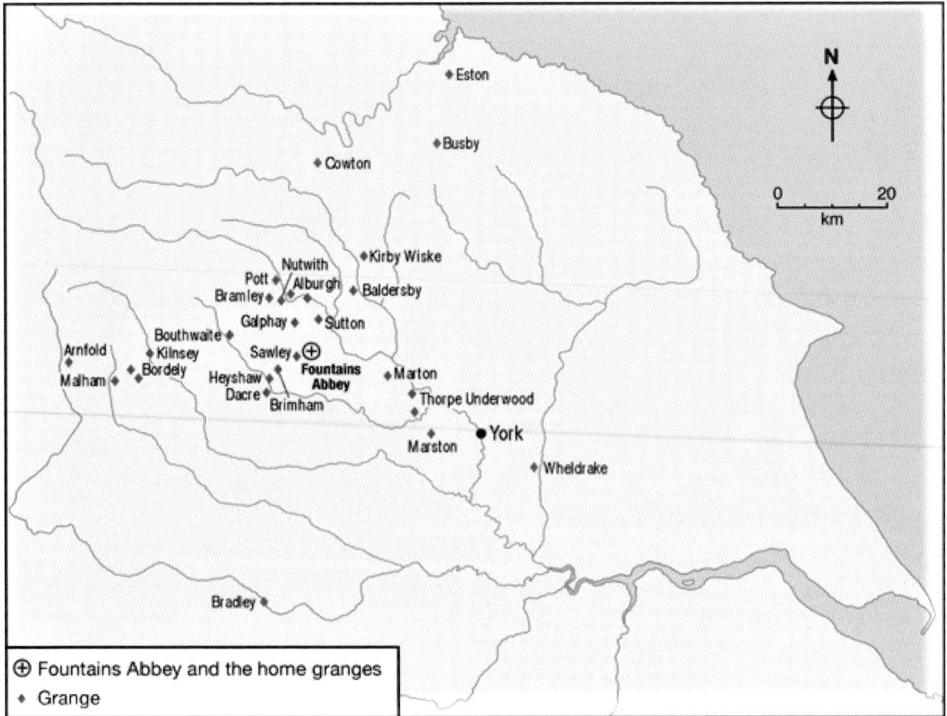

Map showing the distribution of granges belonging to Fountains Abbey in north-east England. (*Cistercians in Yorkshire*)

order with houses in remote districts, which led them into sheep-farming. They took their name from the site of their first foundation at Prémontré, near Laon in north-eastern France (1121), where they sought to live up to the monastic ideal of the 'desert'. Their founder, Norbert, was influenced by St Bernard and the Cistercians, but the order was not strictly speaking monastic. The Premonstratensians were communities of priests living together under the rule of St Augustine, rather than monks. The first Premonstratensian abbey in England was at Newsham or Newhouse (Lincolnshire), founded in 1143 by canons from the abbey of Licques, near Calais. Another nineteen houses were established over the following century. These were mainly in the Midlands, the north of England and Scotland, where there were six houses. Established feudal barons are conspicuously absent from the lists of founders of English Premonstratensian houses, probably because they were already committed to the support of Benedictine, Cluniac or Cistercian houses. The greatest support came from lesser barons and royal administrators, such as Ranulph de Glanville, Chief Justiciar of England in the 1180s, who founded Leiston Abbey, Suffolk; subsequently, another four English Premonstratensian houses were founded by members of his family.

There was only one Premonstratensian house in Wales, at Tal-y-Llychau (Talley), Carmarthenshire. This was located in the Cothi Valley and planned on a grand scale by Prince Rhys ap Gruffydd of Deheubarth in the 1190s. The order had a reciprocal agreement with the Cistercians that no new house of either order should be located close to any pre-existing house of the other order. Although the nearest Cistercian house to Talley was at Whitland, 28 miles away, the monks of Whitland opposed the foundation on the grounds that they had a grange in the same valley. Soon after the canons had settled, they were driven out by Cistercian monks using armed force. When, eventually, they regained the site, the abbey was completed in a much-reduced state; in particular, the church nave had to be drastically reduced in size.[12]

The first Premonstratensian foundations were double houses, that is, for men and women, but the later abbeys were exclusively male. Hitherto, there had been little opportunity for women to join religious orders. The relatively few nunneries were old, selective and often aristocratic Benedictine houses, almost all in Wessex or near London. A few had been added after the Conquest, but the real need was not met until a new order for women was established. The Order of Sempringham – the Gilbertines – was English in origin, though its codes and observances were a combination of Cistercian and Benedictine. This order of nuns was founded by Gilbert, the parish priest of Sempringham (Lincolnshire), in 1131, when he built accommodation for them against the north wall of the church on his land at Sempringham. Later, canons, lay sisters and lay brothers were added to the order. The Gilbertines were the only purely English order and were never particularly large; eventually, something like thirty houses were established, many of them with only a few nuns and canons.

There were several other orders, most of them small with only a few houses, including the Order of Grandmont and the Carthusians, a strictly enclosed hermit group. The Savigniacs and the Tironensians were both offshoot Benedictine reforming orders from north-western France. The Tironensian Order had no houses in England, but five in Scotland and one in Wales. St Dogmaels Abbey, Pembrokeshire, was typical of the fusion of the Celtic and Anglo-Norman Churches and was founded *c*.1114 adjacent to the site of a Celtic church at Llandudoch, where it was built into a steep, easterly-facing slope.

The Savigniac Order began as a hermitage in the forest of Savigny in western Normandy at the start of the twelfth century, developing into an abbey in 1112. The relative scarcity of other orders and the availability of vast areas of unimproved land attracted the Savigniacs to the north-west of England and Wales. The first Savigniac foundation in Britain was at Tulketh (near Preston) in 1124; three years later the monks transferred to Furness. There were other foundations in the north-west at Combermere, Cheshire (1133), and Calder, Cumbria (1134); at Basingwerk (Flintshire) and Neath (Glamorgan) in Wales, and Buckfast Abbey, Devon (*c*.1135). In 1147 the Savigniacs merged with the Cistercian Order.

St Dogmaels Abbey, Pembrokeshire, was founded in 1115 as a Tironensian house. It is believed to occupy the site of a sixth-century monastery founded by St Dogmael, who was reputedly a cousin of St David. (*Trevor Rowley*)

Additionally, quasi-monastic orders, combining religious and military ideals, were founded as a consequence of the Crusades. The uniting of two very different ways of life appealed to Anglo-Norman society. These were the Knights of the Temple of St John of Jerusalem, or the Knights Templar as they are popularly known, and the Hospitallers, the Knights of the Hospital of St John of Jerusalem. Most of the Templars' English houses were small 'preceptories', manned by a few brethren, whose main role was to raise money to send to the order in the Holy Land. Their churches were built on a circular plan, based on the design of the Church of the Holy Sepulchre in Jerusalem. The best-preserved circular church in Britain, apart from the Temple Church in London, is the Church of the Holy Sepulchre, Cambridge, which was built *c*.1130 by the Fraternity of the Holy Sepulchre, a group of Augustinian canons. The castle chapel at Ludlow is also circular and almost certainly influenced by the Templars. (See Plate 14)

The proliferation of monastic orders in the twelfth century prompted the Fourth Lateran Council (1215) to ban the creation of new orders. In future, those patrons who wished to endow a monastery had to choose one of the existing orders, but by this time the great age of monastic sponsorship was over and the geography of English monasticism was virtually complete. By the end of the twelfth century there were more than 600 monastic institutions of different orders in England. They possessed considerable amounts of land and wealth and were to remain a major religious, scholarly, educational and economic institution throughout the Middle Ages, although their political power was rarely to be as great as during the century and a half following the Conquest.

Lesser Priories

Sometimes, small priories were established by lesser lords, often based on existing parish churches. These were either alien priories with mother houses in France or dependencies of English Benedictine or Augustinian houses. Where lesser gentry were unable to afford to build an abbey, they often set up modestly sized priories near to or in their castle or manor house and persuaded a few monks to occupy them. In particular, the Augustinians were prepared to accept small endowments, capable of supporting three or four canons who could be attached to a pre-existing parish church, leading to a considerable saving in building costs. The church of St Andrew at Stogursey (Somerset) began life as a priory church founded by monks from Lonlay in Normandy c.1120. It is a large church with many purely French characteristics, such as the carved capitals and remains of an apsidal chancel, with two apsidal side chapels.

The great Norman abbey of Bec-Hellouin had small priories scattered across southern England from Lessingham in Norfolk to Milburn and Povington

The interior of St. Andrew's Church, Stogursey, Somerset. The church was built by William of Falaise as part of a Benedictine priory (1100-1107) and was a dependent cell of Lonlay Abbey (Orne) in Normandy. (*Michael Garlick*)

in Dorset, giving rise to place names such as Tooting Bec and Weedon Bec (Northamptonshire). These dispersed lands were administered from Ogbourne St George, near Marlborough (Wiltshire). It is doubtful if there was very much of a priory here, as the estates were managed by a single monk from Bec, acting as proctor-general for the abbot in Normandy.

Manasses Arsic, lord of Cogges, just outside Witney in Oxfordshire, established a priory cell next to his newly constructed castle in about 1100, and for a while this was the headquarters for all Fécamp Abbey estates in England. Excavations here indicate that the thegn's hall, which lay adjacent to a small Saxon church at Cogges, was converted into a modest priory. Tensions developed between the priory and Manasses' successors as lords of Cogges, as increasingly and typically Fécamp came to view its English cell as a mere estate office, existing less for the maintenance of religious life than for the collection of revenues. Manasses' heirs resented his generosity to Fécamp, which placed a powerful alien interest on

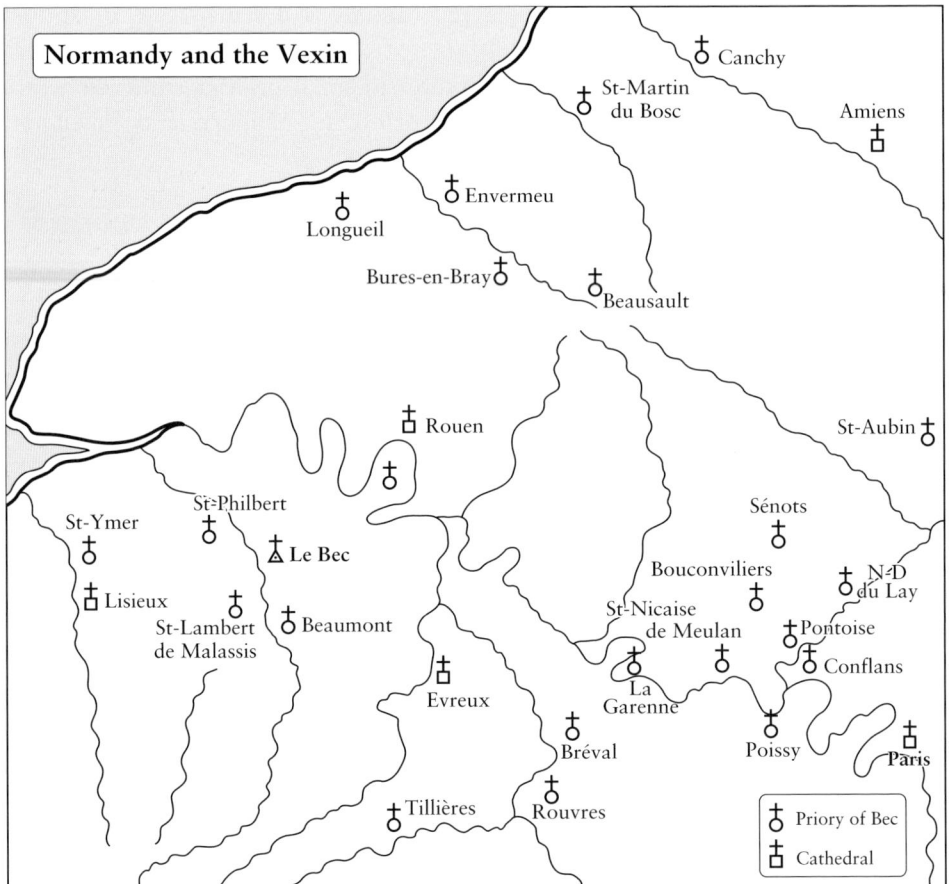

Map showing dependent cells of Bec Abbey in Normandy c.1140. (*Potter, 1998: 180*)

England and Wales

Lincoln

Wilsford

Lessingham

Norwich

Ely

St Neots

Blakenham

Weedon

Cottesford

Stoke by Clare

Goldcliff

Llandaff

Dunton

London

Ruislip

Rochester

Ogbourne

Chisenbury

Tooting

Bath

Wrotham

Canterbury

Salisbury

Winchester

Saltwood

Chichester

Hoo

Bovington

Exeter

Cowick

○ Priory of Bec
● Simple Priory / Manor of Bec
⌂ Cathedral

Map showing dependent cells of Bec Abbey in England *c.*1140. (*Potter, 1988: 180*)

their doorstep and restricted control of their churches and tithes. A remarkable if somewhat exaggerated insight into the situation is provided by a letter written by one of Fécamp's monks to his abbot in the 1150s. The writer, who had been sent to investigate the state of the English properties, vividly describes the dereliction that confronted him: 'When I arrived at Cogges I found the house empty of goods and full of filth … Life itself would be shorter than the tale of woes if I were to recite all the misfortunes of Cogges.'[13] Subsequently, the priory seems to have been staffed by only two or three monks and its importance declined after

The ruins of the Benedictine priory of Alvecote, Warwickshire, founded in 1159 as a dependency of Great Malvern Priory by William Burdet, a crusader. (*David Rogers*)

the 1240s, when Fécamp transferred its English affairs to a new estate centre in Sussex. Excavations here show no trace of formal conventual planning and resemble a small manor house rather than a monastery.

The Monastic Economy

During the twelfth century, British monasteries were involved in virtually every form of agricultural, industrial and commercial activity in the land. In many areas, such as arable farming, they followed the established practices, but in others, such as sheep farming and wool exporting, they were pioneers. Most of the information about monastic involvement in agriculture and industry in Britain dates from the thirteenth to the sixteenth century, well outside the remit of this book. However, many of the characteristics found in the later Middle Ages were established during the Norman era. The Church as a whole held about a quarter of the land of England in 1086 and this grew to about a third as a consequence of the increased number of monasteries during the following century. Estates bequeathed to the abbeys were reorganized and integrated into the monastic farming system. The nature of the exploitation depended upon the regional location of the house and the scale of its endowment. There were also significant differences in the economies between the various monastic orders. Older Benedictine estates tended to lie in fertile, low-lying areas where the emphasis was on arable farming, while reformed orders such as the Cistercians tended to be endowed with land that was largely upland, marshland or woodland, where they developed pastoral farming regimes. Monastic farming practices changed over time and until about 1150 the main role of monastic estates was to provide subsistence to the community and its constituent lay population; thus, crop production was more important than pastoral farming, and cattle were generally more important than sheep. Nevertheless, although the Cistercians are normally credited with the development of large-scale sheep farming in England and Wales, some Benedictine houses already had large flocks by the time of the Domesday Book. Ely Abbey, for example, had 9,000 sheep on its East Anglian estates by 1086, and there were over 3,000 sheep on Glastonbury's Somerset manors alone, while the nuns of the Abbaye-aux-Dames, Caen, had 17,000 sheep grazing on the common early in the twelfth century at Minchinhampton. During the second half of the

Figure carrying a sack of wool, from an account book at Beaulieu Abbey. (*BL. MS Add 487978 f.41 v*)

twelfth century, sheep farming became increasingly important with Cistercian abbeys exporting wool to the Continent and by 1200, Meaux Abbey in Yorkshire had converted some of its cattle sheds to sheepcotes and was turning cow pastures into sheep runs.

By the late twelfth century, monastic houses, mainly Cistercian, held 30 per cent of land in Yorkshire. Land close to the abbeys was used for arable farming, while estates further away were worked by lay brothers from granges and scattered subordinate lodges, characteristic of the Cistercian estates. Sheep farming in bercaries was by far the most common activity in these upland estates, each supporting flocks of 200–300 sheep. Cistercian granges were an essential part in this system; theoretically, they were to be staffed by lay brethren and should not lie more than a day's journey from the mother house. This edict was regularly disregarded, as in the case of the grange at Kilnsey, separated from Fountains by 48km of difficult country. This grange enclosed an area of 25 hectares of pasture, surrounded by a continuous boundary. One or two monks might be based in a grange to minister to the lay brethren and abbey tenants. The granges engaged in a range of activities and specialized according to the resources of the locality. At an early date, Fountains Abbey had granges with industrial specialities: Brimham

Kilnsey Grange, Wharfedale, North Yorkshire. A major grange belonging to Fountains Abbey, which formed the administrative centre of a vast estate mainly concentrating on raising sheep for their wool.

in iron-making and lead-smelting, Bradley in iron-making, Stainburn in arable crops, Horton in horse-rearing, and Kilnsey in sheep and wool production.[14]

In the Cotswolds, all the local abbeys had sheep walks in the uplands; for instance, the abbot of Evesham grazed his flocks around Stow-on-the-Wold, while the lands around Northleach were claimed by the abbot of Gloucester. Even distant abbeys claimed grazing rights in the Cotswolds: Westminster Abbey maintained flocks around Bourton-on-the-Water. These and other suppliers were clearly providing the wool that was processed in Cirencester and other Cotswold wool towns. To some extent it was no accident that wool became associated with monasteries; wool was necessary for monks' habits and cowls in the first instance, but the Cistercians were quick to realize the far greater potential of the wool market.

Specialized dairy farms and cattle-breeding stations, known as vaccaries, were another feature of monastic farming. These often involved seasonal pastoralism and transhumance (movement of livestock). The typical vaccary would handle a herd of 20–80 cattle and would consist of a fold-yard for the livestock, which was surrounded by byres, haybarns and a residence for the granger and any other monastic staff. In northern England, vaccaries were often established at the heads of dales, where they were able to combine the resources of enclosed valley

A prospect of Calder Abbey, Cumbria. (*Matthias Read, 1669 -1747*)

hay meadows and open fellside grazing. Byland Abbey's vaccary at Combe was established in the late 1140s and Meaux had its first cattle farm before 1151. By the end of the twelfth century, Fountains Abbey had developed a well-organized system of vaccaries in Wharfedale and Nidderdale, involving transhumance between upland and lowland pastures. In Cumbria, Furness Abbey had a group of vaccaries in Lonsdale, while there were four vaccaries immediately to the east of Calder Abbey in the Lake District.

The element of continuity and the wealth that characterized the monasteries allowed them to undertake ambitious engineering schemes during the twelfth century as well as to develop farming and industrial techniques to a high degree of competence. Such engineering activity created causeways, dams, feeder channels, ponds and lakes; one notable example was Stuntney Causeway, built by Bishop Hervey of Ely (1109–31) in order to provide access to the cathedral and market town on the Isle of Ely. Early twelfth-century grange sites belonging to Meaux excavated artificial dykes to divide the open fields from marshland or woodland. The other major motive for digging dykes in the Holderness region was to improve communications. At Meaux, in the wetlands of East Yorkshire, a 2km canal called the *Eschedike* was made by the brothers to connect the abbey with the River Hull and the River Humber between 1162 and 1182. In the Somerset Levels, near Glastonbury, the duties of Robert Malherbe, a tenant of Glastonbury in the early thirteenth century, reveal something of the many functions of the monastic waterways:

> He ought to provide a boat that can carry eight men, and be the steerman, and carry the lord abbot where he wishes ... and all his men, and the cook, the hunter with his dog, and all those who can or ought to be carried by water ... He ought to be responsible for the abbot's wine at Pilton, after it has been put in the boat and until it has been brought to Glastonbury ... To look after all waters between Clewer and Street bridges, and between Mark Bridge and Glastonbury. And he ought to look after all the abbot's boats in those waters and keep the waterways in Hearty Moor.[15]

The first generation of Norman prelates, such as Lanfranc, in the south-east often chose to import stone from Normandy for their new churches. In particular, Caen stone was imported in large quantities during the eleventh and twelfth centuries, but the scale of rebuilding was such that many new quarries were opened in England after the Conquest. Most abbeys acquired their building stone locally, often from their own estates; the Domesday Book records that Evesham Abbey obtained stone for its new abbey church from its manor at Offenham, 3km away. Oxen from one of the estate's plough teams were diverted to drag stones, which presumably had been brought along the River Avon from a Cotswold quarry. When stone was not available from monastic estates, temporary rights of extraction were often given. After the Conquest, the stone quarries at Quarr on the Isle of Wight were in the hands of the Crown and William Rufus granted the bishop of Winchester land there, with the right to extract stone. Consequently, the new church at Winchester Cathedral priory was built in its entirety from distinctive grey-white Quarr limestone. Quarr stone was also used at Romsey, Titchfield and Canterbury abbeys and Christchurch, Lewes and Dover priories. Such was its popularity that by about 1120 the best of the Quarr stone had been quarried out and production diminished. The records of the twelfth century abound in references to the right to take and transport stone, often by water, and toll exemptions on building materials were freely given to religious communities. In the twelfth century the abbeys at Ramsey, Crowland and Bury St Edmunds obtained grants of land including concessions and leases of strips of ground in the Oolitic limestone quarries at Barnack (Northamptonshire). Blocks of Barnack stone were transported on sleds to the River Welland and then taken by barge down the River Welland and Fenland waterways; most notably, it was then used in Peterborough and Ely Cathedrals. Sawtry Abbey (Cambridgeshire) had a special canal made from Whittlesea Mere to bring in Barnack stone. Bury St Edmunds had a permanent grant of a right of way from Barnack to the wharves at the Welland ferry, over a mile distant. At Barlings Abbey, on the Isle of Oxney in Lincolnshire, there is evidence that the monks canalized the River Barlings Eau for the purpose of bringing in building stone.

Barnack stone from the ruins of Sawtry Abbey, Cambridgeshire, outside All Saints' Church, Sawtry. (*Alan*)

In 1138 a Cistercian abbey was founded by Waleran de Beaumont in the valley of the River Arrow at Bordesley, Redditch (Worcestershire). The site was low-lying and subject to regular flooding and consequently it was drained and the Arrow was diverted for almost a mile, in a channel dug for it in the northernmost part of the valley. At the same time the bed of the old channel was widened and deepened to accommodate a set of fishponds. Excavations here identified a mill used for metalworking dating to 1174. The mill buildings, with hearths, charcoal spreads and part-finished items of iron and copper alloy, show that this mill and its successors were used for water-powered metalworking, some of the earliest evidence for this process in Britain.[16]

Other abbeys were involved with coal, lead and iron ore extraction from the twelfth century onwards; for example, Kirkstall Abbey had opencast ironstone pits at Seacroft, agreeing to filling them in once all the iron ore had been extracted. Both Byland and Fountains abbeys had acquired iron mines by c.1180. There is also evidence of iron-smelting forges on the granges of Tintern, Fountains and Kirkstead abbeys before 1200. Blacksmiths' forges were commonly found on the home grange or the outer court of many abbeys. Lead was a commodity much in demand for roofs, gutters and a variety of containers on monastic sites and Fountains and Byland abbeys were opening lead works on the moors to the west of Nidderdale in the 1170s.

Monastic Towns

Church leaders were among the most enthusiastic founders of new towns or market extensions to existing settlements, continuing a trend that had started before the Conquest. Bury St Edmunds, which has long been recognized as an early example of a monastic planned town, lies at the confluence of two minor rivers in west Suffolk, the Lark and its tributary the Linnet. It was almost certainly the first Norman planned town and it provided a template for other later monastic towns such as Glastonbury.

The remains of the martyred King Edmund (d.869) were brought here in the early tenth century and the site developed into a shrine. A Benedictine abbey was founded here in 1020 and both town and abbey flourished to the extent that in 1066, the abbey was the fourth in wealth among English foundations. It has been argued that there were two phases of Norman planning; the first in the form of a small regular *bourg* with a marketplace, immediately to the south of the abbey, while the second phase was part of a larger plan, which, together with a new abbey, created a grandiose shrine to the royal St Edmund the Martyr.[17] The scheme was probably devised by Abbot Anselm, a nephew of Archbishop Anselm, during the first half of the twelfth century.

Bury already had 310 inhabitants and a mint by the time of the Conquest. The Domesday Book records how between 1066 and 1086 the town doubled in value:

The town is now contained within a great perimeter, including land which used to be ploughed and sown before the Conquest … Whereon are now 30 priests, deacons and clerks together, 28 nuns and poor people who daily pray for the king and for all Christian people; 75 bakers, ale-brewers, tailors, washerwomen, shoe-makers, robe-makers, cooks, porters and agents … Besides whom are 13 reeves over the lands of the abbey who have a house in the town, and under them 5 bordars. Now 34 knights, French and English, with 22 bordars under them. Now altogether there are 342 houses on the demesne of the land of the abbey, which was all under the plough in the time of King Edward.

Abbot Baldwin (1065–98) was responsible for the great rebuilding of the abbey and the foundation of the new town over part of the old West Field. This was laid out on a grid pattern of streets, immediately to the west of the monumental gate-tower at the entrance to the abbey grounds. The shape of the planned town was determined by the rectangular form of the abbey precinct; presumably, Northgate Street would have run immediately to the west of the abbey church before the precinct was extended after the Conquest. Churchgate Street ran due west from the line of the presbytery and the nave of his great new church,

The Sussex town of Battle was planted at the abbey gate in the late eleventh century, when 'the community of Battle Abbey most urgently needed the community of Battle(town)' (Searle,1991: 1). (*Historic England*)

North
Gate

River Lark

N

Brackland

Risby Gate

East Gate

Great Court

The Vineyard
of the Abbey

Abbey Gate

Abbey Gate Street

St.
James
Church

Abbey
Church

Church Gate Street

Watch
House

Guildhall Street

St. Mary's Church

Normans

Meadows

River Lark

West
Gate

St.
Mary's
Square

Haberden

South Gate

| 0 | | 360 metres |
| 0 | | 400 yards |

Plan of the monastic new town at Bury St Edmunds, Suffolk. Work on the planned town, which was designed around the abbey precinct, started at about the time of the Conquest.

and five streets were laid out in parallel lines from north to south. At the abbey gates, Angel Hill became a marketplace and the site of a great medieval fair (see Plate 15). The Great or Butter Market at the north-west corner of the new town was soon encroached upon by Moyses Hall, whose first floor provided domestic accommodation above a vaulted undercroft that was used for commercial and other functions. The pre-Conquest town to the south, above the meadows alongside the River Lark, was partly destroyed by the new abbey, which developed into one of the six greatest Benedictine foundations in England.[18]

At Battle Abbey, soon after its foundation, William the Conqueror had granted the monks a Sunday market, and went on to found one of the earliest post-Conquest new towns. The *Abbey Chronicle*, compiled a century later, records:

> A goodly number of men were brought hither out of neighbouring counties, some even from foreign countries. And to each of these the brethren who managed the building allotted a dwelling-place of certain dimensions around the circuit of the abbey; and these still remain as they were apportioned, with their customary rent or service.

There follows a list of 115 houses: sixty-five on one side of the main street leading north from the abbey gate, twenty-one on the other side, five houses to the east of St Mary's Church (1107–24), ten more beyond the church and another fourteen facing the church. The rent was 7*d.* for each house. The town's occupants included four shoemakers, three cooks, two bakers, two carpenters, two clerks, a weaver, a goldsmith and a bell-caster. About a quarter of the inhabitants had non-English names and were probably French migrants.

At Evesham (Worcestershire), Edward the Confessor granted the abbey a market in 1055, almost certainly represented by a large, open space called Merstow Green, outside the main west gate of the abbey precinct. A 'new borough' was named in a late-twelfth-century cartulary and this is represented by an irregular, but clearly distinguishable, planned grid of streets to the north of the precinct. Abbot Reginald (1130–49) established a new gate through the precinct wall on this side and it seems probable that he was responsible for laying out a new marketplace here.[19]

The Domesday Book mentions ten traders dwelling outside the gate at Abingdon Abbey. Bond has pointed out that a conspicuous feature of Abingdon's town plan is that the marketplace, believed to be eleventh-century, and roads feeding into it are clearly superimposed over an earlier pattern of roads aligned upon the older minster church of St Helen's at the southern end of the town.[20] The town at Glastonbury has remarkably similar characteristics.

In addition to developing settlements outside their own gates, after the Conquest, Benedictine monasteries founded new market towns on their outlying estates. These often lay at the interface of contrasting landscapes and were thus able to develop new markets at the junction between different economies. For example, in the case of the Cotswolds, between vale arable and wold pastoral. Several successful wool towns, with distinctive planned forms, were founded on the extensive monastic estates found in the Cotswolds. Evesham Abbey held a

The site of the great abbey of Abingdon, Oxfordshire, lies in a small park in the centre of the photograph. The line of the abbey precinct can clearly be seen in the right-angled road which runs to the north and west of the abbey. (*Google Earth*)

large estate at Maugersbury, which included a hill fort skirted by a Roman road. There was a pre-Conquest church sited within the hill fort, known as Edwardstow; Henry I granted Abbot Robert a weekly Thursday market here in 1107–8. At about the same time, the tiny parish of Stow was carved out of Maugersbury in order to create the new town of Stow-on-the-Wold within the former hill fort.[21] Stow later became one of the most successful wool towns in the Cotswolds

Pershore Abbey was granted a market at Broadway (Worcestershire) towards the end of the twelfth century and established a planned borough here soon after. The town, which sits at the foot of the northern scarp slope of the Cotswolds, has a distinctive wide, open high street leading on to a triangular marketplace. There are the remains of numerous burgage plots offset from both market and high street. Broadway developed as a particularly prosperous town based on the flourishing wool trade in the later Middle Ages.

There were several other successful monastic foundations in the region that enjoyed a similar degree of success at the same time. The town and market at Northleach, just 12km to the south-west of Stow, was developed by the cathedral priory of Gloucester, but details of its market and burgesses only appear for the first time in the early thirteenth century. Similarly, the market town at Moreton-

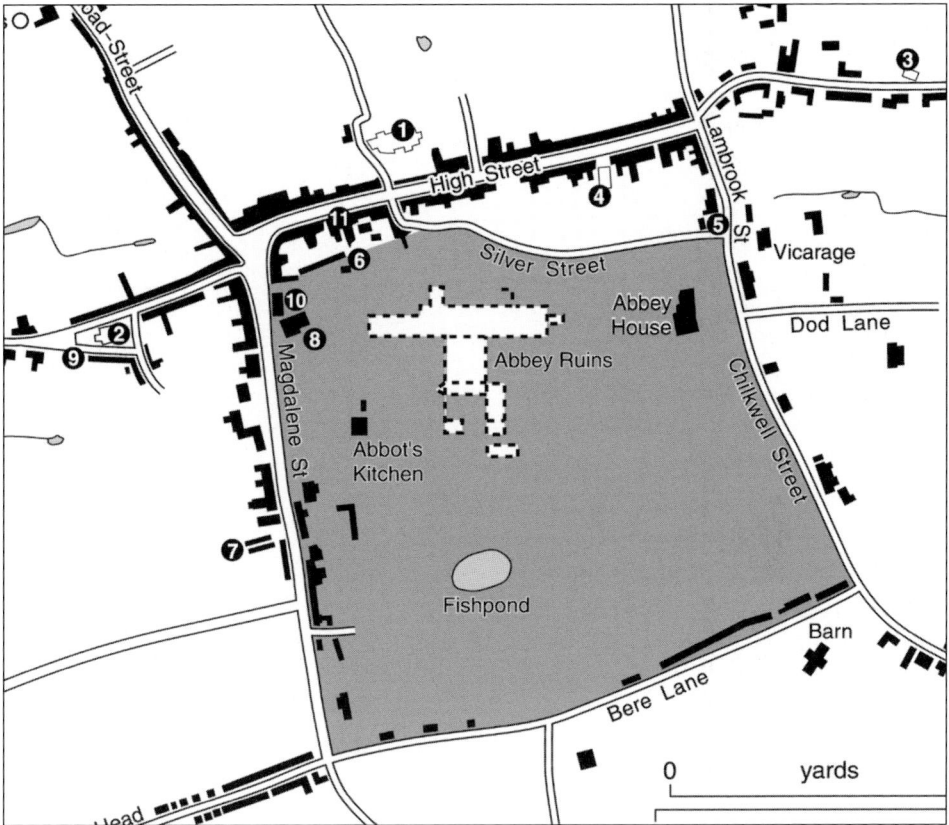

Plan of Glastonbury, Somerset, showing how the abbey has dictated the town topography. (*VCH Somerset, 2006*)

in-Marsh appears to have been laid out in the thirteenth century by Westminster Abbey. The Abbaye aux Dames in Caen was given an estate at Minchinhampton after the Conquest and was probably involved in the establishment of a market town in the late twelfth century, as indicated by its characteristic triangular marketplace and regular burgage plots.

The Landscape of Anglo-Norman Monasticism

In addition to those abbey churches that survived and the majestic ruins of many monasteries, the English countryside contains a wealth of monastic earthworks marking the sites of former churches, claustral buildings, gatehouses, fish and mill ponds, precinct boundaries and parks. Beyond the monastic precinct there was often a home grange or farm court with a great barn, granary, cattle sheds, sheepcote, stabling and perhaps a dovecote. Few of these landscape features can be claimed as exclusively Norman, as monasteries continued to develop right up to the time of the Dissolution.

The earthworks of Sawtry Abbey, Huntingdonshire, are all that survive of a Cistercian house founded by Simon II de Senlis in 1147. The outline of the abbey church and cloisters can be seen clearly at the centre of the photograph. (*Google Earth*)

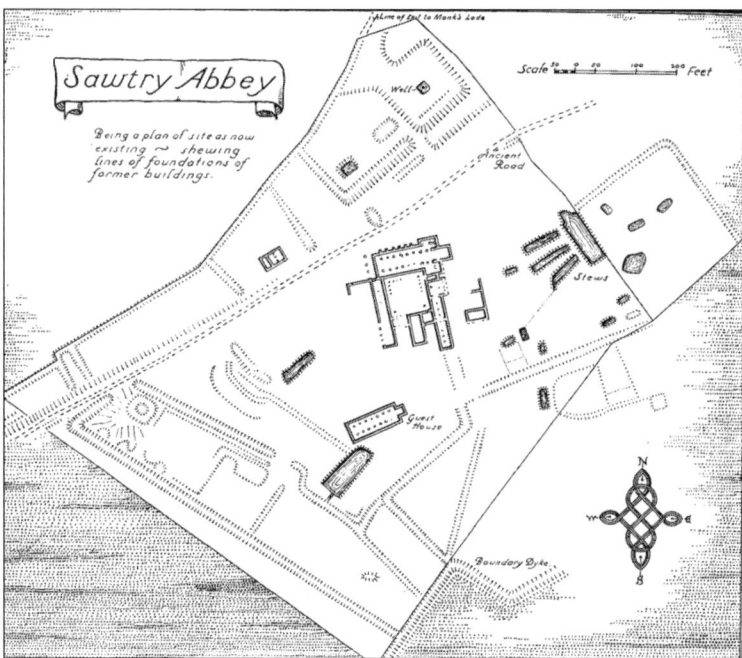

Survey of the earthworks of Sawtry Abbey. The foundation charter stipulated that the abbey should be isolated within a precinct defined by ditches, such as that in the south-west corner of the plan. (*RCHME, 1926: 230*)

Would the floodgates of monasticism have opened so wide in an Anglo-Scandinavian England after 1066? The answer is probably not. The Normans can claim to have provided the impetus that dramatically increased the range of monastic orders and the number of institutions from 52 in 1066 to over 600 by 1200. The cultural affinities between the Anglo-Norman ruling classes and the French homelands from whence the majority of the monastic institutions originated meant that there was an easy transition from mainland Europe to England. The radical redistribution of land after 1066 provided fertile ground for the spread of monasticism. The Conquest resulted in the concentration both of land and of wealth within the hands of a small group of Normans. Overnight it had turned many of them from being local manorial lords into great magnates with a considerable surplus to their accustomed requirements of wealth and land. Traditionally and diplomatically pious by nature, they spent a percentage of this surplus on the endowment of churches and cathedrals, and some of the surplus land, most frequently that which was of marginal agricultural value at the time of endowment, was painlessly given to the newly founded monasteries in order to guarantee a place in heaven.

Chapter 9

Woodland, Forest and Park

Those grey old men of Moccas Park, those grey, gnarled, low-browed, knock-kneed, bowed, bent, huge, strange, long-armed, deformed, hunched-backed oak men that stand waiting and watching century after century, biding God's time with both feet in the grave yet tiring down and seeing out generation after generation.

(Francis Kilvert, Moccas Park,
Herefordshire, 22 April 1876)[1]

How much woodland was there in eleventh-century England? The conventional interpretation of woodland in England recorded in the Domesday Book is that it reflects a countryside that was still fairly heavily wooded. It was recognized that this woodland was not necessarily uncleared virgin forest but vegetation that had naturally reoccupied land that had been managed during the Roman era. Rackham argued that far from being

An ancient oak in Moccas Park, Herefordshire. There has been a park here since at least the thirteenth century, but some of the trees may be older. (*naturebfib*)

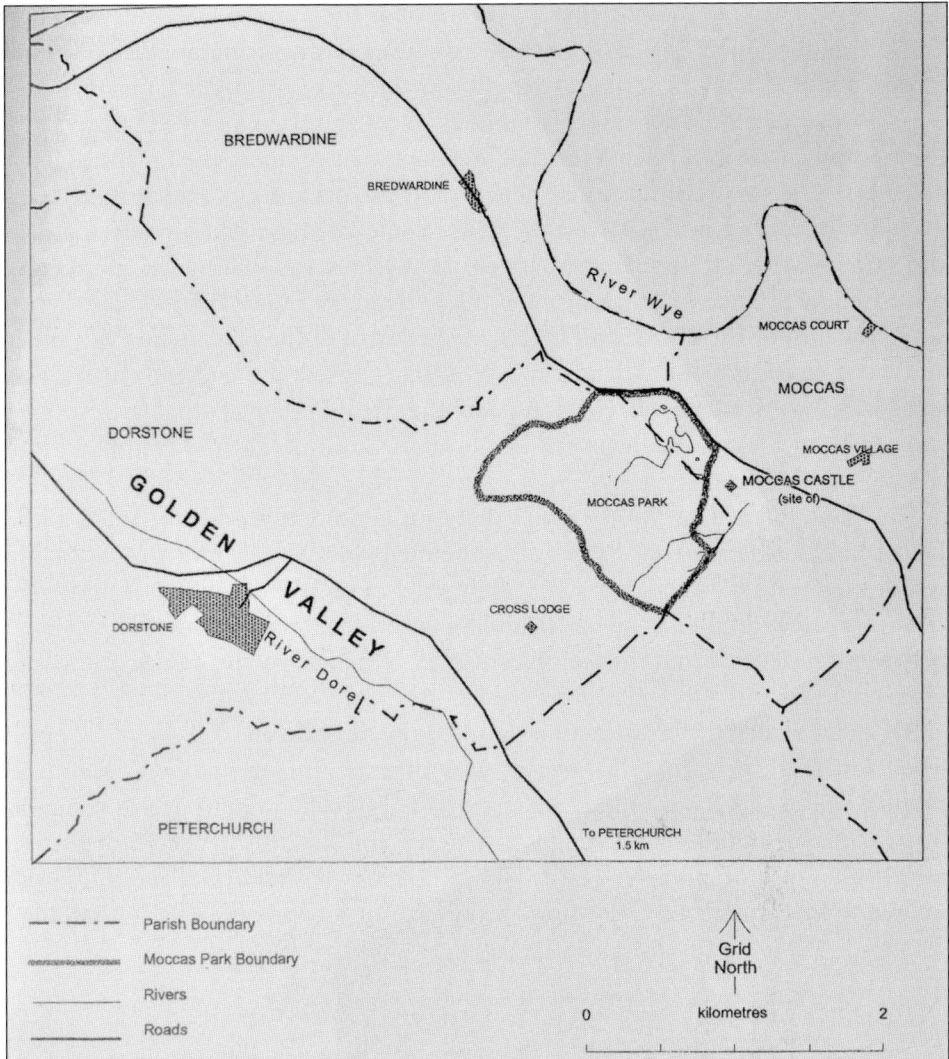

Plan showing the location of Moccas Park in relation to the site of Moccas Castle. The castle is first recorded in 1294 but was probably built *c*.1100 by the de Fresne family, and it seems likely that the park was created soon after that. Alternatively, it could have been the work of the border baron, Barnard de Neufmarche (*d.c.*1125). (*Harding and Wall, 2000: 42-3*)

heavily wooded, England was relatively open in 1086, and that perhaps no more than 15 per cent of the countryside carried a woodland cover. Warwickshire, Worcestershire and Staffordshire had more woodland than the national average, while only about 7 per cent of Huntingdonshire was under woodland and Lincolnshire had just 3.5 per cent. By 1066, apart from on the steepest slopes and in northern England, there was little woodland left that was not managed in some way.

Different forms of measurement were used for each of the Domesday circuits as the commissioners variously recorded wood in terms of the number of swine it would support, or in terms of length and breadth, or leagues, furlongs and perches, or in acres. There were a number of other variants and idiosyncrasies, for example, in terms of wood for fuel, for the repair of houses or for the making of fences. The survey also records denes, or swine pastures, of which there were over fifty recorded in the Weald of Kent. Some of these had already fostered the development of permanent hamlets or villages by 1086; such pioneering settlement was allowed in return for dues, monetary fines, heriots and rents, while the lord of the manor still maintained control of the exploitation of timber and wood in these areas. A landscape of assart (cleared of woodland) fields with smaller areas of woodland characterized the Weald, representing an evolving process of enclosure, which started in the later Saxon period and continued into the thirteenth century.

Woodland formed part of the lord's demesne and is extensively recorded in the Domesday Book and about half of all settlements in 1086 are recorded as having woodland. Areas of woodland were often sited close to manor houses and were relatively stable elements in the landscape after their boundaries were defined between the eleventh and thirteenth centuries. This was partly because they were often enclosed with large perimeter banks.

Rackham argued that a distinction should be made between *silva minuta*, coppice woodland that was properly farmed, and *silva pastilis* or *pascualis*, woodland pasture where there was limited management. Typically, wood-pasture common was grassland or heather scattered with trees and bushes. It provided grazing for a wide range of animals – cattle, sheep, horses, pigs and even geese – whose numbers were restricted according to the size of an individual's landholding.[2]

Earthwork of a medieval park boundary at Slindon Park, near Arundel, Sussex. The park belonged to the archbishops of Canterbury, who had a hunting lodge here from the early twelfth century. (*National Trust*)

In some counties, such as Derbyshire, woodland pasture occupied a quarter of the land area, but in upland Lincolnshire it was only 2 per cent.

Woodland pasture was found in open forest glades and deer parks in particular, where trees were pollarded to produce crops of wood, out of reach of deer and other grazing animals. Coppicing, the most widespread form of woodland management, required trees to be cut to ground level at regular intervals. The extensive communal wood pasture recorded in the Domesday Book diminished during the twelfth and thirteenth centuries. Population pressure led to an expansion of arable, and non-arable land tended to be defined more precisely. Overgrazing turned some areas into heathland or open pasture while other areas were turned over to dedicated coppice wood, and others were taken over for deer parks or had been assarted for arable cultivation. Domesday may be hinting that this process was already under way; for example, in Norfolk the number of swine that could be fed on woodland fell by half in 35 vills between 1066 and 1086, including North Elmham where they fell from 1,000 swine to 500. It is possible that the reductions reflect the enclosure of some woodland for coppice management, thus limiting the area available for pannage. Alternatively, these changes may have been caused by undermanagement or unrestrained felling as a direct consequence of the disruption brought about by the Conquest and its aftermath.[3]

It has been plausibly argued that what is known as 'ancient woodland' actually comes into existence between the eleventh and thirteenth centuries with the stricter demarcation and management of woodland landscapes.[4] The creation of dedicated coppice woods and deer parks was accompanied by the enclosure of other woodland by manorial lords, as the overall area of woodland diminished. From this period onwards until the nineteenth century, virtually all woodland was carefully managed. Furthermore, the measures the Normans introduced relating to hunting landscapes resulted in the partial survival of ancient woodland landscapes, rich in diversity. The concept of the Normans as unwitting agents of conservation and biodiversity is a difficult one to swallow, but the Norman regulation of forest, chase and park, in order to monopolize the king's and lords' hunting rights, inadvertently initiated a process of conservation from which countrysides rich in 'vert and venison' have survived.

Typically, oak and ash trees were found in medieval woodland pasture, where they grew in stands with coppice underwood of alder, beech and maple. This combination was particularly valuable in providing winter food and shelter for the fallow deer which, having been introduced from warmer environments, would not have survived the English winter without such protection. Norman management of forest and park created an arboreal culture that has led to the survival of many ancient trees; for example, medieval deer parks were by far the most important land use associated with ancient and veteran oaks in England. Some 35 per cent of oaks with a girth of 6m are associated with medieval deer parks, and twenty of the twenty-three most important sites for ancient oaks originally lay in deer parks.[5] Very few oak trees alive today date from the Norman period, but within the context of ancient forest and deer park, oaks have germinated, grown and died in a continuing cycle. Thus, this continuum will have operated on a site for longer than the oldest oaks now present, and is of critical importance for biodiversity. Ancient trees, and particularly oaks, collectively support greater diversity, in the form of fungi, lichens and invertebrates, than any other type of habitat in Europe.[6]

Oak trees in woodland pasture were particularly important for pannage; tame pigs were fed on acorns in the autumn before being slaughtered and their meat salted. Pedunculate oak (*quercus robur*) was the most suitable tree for pigs because it produced a superior crop of acorns to the sessile oak (*quercus petraea*). Swine herds could be large; the Domesday entry for Luton, Bedfordshire, records two woods that could feed a total of 2,050 pigs, while in the heavily wooded county of Essex there were many vills with wood for 1,000 swine. In parts of northern England and the Weald of Kent and Sussex, where woodland was extensive, pig-keeping was the primary form of farming. In the foundation charter of Lessay Abbey (1056) in Normandy, it is recorded that the monks were permitted 'to have pasture for all their animals and all their pigs, as well as pasture for the animals of the servants who take care of the monks' herds. ... The monks shall have the right to freely graze one hundred pigs from Martinmas [11 November] to Lent.'[7] This indicates that pigs were fed in wood pastures, both during the autumn mast season when acorns were available and at other times as grazing fields.[8]

One of the ancient oaks in woodland pasture in Savernake Forest, Wiltshire. It has been estimated that at least three trees in the forest may have originated before the Norman Conquest. (*Lennon, 2014: 234*)

The Normans made one monumental and lasting change to English woodland – in the way that hunting landscapes were managed. They created the royal forest – an extreme form of landscape privatization, governed by its own laws. Forests consisted of large areas of land over which the Crown had a monopoly of hunting rights, alongside which they developed the private deer park as an important seigneurial symbol of status.

The Evolution of the Forest

References to forest (*foresta*), as opposed to woodland, first appear under seventh-century Frankish Merovingian rulers. In 648 the Ardennes region was defined as forest and characterized as a vast solitude and home to wild animals. The Merovingian forest appears to have derived from the Roman *saltus*, which covered areas that were uncultivated and lordless and consequently directly subject to the Roman emperor.[9] There is little evidence that the Merovingian forests were intended for hunting, but in the eighth-century *Life of St Columbanus*, Duke Gunzo complains that, in the kingdom of the Franks, Christian hermits settling in the forest were disturbing the royal hunting. This is one of the earliest references to forest hunting as a royal prerogative.[10]

Under the Carolingian kings, ideas relating to royal forests and hunting crystalised and were adopted by Norman dukes; thus many of the features of the post-Conquest forests in England were present in Carolingian law. In 768, Pippin III granted to the monastery of Saint-Denis the imperial forest of Yvelines, with defined boundaries. The grant incorporated rights over serfs living in the forest, over water (for fishing), over pastures and over wild beasts, and also included command of the forest officials (*forestarii*) and their services. Imperial hunting rights in forests were firmly upheld and fines were imposed on those illicitly catching wild animals there. Clearance and settlement within the forest were strictly controlled, and charges were imposed for animals driven into the forest to feed on acorns and beechmast, except where this was prohibited completely. No one was allowed to release dogs from their leashes in the forest. (See Plate 16)

The Carolingian emperor's seat at Aachen lay at the heart of an imperial estate of which forests formed a major part, and the ritual of the hunt was employed to reinforce royal displays of power. The relationship between imperial palace and forest established a close configuration that was repeated later in England between royal castle or palace and forest. Hunts were often preceded by feasts and processions in which the king's authority over his court and submissive subjects was demonstrated.[11] Subsequently, hunting and its symbolism were extremely important in courtly circles throughout the Middle Ages. The forest was also an important source of revenue for the palace; the *Capitulare de Villis* makes it clear that it was the stewards of the royal vills who were responsible for managing the cleared and woodland parts of the forest, caring for the game and collecting the appropriate royal dues, principally those payable for the pasturing of pigs.

In the region that became Normandy during the Carolingian era, the forest of Jumièges appears as *Saltus Gemmeticensis*, and on the opposite bank of the Seine *Saltus Arelaunensis* the forest of Brotonne. During the twelfth century, when Brotonne was in the hands of the Earl of Leicester, the forest brought in over £100 revenue annually.[12] In eleventh-century Normandy, the duke, counts and lesser lords could all hold forest rights of grazing, hunting and wood collection. Pre-Conquest forests in Normandy appear to have been 'areas of wide-ranging resource management under the authority of various nobles and often controlled by foresters'.[13] One significant difference between Norman ducal forests and England's royal forests was that in Normandy the forests were, broadly speaking, ducal demesne, that is, land belonging to the duke, while in England a great deal of non-royal land was under forest law.

The Anglo-Norman Forest and Chase

Although elements of forest law were present in England before the Conquest, it is generally accepted that the Norman kings introduced forests and forest laws into England. Initially, these gave the Crown sole authority over designated forest areas. In Saxon England, hunting for wild boar, hares and deer was a popular pastime for the Crown and nobility, but hunting rights were not a function of kingship. They were a prerogative of landownership, and while pre-Conquest kings had enjoyed the right to hunt freely on their own lands, this was true of any landholder. A forged twelfth-century document attributed the forest laws to the Anglo-Danish king Cnut, and was used to imply their respectable antiquity, but the Saxons had no word for forest, although the concept of the king's wood was not a new one. Kingswood in the Weald of Kent was so called from the mid-Saxon period and specific areas such as Woodstock Chase in Oxfordshire were closely associated with the hunting activities of the Saxon monarchy.

Within the demarcated royal forest, the king and his kinsmen had the right to hunt game, regardless of private landownership. The creation of royal forests represented the symbolic privatization and taming of the wild landscape for the king and his courtiers. Such a demarcated area of wilderness represented 'a separate and privileged world, governed by its own laws, and providing delight and recreation to the court'.[14] Forests normally covered vast areas incorporating land that did not for other purposes belong to the king or noble. Unlike deer parks, forests and chases were not enclosed by a fence or wall. Some forests were demarcated by natural features such as rivers and streams, and occasionally wide ditches can be identified on the ground. The regulated nature of the royal hunt, with its own distinctive ceremonial and symbolism, required extensive managed

Boar hunting from a ninth-century Salzburg calendar. (*Goldberg, 2020: 145*)

landscapes that were protected under law. The forest laws were quite separate from the common law and restricted a whole range of activities, granting the king exclusive and extensive powers within the designated areas. Only the Norman kings at the very height of their authority could have imposed and maintained a system such as this and thus the forest must be seen very much as a phenomenon of Norman England.

Up until the Conquest, wild animals were *res nullius*, nobody's property; afterwards, all game within prescribed forest areas belonged to the king. Forest law gave the Crown the right of 'free chase', that is, the exclusive right to hunt all wild animals in the forest. Protected beasts of the chase, in addition to red, roe and fallow deer, included the hare, fox, marten, wild boar and wolf. The laws also protected game birds such as pheasant and partridge as well as *vert*, that is, the greenery that sustained the forest animals. Forest laws were enforced by royal officials and cases were heard at forest courts. The forest was the most intensively governed and closely managed component of the king's realm.

Forests also had an important material role in supporting the Crown and its itinerant court. Early medieval kings and their courts consumed large quantities of venison and other game and were clearly prepared to devote much of their territory to its protection. An examination of royal itineraries demonstrates that one of the main concerns of the Crown was to remain close to royal forests. From the middle of the twelfth century, the Pipe Rolls contain references to large quantities of venison killed, the preservation of meat by salting and its transportation; for example, in 1210, King John hired a ship to transport venison from Torksey (Lincolnshire) to York, for the benefit of the court. Live animals were also moved around the country, either to provide guaranteed hunting success for the king and court or as gifts to stock or restock his barons' deer parks.

One of the persistent accusations levelled against Norman kings, both by contemporary chroniclers and by later historians, was that they imposed a draconian system of forest law over much of England. The *Anglo-Saxon Chronicle* for 1087 complains that: 'The King, William, set up great protection for deer and legislated to that intent that who so ever should slay hart or hind should be blinded … . He loved the high deer as if he were their father.' It is generally agreed that the suffering imposed on the English by the imposition of forest law has been somewhat exaggerated. Twelfth-century chroniclers declared that in creating the New Forest, William had reduced a flourishing district to a wasteland by the wholesale destruction of villages and churches. The Domesday Book record of 'waste' seems to confirm this description, and the perception that the creation of the New Forest led to mass evictions seems to have been confirmed by John of Worcester, writing about 1100:

> In old times past … that area fruitfully abounded with people … and with churches, but on King William the Elder's command, men were expelled, homes cast down, churches destroyed, and the land was made habitable only for wild animals.

Darby recognized that this scale of devastation was unlikely, given that the greater part of the forest area lay on infertile sands and gravels, which could not have supported a flourishing network of settlements.[15] It has been pointed out that land in the forests no longer paid geld and that references to 'waste', in this context, meant that the Domesday commissioners were not interested in making the usual record.[16] This does not mean that the Normans did not destroy settlements in the interests of hunting, and there are several references to a manor being placed *in foresta* or *in foresta regis*, followed by its disappearance from the record. In Staffordshire, the lost settlements of *Haswic* (Ashwood) (assessed at eight ploughs), Chasewood (assessed at two ploughs) and 'Cippemore' were said to be waste, as they had been placed within the forest of Kinver. Both Ashwood and Chasewood are recorded as possessing 'hays', used to corral deer before a hunt.[17] In the New Forest there appears to have been limited depopulation following legal afforestation, but inhabitants were still permitted to exercise commoners' rights. Such rights almost certainly predate the Conquest. However, lords were not allowed to convert their land from pasture into arable, clear land of trees and scrub or make enclosures to exclude game.

When Henry II expanded the area under forest law to cover about one third of England, it clearly was not to meet his hunting requirements. If we rule out straight megalomania, then the most probable explanation is that he saw a financial advantage in his actions. Forests were an important source of revenue in terms of timber and mineral resources, but also through the imposition of multiple 'fines' for the infringement of forest law, many of which appear to have been sanctioned by the Crown. A tenant of land within the forest needed royal permission or supervision for collecting wood or grazing animals there. Those who committed offences against the laws of the forest were penalized, and the laws of the forest had their own particular character. The Pipe Roll of 1130 records forest fines amounting to £1,400 and by 1175, Henry II was able to raise £12,000 from fines and infringements of forest law. Eventually, it was not a response to

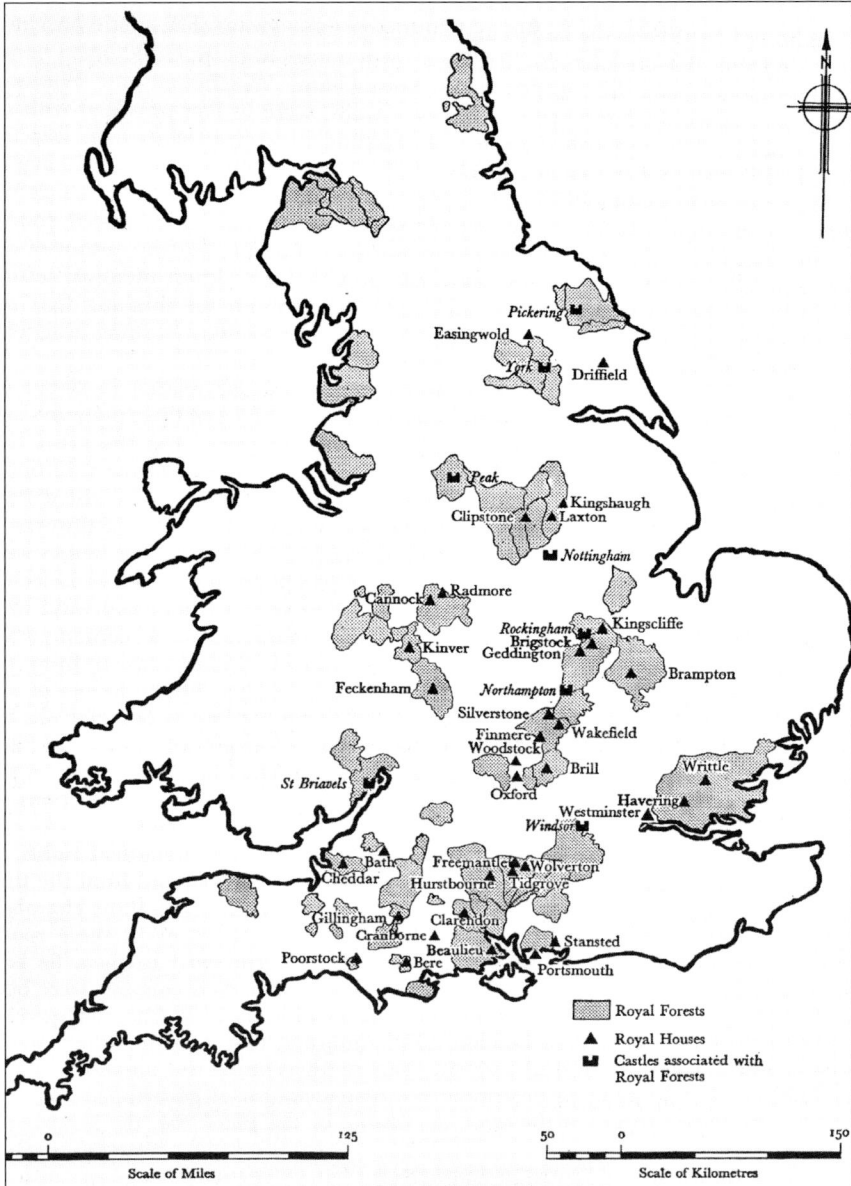

Map of Royal Forests and Royal Houses, *c.*1200. (*Colvin, 1963a: 85*)

the persecution of peasants contravening forest law that brought problems for the Crown, but conflicts of interest between the king and owners of estates within the forest. More frequently than not the king's hunting grounds overlay the lordly demesne of his subjects. 'The competing interests of royal sport and revenue and those of the political elite combined to make the forests a toxic political issue in a way not paralleled in Normandy.'[18]

Royal forest could contain not only woodland, but heath, grassland and wetland, as well as settlements and agriculturally productive land. There were comparatively few forests in the largest concentrations of surviving woodland in England, that is, the Weald, the Chilterns and Arden, and they appeared to be most numerous in moderately wooded counties such as Hampshire, Wiltshire and Shropshire. There were, in addition, mountain and moorland forests, such as Dartmoor, Exmoor, the Pennines and the Lake District, which were almost treeless. Some forests consisted of fenland, such as Kesteven (Lincolnshire) and

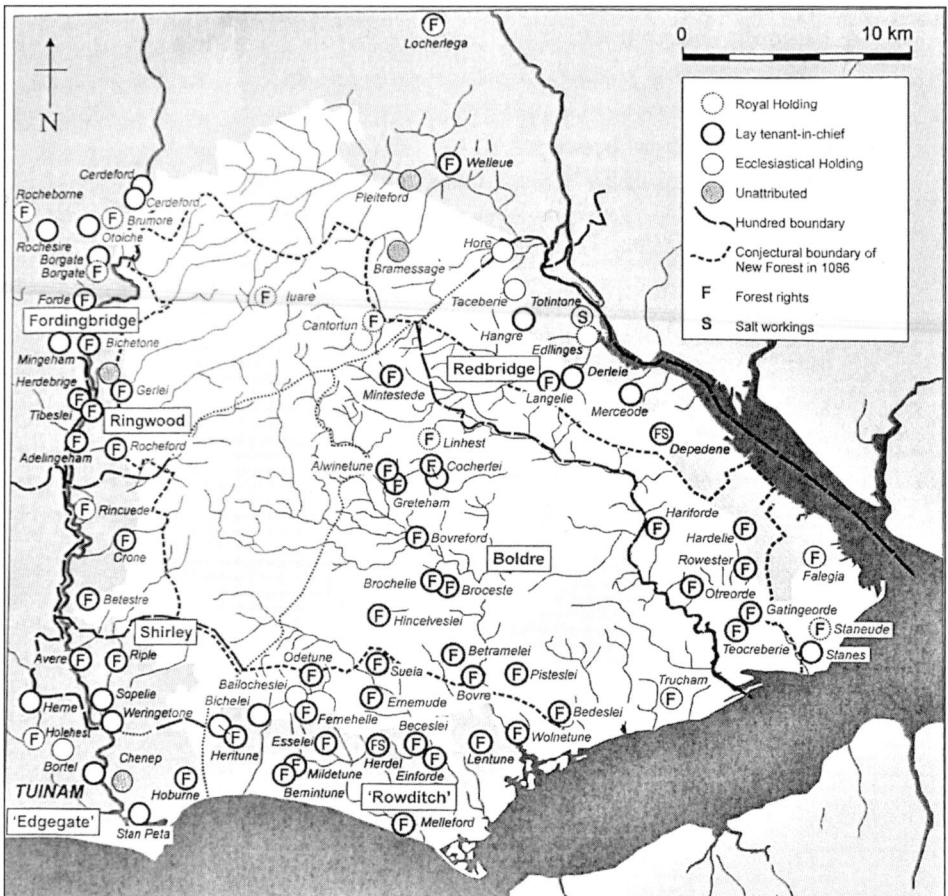

Plan of the New Forest in 1086 showing Domesday holdings and forest rights. (*Cook, 2017: 83*)

Hatfield Chase near Doncaster, while others consisted of heath, like Woolmer (Hampshire) and Rudheath (Cheshire), and still others appear to have consisted largely of arable land in places such as the Wirral (Cheshire) and Corfe (Dorset). Although the choice of forest areas seems to have been somewhat arbitrary, in some cases incorporating whole counties, in general they tended to be based on large Crown-held estates, which often included well-wooded or mountainous areas. Prosperous and densely populated counties such as Norfolk, Suffolk, Hertfordshire and Middlesex had no forest land.

The largest forests were the New Forest, with about 32,000 hectares of heath and woodland, and Sherwood, with about 20,000 hectares of woodland. Several, such as Weybridge (Huntingdonshire) or Hatfield (Essex), had as little as 400 hectares of woodland pasture, while others, such as Chute (Wiltshire), appear to have been scattered patches of land with no identifiable nucleus.

Once a forest had been created, it needed to be administered and managed. In addition to foresters, among those employed were hunters, hawkers, falconers and archers. Within the New Forest there were seven cattle farms (*vaccaria*), each of which was allowed twenty cows and one bull; the tenants were expected to pay a specified amount of cheese to the king each year. Forests were subdivided into

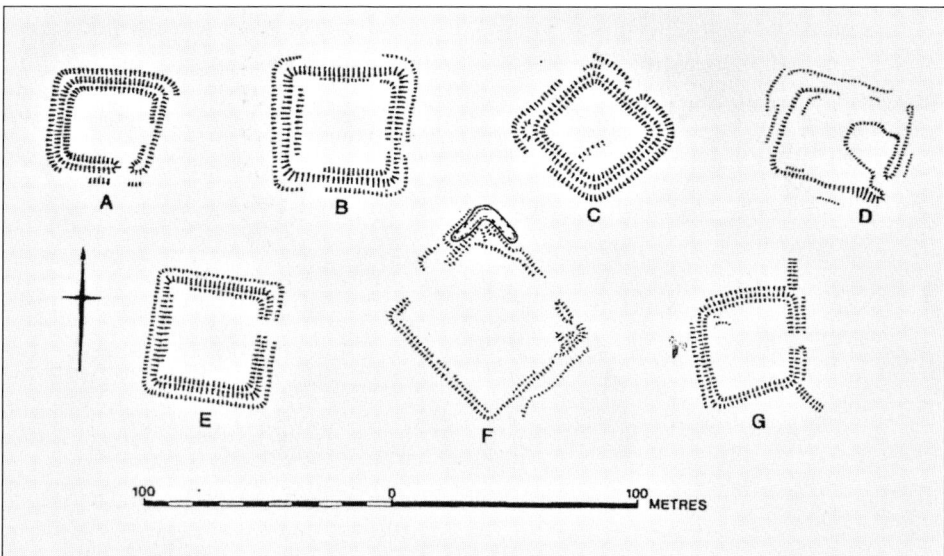

Plans of the earthwork remains of New Forest hunting lodges. Some of these earthworks were mistakenly believed to have been churches belonging to settlements destroyed by William the Conqueror, hence the church names. They are undated but were in use between the twelfth and sixteenth centuries.

A. Church Place, Denny; B. Church Place, Ashurst; C. Church Place, Sloden; D. Boulderwood; E. Studley Castle; F. Queen Bower; G. enclosure at King's Passage, Matley. (*Cook, 2017: 91*)

'walks' or 'bailiwicks' – forest districts in which a keeper had responsibility for the game and the woods. The actual woods were often called coppices. Between coppices were 'ridings' and 'plains', which were open and with extensive zones of grass and scattered trees providing herbage for deer. 'Lawns' were enclosed plots of grassland managed to provide hay and pasture for deer and were normally situated close to the keeper's 'lodge'. Such lodges, which by the thirteenth century were often moated for defence against poachers, were scattered throughout the forest as isolated dwellings.[19] Archaeological evidence for poaching through the analysis of bone evidence has been found at Wakefield, Yorkshire, where an unusual assemblage of whole and young deer strongly suggests illicit activity.[20]

Although the vast majority of forests were under royal control, there were a few in the hands of senior barons. The term 'chase' is inconsistently used to distinguish the forest of a subject from that of the Crown. The forest was the supreme status symbol for the noblest of families, such as the earls of Richmond, and among churchmen only the bishops of Durham and Winchester achieved proprietorial rights. From the beginning of the twelfth century the Bishop of Durham enjoyed unique hunting rights for all the forests between the Tees and the Tyne, with the same weight and legal protection as the king's own New Forest. In the autumn there was an elaborate month-long hunt called the Great Chase in the forests of Upper Weardale, starting with a grand ceremonial procession out of Durham. A number of the bishop's chosen tenants, from across the diocese, provided forest service, normally consisting of forty days in the fawning season and forty days in the rutting season. During the chase itself they were to provide hunting dogs and

Ludgershall Castle, Wiltshire. King John converted an early ringwork castle into a hunting lodge for the nearby Forest of Chute. (*English Heritage*)

Deer house dating from 1767 on the Bishop of Durham's estate at Auckland Park. The bishops were given a deer park here by Henry I in 1109. This ornate structure was designed to entertain the bishop's guests, who watched the deer feeding, continuing the tradition of hunting entertainment which started under the Normans. (*Historic England*)

equipment, typically, two greyhounds, a horse and five ropes each. Additionally, the tenants of Stanhope, in the heart of the forest, were obliged to help construct temporary wooden buildings for the bishop and his retinue. These consisted of a great hall and chapel, kennels, a buttery and butchery, a kitchen and chambers. They would have been erected on the sites of established lodges scattered throughout the forest. Other services listed in the *Boldon Book* (1183), which gives details of the scale and pomp of the Grand Chase, included the provision of litter for ground cover, carriage of goods and transport of venison. This momentous annual event would have served as a testament to the power of the prince-bishops across the palatinate of Durham.[21]

In Cheshire, the forests of Wirral, Delamere, Mondrem and Macclesfield were all in the hands of earls. In the palatine earldom of Chester, five places were said to be in Earl Hugh's Forest, in what became Delamere Forest. To the west, in Atiscross hundred (now in Flintshire), the earl had put all the woods into his forest, whereby the manors were much depreciated. Further west still, he and his tenant, Robert of Rhuddlan, shared between them all the forests that did not belong to any vill in the manor of Rhuddlan.

Deer Parks

Deer parks were part of the landscape of lordship, representing 'powerful symbols of lordly appropriation of the remaining areas of wild land'.[22] (See Plate 17). Although there were some parks for beasts of the chase in existence before 1066, such as those at Holt and Costessey (Norfolk), the deer park in its established form seems to have developed after the Conquest. A number of regular deer parks are known from Normandy from before the Conquest; for example, episcopal deer parks have been identified in Normandy belonging to the Bishop of Coutances at Saint-Ébremond (1060), the Bishop of Avranches at Sainte-Pience (1050) and the Bishop of Bayeux at La Haia de Perchet, Neuilly (1035). The Domesday Book records over 100 *haiae* (hays) or animal enclosures, mainly in the Welsh borders and the West Midlands, many of which must have been in existence before the Conquest. Domesday *haiae* were never located in forests, though they were often associated with lordly woodland. At Corfton (Shropshire) there was a '*haia* for catching roe deer' and several of the Shropshire and Cheshire references appear alongside hawks' eyries; elsewhere, they are often mentioned beside mills and fisheries.[23] At Ongar (Essex) there was a *derhage* recorded in 1045, which emerged after the Conquest as Ongar Great Park.[24] There are also records of 'hays' (hedged enclosures) and leap gates in pre-Conquest charters.

After the Conquest, deer parks in England and Wales were held by the Crown, the nobility, monasteries and bishops, and lesser lords. Deer parks provided an environment for social and leisure activities – 'the supreme status for aristocratic families'.[25] A park differed from other demesne woodland mainly in that it contained deer and other animals of the chase, and was securely fenced. In 1086, 40 deer parks were recorded in England; by 1200 there were several hundred and there were about 3,200 by 1300. Many of the parks that were first documented in the thirteenth century had actually been founded at an earlier date, but only appeared then because the Crown tightened its requirement for lords to buy an imparking licence.

In addition to *haiae*, game parks (*parcus bestiarum silvaticarum*) appear sporadically in almost every county in the Domesday Book, implying that in addition to deer, other large mammals such as boar were also hunted. Three Hertfordshire parks recorded in Domesday 'for woodland beasts' belonged to St Albans Abbey and may also have been pre-Conquest.[26] Although churchmen were discouraged from hunting themselves, monastic and cathedral deer parks were common. Abbot Sampson of Bury St Edmunds (1135–1211) did not hunt or even eat venison, but he created and stocked parks and he and his monks would watch the chase when hunts were set up for visiting guests. His contemporary, the Bishop of Durham, Hugh de Puiset (1153–95), had no such qualms about participating in the chase and was known as an enthusiastic hunter, responsible for building Auckland Castle as a hunting lodge and formalizing the Great Chase.

The two native deer species in Britain before 1066 were the roe and the red deer, neither of which was well suited for keeping in parks. Red deer were always greatly prized, but they did not adapt to being kept in enclosed parks, as they were prodigious jumpers, able to clear 2m-hurdles with ease. Roe deer were notoriously difficult to confine and generally regarded as unsuitable for controlled management within parks. The fallow deer, an exotic species that was not found in Britain before the Conquest, apart from a few imports by the Romans, was particularly well suited to parkland. They were gregarious, adaptable, able to fatten on poor land

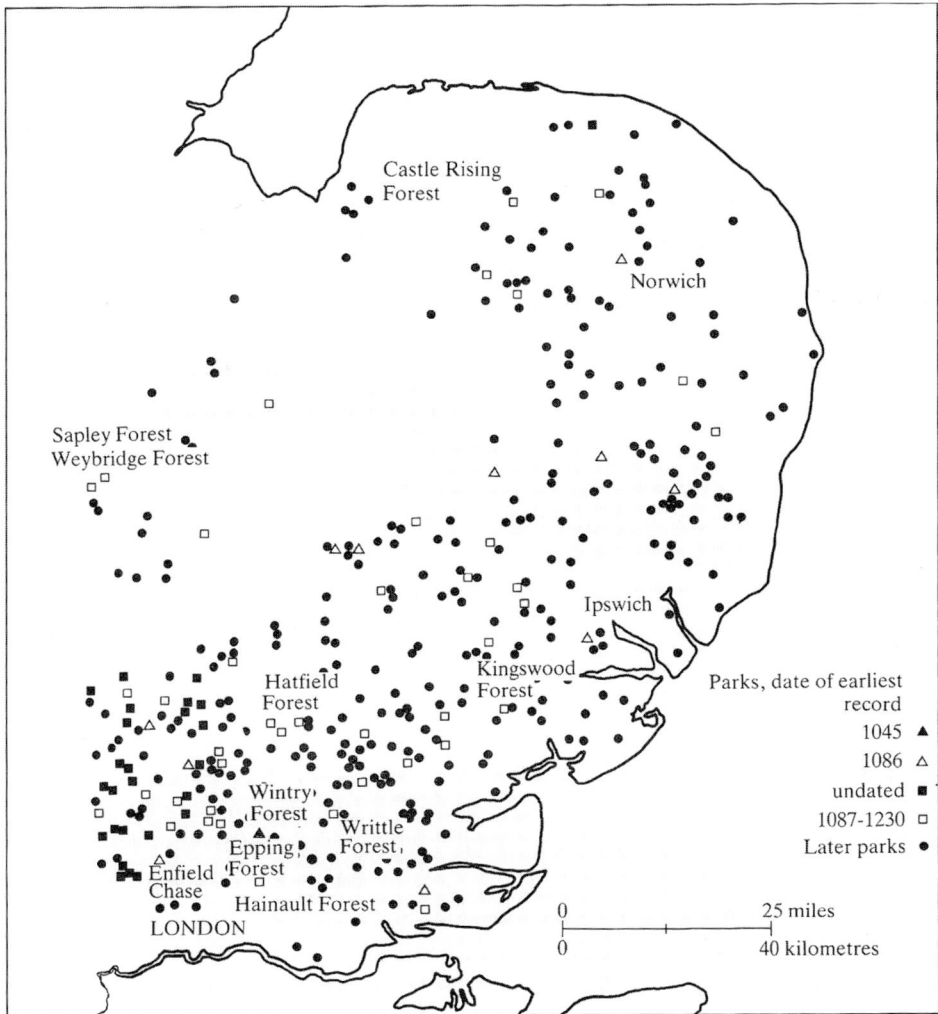

Medieval deer parks and forests in Eastern England.

and less dangerous than red deer in the rutting season; they also produced excellent venison. They were introduced from areas with Norman contacts, either Antolia or the Levant, as a means of producing meat from poor agricultural land. Fallow deer are not mentioned as one of William the Conqueror's favourite animals in the *Anglo-Saxon Chronicle*'s obituary in 1087, and it has been surmised that they were first introduced in the late eleventh or early twelfth century as part of a second phase of park and forest creation. It has recently been argued, based on isotope analysis, that when fallow deer were first reintroduced to England they were kept not for hunting, but as prized exotica.[27] The age profile shows that, in the eleventh and early twelfth centuries, the small number of fallow deer that were in Britain tended to live long lives, possibly in menageries.

It may be significant that the fallow deer was not found in Normandy or elsewhere in north-west Europe until the thirteenth century. Its importance in Norman England was unique in the twelfth century and indicates that the aristocratic culture of the country had developed in a different direction from that of the homeland.[28]

Although medieval parks were intended primarily for the production of venison, they did accommodate other game such as rabbits (from the late twelfth century), pheasants, peafowl, partridges and swans. The first four of these species were non-native animals and were particularly prized because of their rarity. Parks also provided timber for fuel and building and grazing for farm livestock. Cattle, sheep and horses were all grazed within deer parks. The Normans took considerable care to breed and train horses, sometimes in specially designated parks, importing thoroughbreds from Muslim Spain; Duke William reputedly rode one such Spanish horse at Hastings. Horse studs were sometimes established in deer parks, which were prized for their grazing and for the extra protection provided by their boundaries. Several of the greater Norman abbeys founded in forest regions were actively involved in horse-breeding. After the Conquest, a number of English monasteries had horse-breeding programmes for palfreys as well as draft animals. Earthwork remains of stud complexes for mares, foals and stallions have been identified at several sites in Yorkshire, although it is not possible to link these specifically to the Norman era.[29]

To avoid sacrificing prime agricultural land, deer parks were often located on the margins of the manor, frequently on less fertile ground. Of approximately sixty-six medieval parks in Hertfordshire, virtually all were located on high plateaus or valley sides, at remote locations within the manor.[30] Early parks usually consisted of uncompartmented wood pasture and, although they varied greatly in size, typically they were between 40 and 120 hectares. Substantial boundaries were needed to contain the deer, some varieties of which can leap up to 2m vertically or 6m horizontally. The classic form of boundary was a high bank surmounted by a paling fence with a deep, wide ditch on the interior, though stone walls and hedges were also employed. Because of the labour and expense of constructing and maintaining a deer-proof boundary, their ideal shape was circular or oval, maximizing the interior area of pasture while minimizing the length of boundary. The upkeep of the park pale was a constant and considerable expense, and sometimes it was made a customary work or labour service, particularly where tenants enjoyed common rights within the park. The bounds of many of these parks can often be readily reconstructed from the surviving earthworks of park pales, the alignment of roads, property boundaries and parish boundaries as well as place-name evidence. The functions of the great monastic park attached to Fountains Abbey illustrate the variety of uses such enclosures could be put to. It was devoted mainly to timber production, fish ponds, a water supply, a horse stud and a rabbit warren.[31]

Woodstock

There were royal hunting grounds at Woodstock (Oxfordshire) before the Conquest. Ethelred II held a council at Woodstock 'in the land of the Mercians' and there is a reference in the Domesday Book to the extent of the king's demesne forests of Woodstock, Cornbury and Wychwood. It is recorded that Henry I came here on many occasions and that it was 'the favourite seat of his retirement and privacy'. A grant of Abingdon Abbey, which is dated 1110, was signed 'at Woodstock in the park', and according to later accounts it was in this or the following year that Henry I enclosed the park with a stone wall. There are frequent references during the twelfth century to work on the wall and in 1164–5,

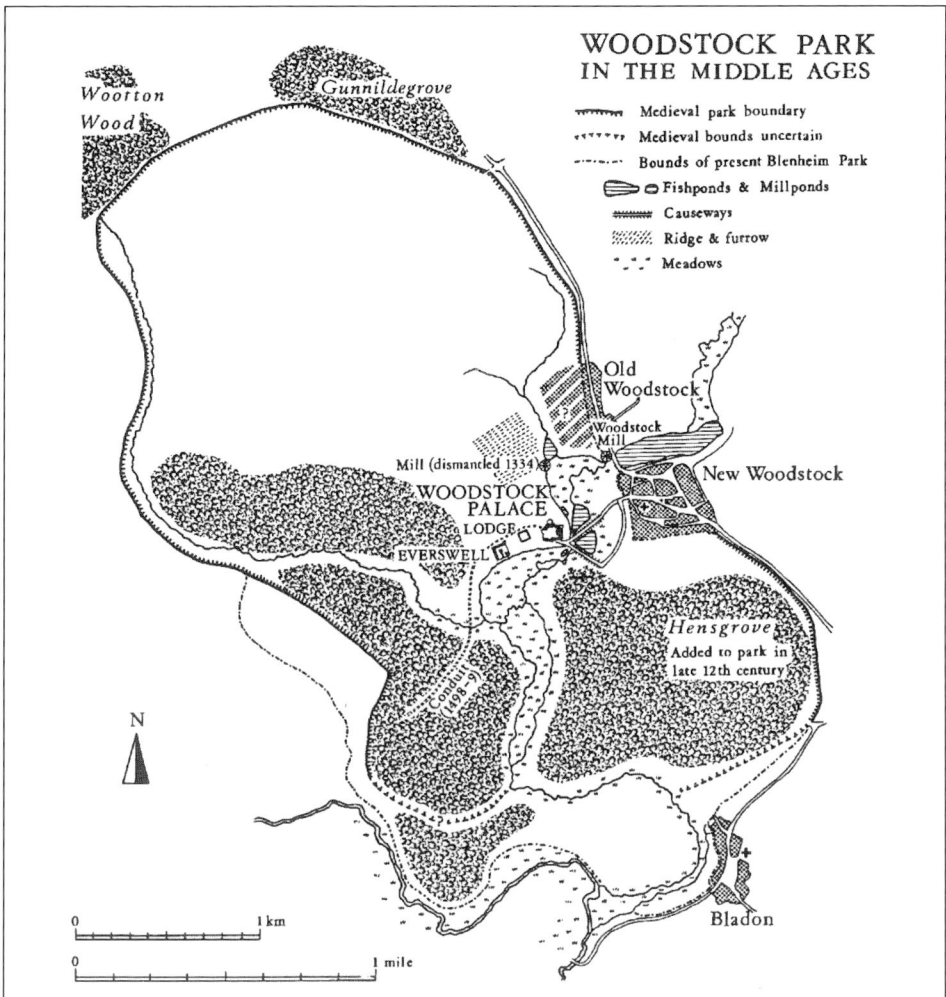

WOODSTOCK PARK
IN THE MIDDLE AGES

- Medieval park boundary
- Medieval bounds uncertain
- Bounds of present Blenheim Park
- Fishponds & Millponds
- Causeways
- Ridge & furrow
- Meadows

Wootton Wood

Gunnildegrove

Old Woodstock

Woodstock Mill

Mill (dismantled 1334)

WOODSTOCK PALACE

LODGE

EVERSWELL

New Woodstock

Hensgrove
Added to park in late 12th century

N

Bladon

0   1 km

0   1 mile

Woodstock Park in the Middle Ages, showing the location of Woodstock Palace. (*Bond and Tiller, 1997: 29*) for example, £30 was spent on its maintenance. Henry of Huntingdon refers to Woodstock as 'a remarkable place which he had made a dwelling-place for men and beasts' and William of Malmesbury elaborated on this by describing 'a park called Woodstock' in which the king kept wild animals, brought from abroad, including a porcupine sent to him by William of Montpellier. Within the park there appears to have been a menagerie of exotic wild animals as well as water gardens, fish ponds and, later, pavilions and it has been argued that one function of these early Norman parks may have been to serve as menageries.[32]

Later, King Henry II visited the manor house of Woodstock 'for love of a certain woman called Rosamund' and created a new town here, probably in the years 1174–6: 'And there was a waste place without the said park and manor and because men lodged too far, the king gave places to diverse men to build hostelries there for the use of the King's men.'[33] It is clear from later documents that Woodstock Park was much more exotic than the average deer park. It had a royal palace, gardens and pavilions, some of which in the Moorish style used

The Fountain Hall at La Zisa, Palermo, a summer hunting palace built for the Norman kings of Sicily in the second half of the twelfth century. The upper frescoes on the wall show hunters with bows shooting at birds in the trees. (*Ariel Fein*)

Rosamund's Well, Everswell, Woodstock Palace, whose original design by Henry II may have been based on Norman Sicilian examples. Henry's daughter Joan was married to King William II of Sicily. (*David C. Woods*)

water as a principal design element. The water gardens were centred around a spring known as Everswell, later called Rosamund's Bower. It has been suggested that the gardens here were inspired by the twelfth-century romance of *Tristan and Isolde*, a version of which was probably written for Henry II. The most likely source of inspiration, however, was Sicily. Henry II's daughter Joan was married to William II of Sicily, where the Norman kings had a series of exotic pavilions built within easy reach of their capital, Palermo. One of these, the Palace of La Zisa, had a central court across which water from a spring ran through a series of basins set in the floor, a design which the Normans had copied from the Muslims.

The Hunt

William of Malmesbury claimed that Edward the Confessor's sole worldly pleasure was his love of birds and hounds, which he inspected daily after mass. Hunting narratives also weave their way through William the Conqueror's life; reputedly, the duke was out hunting when he received the unwelcome news that Harold had been crowned king of England. Hunting and falconry represented both power and pleasure for Norman kings and their nobility. Many royal itineraries were arranged to incorporate hunting and a number of royal castles, such as that at Rockingham in Rockingham Forest, were built with hunting considerations in mind. Certainly, almost all the major royal forests had a castle or palace close at hand, and Norman kings and their immediate successors took advantage of these facilities whenever possible.

Hunting was important in preparing the king's vassals for warfare, by giving them skills and proficiency both in handling horses and in the use of weapons to prepare them for battle. In the Carolingian world, hunting had been the chief form of military training for the nobility. The Crown could also use hunting privileges as a payment or bribe to its followers; for example, in 1088, William Rufus appealed to the English nobles to support him against his brother Robert by offering them free hunting.

Prior to the Conquest, the most common form of hunting technique was the drive, where deer were chased into enclosures called *haiae* and then killed with knives and spears; the whole of the body was taken back to high-status sites such as Cheddar royal palace and Eynsham Abbey. In Saxon England, hunting appears to have been centred on enclosed, wooded spaces, to which the roe deer was well suited and was accordingly the prime target of the pre-Conquest hunt. The introduction of the forest, which extended over a variety of terrain including

Earl Harold riding with hounds and hawks as depicted on the Bayeux Tapestry. Hunting is clearly portrayed here as an aristocratic pursuit.

Red deer stags from the *Utrecht Psalter*. Red deer were not suitable for enclosed parks as they can jump up to 2 m high. They would have been chased over a variety of terrains, running up to speeds of 35 km at a time.

open heath, moor and agricultural land, favoured the red deer; thus, hunting strategies changed after the Conquest.

Relatively few deer parks are large enough to allow for an uncontrolled chase to the kill *par force de chien*, and it is probable that some enclosed parks lying next to heathland or open woodland were used simply to retain deer, who would be released into the open to be pursued by mounted hunters and dogs. Alternatively, the animals could have been lined up and then shot at by a group of hunters holding bows; it has been condescendingly suggested that this activity would have been particularly suitable for women, rather than the hurly-burly of the open chase. It has also been suggested that falconry would have been a more feminine pastime.[34] Various other activities are known to have taken place within medieval parks, such as coursing, the chasing of a single deer or hare along a defined track.

Royal forests and parks were able to provide a regular supply of game for consumption by the itinerant court. Studies of animal–bone assemblages suggest that by the twelfth century the diet of high-status households was increasingly rich in game. Red deer are better represented in early post-Conquest contexts, but the proportion of fallow deer consumed rose rapidly, becoming much more important by the late twelfth century. Venison was regarded as an exclusively aristocratic dish (though deer poaching was widespread) and it assumed the status of a currency, used to reward and to bribe.

The sociological dimension of hunting has been emphasized in recent research. There were rituals associated with those who made the kill and who claimed the finest joints of meat. Great importance was placed on different parts of the deer carcass and the kill was followed by an 'unmaking ceremony'; the body of the animal was broken up and distributed according to status.[35] Later hunting manuals describe how the huntsmen distributed the parts; choice parts such as testicles and tongue were reserved for the king or lord, and the right and left shoulders given respectively to the best hunter and the chief forester. The skeletons of deer found at elite sites are often missing the shoulder and leg bones. A preponderance of hind leg bones has been found at several high-status sites – Sandal Castle, Dudley Castle, Okehampton Castle and Launceston Castle.[36]

By the twelfth century, a wide variety of animals and birds were being eaten by the nobility, including peafowl, pheasants, fallow deer and rabbits. The language of the chase changed and became essentially French in character. For example, 'venison' is derived from the Anglo-Norman *venesoun*, literally, 'the product of hunting'. While the lords consumed the prize portions of hunted animals, the remaining offal or 'umbles' were offered to the hunt servants; thus, the saying 'to eat humble (umble) pie' is derived from the link between the eating of poorer cuts of deer with low status.[37] It has been suggested that the change of diet together with changes in hunting practice would have excluded the English. Combined with forest law, hunting provided the Normans with a means to emphasize their separateness and their Frenchness. By embedding social status and ethnicity in law, landscape and language, hunting represented a powerful statement of Norman identity. It is no accident that 'love of the chase' has become a characteristic symbol frequently attributed to the Normans.[38] Hunting presented an opportunity to demonstrate control over the natural environment only for the elite who could afford to create parks, chaces and forests.

These practices were introduced into England by the Normans and knowledge of these ceremonies and the Norman-French terminology that was attached to them was seen as a mark of nobility. Some historians claim that hunting became symbolic of the French cultural takeover, and the rituals and associated language introduced from France came to represent not only control over the wild, but also over the English.[39] John of Salisbury, writing in the mid-twelfth century, complained of pretentious hunting terminology and warned his readers to be wary when using it, 'because you will be beaten or condemned for ignorance of all good things, if you do not know their *figmenta*'.

In order to service its hunting requirements, the Crown kept large numbers of horses and an even larger number of hunting dogs. The most common were greyhounds that hunted by sight; pack dogs or running hounds that pursued deer by their scent; and lymer dogs and brachets, used to start the hunt by sniffing out prey. There are also references to boarhounds, wolfhounds, foxhounds, setters and Spanish dogs. Detailed information about the make-up of hunting packs only becomes available in the early thirteenth century. We hear that when hunting on 28 December 1213, King John dispersed 438 dogs (273 greyhounds,

King John on horseback in a forest. His pack of hounds pursue a stag, while birds and rabbits are also portrayed. (*BL Cotton Ms Claudius D ii f116*)

King John's House, Tollard Royal, on Cranborne Chase, Wiltshire, which traditionally has been known as a royal hunting lodge. General Pitt Rivers investigated the manor house, on whose estate it lay in 1899, demonstrating that parts of it at least dated to the twelfth century. For much of the Middle Ages, Cranborne Chase was in the hands of the earls of Gloucester.

158 pack dogs and 7 unspecified) in three packs through the countryside. With so many animals the king required a large retinue of huntsmen: eleven named huntsmen, fifty-six dog handlers plus fifteen other helpers.[40] Despite the Norman kings' much heralded love of the chase, references to the king hunting in person are surprisingly rare, but there is much more information about King John than his predecessors and it is clear that he was a prolific hunter. For example, in early December 1205, John and his huntsmen took one hundred fallow deer and seventeen feral pigs in the king's park at Havering (Essex). Even during the most troubled episodes of his reign he took time off to hunt. There are a number of locations which claim to have been hunting lodges associated with John, including Kings Clipstone (Nottinghamshire) and Tollard Royal (Wiltshire).

Some animals, such as the wolf, otter and fox, were hunted largely because they were considered 'noxious animals', although their pelts were of some value. The abundance of wolves in pre-Conquest England is confirmed by the Saxon name for January – 'Wolf Month'; there was no close season for hunting vermin and the wolf provided a popular prey in winter months in Norman England, when beasts of the chase were out of bounds. Wolves were generally trapped, but Henry I kept a dedicated wolf hunt, consisting of wolf huntsmen, eight greyhounds and twenty-four racing dogs; £6 a year was set aside for buying horses and 20d. a day for the huntsmen's clothes.[41] Outside royal forests and parks there was no restriction on the hunting of wolves and William the Conqueror granted the lordship of Redesdale (Northumberland) to Robert de Umfraville on the specific condition that he defended the land from enemies and wolves.

Falconry and hawking were as popular with the nobility as hunting with hounds because they could take place in a wider variety of landscapes, but were most closely associated with rivers, where large wading birds, such as cranes and herons, were a favoured prey. The second scene of the Bayeux Tapestry shows Earl Harold riding to Bosham, accompanied by hunting hounds and hawks. This picture clearly identified Harold as a wealthy noble, able to afford the costly pastime of gamehawking. The Domesday Book lists six of William the Conqueror's hawkers in East Anglia and the South East, as well as hawk eyries in eight counties. Hunting hawks were specially bred and trained for royalty and the aristocracy; the *Boldon Book* (1183) records hawk eyries in the bailiwick of Ralph the Crafty, at Frosterley on the eastern edge of the Bishop of Durham's forest of Weardale. Winchester, close to the New Forest, was an important centre for hunting birds and Henry II built a mews extension, the New Close, for hawks, falcons and sparrowhawks and their keepers. In Norman England at least twelve royal residences had mews for hunting birds.[42] In 1179, Henry II acquired ninety-six hawks and six gerfalcons (the great northern falcon) and spent £35 6s. 8d. on purchasing miscellaneous hunting birds, while King John favoured gerfalcons, peregrine falcons and goshawks, all expensive birds of prey, many of which were imported from Iceland and Norway. Such birds were sold at the great fairs of eastern England – King's Lynn, Yarmouth and Boston.

October's task of hawking, from an eleventh-century calendar. (*BL Cotton MS Julius A VI f7r*)

During the Norman period, levels of game-bird consumption on elite sites increased dramatically. The species of bird also changed with an increase in the representation of peafowl, pheasants and domestic doves in animal-bone assemblages. It appears that all of these birds were introduced into England by the Normans. Animal bones from elite sites show that the nobility consumed a wide range of wild birds, implying that a wide variety of species were hunted.[43]

Although the forest hunting culture matured in England after 1066, the Crown and barons such as the earls of Leicester continued their hunting interests in Normandy. The first earl, Robert de Beaumont (*c*.1045–1118), was probably the greatest owner of forest in England and Normandy after the king, and was part of the hunting party in the New Forest when William II was killed. Henry II had hunting lodges and palatial dwellings near his Norman ducal forests and John sent

Hunting with different kinds of net was common. This ninth-century image from the *Stuttgart Psalter* shows huntsmen using a purse net, which tightened with retractable cords. (*Goldberg, 2020: 136*)

fallow deer and other game from England to restock his parks in Normandy.[44] Hunting birds from Winchester were frequently shipped to Normandy during Henry's reign, and when the king crossed the Channel to France, he was accompanied by caged hawks and falcons.

Landscape evidence for hunting endures in place names and field monuments, although it is difficult to distinguish specific Norman forest landscape features from later medieval elements. Funnel-shaped enclosures used for corralling animals are a feature of forests such as Neroche and Hatfield. Some sections of forest were fenced and gated; others were marked by signs cut into trees. The complex nature of forest demarcation has shown that seasonal as well as permanent barriers were used.[45] Clarendon Park, Wiltshire, was divided up into more than a dozen compartments with lodges sited around its perimeter and a royal hunting lodge, later a palace, at its centre. There would also have been stables, kennels and accommodation for the large retinue of helpers required for a royal hunt.

Chapter 10

Landscape and Empire: The Impact of the Roman World

Imitation of Rome and the construction of grand buildings were an expression of moral superiority and a higher civilization.[1]

William the Conqueror and his Norman successors held power on a grand scale. The Crown operated a monopoly of coinage, controlled economic and mercantile activity, was the paramount lawmaker in the realm and held military supremacy. William had graduated from a duke to a king by means of military and political success. Normandy had emerged from the world of Carolingian emperors and monarchs. Such was William's reputation by the twelfth century that he was frequently likened to a Roman emperor, and just as emperors had used symbolism to enhance their prestige, so too did Norman kings.

Rome was at the heart of the western Church and newly appointed archbishops were required to travel to the city to acquire a symbol of their status, the pallium, directly from the pope. After Archbishop Sigeric of Canterbury (990–994) recorded his journey to Rome, along what became known as the *Via Francigena*, the 'Eternal City' attracted pilgrims to Rome in increasingly large numbers. These included many senior ecclesiastics as well as secular rulers, such as King Cnut, who went on pilgrimage to Rome in 1027. Anglo–Norman clerical leaders saw themselves as directly descended from the founders of the Latin Church; Abbot Anselm of Bury St Edmunds (d.1148), for example, notably signed himself, 'son of the Church of Rome'.

Although some of its glory had faded, the city and its reputation were still held in awe and envy by emperors, kings and princes. Legends of the Roman and Carolingian empires and their predecessors cast a long shadow over ruling dynasties, who wanted to be seen within a comparable heroic framework. Throughout the Middle Ages, rulers were anxious to trace their lineage back to antiquity and chroniclers were encouraged to measure contemporary rulers against historical and legendary heroes. It was commonplace for hagiographers to compare their subjects favourably with classical models. The language and imagery associated with empire can frequently be seen in art, architecture and chronicles after 1066. Fernie argues that Romanesque was a continuation of the Roman Empire and 'formed part of an extended tradition of building in stone which was so pervasive that every feature in masonry buildings up to the middle of the twelfth century may be Roman in origin'.[2].

The narrative of the Norman Conquest of England lent itself to classical comparisons, involving as it did a naval invasion across the Channel. Contemporaries claimed that it surpassed the Roman conquest of Britain as it was achieved following a single decisive victory on the battlefield and the successful occupation of a foreign country, larger and wealthier than the homeland. Furthermore, perceptions of a Norman diaspora across Europe and the Middle East readily led to comparisons with former empires, particularly that of Rome. King William I's own epithet, 'the Conqueror', encouraged images of imperial expansion and it is difficult not to see the White Tower or Durham Cathedral as expressions of colonial triumphalism. Before 1066, William was already building churches in Normandy on a scale unknown in the duchy since the Romans. To some extent he was imitating his peers in Western Europe, but his victory at Hastings must have persuaded him that he was in fact greater than them, and this should be manifested through the scale of his palaces, castles and cathedrals.

In the first instance, the Norman kings of England and their compatriots in southern Italy may not have seen themselves as imperialists; they were above all opportunists, but eventually a form of empire is what they bequeathed to their successors. Much has been written about the 'Norman empire' and 'Norman colonization' and recently David Bates has persuasively argued that there was a Norman empire, which was cultural rather than military in character.[3] This chapter examines how far that imperialism can be detected through literature, architecture and landscape.

William the Conqueror, sitting in state, receiving a copy of *Gesta Normannorum Ducum* (Deeds of the Dukes of Normandy) from its author, William of Jumièges, c.1070.

Norman Chroniclers and the Classical World

The Norman dukes were well aware of their notorious Viking ancestry and the earliest chronicler of Norman history, Dudo of Saint-Quentin (*c*.965–*c*.1040), attempted to remedy this. He traced the Norman dukes' forebears back through a spurious family line, linking them to Scandinavian aristocracy, and portraying the first ruler, Rollo, as 'a Christian Aeneas' – a hero founder of a new dynasty.

Later, Norman chroniclers were able to see and assess the Norman achievement beyond the conquest of England. The success of the Normans in southern Italy and Sicily, as well as their achievements on crusade, which saw the establishment of the principality of Antioch in the Levant, provided a broad canvas to portray valour and empire-building.

Not only was literary analogy common, but appearance, presentation and ritual all borrowed consciously from classical or imperial roots. One of the most impressive illustrations of this conceit is the portrayal of the Norman king Roger II of Sicily in a mosaic in the Church of the Martorana, Palermo, wearing the robes of a Byzantine emperor, being crowned by Christ (see Plate 18). Henry of Huntingdon (1088–*c*.1157) went one stage further and seated William the Conqueror 'on the right hand of God, a place reserved only for a truly imperial figure'. Henry observed that William was greater than all the kings that preceded him.[4]

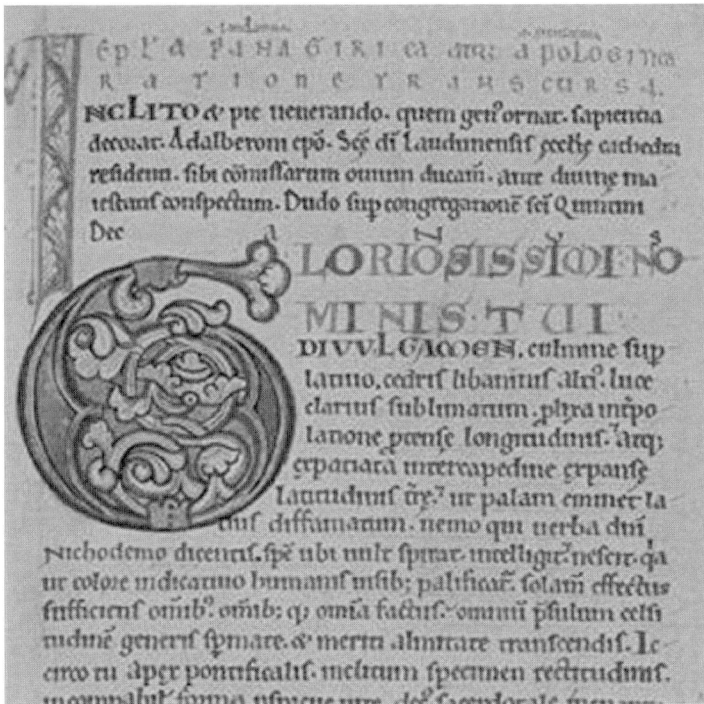

Opening page of Dudo of Saint-Quentin's *Historia Normannorum*. (*Museum Plantin-Moretus, Antwerp, MS 17.2, f, lv*)

The Classics formed the basis of literary education and references to popular heroes and events such as Alexander the Great, the Trojan Wars and Charlemagne were commonly adopted by the chroniclers, who wrote narratives based on classical texts to reinforce William the Conqueror's right to the throne of England and his abilities as a ruler. Throughout medieval Europe, Trojan origins were claimed for cities and territories in order to provide a sense of collective solidarity, to imbue their lineage with authority and to establish a connection with the ancient world. Hagiographers were only fulfilling their brief when claiming that their hero's bravery and achievements were equal to or surpassed those historical and classical figures to whom they were compared.

In the earliest surviving account of the Battle of Hastings, the *Song of the Battle of Hastings*, Duke William is compared to Julius Caesar and his invasions of England from Gaul in 55 and 54 BC; King Harold is likened to Pompey, whom Caesar defeated at the Battle of Pharsalus in 48 BC, an event that was partly instrumental in the transformation of the Roman republic into an empire. Another echo of Pharsalus, according to the *Song*, is that after winning the battle, William, like Caesar, spent the night on the battlefield.

William of Poitiers, another early chronicler, has been dismissed as being 'nauseatingly sycophantic' in his coverage of William the Conqueror in his *Gesta Guillelmi ducis Normannorum et regis Anglorum* (*c*.1070).[5] It has recently been argued that these analogies did not represent superficial flattery but were consciously constructed to serve a number of purposes.[6] Poitiers used a classical literary format as found in writers such as Cicero, Sallust and Virgil to claim that William had delivered England from the tyranny of Harold. He was citing Cicero when he claimed that to kill a tyrant (Harold) was 'the finest of all glorious deeds'. Throughout the *Gesta*, Poitiers quotes and alludes to classical works and heroes – Aeneas, Caesar and Theseus – using their stories to underline Harold as a usurper and William's legitimacy. 'Poitiers finds significant parallels between the intention, destination and morality of these heroes' sea voyages and William's conquest.'[7]

Discussing the voyage to England, Poitiers claims William's superiority to ancient sea venturers Agamemnon and Xerxes: 'We protest' that William had more ships than Agamemnon and 'we proclaim' that William linked Normandy and England, whereas Xerxes linked two towns with a boat bridge. In comparing William with Caesar, Poitiers implies that the Roman was not a strong enough leader to provide adequately for his troops: 'Caesar limited himself to commanding his troops, rarely fighting himself; William participated in battle as a commander and fighting knight.'

[Caesar] who twice crossed over to this same Britain with a thousand ships did not perform deeds as great as this the first time, nor did he dare to advance far from the coast or to stay long on the coast, although he fortified a camp in the Roman fashion. He crossed over at the end of summer and returned before the following equinox. His legions were overcome with great fear when his ships were partly broken up by the tides and waves of the sea.

William was also a more vigilant leader who never neglected his duty; he was accomplished, strong when necessary and compassionate when appropriate:

The Britons often gave battle to Caesar; whereas William crushed the English so thoroughly in one day that afterwards they could not muster the courage to fight him again.

Contrary to other sources, which tell stories of Norman brutality, Poitiers went on to claim that:

Caesar sent out his cavalry to lay waste the fields with fire and plunder … William, on the other hand, made peace offerings to the people, and so preserved with its inhabitants the land which he could have devastated in a short time.

Poitiers also compared Caesar's transformation from consul to emperor with William's elevation from duke to king. The chronicler compared William favourably with Aeneas, who left Troy to found Rome, Achilles, Xerxes, Cicero and Pompey; he also likened the king's advisors to the Roman senate.

Poitiers claimed William matched Caesar Augustus in his love of his country and his country's love of him: 'It was doubtful which was the greater, his country's love for him or his love for his country, just as it was once doubted of Caesar Augustus and the Roman people.' Also:

When he entered his metropolitan city of Rouen, old men, boys, matrons and all the citizens came out to see him, they shouted out to welcome his return, so that you could have thought that the whole city was cheering, as did Rome formerly when it joyfully applauded Pompey.

Poitiers uses a classical allusion when William refuses money from Harold's mother for Harold's body. It made him more noble than Achilles, who had accepted King Priam's offer for his son Hector, whom Achilles had killed in single combat and to whom Poitiers had compared Harold.

William of Malmesbury (c.1095–c.1143) was interested in ancient Rome and was able to write of the broader Norman achievement within a classical context: 'Let eulogistic poets and ancient fables no longer praise the old heroes … Nothing that was done in those or any times can compare with the glory of what these men

William the Conqueror's great seal shows the king sitting in state on one side and mounted as an equestrian figure on the obverse. William appears to have been the first monarch to have used the equestrian image. (*Nieus, 2016*)

have achieved.'[8] Furthermore, he claimed that: 'If you look closely at the deeds of that Roman [Caesar] and those of our leader, you will rightly say that the Romans took risks and trusted too much to luck, whereas William always acted with foresight and succeeded more by good planning than by chance.'[9]

The portrayal of William's minority as a time of serious danger for the young duke by Orderic Vitalis and other chroniclers may have been intended to echo the precarious youth of Julius Caesar as recounted by the Roman writer Suetonius in *The Twelve Caesars*. Likewise, the anecdote told by William of Malmesbury relating how William tripped while disembarking at Pevensey could be interpreted as another classical reference. A knight next to the fallen duke exclaimed, 'You have England in your hand, duke and shall be king' – there was a remarkably similar episode told by Suetonius when Julius Caesar landed in Africa.

It is possible that stories of William's harsh treatment of opponents were also influenced by a story found in Caesar's *Gallic War*. When besieging the town of *Ulexodunum* in the Dordogne, he deprived the citizens of water by diverting the river, thereby bringing about its surrender:

> Caesar knew that his leniency was universally known, and so he was not afraid that if he acted somewhat harshly he would appear to have done so out of any innate cruelty ... For this reason he decided upon making an example of the townspeople in punishing them, so as to deter the rest. He allowed them to live, therefore, but cut off the hands of all those who had carried arms against him.

Similarly, Duke William had mutilated the defenders of Alençon, which he besieged *c.*1050, for mocking the humble origins of his mother. The next town to be threatened, Domfront, then surrendered immediately without a fight in fear of a similar punishment if they did not yield. Caesar was held up as a role model for medieval rulers and William employed similar methods to the Romans in order 'to deter the rest'.

Goscelin de Bertin, a Benedictine hagiographer from Flanders, claimed *c.*1090 that England was 'an imperial kingdom ruled augustly by the Caesars, who boasted that they had their seat as much here as in Rome'. Furthermore, he argued that both Rome and Troy would have been vulnerable to a hero like the Conqueror. Goscelin's account of the surrender of Domfront after the destruction of Alençon echoes Caesar's sack of Gomphi and the subsequent surrender of Metropolis in his war with Pompey.[10]

The Anglo-Norman chronicler Geoffrey Gaimar suggested *c.*1136 that 'had William Rufus been able to reign a little longer, he would have marched on Rome to reclaim the country', while an anonymous mid-twelfth-century poem written for Geoffrey Plantagenet, Empress Matilda's husband, portrayed Rouen as the new Rome, served by conquered Britain with the English, Scots and Welsh bringing gifts to the empress. The author of the last Latin narrative history of Normandy, Stephen of Rouen (d.*c.*1169), gave the Normans a Trojan ancestry. He likened both William the Conqueror and Henry II to second Caesars, and Rouen to 'the city of Caesar'.

Favourable classical comparisons were not restricted to the monarchy; Orderic Vitalis extended them to the Norman barons. He claimed that the Norman magnates had 'inherited the warlike courage of their ancestors and excelled in judgement and wise counsel' and 'would have yielded nothing to the Roman Senate in talents or experience'.

In the late 1140s, Rouen was likened to Rome: 'Has not the Norman people indeed chosen Rouen for its capital, whence it has reduced to tribute Brittany and England, Scotland and Wales?' During the Anarchy, Henry of Huntingdon attributes a speech to Ralph, Bishop of the Orkneys, before the Battle of the Standard fought in Yorkshire in 1138 between an Anglo-Norman army led by William of Aumale and a Scottish army led by King David I:

> Noblemen of England, renowned sons of Normandy, before you go into battle you should call to mind your reputation and origin: consider well who you are and against whom and where you are fighting this battle. For no one has resisted you with impunity. Bold France, when she had put you to the test, melted away. Fruitful England fell to your conquest. Wealthy Apulia, gaining you, renewed herself. Jerusalem, the celebrated, and famous Antioch both submitted to you.[11]

It is clear that such ideas were current among the higher Norman aristocracy, the 'dominant and exploiting group', and represent their attitude to what has been described as 'the Norman achievement'. Such sentiments go some way to justify the use of the term 'Norman Empire' to describe the complex of dominion and lordship which William the Conqueror and Henry I built up on either side of the English Channel.[12]

A new generation of landscape historians looking at the chroniclers locate them in the tradition of classical writers – their aim is to place William the Conqueror's achievements within the context of the heroic. For instance, it is argued that when describing royal journeys, such as William's campaign during the Harrying of the North, they are not trying to provide a detailed itinerary; they are instead showing that the new king needed to establish his authority over the landscape as much as over the people.[13]

Another episode underlines the Norman perception of their elite place in the world and of the unlimited rewards available to the opportunistic Norman leaders. William the Conqueror's half-brother Bishop Odo of Bayeux was second only to the king in wealth in England. During the early years of William's reign Odo had acted as regent of England during William's absence in Normandy. Later in the Conqueror's reign, Odo played a smaller role and clearly developed itchy feet. In 1082/3 he appears to have raised an army with the intention of sailing to Rome in order to secure the papacy. Odo already had a palace in Rome and it was claimed that he had spies there as well. He was arrested on the Isle of Wight by Archbishop Lanfranc for raising a private army, before his troops could embark, and subsequently he was imprisoned in Rouen until the Conqueror's death in 1087.[14]

It has been suggested that the Bayeux Tapestry, for which Odo was almost certainly responsible, was itself a work with Roman imperial overtones. Comparison has been made between the contents of the tapestry and Trajan's Column in Rome; both show elaborate preparations for a military campaign. It has even been suggested that some scenes from the tapestry have been taken from the column in Rome.[15] The monument, which was erected in AD 113 to commemorate Emperor Trajan's Darian wars, bears carved accounts of Roman military victories, arranged in spiral strips around a cylindrical pillar. As in the tapestry, the narrative is divided into discrete episodes, bounded by trees and buildings. Originally, the frieze sculptures on the column would have been coloured and even by the eleventh century the resemblance to the tapestry would have been more obvious than today.[16]

William the Conqueror and the Normans had their own twentieth-century hagiographer in that great Norman scholar R. Allen Brown, who claimed that: 'The Norman ecclesiastical revival of the eleventh century, moreover, included a programme of church-building on a majestic – indeed imperial scale … Such buildings surely show that the Normans were not merely the Romans of their world, but also the Greeks.'[17]

Allen Brown argued that 'Normanitas' was characterized by strong, ambitious fighters and diplomats, who left their distinctive mark throughout Europe

Detail of Trajan's Column, Rome, showing Roman soldiers preparing for battle. (*Kenneth Garrett*)

Extract from the Bayeux Tapestry showing Norman troops preparing for battle. Although there is little stylistic similarity between the two pictures, they are covering the same activity.

and the Near East from the tenth to the thirteenth centuries. In invoking the original Viking spirit of the Normans and praising their 'daring, adventure, land-hunger and wanderlust', Allen Brown may have taken his enthusiasm a step too far. The term has attracted criticism as it was felt to have overtones of racial superiority.

It is questionable how far the replacement of Old English by French and Latin can be seen as an imperial imposition or simply a natural consequence of the Conquest, but it has been argued that the making of the Domesday Book could be viewed as an imperial project. It can be placed within a tradition of *descriptiones* going back to Caesar Augustus. It is known that Charlemagne commissioned a survey of conquered lands in Istria, which included references to conditions under the previous rule of the Byzantine emperors. Was William in part moved to compile the great survey because he was conscious that great emperors had done these things in the past? The impact of William's conquest and of his subsequent activities as king of England certainly created an imperial impression, as expressed by the poet and cleric Baudri of Bourgueil: 'In the end his power was so great that his name alone made the entire earth tremble and bow to his rule.'[18]

The Normans and Roman Monuments

How far did the Normans imitate the Romans in an attempt to capitalize on the imperial reputation of their 'illustrious' predecessors? There appear to be several examples of deliberate imitation; for example, the spiral columns to the east of the transepts at Durham Cathedral have been likened to those at Old St Peter's, Rome, where in the fourth century Constantine used such columns to mark the tomb of the Apostle. Their presence at Durham could be an implication that St Cuthbert was a figure of parallel importance. The westernmost columns of the nave have twenty-four flutes, the number given by Vitruvius for the flutes on an Ionic column. Similarly, facades with three large arches, such as those at Bury St Edmunds, could well have been symbolic allusions to Roman triumphal arches, suggesting that Abbot Anselm, who was responsible for the buildings, was deliberately linking St Edmund with Constantine, as fellow Christian kings. The gate tower and west façade, which formed the ceremonial entrance to the royal burial site of St Edmund, incorporated Roman features relating to Constantine's Old St Peter's in Rome. It has also been argued that at Rievaulx Abbey, Abbot Aelred (1147-67) appears to have based the design of the simple chapter house on the Basilica of the Apostles in Rome, a church with which he was familiar.[19] In particular, the west front at Lincoln Cathedral, built by Bishop Remigius, probably drew upon the Arch of Constantine in Rome for inspiration.[20] Norman builders tended to use plain, Roman-inspired surface decoration such as *opus reticulatum*, which was borrowed directly from Romano-Gallic temples and aqueducts still standing in France and Britain, as can be seen on the west front of Rochester Cathedral.

It was above all the size and dominant siting of many of the new buildings that fostered the perception of empire. At Winchester, the austere, powerful architecture found in the cathedral transepts would have been echoed in the contemporary Winchester castle: 'With the cathedral of St Peter at Winchester, William's kingdom takes a step into a different league, and it is possible to talk of imperial pretensions.'[21] The mighty drum columns of the nave of Shrewsbury Abbey were replicated in Shrewsbury Castle, both built by Roger de Montgomery in the later eleventh century, transforming the townscape of the Saxon borough, possibly in response to the ruins at Wroxeter (*Viriconium Cornoviorum*), which lies a few kilometres further down the River Severn. It has also been suggested that in building Westminster Palace, the biggest hall seen in Europe since Roman times, William Rufus wanted not only to surpass his father and his contemporaries among western rulers, but also Charlemagne at Aachen.

One means of claiming a direct association with the Roman past was by reusing material from Roman buildings, known as *spolia*. The value of reusing Roman material and sites was normally for pragmatic reasons, but there could have been more to it than that and it can be argued that the reuse of Roman structures had an added symbolic significance. The Normans were aware of the Roman legacy in Europe and may have consciously used Roman sites to relate to their military successes and to indicate that they too were an imperial power. The reuse of Roman structures implied an element of imperial authority, antiquity and continuity.

Stones brought from Rome itself conferred an aura of antiquity upon new buildings and associated their sponsors with the authority and legendary splendour of the past; for example, Charlemagne had material brought from Rome and Ravenna for his palace at Aachen. Perhaps the most high-profile activity of this nature in the Norman era was undertaken by Bishop Henry de Blois of Winchester in the 1140s. John of Salisbury, in his *Historia Pontificalis*, claimed that Henry loaded up an entire ship at Rome's port of Ostia with statues and other *spolia* taken from the ruins of ancient Rome, with the intention of furnishing his palace at Winchester with this symbolic material.[22]

In the eleventh century, surviving Roman structures were plentiful and substantial in Normandy, England and Wales. Defensive walls survived, sometimes to their original height, in many Roman cities, as well as decayed public buildings, bath houses and temples. Stone and brick structures of Roman Britain were bonded with hydraulic lime-mortar, which sets like hard rock. Many Roman buildings were still roofed with vaults. Roman sites provided a ready quarry of worked stone, brick and tile as well as a plentiful supply of rubble for foundations and wall fillings. For the Normans in England building in stone on a large scale, the remains of Roman buildings proved particularly important.

Time and weather had been the most virulent destructive agents of the Roman structures that had been constructed throughout the imperial-occupied areas of north-west Europe. The nearest we can get to a description of Roman remains in Saxon Britain is the poem 'The Ruin', which graphically describes the impact of decay upon a once great Roman city. The poem consists of forty-nine lines describing decayed, broken buildings. The writer/speaker imagines how towers, walls, baths and palaces appeared at the time of their completion and contrasts this with the desolate reality, brought about by time and fate. It was written in the eighth or ninth century and appears in the tenth century in the *Exeter Book*, an anthology of Anglo-Saxon poetry.

> These wall-stones are wondrous –
> calamities crumpled them, these city sites crashed, the work of giants
> corrupted. The roofs have rushed to earth, towers in ruins.
> Ice at the joints has unroofed the barred gates, sheared
> the scarred storm-walls have disappeared –
> the years have gnawed them from beneath.

It is generally agreed that the city depicted in the poem is Roman Bath, although several other possibilities, including Chester and Hadrian's Wall, have been suggested. References to a hot spring, many bathing halls and a circular pool seem to confirm that Bath, the foremost spa town of Roman Britain, was the inspiration for the poem. Although two or three more centuries elapsed between the Saxon verses and the Norman Conquest, there is every reason to believe that

The Old Work at Viriconium (Wroxeter) in Shropshire, which was the south wall of the Roman basilica. It is the largest example or Romano-British civil masonry still standing in Britain. (*David Dixon*)

St Andrew's Church, Wroxeter, which uses Roman columns as gateposts for the entrance to the churchyard. Large stones from Roman buildings have been used in the fabric of the church, which sits in the south-west corner of the Roman town. (*Trevor Rowley*)

the 'lichen-grey and rust-stained' walls of the poem were still a prominent feature of the post-Conquest townscape. There are relatively few surviving examples of large-scale civil Roman architecture in Britain; two remarkable exceptions are the Jewry Wall in Leicester and the Old Work at Wroxeter.

Another tenth-century poem from the *Exeter Book*, 'The Wanderer', includes references to decaying buildings, emphasizing the transitory nature of human achievements:

> The walls stand, blown by the wind,
> crushed by frost, the buildings snowswept.
> The wine halls moulder …
> And so the Shaper has laid this Middle earth to waste
> until the ancient works of giants stood empty,
> devoid of the revelry of their citizens.

After the Conquest, Gerald of Wales described how at Caerleon in south Wales, significant parts of the Roman fort, most notably a roofed bath house and a tetrapylon (a four-way triumphal arch), survived:

> You can still see many vestiges of its one-time splendour. There are immense palaces, there is a lofty tower, and beside it a remarkable hot bath, the remains of temples and an amphitheatre. All is enclosed within impressive walls, parts of which still remain standing.[23]

The use of Roman altars, milestones, statues and tombstones within some Anglo-Saxon churches may well have been a conscious attempt by the Church in the early Middle Ages to deliberately promote *Romanitas* – to reflect past imperial grandeur.[24] The Normans appear to have continued the practice. 'Ancient places…. represented important points of reference which helped define and maintain the collective identities of local communities', used by the Normans to enhance their rights 'to people, place and power'.[25] It is difficult to determine how often Roman sites were deliberately reoccupied and in what circumstances Roman material was used for symbolic reasons. There are, however, clear examples where other, more suitable sites were available and building material was more readily accessible than Roman *spolia*, but where the Roman option was preferred.[26]

A strong case has been made out for the conscious reuse of Roman *spolia* in the castle keep at Chepstow, which was built within a few years of the Conquest on a strategic and symbolic site on the route into south Wales.[27] It has even been suggested that there may have been a Roman temple on the site where the castle was erected.[28] What is clear is that the Great Tower at Chepstow, dominating the River Wye and the entrance to Wales, was an imperial statement by the Normans. On the basis of the Domesday evidence, it was believed to have been the work of William the Conqueror's right-hand man William fitz Osbern. It now appears much more likely to have been a royal castle, commissioned by William himself.

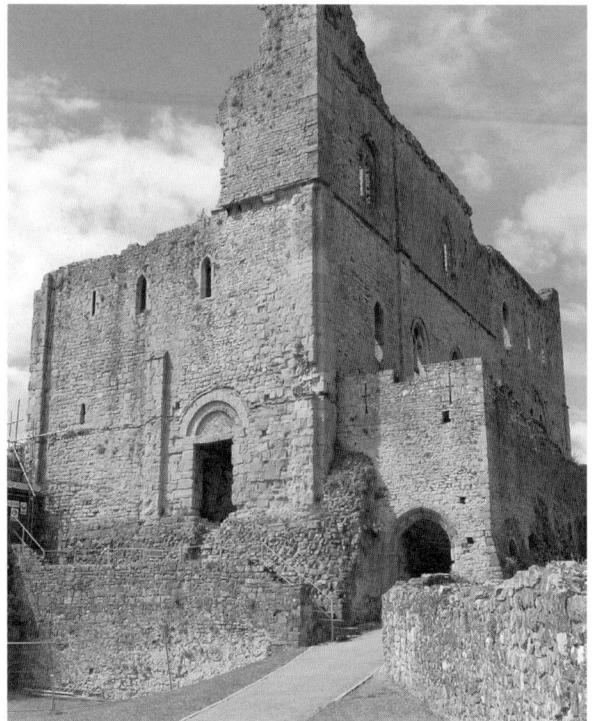

Chepstow Castle, Monmouthshire, was one of the first stone castles built by the Normans in Britain. It stood proud on a cliff above the River Wye at the entrance to Wales and made extensive use of stone brought from the Roman town of Caerwent (*Venta Silurum*), 8 km away. A course of reused Roman tile runs above the Great Hall doorway. (*Andrew Tivenan*)

It has been convincingly argued that it was built as much as a ceremonial building as a strategic military fortress, representing the presence of the English king at the entrance to south Wales. The historical context for the erection of the Great Tower at Chepstow was probably the expedition William made with an army through south Wales in 1081. It was ostensibly a pilgrimage to the shrine of St David, but it was more a show of strength and an opportunity to exact tribute from the prince of south Wales, Rhys ap Tewdwr (d.1093). For almost a thousand years, those travelling to south Wales, having passed through the Forest of Dean, would have been presented with the Great Tower at Chepstow, towering over the cliffs of the Wye estuary. Like the Tower of London, the Great Tower at Chepstow with its imported Roman stone from Caerwent was built for its appearance as much as its function.[29]

The use of polychrome banding at Chepstow may have represented a deliberate evocation of the standing ruins the Normans would have encountered in Britain and Gaul, and furthermore, not only did the design have imperial connotations, but the use of antique building material may have been an integral part of the symbolism.[30] The banding at Chepstow takes the form of a three-deep string

The heavily robbed town walls at Caerwent, built c.300. Soon after the Norman Conquest, a small motte and bailey castle was built in the south-east corner of the Roman defences. A portion of the Roman wall was demolished and the motte built over its foundations, while the Roman ditches were reused as defences. A ditched bailey was created inside the walls. (*Paul R. Davis*)

course in Roman brick around the exterior of the castle, coursed in the *petit appareil* style characteristic of the nearby Roman town wall at Caerwent.

Cardiff Castle was built during the same expedition and occupied the remains of a third-century Roman fort. It was the largest motte and bailey in Wales. The Normans used the remains of the collapsed Roman walls as the basis for the outer castle perimeter, digging a defensive trench and throwing up a 27ft (8.2m) high bank of earth over the Roman fortifications. They further divided the castle with an internal wall to form an inner and an outer bailey. In the north-west corner of the castle, a wooden keep was constructed on top of the 40ft (12m) tall earth motte, surrounded by a 30ft (9.1m) wide moat.

Although material and designs taken from Roman contexts were normally used to enhance the prestige of the Normans, occasionally they were harnessed in opposition to Anglo-Norman lordship. At Caerleon the Roman ruins were adopted as a symbol of Welsh opposition to Norman rule. For much of the twelfth century, and the first decade of the thirteenth, there were persistent efforts to assert Welsh lordship and at times kingship at Caerleon, with the castle changing hands between the Anglo-Normans and Welsh on several occasions. In the thirteenth century, however, they were systematically destroyed by the English, 'a victim of the deliberate erasure of memory'.[31]

Some Roman towns, such as *Durovernum Cantiacorum* (Canterbury), had already been heavily robbed for building material in the Saxon period and by the twelfth century relatively little survived above ground level.[32] Churches erected in and around Canterbury – St Peter and Paul's (*c*.597–619), St Pancras (late seventh century) and St Martin's (seventh century) – had all made extensive use of Roman *spolia*, but there was clearly sufficient left for the Normans. Both St Augustine's Abbey and the cathedral church of Christ Church were completely rebuilt after the Conquest; the new St Augustine's, just outside the Roman city walls, like its Saxon predecessor made extensive use of Roman material.

Abbot Paul of Caen, the first Norman abbot of St Albans, rebuilt the abbey church on a massive scale; it was one-third larger than Canterbury Cathedral. Unlike any other major monastic church in England from the late eleventh century, St Albans was built almost entirely with reused Roman building material from the Roman city of *Verulamium*. The material used in the abbey comprised primarily Roman brick tiles and unknapped flint with small amounts of limestone, mostly obtained from the city walls. Some of this *spolia* appears to have been excavated by the eleventh-century Saxon abbots Ealdred and Eadmer. Matthew Paris, who was a monk at St Albans in the mid-thirteenth century, gives an account of the finds of these early monk-archaeologists, including the discovery of a dragon's cave. Apart from these flights of fancy, he noted how they stored the Roman stone and perfect bricks, which were then utilized after the Conquest. He wrote:

The outline of St Augustine's Abbey, Canterbury. In 1070, Scolland, a monk from Mont Saint-Michel, became abbot and began reconstructing the building in the form of a large Norman Benedictine foundation. The Normans made extensive use of Roman material, as did their Saxon predecessors. (*John Fielding Aerial Images*)

> The city was floored of stone, with roof tiles and columns ... The diggers found in the foundation of the ancient building, underground cavities, jugs and amphorae ... likewise vessels of glass.

It is also believed that Robert Mason, the Norman builder of the abbey, may have used the standing Roman buildings as an inspiration for some construction techniques. It is therefore possible that the Roman ruins of *Verulamium* not only provided the raw material for the building, but also some of the techniques of building and decoration. 'Roman remains were used to commemorate the antiquity and authority of the abbey.'[33]

The symbolic significance of locating the White Tower within the corner of London's Roman walls on the Thames would have been self-evident. Although this was the obvious strategic location for the capital's premier castle, its size dominating the former city defences would have sent a clear and powerful message to London's population. While at Colchester (*Camulodunum*), the castle keep was located on the podium of a classical temple to the Divine Claudius Caesar, which had later been used by Saxon kings. Excavation combined with architectural

The central Norman tower of St Alban's Cathedral, Hertfordshire (an abbey up to its dissolution in 1539), is the only eleventh-century great crossing tower still standing in England. It was built by Abbot Paul of Caen (1077-1093), making extensive use of brick and tile from the nearby Roman town of *Verulamium*. (*Trevor Rowley*)

analysis of the keep, which incorporates much reused Roman masonry, indicated that the monumental structures surrounding the temple had survived to a considerable height up until the castle was built. It is possible that the Normans were well aware that Colchester had been the site of one of the greatest rebellions against the Romans, that of the Iceni tribe led by Boudicca in AD 61. Furthermore, one of the reasons for the revolt was the use of forced native labour to build the

Claudian temple. If they were not aware, it was a fortunate coincidence that the largest stone castle in the land was on the site of a suppressed rebellion against a foreign occupation.

Not only was the castle sitting on a former Roman temple dedicated to the Emperor Claudius, but it also occupied what became the core of a late Saxon *villa regalis* (royal manor).[34] The mid-fourteenth-century *Colchester Chronicle* recounts that William the Conqueror's steward Eudo Dapifer built the castle in 1076 on the foundations of the palace of Coel, 'formerly king', a reference to a legendary late or post-Roman British leader. A later medieval legend claimed that Coel was St Helena's father, and thus the grandfather of Constantine the Great. The chapel of St Helen's, which lies to the north-west of the castle keep, stands on the foundations of a Roman theatre. Although the present building dates from the thirteenth century, the *Colchester Chronicle* states that it was repaired by Eudo Dapifer in 1076. During the twelfth century, town houses were built throughout Colchester, at least seven of which contained reused Roman material, and archaeological work in the city indicates that such was the scale of Norman reuse of Roman material that by the end of the twelfth century, standing Roman buildings were becoming scarce.[35]

As in London, the building of Colchester Castle within a Roman context overshadowing anything that had been seen since the Romans was an unambiguous statement of William the Conqueror's imperial ambitions.[36] The great keep here was one and a half times larger than the White Tower of London and displayed

A Victorian reconstruction of Colchester Castle, Essex. (*Nichols, 1882*)

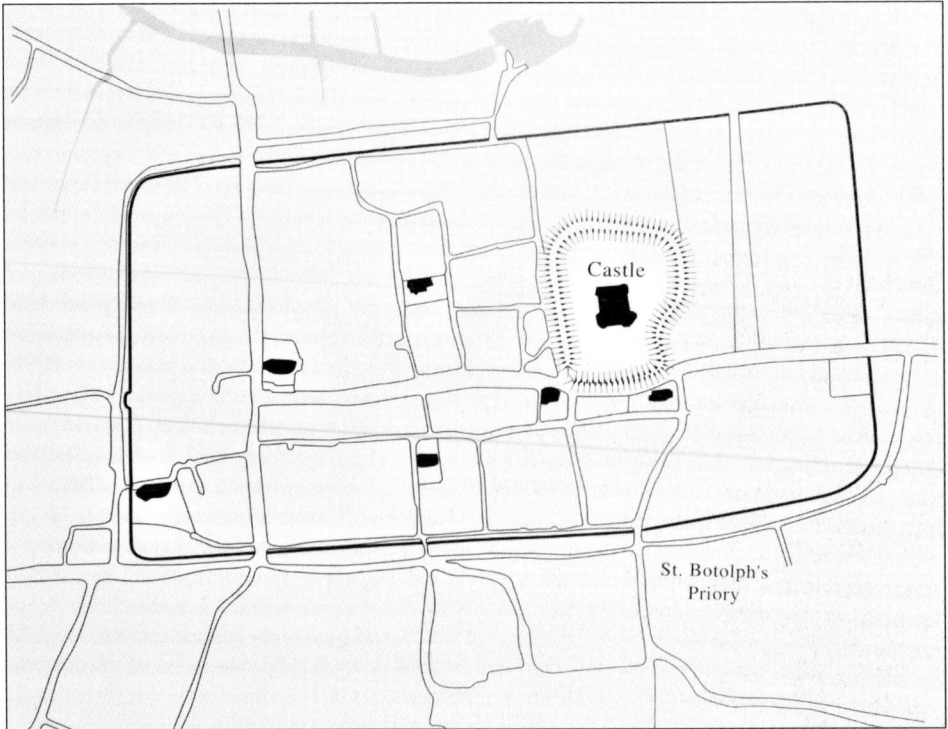

Plan showing the location of Colchester Castle within the Roman town of *Camulodunum*. The Norman fort is built directly on the foundations of a Roman temple dedicated to Claudius.

clear architectural links to the great palaces of the Carolingian empire. Close by, at Colchester, St Botolph's Priory (1100–30) was also built using material from the Roman defences on which it abutted and these walls had been almost entirely robbed. Today, the ruins of the priory with its row of double arches of red and brown *spolia* look very much as 'The Ruin' must have looked to the Saxon poet, with its 'houses of red vaulting' that had 'drearied and shed their tiles' (see Plate 19). At Chester, the Norman cathedral of St John's used a considerable volume of salvaged Roman building material. Most of this was excavated from the adjacent Roman amphitheatre with which the church shared a precinct wall until the later Middle Ages.

The Norman desire to replace existing Saxon structures sometimes capped any reverence for the Roman past. At Canterbury, for instance, the rebuilding of the cathedral involved the destruction of its Saxon predecessor, which had almost certainly incorporated Roman architectural features, as Bede stated that Augustine had reused a Roman church when he founded Canterbury Cathedral in 597. The chronicler Eadmer, who had known the Saxon cathedral as a boy, wrote that its design was similar to that of St Peter's in Rome – a basilica with an eastern apse.

St Botolph's, Colchester. The main west door, known as the Pardon Door, was where pardons were granted on the Feast of St Denis.

At Lincoln, located at an important strategic site on Ermine Street and the Fosse Way, the castle was erected within the surviving remains of a Roman fortress for retired soldiers (*Lindum Colonia*). In 1068 it was erected as a motte, using the Roman defences for its western and southern boundaries. On the south side, where the Roman wall stands on the edge of a steep slope, it was retained partly as a curtain wall and partly as a revetment to retain the two mottes. On the west, the Roman wall was buried within an earth rampart and extended upward to form the Norman castle wall.

The adjacent cathedral, rebuilt by the Normans (1088 onwards), was located within the Roman fortifications, and the twelfth-century bishops' palace immediately to the south of the cathedral was also bounded on the east by the line of the Roman defences. The castle with its bailey and the cathedral with its close occupied the whole of the upper part of the Roman defences, called the Bail. The core of ancient Lincoln, as at Winchester, was taken over by high-status

Norman structures. Henry of Huntingdon described the Norman cathedral at Lincoln as 'strong as the place was strong … and invincible to enemies'. The giant arches have been compared to Roman monuments such as the Porte de Mars in Reims. Other analogies include the fortified churches in the south of

Right: Reconstruction of Lincoln Cathedral's eleventh-century west front, seen from the south-west. (*W.T. Ball and R.D.H. Gem*)

Below: Plan showing the location of Lincoln Castle and the alignment of the cathedral respecting the Roman town defences. Lincoln Castle was unusual as it had two mottes. (*Lindum Colonia*). (*Gem, 1986: 21*)

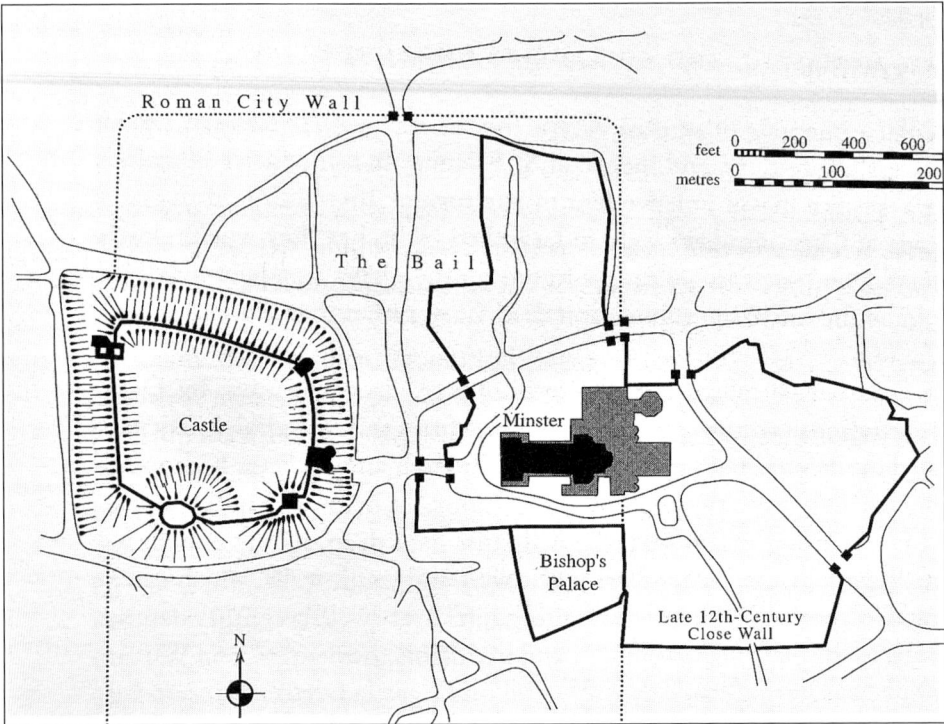

Lincoln Cathedral and castle from the east. (*Lincolnshire County Council*)

France, which are constructed in a similar manner to the west end of Lincoln, with deep buttresses and machicolations.[37] It has also been suggested that the western tower was originally built as a stand–alone defensive structure before being incorporated into the cathedral. The first Norman bishop, Remigius, was also the principal secular lord of Lincoln, obliged to provide twenty knights for the castle guard. 'In building it [the tower], Remigius was behaving not as a bishop, but primarily as a conventional great Norman lord in a newly conquered former Roman city; symbolizing his lordship in the conventional Norman way, by constructing a massive, dominant, new great tower, a donjon in a newly fashionable, self-consciously Roman style.'[38]

Roman material was used in the construction of many other castles. Carisbrooke Castle on the Isle of Wight used faced greensand blocks from a nearby Roman villa, while at Eynsford, Kent, extensive use was made of recycled Roman material by William de Eynsford for his castle in the late 1080s. It appears that William also tried to replicate Roman building styles with selective use of Roman tile and brick in archways and supporting piers.[39]

There are several Romanesque parish churches in Lincoln that use Roman squared stone (*saxa quadrata*) in their towers, which are dated to the Saxo-Norman overlap. These include St-Mary-le-Wigford, which has a Roman tombstone with a truncated Latin inscription, set to the right of the west doorway in its tower. Above it is a Saxon inscription: 'Eirtig had me built and endowed to the glory of God and St Mary'. St Peter-at-Gowts has an early-eleventh-century tower, reusing Roman stone with post-Conquest modifications, while worn Roman sculptures and inscriptions have been reset in the church walls.

At Rochester the first castle was in the form of an earth and timber ringwork, which lay in the south-west corner of the Roman town of *Durobrivae* and was comparable with the earliest phases of other important castles such as Exeter, the Tower of London and Winchester. The ringwork enclosed an area of around 1.7ha; there is no evidence of a motte here, although there does appear to have been a second, somewhat smaller, outwork or bailey to the south, known as Boley Hill. Excavations in the 1970s identified a massive rampart, incorporating a section of Roman wall, and a ditch, which was almost 7m deep.[40] It would have been in this earth and timber castle that Odo and the barons held out against William Rufus in a rebellion in 1088.[41] Odo's castle was replaced by a castle built by Gundulf, Bishop of Rochester, in the late 1080s; this in turn was superseded by the great stone keep built by William de Corbeil, the Archbishop of Canterbury, *c*.1130.

Norman keep castles were later built on other important Roman sites, notably in the impressive forts of the Saxon Shore, including those built at Pevensey, Portchester and Burgh. The first two were originally built in earth and timber in the eleventh century, but later rebuilt in stone, while Burgh Castle had a large motte built in the south-west corner of the Roman fortification. In 1770 this motte was partially destroyed and the remainder completely levelled in 1839.

Many of the buildings that were built reusing Roman material were located in eastern England, in areas where good building stone was not readily available. A more mundane explanation for the extensive reuse of *spolia* in Norman

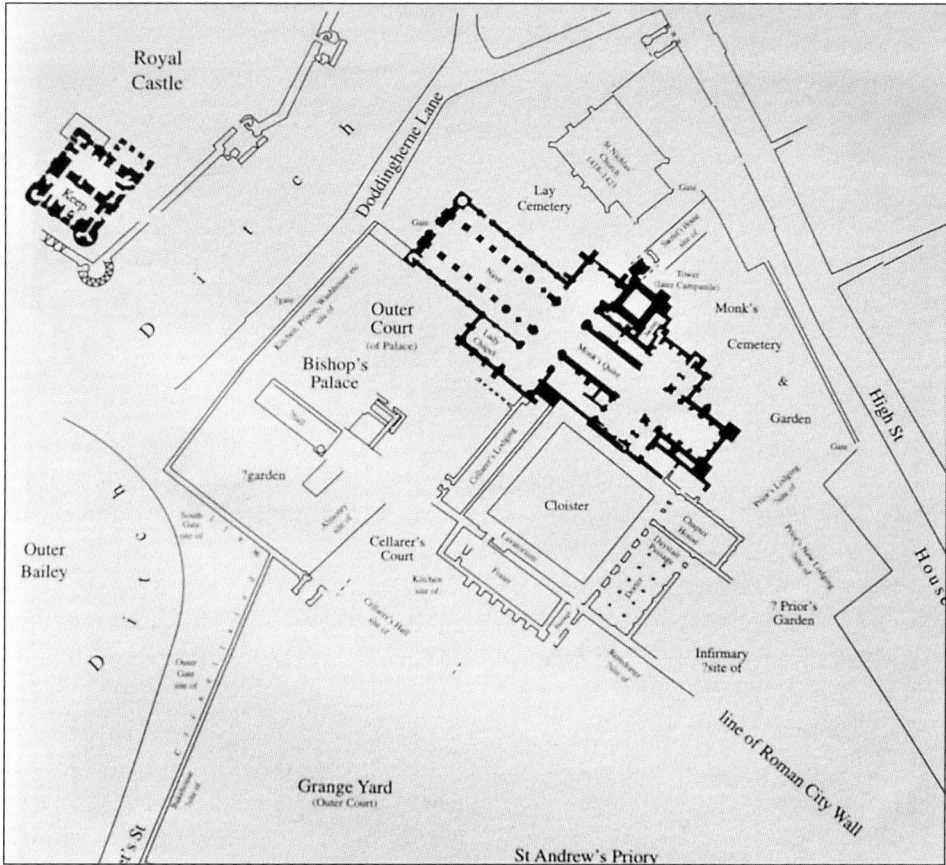

Plan of Rochester Cathedral, Bishop's Palace and Castle in relation to the city defences of Roman *Durobrivae*. (See Plate 20) (*Jill Atherton*)

buildings is provided by a study of churches in the London Basin that contain reused Roman brick and tile. It is true that out of 144 churches where the work could be dated in the study region, 86 were Saxo-Norman or Norman, but an even more telling feature was the relationship of the churches to geology. The vast majority of the churches lay in northern Essex in an area where there was no solid geology; that is, there was no stone building material to hand. This does not mean that higher-status buildings did not deliberately reuse Roman *spolia*, but in the case of lesser constructions perhaps pragmatism was more important than symbolism in the end?[42]

Although the majority of standing stone structures were Roman, Norman builders used *spolia* from Saxon buildings as well, indicating that it was normally used for pragmatic reasons. Southwell Minster, Nottinghamshire, one of the best surviving examples of a Norman Romanesque church in Britain, made extensive use of stone from an earlier Saxon church on the site.

Southwell Minster, Nottinghamshire. The great twelfth-century church reused stone from an earlier Saxon building on the site.

Reused tympanum at Southwell Minster. The carving of St Michael fighting a dragon may be *c*.1100, but the stone was originally used as a Saxon grave cover. (*Brett and Woodman, 2015: 343*)

The Reuse of Roman Roads

In addition to the surviving remnants of Roman buildings and defences, much of the Roman road infrastructure was still in place. The Laws of Edward the Confessor, written down in the twelfth century, confirm that the king's peace prevailed over the four great routes of the kingdom. Three of these, Watling

Street (Dover to Chester), Ermine Street (London to Lincoln) and the Fosse Way (Exeter to Lincoln), were originally Roman and the fourth, the Icknield Way, was a Romanized prehistoric trackway, running beneath the Chiltern escarpment. The earliest map of England, the Gough Map (*c*.1360), shows that something like 40 per cent of the marked routes corresponded to Roman roads. It is true that no systematic programme of repairs had been carried out for six centuries and as a result significant sections of road would have been overgrown and fallen out of use. For instance, the western part of the road between *Noviomagus Reginorum* (Chichester) and *Venta Belgarum* (Winchester) had been lost by the eleventh century.

The Norman use of Roman roads was purely pragmatic. William the Conqueror and his successors would have travelled by the most serviceable route available both during the Conquest and subsequently on their extensive royal itineraries. After the Battle of Hastings, William would have used Watling Street to move his army from Dover to London and the Lower Icknield Way from Wallingford to Berkhamsted.

On his return from York following the Harrying of the North, William the Conqueror followed the Roman Ermine Street and the *Via Devana*, founding castles at Lincoln, Huntingdon and Cambridge along his way. Roads linking towns that had ceased to exist, such as *Calleva Atrebatum* (Silchester), tended to disappear. Others, linking settlements that continued in one form or another, were more resilient; Watling Street running from *Dubris* (Dover) to *Londinium* (London), linking Canterbury and Rochester, remained an important routeway throughout the Middle Ages. The itineraries of early medieval kings show that stretches of Roman road were regularly used by large caravans of vehicles transporting the royal court around the kingdom. Some Roman bridges also survived into the Middle Ages. The bridge at Worcester over the River Severn became a focal point for medieval roads and survived into the eighteenth century. The collapse of a bridge or disappearance of a fording point often led to the diversion of routes away from their Roman origins.

William had undoubtedly used the Roman road system in Normandy in the run-up to the invasion. Roads linking the former Romano-Gallic towns of *Baiocassensis* (Bayeux) and *Rotomagus* (Rouen) provided a sound infrastructure to build up his army and ordnance depots. It was during the preparations for the invasion of England that extensive use was made of both Roman fortifications and roads. It seems probable that William deliberately intended landing at the Roman Saxon Shore fort of *Anderitum* (Pevensey). The 3.7-hectare enclosure would have provided a safe base for his command and perhaps the cavalry horses during the first phase of the conquest. King Harold had garrisoned the fort during the summer, but had withdrawn his troops by the beginning of September 1066. Following the Battle of Hastings, the Norman army had moved along the south coast to Dover, where they occupied a large prehistoric enclosure on the clifftop which had been adapted by the Romans and incorporated a Roman lighthouse next to the Saxon church of St-Mary-in-Castro – an apparent attempt by the Normans to appropriate the symbolic importance of the Roman monument. The march to London followed Watling Street, passing through former Roman towns at Canterbury and Rochester.

It has long been recognized that there was a close association between Norman castles and Roman roads, but the siting of fortifications at Romano-British focal points and in already defended contexts would have been the choice of any successful invader. Nevertheless, the siting of 80 per cent of Hampshire castles on or within close proximity to a Roman road demonstrates that these routes survived as visible landscape features, as well as forming the backbone of the medieval communications system. For the most part, this siting reflected the use of the old roads for transport rather than to establish strategic control of

The Roman lighthouse at Dover Castle. (*Michael Coppins*)

Goodrich Castle, Herefordshire, overlooking the site of a Roman ford over the River Wye. (*CastlesFortsBattles.co.uk*)

the communications network. There are a few examples of the importance of control being the motivating factor behind the location of Norman fortifications, such as the castle at Skipton (North Yorkshire), which lies at the head of the Ribble, commanding the passage of a Roman road through the Aire Gap.[43] In Herefordshire, Goodrich Castle overlooks the fording point of the Wye on the Roman road from Gloucester to Caerleon.

Chapter 11

The Cultural Landscape of
Anglo-Norman England

*The Normans ... altered the development of English and immeasurably
enriched its lexical resources ... the ultimate victor of the Battle of Hastings
was English.*[1]

How was the cultural landscape of England changed by the Norman
Conquest? All aspects of cultural life were affected by the imposition of
a new French elite at the head of English society. The most noticeable
impacts were on architecture, literature, law and language. French replaced
Anglo-Saxon as the language of the aristocracy and remained the courtly tongue
for several centuries. After 1066, literature, religion, law and much commerce
were all largely conducted in languages other than English and this usage filtered
through into place names. In 1066, settlements and topographical features already
had established names, but afterwards markedly French names were given to
castles, estates and monasteries; for example, Belvoir, Grosmont, Richmond and
Barnard Castle. Personal names also took on a distinctly French complexion after
the Conquest and as early as 1100, Williams and Richards easily outnumbered
Aethelreds and Edgars as popular boys' names.

Continental territorial boundaries were constantly moving and rarely policed,
meaning that people's movements between territories were hardly ever restricted
by ethnic or political considerations. The cosmopolitan nature of European
society was particularly evident at the courtly level where intermarriage
between the different ruling groups was not only common, but was expected.
Accordingly, many aspects of eleventh- and twelfth-century cultural life,
particularly in the areas of music and literature, were not restricted to one
territory or another, but were found throughout Europe, albeit with marked
regional variations. Nevertheless, in the area of social manners, later historians
often regarded the Normans as a 'rude and somewhat barbarous people'.[2] This
negative view of Norman cultural achievements has to be revised, particularly in
the field of architecture, but also in literature, where Dudo of Saint-Quentin's
Historia Normannorum, *c*.1000, for long dismissed as a virtually worthless
hotchpotch collection of fiction and legend, is increasingly admired as the
earliest illustrated Latin history.[3]

Anglo-Norman Architecture

Anglo-Norman Romanesque architecture (see Plate 21) has been the subject of many books and can only be touched on here. The Norman conquest of England produced one of the most distinct changes in architectural style found anywhere in eleventh-century Europe. After 1066 there was an explosion of new building – castles, cathedrals, abbeys, churches and even some domestic houses were all constructed in the new style. In Britain this form of architecture became known as Norman or Romanesque, while in France it is known simply as Roman. The adoption of Romanesque from the tenth century onwards extended well beyond Britain and Normandy and was largely contiguous with the lands of the Roman Latin Church. It coincided with a period of economic and population growth in western and central Europe, when the conditions for building in the new style in stone developed, stimulating an infrastructure of quarries, transport and manufacture that had been largely absent in the previous five centuries.

It was a coincidence that the Norman Conquest came at a time when the neoclassical Romanesque was developing as the dominant architectural style across much of Europe. It was a brash, dominant style that in the hands of the victorious Normans took on a distinctly triumphalist complexion in Britain. The new Norman rulers in Britain were anxious to be at the forefront of European architectural development and many of their buildings were constructed on a scale unknown since the Roman occupation. The frenzy of building activity between 1066 and 1200 was not to be equalled in Britain until the Industrial Revolution. Finally, we should dwell on the sheer scale of the Norman achievement. Every cathedral was built afresh, hundreds of completely new monasteries were erected and perhaps thousands of parish churches were built or rebuilt in stone before 1200. The magnitude of the achievement in logistical and architectural terms is breathtaking and without doubt forms the most impressive artistic legacy of the Normans in Britain. Apart from the new, distinctive architectural style, many buildings such as parish churches and abbeys that had previously been built of wood were replaced by stone structures, often of a size unknown in late Saxon England.

The Old Minster at Winchester, whose plan is laid out next to the later cathedral, would have been one of the largest churches in England for its time, yet it is dwarfed in comparison with its Norman successor. Apart from its size, it also had fundamental design differences. The Norman cathedral was an integrated whole, with a large nave leading into the choir and apse; one vast room divided by screens, broken up by the transept, but essentially a single building. In contrast, the Old Minster was a succession of modest-sized churches joined to each other, without a substantial open hall or nave. It has been argued that while the Normans placed much importance on spaciousness, the English had

Interior of Tewksbury Abbey church with its great Norman drum columns. (See Plate 21) (*Trevor Rowley*)

valued fine and costly decorative objects. William of Malmesbury observed that the Normans lived frugally in large buildings, while the Anglo-Saxons lived extravagantly in small ones. The work of the Winchester School of illumination used a wide range of colours, including much gold and silver, to achieve a unique decorative effect.

While many of the newly applied ideas came via Normandy from Burgundy, the majority of masons and craftsmen used in the construction of the new buildings were English. The distinctive Anglo–Norman school that developed soon came to dominate the homeland and subsequently spread back to Normandy and other parts of Europe. The Anglo–Norman achievement is a landmark in architectural history for western Europe in which Durham Cathedral, being the first building to be roofed with ribbed vaulting, represents the apotheosis. This technique of vaulting was taken back to Normandy and thence to the Île de France where it laid the foundations for Gothic architecture.

The influence of the Anglo–Saxon decorative tradition is more clearly seen in eleventh-century parish churches than contemporary cathedrals. Although the earliest Norman parish churches in England, such as Lastingham, North Yorkshire, were very similar to contemporary buildings in Normandy, gradually the survival of the English emphasis upon surface enrichment resulted in a growing divide. The blending of the English decorative tradition with Norman architectural skills led to a form of architecture that was different from its austere

The footings of the Saxon Old Minster, Winchester, are dwarfed when seen against the north wall of the later cathedral, which lies on the footprint of its Norman predecessor.

Norman counterpart. Later, they were to adopt many of the richer and freer surface embellishments found in England. Some architectural devices, such as the use of cushion capitals and the beak-head ornament found principally in northern parish churches, were taken from England back to Normandy. In the words of Zarnecki: 'The Normans were not totally unfriendly to local achievements and once they adopted a feature from Anglo-Saxon buildings, they used it widely.'[4]

In the twelfth century there was a fresh burst of architectural inspiration. The growing prosperity of monasteries meant that recently built monastic churches needed to be enlarged. Lanfranc's cathedral at Canterbury, for instance, which had been built in the 1070s, was enlarged with a new 'glorious choir' and dedicated in the presence of Henry I in 1130. The few Anglo-Saxon churches that had escaped the first great rebuilding campaigns, such as Lichfield and Peterborough, were levelled and new buildings erected. The principal characteristic of these churches distinguishing them from their eleventh-century equivalents was the extensive use of decoration. This displayed an exuberant blend of classical, Scandinavian, Anglo-Saxon and even Muslim elements. Doorways, chancel arches, corbel tables and other surfaces were eventually covered with a profusion of ornament. In some cases, this was a wild mixture of abstract, Christian and pagan ornament.

Above: St. Mary and St. David's, Kilpeck, Herefordshire, was described by Pevsner as 'one of the most perfect churches in England'. (*Brooks and Pevsner, 2012: 384*)

Right: The magnificent tympanum and south door decoration are attributed to the twelfth-century Herefordshire School of stonemasons.

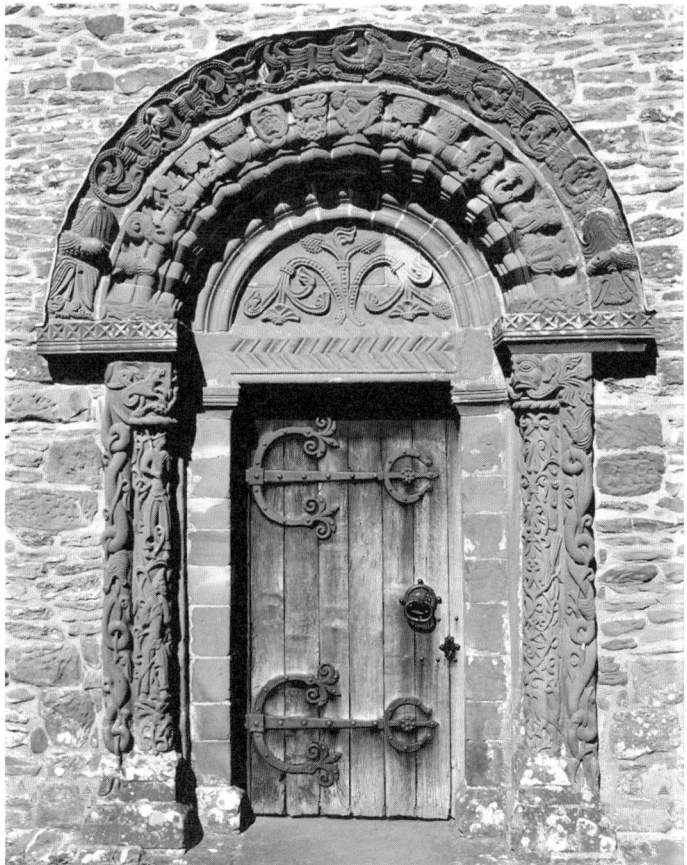

Generally speaking, it was far more inventive and less stylized than contemporary French work.

The work was executed by native masons and by the mid–twelfth century, the work of several local schools, such as those based in Herefordshire, Northamptonshire, Canterbury and East Anglia, can be identified. At Kilpeck (Herefordshire), the influence of Anglo–Saxon manuscript decoration is clearly demonstrated around the doorway, where the entwined creatures are extremely well preserved.

The combination of geometric design and colour played a vital part in Muslim architecture, which was seen by the Normans during the crusades, in Sicily and North Africa. The prevalence of geometric motifs in Islamic art may well have been the inspiration for some subsequent Romanesque decoration. And it is worth noting that although the decorative motifs of Romanesque sculpture have been much studied and debated, the fact that colour, which was extensively applied but rarely survives, played a vital part is often ignored. The sources of inspiration, however, were not solely architectural. The double quality of decoration and colour seen in contemporary manuscripts, both in England and on the Continent, was extremely influential. This may be seen most clearly in the development of Romanesque sculpture, which relied heavily on the figurative depictions seen in illuminated manuscripts. (See Plate 22)

The west doorway of Rochester Cathedral appears to have originally been constructed with an elaborate design *c*.1140, and then modified two decades later in response to significant changes in French portal fashion. (Baxter, 2006: 85). (*ChrisO*)

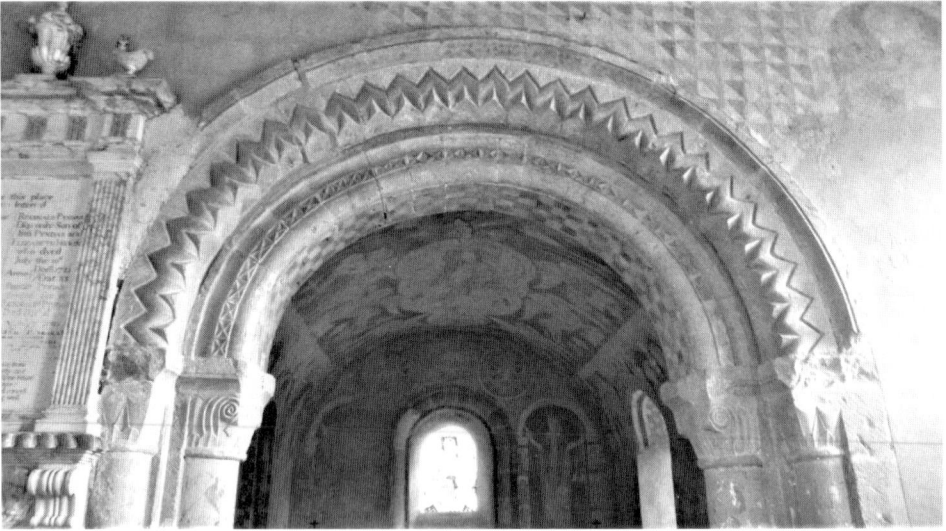

The decorated chancel arch at St Mary's, Kempley, Gloucestershire. The church was built by Hugh de Lacy in the early twelfth century and contains the most complete set of Romanesque paintings in northern Europe. (*Paul E. Williams*)

Anglo-Norman Language

William the Conqueror and his followers brought with them a variety of languages and Anglo-Norman England became multilingual. Those who came from Normandy and elsewhere in northern France spoke a range of *langues d'oil* (Gallo-Romantic), one of which was Old Norman or Old Northern French. Others spoke varieties of the Picard language or forms of Old French. These, together with elements of Anglo-Saxon and Anglo-Scandinavian, developed into Anglo-Norman, which was used for literary and administrative purposes from the eleventh to the fifteenth century. Additionally, a large number of loan words were taken over into English at a time of sustained language contact between English and French.

Post-Conquest England encompassed a trilingual culture. Latin, the international language of the Church, scholarship and the law, became the language of government in place of English, but it was Latin that became infiltrated by French and English words. Anglo-Norman became the language of the rulers and of polite society, but gradually changed from the French spoken on the Continent. English was largely employed as the vernacular language of the country. Even before 1066 it is estimated that about 9 per cent of English words were derived from French; this increased to about 21 per cent after the Conquest and even more later on.[5] The cosmopolitan character of society is reflected in the Domesday Book, which has been called 'the most remarkable multilingual event in the history of the English state'. Its name, *Domesdei*, was given by the English to a book written in Latin for a French-speaking colonial elite.[6]

The language of literature changed too, from Early English to Latin. In Edward the Confessor's time, the *Anglo-Saxon Chronicle* had been kept up at some half-dozen monasteries and, in a few, the native language survived the coming of the Normans for some time, although Latin rapidly gained ground over the vernacular. In about the year 1100 a version of the *Chronicle* was copied bilingually at St Augustine's, Canterbury. The scribes at Christ Church, Canterbury, retained the native language until 1110, when the *Chronicle* started to be written in Latin, with some occasional English entries; while at Peterborough it continued in English right up until the accession of Henry II in 1154. Other bilingual documents included a writ of Henry I confirming the privileges of London to Bishop Anselm, which appears in both Latin and English. English was used in county courts in the first decades of the twelfth century, while some estate boundaries continued to be described in English until the reign of Henry II. Eventually, a simplified version of Anglo-Saxon emerged as what became known as Middle English. Some early Norman documents written in England appear in both French and Latin.

Although French was the dominant aristocratic language, English was spoken in some households of the Norman nobility. Many Normans took English wives, and it is reasonable to assume that sections of society, even of the aristocracy, were bilingual. Many of the higher clergy spoke and preached in English, and it has been argued that 'the pulpit was the cradle of English prose'.[7] Indeed, it was devotional literature in the vernacular that preserved the tradition of English prose writing during the Anglo-Norman period. At Worcester, owing to the influence of the English Bishop Wulfstan, who held the see until 1095 and whose

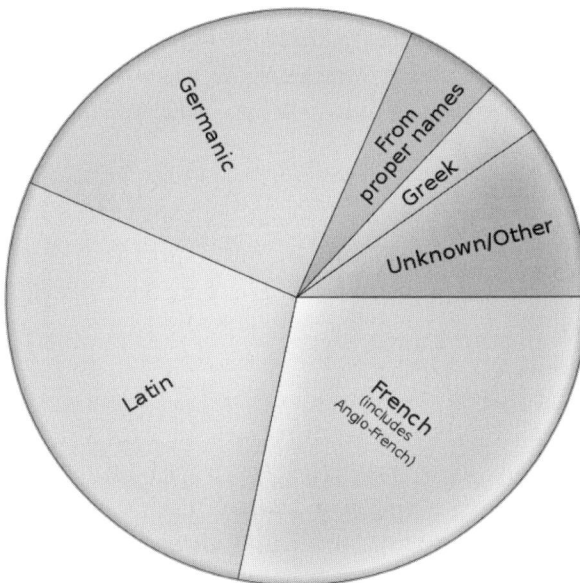

The origins of the English language shown on a pie chart. About 30 per cent of English words are derived from French, roughly the same as Latin. These figures are based on a computerised survey of roughly 80,000 words taken from the *Shorter Oxford Dictionary* 3rd Edition.

own life was written by a Worcester monk in Anglo-Saxon, the persistence of the native language in religious works was particularly strong. Collections of sermons, Anglo-Saxon versions of sections of the Bible, service books and lives of saints continued to be copied there in the twelfth century. However, Anglo-Norman gained rapidly over English as the language of romance poetry, commerce and architecture.

Norman Place Names in England

Conventionally, it has been argued that the Normans had relatively little impact on English place names and it is true that most places retained their pre-Conquest names, sometimes modified to suit the French tongue. For example, *Grantebrige* became Cambridge and *Dunholme* became Durham. Such place-name spellings to some extent represent an attempt by French-speaking clerks to render the pronunciation of English country people. Although the influence of Norman scribes is generally very strong in the Domesday Book, specific Norman place names are rare. Gulpher and Boulge (Suffolk) are exceptional Domesday entries; the former meaning 'fox's den', while *boulge* means 'a piece of land covered with heather'.[8]

When eleventh- and twelfth-century French clerks came across sounds or combinations of sounds that were absent from French or Latin, they would tend to substitute for them the nearest sounds in those languages. Many earlier Old English or Scandinavian names were affected by this process. For example, the simplification of 'ch' to 'c' has resulted in many names that might have ended in 'chester' finishing in 'cester', as in Gloucester, Cirencester, Worcester, and is the reason for 'cer' in Cerne and Cerney. Similarly, Old English names beginning with 's' followed by a consonant were liable to be affected by this process; sometimes the 's' was dropped, thus Snottingham becomes Nottingham and Studbury becomes Tutbury. The combination 'shr' as in Shrewsbury was

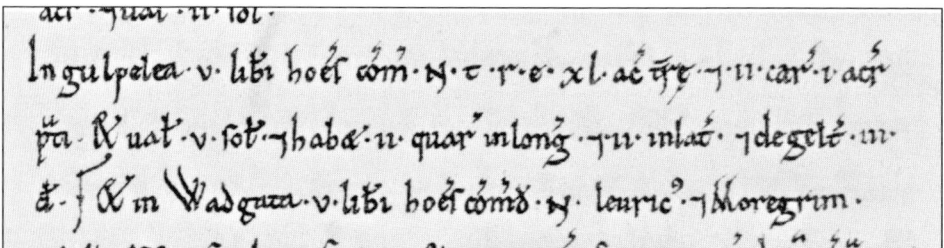

Domesday entry for Gulpher, on the edge of Felixstowe in Suffolk. A rare occurrence of a Norman French place name in the survey. This small manor of five freemen was held by the Norman Roger Bigod and, unusually, Northmann the Sheriff was the occupying tenant in 1086 as he had been in 1066.

particularly difficult for French speakers and the scribes resorted to Salop, an alternative name that has survived. 'Cn' was made easier by the insertion of a vowel, and Cnock became Cannock. The initial sound of place names beginning with 'y' did not exist in Norman French; place names such as Jarrow and Jesmond would have been Yarrow and Yesmond if they had not been subject to French influence. The initial sound 'th' was also unknown to the Normans; this they replaced by 't' or 'ch', thus French pronunciation has survived in some names such as Chilsworthy and Tingrith which otherwise would have been Thilsworth and Thingrith. There is a concentration of Anglo-Norman pronunciation in the Durham area; for example, in addition to Durham itself, Whorlton, Lintz and Jarrow might indicate a concentration of French-speaking population in that area after the Conquest.

Some castles were given French names. For instance, Alan Rufus, a Breton leader at Hastings and a cousin of William the Conqueror, laid the foundations of his great castle overlooking the River Swale in north Yorkshire. The original name of the settlement here was *Hindrelaghe*, which was changed to Richmond (Fr. *Richemunde* 'strong hill'). The Conqueror's standard-bearer's brother, Robert de Todeni, founded his castle and priory on a commanding headland in the Leicestershire Wolds and called it Belvoir (Fr. *Belveder* 'beautiful view'). Beaudesert Castle (Fr. 'beautiful wilderness') is sited on a mount overlooking Henley-in-Arden (Warwickshire) and is in the form of a motte and bailey located within a pre-existing hill fort, built by Thurstan de Montfort in the first half of the twelfth century.

In addition to castles, new towns, monasteries, hunting parks and chases were often given French names. Newly founded religious houses were frequently given French or Latin descriptive names; Beaulieu (Hampshire) 'beautiful place' is a Cistercian abbey founded by King John and was known as *Bellus Locus Regis* 'the beautiful place of the king'. Another example, Beauchief Abbey (Derbyshire) 'beautiful headland', was a Premonstratensian monastery on the edge of Sheffield, founded *c*.1170. The element *beau* is also found in Beamish, Beaumanor, Bolasis, Belper, Belvoir and Beachy Head. There are numerous Beaumonts and Belmonts, and these continued to be applied well beyond the Norman era. Two Yorkshire monasteries, Jervaulx and Rievaulx, have hybrid names in which the old river names Ure and Rye precede the French *vals* 'valley'. Charterhouse on the Mendips in Somerset was named after the great monastic house at Chartreuse.

There are a considerable number of village names where an aristocratic French family name has been attached to an Old English settlement name, thus providing us with some of our more exotic and bizarre place names: for example, Stoke Mandeville, Berry Pomeroy, Ashby-de-la-Zouch, Croome d'Abitot and Shepton Mallet. Occasionally, the names have coalesced, as in the case of Stokesay (Shropshire), which comes from Stoke-de-Say, derived from the de Say family, tenants of Stoke in

The ruins of Beaumont Palace, Oxford, in 1785. The palace was originally built by Henry I outside the city's north gate, close to his royal hunting lodge at Woodstock. No trace of the palace survives today apart from its name, in Beaumont Street.

the Domesday Book. Other combined names of interest include Chapel-en-le-Frith and Haughton-le-Skerne. One uniquely exotic place name that dates from this period is Baldock (Hertfordshire), which comes from the Old French name for Baghdad – *Baldac*. The name, which came to England by way of the Crusades, was given by the Knights Templar, who held the manor in the twelfth century.

It has generally been accepted that there are no or very few Norman field names, because the spoken French language was largely restricted to the aristocracy and landed class. Field names tend to develop from the vernacular, which was largely Anglo-Saxon and Anglo-Scandinavian during the Norman era. Some recent analysis suggests that Norman field names may be more common than previously thought: Bruera (Cheshire), Temple Bruer (Lincolnshire) and Bruern (Oxfordshire) all refer to 'heathland'; Kearnsey (Kent) 'place where cress grows'; and Salcey (Northamptonshire) 'a place abounding in willows'. The field name Cangle/Kangle derives from 'chancel' and means 'rail, lattice', 'fence-boundary' or 'fenced enclosure'. Examples are found in Kanglecroft (Hertfordshire), le Cangel (Essex) and Cangle (Oxfordshire). The place-name element *ewe*, Anglo–Norman for 'water', is very close to the Anglo–Saxon ĕa, but can be found at Belewe and Caldew in Westmorland.

Stokesay Castle, Shropshire. The manor was known simply as Stoke up until *c*.1200, when it acquired the affix from the de Say family, who held the estate for much of the twelfth century. The addition of a French family name on to existing Saxon place names increasingly occurred as the volume of written records grew from the mid-twelfth century onwards. (*Trevor Rowley*)

Similarly, *mond* 'hill' has replaced various Old English and Old Norse words: Old English *mūoa* in Jesmond (Northumberland), formerly *Gesemuthe* 'mouth of Ouse Burn'; Old Norse *mot* in Beckermonds (Yorkshire) 'confluence of the streams'; and Old English *mōt* in Eamont (Cumberland) also 'junction of the streams'. The commonest alternation is that of French *ville* with Old English *feld* 'open land', especially in the south and west. Surviving examples include Clanville (Hampshire, Somerset) 'clean open land', Enville (Staffordshire) 'level open land', Longville (Shropshire) 'long open land', as contrasted with Tovil (Kent) 'sticky open land'. A surprising number of field names containing Anglo-Norman elements, such as 'close', have been found in an examination of place names in Cumbria. It would seem that the occurrence of such place-name elements points to a rather deeper penetration of the Anglo-Norman language into the English countryside than has been assumed.[9]

Personal Names

After the Norman Conquest, radical changes took place in the types of personal names used in England. Anglo-Saxon personal names rapidly fell out of fashion

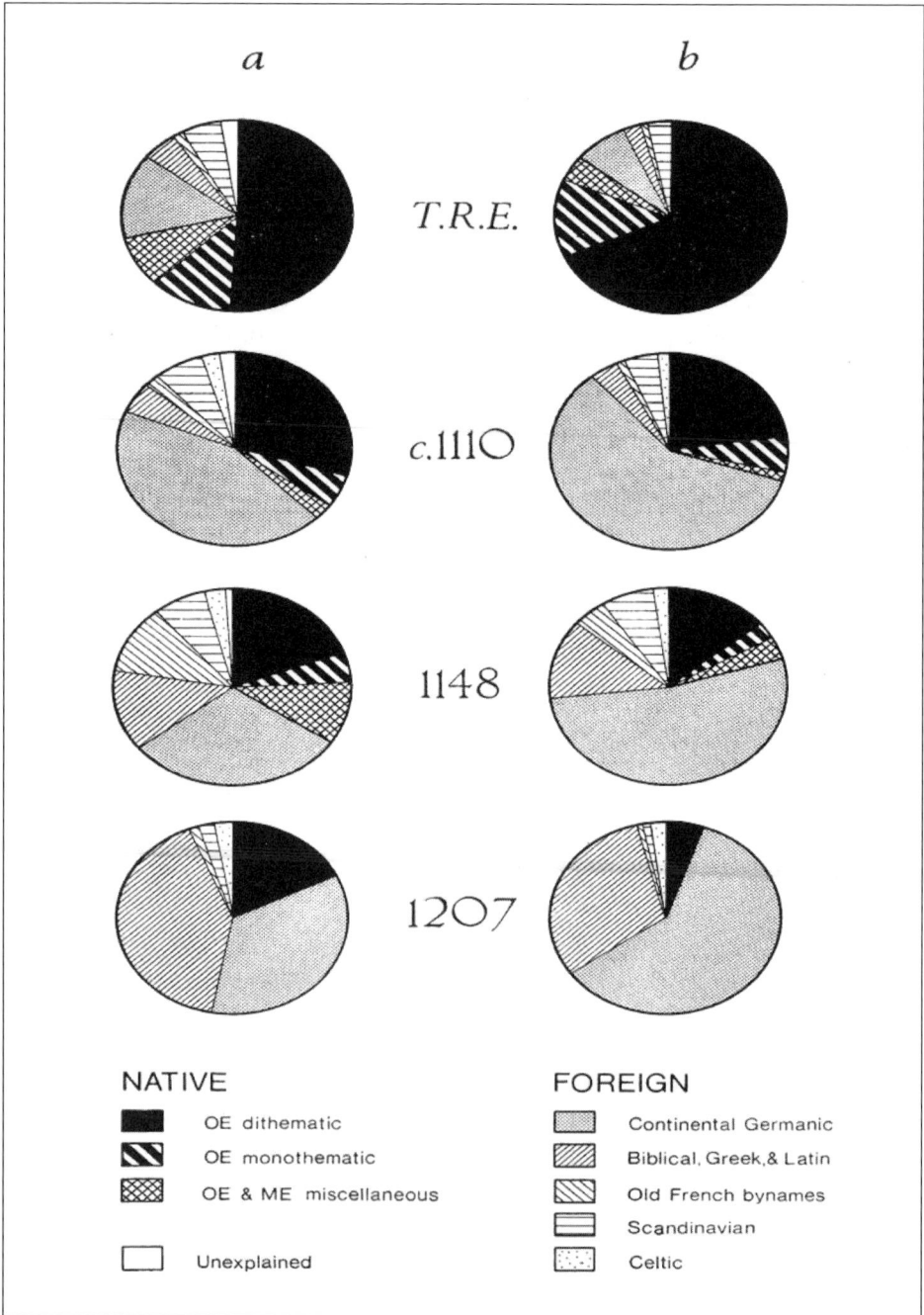

The changing character of personal names in Winchester between 1066 (T.R.E.) and 1207 is clearly shown in these pie charts. The analysis is based on names which appear in the *Winton Domesday*, two surveys of Winchester; one made *c*.1110 and the other in 1148. The charts in column (a) record the numbers of different names, while those in column (b) are estimates of the number of occurrences of the different categories. (*Biddle, 1976: 186*)

and were replaced by Norman alternatives, which were primarily of French or Continental German origin. A little later there was a fashion for biblical names, which had been rare in Saxon England. In Winchester, for example, Norman personal names were in the majority soon after the Conquest, when they were widely adopted by the Anglo-Norman population. Though Old English names continued in use for some time – indeed, one or two have had a continuous history to the present day – for the most part they gradually fell into disuse.

There are very few place names that incorporate a Norman personal name. A rare example of a place name that is made up exclusively of a Norman lord's name is Holdgate (Shropshire), which up to 1066 was called Stanton. Helgot de Reisolent, a tenant of Roger de Montgomery, was the holder of the manor with a castle here in 1086. Roger gave his name to the town founded a few miles to the west of Offa's Dyke in Wales. More common are instances where Norman personal names were attached to an earlier Anglo-Saxon place-name element. The largest group is that compounded with Old English *tun* 'farmstead, village' and, later, also 'manor': in the north and Midlands, names such as Williamston (Northumberland) from William, Howton (Herefordshire) from Hugh, Rowlstone (Herefordshire) and Rollestone (Wiltshire) from Rolf, Walterstone (Herefordshire) from Walter and Botcheston (Leicestershire) from Bochard; in the south of England, Marlston (Berkshire) from Martel and Mainstone (Hampshire) from Matthew; in Wiltshire, Faulston from Fallard, Flamston from Flambard and Richardson from Richard; while Dorset has Bryanston from Brian (a Norman name of Breton origin), Ranston from Randulf and Waterston from Walter. In the south-west there are also places that use a family name as the first element. These include Drewston from Drew, Johnstone from John, Jurston from Jordan, Penson and Penstone from Pain and Stevenstone from Stephen. Post-Conquest personal names are only rarely compounded with other English elements for habitations, as in Painswick (Gloucestershire) 'Pain's Farm'.

Anglo-Norman Literature

The growth and influence of Anglo-Norman literature should be seen against the broad cultural relationship between Normandy and England, beginning in the decades before the Conquest (see Plate 22). The influence was mutual; Norman art and sculpture show the influence of English design and English skills in such differing areas as coinage and embroidery, and these were developed by the Conqueror. The vernacular literature of Anglo-Saxon England was well established with an output unequalled by any other European principality. In contrast, there was relatively little pre-Conquest literature from Normandy, although after the Conquest, Norman writers turned to Anglo-Saxon literature, law and cultural traditions for inspiration and information. Anglo-Saxon writing provided the Normans with a plentiful source for serious, high-quality literature, written in the vernacular for the education and entertainment of the aristocracy.

The opening of Robert Wace's Norman-French verse *Roman de Brut* from the earliest manuscript of the poem, dating from the late twelfth century. Brutus of Troy was the legendary founder of Britain and appears in several early medieval 'Brut' accounts of the islands (*c*.1110–*c*.1174). (*Durham Cathedral MS C. iv.27*)

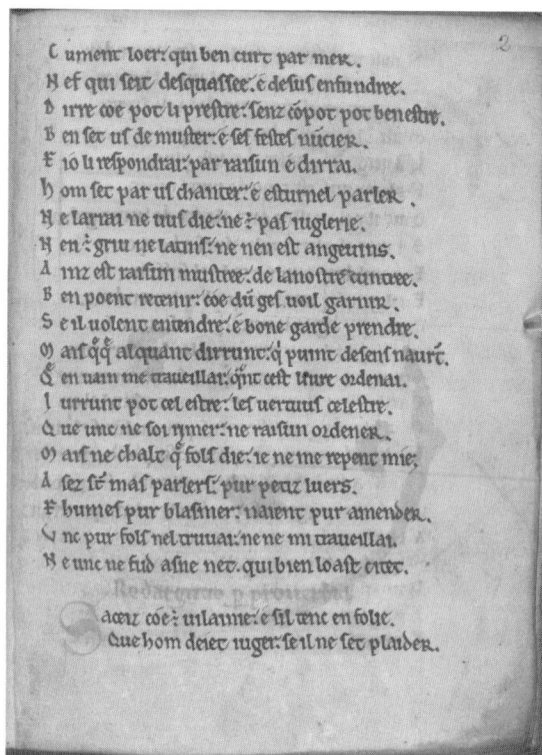

In the post-Conquest period, the choice of language was dictated by the taste of the expected audience or patron, or by the nature of the topic. Importantly, language was not yet perceived as part of national identity. The material moves easily from one vernacular to another within the same manuscript or even within the same poem. This flexibility is demonstrated by the large intake of Romance vocabulary into English throughout the Anglo-Norman period and means that its literary influence is pervasive rather than distinctive. Anglo-Norman literature developed more through its response to Latin rather than to English, often representing the popularization of more scholarly Latin writing. (See Plate 23)

The literature of the first century after the Conquest is small in quantity, but significantly ahead of developments on the Continent. From its beginning, Anglo-Norman narrative literature presented the ecclesiastical and secular rulers of Anglo-Norman England with material about the land they now ruled. This perspective is first apparent in the work of the early-twelfth-century historians in England and Normandy, for instance, William of Malmesbury, Henry of Huntingdon and Orderic Vitalis. In 1155 the Norman poet Wace completed his *Roman de Brut*, a highly influential account of British history, which was later translated into English. He then moved on to Norman history with the less well-known *Roman de Rou*, *c*.1160–70.

Anglo-Norman literature flourished in the reign of Henry II when the Angevin court was the dominant literary centre of Europe. The Angevin succession, together with the inheritance of Aquitaine, placed England within an empire that extended from the Welsh Marches to the Pyrenees and gave access to all the cultural diversity associated with those lands. The Anglo-Norman *Tristan and Isolde* was the most striking of the new literary achievements. Its sympathetic account of doomed and passionate adultery and the absence of judgemental elements commonly found in other medieval writings meant that contemporary literary reaction tended to be largely negative, although historical criticism has been much kinder. Some of the major narrative works of the following decades have been interpreted as being responses to the morality of *Tristan*. Nevertheless, the story of Tristan and Isolde spread to become one of the important statements of passionate love in European literature.

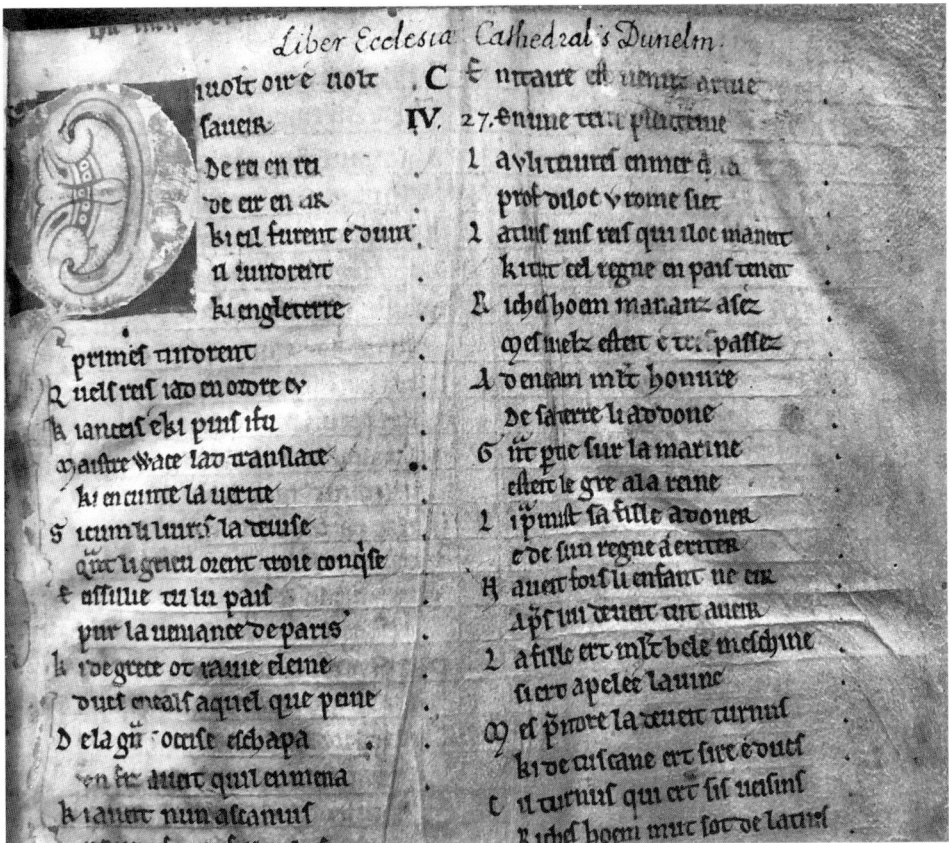

Extract from the *Comput*, written in 1113 by Phillipe de Thaon, the first poet to write in the Anglo-Norman vernacular instead of Latin. The composition discusses the calendar and was compiled in order to help secular priests provide pastoral care. This version was copied at Holme Cultram Abbey, a Cistercian house in Cumbria. (*BL Cotton MS AV. f 2rCIII3*)

Much early literature was written for the immediate circle of the royal court, but at the same time there was a development of romance written for specific baronial patrons. This was directed towards a more provincial audience with elaborate treatment of the so-called 'Matter of England romances', partly based on genuine Anglo-Saxon or Scandinavian legend. Largely fictional work, appearing from the late twelfth century onwards, such as *Haveloc the Dane* and *Romance of Horn*, represents the best products of this genre. *Boeve de Haumtone* (Bevis of Hampton) and *Guy de Warewic* are possibly connected with the family interest of the owners of Arundel Castle and the earls of Warwick respectively. Both were later translated into English for a wider audience. Such romances demonstrated in their plots the broader interests of an incoming feudal dynasty, the hero acquiring lands by marriage with an heiress, holding his own in conflict with the centralizing power of the monarchy, and borrowed the names and geography of England to establish authenticity.

Alongside secular narratives, saints' histories were written for monastic and lay audiences, generally with courtly taste and an interest in tales of those pre-Conquest saints who had shrines in the new cathedrals. The patronage of successive queens supported such twelfth-century works as Benedeit's *Voyage of St Brendan the Abbot* (*c*.1118–21), a colourful account of the Celtic saint's miraculous journeys, and Denys Pyramis's *Life of St Edmund the Martyr*. Drama also evolved in the twelfth century with the *Jeu d'Adam* (1180), the oldest extant play written in any Old French dialect. The *Seinte Resurrection* (*c*.1200) is another liturgical play that shows a high level of literary ability and conscious stagecraft.

Historical writing in the vernacular continued in the late twelfth and thirteenth centuries with the *Brut* tradition of British history, lively accounts of contemporary events such as Jordan Fantosme's *Chronique* and *The Scottish Wars of Henry II*, a heroic play on the conquest of Ireland, and a popular biography of Richard I. The Anglo-Norman literary tradition did not, of course, stop with the early Plantagenets. Up until the time of Chaucer and beyond, the royal court continued to keep up with the dominant fashions of France. However, outside that circle, in baronial halls, manor houses and monasteries in England, the literary development of chronicled romance and saints' lives provided a continuing tradition of vernacular provincial writing.

Music in Anglo-Norman Society

The Normans were accustomed to a range of music, both liturgical and secular; nearly everyone would have been exposed to sung Masses, Offices and liturgical drama set to Latin texts. Members of the clergy and the aristocracy would have also enjoyed secular and devotional songs, set to Latin and/or vernacular texts, and instrumental music as entertainment (see Plate 24). Music of the times was relatively simple in that there was often only one voice part, monophony, and this was usually unaccompanied. Much of the music was vocal, and the text, usually sacred or devotional, was the source of the rhythm as well as of the melodic line. However, there were also liturgical dramas and other entertainment whose music was more complex, with instrumental accompaniment on bowed and/or plucked instruments, drums and pipes, and with two or more voice parts either singing together or in alternation. In the case of secular songs, the language was often vernacular and the subject matter far from liturgical. Purely instrumental music was also heard and danced to by the upper classes. Music was, like everything else for the Normans, something to be exported, imported and, perhaps most of all, assimilated.[10]

This Cluniac tradition was the recognized source of 'correct' liturgical practice, and was exported by the Normans to England. Liturgical drama and secular music, in the form of songs, either unaccompanied or accompanied by bowed or plucked instruments, drums or pipes, was also an important part of Norman life, especially among the aristocracy. The vernacular texts set in these songs trace the intermingling of conquerors and conquered, characteristic of the Norman pattern of invasion followed by assimilation. It would appear that in their music, as in so many other things, the Normans both influenced and were influenced by what they encountered in the countries they invaded. This phenomenon of mutual influence is a major contributory factor in the relative homogeneity of style that characterizes this period in Western music history.

The 'most powerful impact of the Conquest on liturgical music [in England] came from the wholesale replacement of senior monastic officials by Norman monks, with a resulting Norman influence in liturgy, ceremonial and chant in which the practices of Cluny and Bec were particularly important'. But even as they exported their own practices, the Normans also assimilated local practice. 'Eleventh-century English and Norman monks also continued the tenth-century Benedictine literary and musical tradition of writing hymns, sequences and full rhymed Offices for Anglo-Saxon saints' and 'many Continental tropes [additional texts set to music interpolated into existing Mass texts as commentaries] have been reworked ... to suit local needs and tastes.'[11]

Liturgical Music

Mass and Office settings, always of Latin texts, were largely monophonic, with one voice line, but examples of simple note–against–note polyphony with two or more voices also survive from the late eleventh and early twelfth centuries, one each from Canterbury and Winchester, both of which remained centres of musical creation and scholarship. Later on, liturgical music was influenced by practices and the musical repertory at the cathedral of Notre-Dame in Paris. These practices were centred on the two-voice polyphony for all major feasts of the Church year as set out in the famous source, *Magnus liber*, composed by Leonin in the 1170s and early 1180s. The Normans and those they ruled surely must have heard these Mass and Office settings as well as the liturgical dramas associated with the celebration of the

Nativity and the Resurrection. Based on the biblical story of the 'empty tomb' and the question *quem quaeritis?* that asks where the resurrected one had been taken, this drama typically consists of alternating sung lines and voices and was performed in monasteries throughout northern France before the closing hymn in the service of Matins. Other liturgical dramas, including the Magi plays and Easter Pilgrims' plays, abounded during this time. The texts and music were characterized by a regular rhyme scheme and systematic melodies that combined poetry with distinct melodies. These liturgical dramas provide a 'bridge' from the purely liturgical, Latin-texted music to the non-liturgical and, sometimes, vernacular-texted medieval songs that were doubtless also heard and performed by the Normans.

These musical developments were not welcomed by everyone. In his *Speculum caritatis* (*c.*1142–3), Abbot Aelred of Rievaulx warned his novices about the artificialities and excesses in the performance of contemporary music. John of Salisbury, in *Policraticus* (1159), condemned the 'unnatural' vocal timbres and 'florid' tunes indulged in by the singers. They were complaining about the ad hoc ornamentation of slowly sung chant by one or more of the singers simultaneously, before it began to be codified in the written record.

The Play of Daniel. A twelfth-century illustration from a liturgical drama text. (*BL. Add MS 11695*)

Non-Liturgical Music

Anglo-Norman non-liturgical music is made up of devotional and quasi-sacred songs, secular songs and instrumental pieces. Song texts were in the vernacular, and a consideration of such texts reveals that there was considerable influence both from the Normans on those they conquered and vice versa. In England 'the first hundred years of Norman rule saw the introduction at the highest level of society of a new vernacular with its own tradition of secular entertainment music. These included Anglo-Norman and Middle English verse chronicles, epics, [and] romances.'[12] Devotional monophonic Latin songs were also written, and the monastic rhymed Office for St Thomas of Canterbury, written in the late 1170s, continued that Anglo-Saxon and early Norman tradition of writing in this form in Latin text. While Latin remained the language of choice for most non-liturgical devotional songs, French was the language of social intercourse and literature among the aristocracy in England after the Conquest. Therefore, the ubiquitous romance song both in Normandy and in Britain at this time invariably had a French or Anglo-Norman text. Songs were both unaccompanied and accompanied by plucked and/or bowed instruments (e.g. by *harpa* or early lute and/or viols, pipes and drums).

During the twelfth century, although there was 'a wider musical culture embracing Anglo-Norman England and northern France', there was, as time went on, a 'drift of Anglo-Norman away from mainland French dialects, and [this was] a process for which one can find parallels in politics, the fine arts, architecture, and music'.[13]

A Note on the Visual Arts

As in so many other areas, the immediate impact of the Conquest on the visual arts was negative. Not only was much illuminated literature, murals, tapestries and jewellery stolen or destroyed, but in these creative areas, unlike architecture, the Normans had nothing to replace the prolific, accomplished output of the Anglo-Saxons. Accordingly, in the decades after 1066 there was little produced that was not derived from English sources, in one way or another. (See Plate 25)

The best known and most notable example of this process was the Bayeux Tapestry, a Norman pictorial narrative of the Conquest created by English craftspeople. To many, the embroidery portrays the quintessential story of the Norman takeover, its images definitively marking the end of Anglo-Saxon England, with the defeat of the English army and the dramatic death of King Harold. Yet it was almost certainly produced at St Augustine's, Canterbury, by English craftswomen and men. Much of its imagery was derived from English illuminated manuscripts, and there are many other indications that it was essentially an English product.[14] There are examples of post-Conquest murals which display a similar flamboyance to the tapestry, but are not as skilfully executed. At Claverley in Shropshire the murals have a similar theme of knightly warfare, apparently retelling the *Song of Roland*.

After 1066 the English School of illuminated manuscripts slowed in its scale of production and there was a move towards more distinct regional styles at places such as Canterbury and Winchester. The richness of colour and materials found in pre-Conquest art was not resumed until the twelfth century, but the Normans were influenced by what they found in Britain. Anglo–Saxon monk illustrators seem to have travelled to Normandy and there is some evidence of books at Fécamp, for example, being written on one side of the Channel and illustrated on the other. Illumination both in Normandy and in England between 1066 and 1100 was highly redolent of Anglo–Saxon work in terms of both figure style and decoration.[15]

Nevertheless, it is not until the twelfth century that a vibrant new Anglo–Norman visual art emerges, exemplified by the Eadwine Psalter, which was illustrated at Canterbury Cathedral (1160–70). It contains the Book of Psalms in three languages, Latin, Old English and Anglo–Norman, and is named after a Canterbury monk-scribe who was involved in its production. It bears some resemblance to the Carolingian Utrecht Psalter, which was kept at Canterbury for some time. Among the images contained within the psalter is an inset of Eadwine at work and the remarkable plan of the water works of Christ Church, Canterbury. (See Plate 25)

Extract from the Bayeux Tapestry showing the death of King Harold during the Battle of Hastings. The tapestry (in reality it was an embroidery) was almost certainly commissioned by Bishop Odo of Bayeux, William the Conqueror's half-brother. Odo was also Earl of Kent and the tapestry is thought to have been created at St Augustine's Priory, Canterbury.

Above: Wall paintings at All Saints, Claverley, Shropshire, created *c*.1200. The featured photograph shows 15 metres of fighting knights, possibly as part of a version of the *Song of Roland*. (*Mike Searle*)

Left: Prior Wilbert's twelfth-century octagonal water tower on the north side of Canterbury Cathedral. The tower formed part of the system devised to provide clean water to the priory (see Plate 26). (*Whn64*)

Conclusion

The analysis of historic landscapes of all ages has changed significantly since W. G. Hoskins used his inspired eye to establish the basis of the discipline in the 1950s. As we move into the third decade of the twenty-first century, intuitive interpretation is increasingly rejected as scientific modelling and advanced technology move centre stage. A victim of these developments is reader accessibility; one of the joys of the Hoskins approach was its simplicity and openness, appealing to audiences well beyond the professional archaeologist, geographer or historian. The new landscape histories tend to adopt vocabularies that exclude all but the specialist. Brian Roberts, a historical geographer who has been applying specialist analytical tools to settlement studies for decades, admitted with commendable frankness that, 'For many years the author has been creating and publishing settlement models that are on the edge of viability, i.e. they are too complex to be understood without great effort and some experience, and indeed, some, like that line in Browning's poetry, are eventually a puzzle for him!'[1]

The Norman conquest of England opened the country to stronger influences from France and Continental Europe; although the links with Scandinavia were not completely broken, they were weakened to the point that another Danish or Norwegian king was unlikely. It was the Norman connection that was by far the strongest in the century and a half following the Conquest. There was what Lefferts calls 'a wider culture embracing Anglo-Norman England and northern France'; there was, as time went on, a 'drift of Anglo-Norman away from mainland French dialects, and [this was] a process for which one can find parallels in politics, the fine arts, architecture, and music'.[2] In England 'the first hundred years of Norman rule saw the introduction at the highest level of society of a new vernacular with its own tradition of secular culture. These included Anglo-Norman and Middle English verse chronicles, epics, [and] romances.'[3] Devotional monophonic Latin songs were also written, and the monastic rhymed Office for St Thomas of Canterbury, written in the late 1170s, continued that Anglo-Saxon and early Norman tradition of writing in this form in Latin text. While Latin remained the language of choice for most ecclesiastical activities, French was the language of social intercourse and literature among the aristocracy in England after the Conquest.

England readily and rapidly absorbed the new monastic orders, such as the Cistercians, that developed and spread rapidly during the twelfth century.

The manorial system, which had been evolving before the Conquest, became widespread. Landscape features specifically associated with the seigneurial class became common. Manor houses, many of them moated and some of them fortified, with assemblages of fishponds, dovecotes, rabbit warrens and deer parks, were widely spread across the country by 1200.

The apparent absence of change in the archaeological record has led to the perception that 'the archaeological signature of the Norman Conquest was minimal'.[4] Archaeology is capable of providing answers not deducible from other sources, but in the past its application to the Norman era has been constrained. The material record of the period – coins, pottery, burial practice and vernacular architecture – shows little apparent change after 1066. The relatively short time span covering the Conquest and its aftermath has restricted the perceived capacity of material evidence to be sufficiently precise. Dating for the period has traditionally relied heavily on pottery analysis, and while contemporary pottery is commonly found in southern and eastern England, it is less frequent in the north and west, where there are areas that remained aceramic until the late twelfth century. Hence, there are marked regional differences in the value of ceramic studies. Furthermore, where it is found, Saxo-Norman pottery often changed little in form between the tenth and early twelfth centuries, making it difficult to distinguish between pre- and post-Conquest strata.

More recent work, which has adopted a multidisciplinary approach to the material evidence for the period 1000–1200, is producing exciting results.[5] Archaeobotanical and zooarchaeological evidence suggests it is possible to identify cultural and agricultural changes over a broader time span, indicating that there are significant regional differences in changes in land use in England before and after the Norman Conquest. Important trends in the production and consumption of some commodities stretching over the eleventh and twelfth centuries can be identified. For example, over the two centuries there was a move from barley towards wheat, a move from cows to sheep and goats, and a growing demand for maritime fish. Changes in diet after the Conquest are revealed by the analysis of animal–bone assemblages from archaeological sites. There appears to have been an increase in the consumption of pig, chicken and game after 1066, particularly on elite sites. The types of fish consumed also changed, with a far greater emphasis on coastal fish after 1066. The impact on the landscape of these developments may at first seem marginal, but they link in to agricultural practices, afforestation, emparkment and significant changes in fishing patterns in the twelfth century. They also link in to cultural changes whose impact on the contemporary environment is difficult to discern, but new ways of examining the evidence are leading to greater understanding of their importance. It would appear that new archaeological techniques designed to identify more nuanced changes are ideal for unravelling landscape changes for such a complex period.

Although the Normans inherited and adapted much from the Anglo-Scandinavian world, the English landscape in 1200 was very different from that of 1066 and this would not have happened if Duke William had not defeated King Harold at the Battle of Hastings on 14 October 1066. When Henry II became king in 1154, the Norman dynasty in England came to an end, but not Norman England. Many of those military, administrative and ecclesiastical innovations continued, developed and flourished. Virtually every aspect of English life had been touched by the Normans. The landscapes in 1200 of village and field, of town, castle and market, and of cathedral, monastery and parish church were not of themselves all the result of the Norman Conquest, but they had all been affected and altered by the Conquest. The Normans can be viewed as catalysts, responsible for changing the Saxon landscape into the medieval landscape, as one great Anglo-Saxon scholar observed that 'sooner or later every aspect of life was changed by the Norman Conquest'.[6]

Endnotes

Introduction

1. Gransden 1995: 1–52.
2. Abrams 2012: 45–64.
3. Rowley 1983: 32.
4. Hoskins 1955.
5. Liddiard 2018; Hoskins 1976: 233; Hoskins 1973: 23.
6. Le Patourel 1976.
7. McClain and Sykes 2019.

Chapter 1

1. Lennard 1959: 1.
2. Muir and Turner 1998: 9–12.
3. Goscelin, *Hist. Augustine*, col 51.
4. *Liber Eliensis* 2005: 213.
5. Gillingham 2012: 47–8.
6. Sawyer 2013: 1.
7. Lewis 1994.
8. Wickham 2005.
9. Earl is the Old English form of the Scandinavian *jarl*.
10. Rowley 1983: 59.
11. Roffe 2007: 67.
12. Knowles 1994.
13. Darby 1977.
14. Roffe and Keats-Rohan 2016.
15. Baxter 2017: 226.
16. Loyn 1978.
17. Baxter 2001.
18. Barlow 2011: 19–36.
19. Stafford 1985: 34–9.
20. Gerrard and Aston 2007.
21. Stamper 2009: 343.
22. Rowley 1981; Hall 2014.
23. Hall 2014: 181.
24. Stamper 2009: 341.
25. Oosthuizen 2005.
26. Cantor 1982: 17–18.

27. Sawyer 2013: 15-20.
28. Darby 1977: 167,163.
29. Darby 1977: 129, 144, 148.
30. 'The Fisherman's Dialogue' from Aelfric of Eynsham's *Colloquy*, *c*.998. Although whalebone artefacts have been found in Anglo-Saxon contexts, there is little other evidence for whaling in England. The Normans had whaling fleets based at Dives and at Fécamp.
31. Bond 2004: 185.
32. Jervis *et al.* 2017: 250.
33. Historic England 2018.
34. Fowler 1922: 72.
35. RCHME 1972: 60–1; 137–8.
36. Darby 1977: 287.
37. Alexander 2007.
38. Alexander 2007.
39. Watts 2017: 185.
40. Keen 1988: 133–80.
41. Keen 1988: 133–80.
42. Unwin 1990.
43. Lamb 1977: 435–49.
44. Bond 2004: 165–9.

Chapter 2
 1. Hewitt 2018: 75.
 2. VCH Sussex, 1905.
 3. Hewitt 2016.
 4. Robinson and Williams 1983.
 5. Foord and Clephane-Cameron 2015.
 6. Fields 2006; Combes and Lynes 1995.
 7. Jamieson 2019.
 8. Gillingham 2018.
 9. Combes and Lynes 1995.
10. Fradley 2011.
11. Allen Brown 1989: 127.
12. Haslam 2021.
13. Rowley 2016: 140–6.
14. Morillo 1994: 102.
15. Roberts 2008: 143.
16. Palmer 1995a: 23–44.
17. Hooke 1998: 142–4.
18. Searle 1974: 22.
19. Welshman 2019.
20. Searle 1980.

21. Hewitt 2018a: 1–25.
22. www.channel4.com.
23. Gillingham 2018.
24. Hewitt 2016.
25. Winkler 2020: 1–22.
26. Palmer 1995b: 23–44.

Chapter 3
1. Bates 2016: 296–7.
2. Dyer 2002: 89.
3. Darby 1951: 173.
4. Darby 1977: 238–9.
5. Williams 1997: 92.
6. Williams 2004.
7. Prior 2007: 82–4.
8. Williams 2019: 14–19.
9. Williams 1997: 39.
10. Kapelle 1979: 3.
11. Williams 1995: 43–4.
12. Baring 1898.
13. Palmer 1995a.
14. Darby 1977: 261–3.
15. Hallam 1988; 135.
16. Dalton 2002: 23.
17. Darby 1977: 251–2.
18. Donkin 1978.
19. Palliser 2014: 91.
20. Allen 2012: 1–22.
21. Hinton 1990: 121.
22. Creighton and Rippon 2017: 71–2.
23. Kapelle 1979.
24. Allison 2003.
25. Roberts 2008: 146.
26. Austin 1990: 141–50.
27. Roberts 2008: 144.
28. Rex 2014: 120–79.

Chapter 4
1. Wickham 2016: 103.
2. Harvey 2014: 264.
3. Dodgson 1987: 123.
4. Roffe 2007: 167–8; Oksanen 2016:213–18.
5. Clover and Gibson 1979: 166–7.

6. Williams 1995: 12.
7. Lennard 1959: 67.
8. Williams 1995: 79, 89.
9. Williams 2018: 124.
10. Williams 1997: 104.
11. Williams 1997: 107.
12. Baxter 2012: 271–308.
13. Rowley 2013: 116–7.
14. Ivens 1980.
15. Bates 1975.
16. Barlow 1997.
17. Creighton 2005: 98.
18. Jervis 2016: 219–33.
19. Campbell 1975.
20. Hewitt 2010: 130–44.
21. Roberts 2008.
22. Roberts 2008: 147–9.
23. Creighton and Rippon 2017: 64–5.
24. Verbeckmoes 1988: 725–56.
25. Le Patourel 1976: 58.
26. Green 2004.
27. Rippon 2008: 242–5.
28. Laws 1888: 107.
29. John 2020.
30. Rippon 2008: 242–5.
31. Kissock 1997.

Chapter 5
1. Bartlett 2002: 270.
2. Jamieson 2019.
3. Leary et al 2013.
4. Creighton 2002: 3.
5. Allcroft 1908: 401–2.
6. Creighton 2002: 160.
7. Creighton 2002: 198.
8. Wright et al. 2017: 6-25.
9. Lovelock 2013: 287–9.
10. *Liddiard 2002: 27.*
11. Williams 2003.
12. Renn 1994: 177–98.
13. Blair 2018: 390–5.
14. Blair 2018: 399.
15. Poore *et al.* 2009: 1–18.
16. Flight and Harrison 1978.

17. Paul Drury Partnership 2009: 12–17.
18. Ivens 1984: 118.
19. Colvin 1963b: 3–4.
20. Jope and Threlfall 1946–7; Ivens 1984.
21. Armitage 1912.
22. Wyeth 2018.
23. Pettifer 1995: 98.
24. 21 Impey and Parnell 2000.
25. Barlow *et al.* 1976: 325–7.
26. Steane 1993: 72.
27. James 1990: 42.
28. Lilley 2017: 30–56.
29. Hope 1909.
30. Pounds 1994: 11.
31. Lilley 2002: 140–2.
32. Goodall 2006.

Chapter 6

1. Liddiard 2005, 36.
2. Bond 2007: 172–3.
3. Schofield 1991.
4. King 2002: 6.
5. Bony 1992: 486.
6. Allen 2012: 12.
7. Allen 2012: 20.
8. Sergeant 1899: 6.
9. Biddle 1986.
10. Palliser 2014: 91.
11. Ayers 2004: 13.
12. Ayers 1994: 41.
13. Historic Towns Atlas 1975.
14. Harper-Bill, 2004.
15. Rawcliffe and Wilson 2004: 19.
16. Strutt *et al.* 2018.
17. Gauthiez 1998.
18. Linsley 2005: 112.
19. Rowley 1972: 181.
20. Beresford 1967.

Chapter 7

1. 1 Bates 1982: 248.
2. Brooke 1999: 175.
3. Reilly 1996: 335–52.
4. Bartlett 2002: 407.

5. Matthew 1962: 19–26.
6. Knowles 1940.
7. Lefferts 1990.
8. Dodwell 1982: 216.
9. Dodwell 1982: 219–20.
10. O'Sullivan 2011.
11. Browett 2016: 183–202.
12. Gransden 1982: 89.
13. Hayward 1998.
14. Styler 2019.
15. Bates 2014: 11.
16. Brooke 1999: 147.
17. Bates 2016: 306.
18. Pounds 2000: 174.
19. Round 1964: 268.
20. Bartlett 2002: 262–3.
21. Chaplais 1987: 65–77.
22. *British Archaeological Association 1978: 17.*
23. Morris 2018: 548–9.
24. Rowley 1972.
25. Drury and Rodwell 1978: 133–51.
26. Cragoe 2010: 20–38.
27. Mason 1963: 1–28.
28. Roffey 2017.

Chapter 8

1. Knowles 1940.
2. Cowdrey 1969.
3. Fleming and Barker 2008: 261–90.
4. Green 1997: 409.
5. Hill 1968: 36–41.
6. Hall 1895: 78.
7. Platt 1984: 48–29.
8. Platt 1984: 41.
9. Page, 1974: 150.
10. Donkin 1978.
11. Bond 2004: 247.
12. Bond: personal comment.
13. Blair and Steane 1982: 37–127.
14. Muir 1997: 148.
15. Williams 1970: 65–6.
16. Aston 2000.
17. Gauthiez 1998.
18. Gransden 1998.

19. Bond 2004: 282.
20. Bond 2004: 279.
21. Bond 2004: 287.

Chapter 9
1. Plomer 2006.
2. Rackham 2003.
3. Barnes and Williamson 2015: 38.
4. Barnes and Williamson 2015: 26.
5. The Ancient Oaks of England, Herbaria.plants.ox.ac.uk/bol/ancientoaksofEngland/ deerparks accessed 18 December 2021.
6. Farjon 2017: 274.
7. Bates 1998: 175.
8. Jørgensen 2013.
9. Rollason 2016: 137.
10. Langton 2010: 36–67.
11. Hoofnagle 2017: 25.
12. Crouch 1986: 178.
13. Jørgensen 2009.
14. Saunders 1993: 10.
15. Darby 1977: 232–59.
16. Darby 1977: 198; Roffe 2007: 199.
17. Hawkins and Rumble 1976.
18. Green 2013: 416.
19. Taylor and Muir 1983: 314–15.
20. Holmes 2015: 200–7.
21. Austin 1982.
22. Barnes and Williamson 2015: 98.
23. Liddiard 2003: 4–23.
24. Rackham 1986: 125–7.
25. Battles 2013: 86.
26. Rowe 2007: 128–30.
27. Sykes and Carden 2011.
28. Sykes 2007: 79.
29. Moorhouse 2007: 114–15.
30. Rowe 2007: 144.
31. Moorhouse 2007: 102.
32. Sykes 2007: 49–62.
33. Beresford 1967: 478.
34. Liddiard 2007.
35. Battles 2013: 85.
36. Holmes 2015.
37. Goody 1982: 142.
38. Sykes 2007.

39. Sykes 2007.
40. Thomas 2020: 26–7.
41. Griffin 2007: 21.
42. Oggins 2004: 50–63.
43. Sykes 2007: 65.
44. Thomas 2020.
45. Langton 2014: 5–30.

Chapter 10
 1. Bates 2013.
 2. Fernie 2000: 5.
 3. Bates 2013.
 4. Bates 2013: 21.
 5. Gillingham 1989: 141.
 6. Winkler 2016.
 7. Winkler 2016.
 8. Gillingham 2012: 46.
 9. William of Malmesbury 2002.
10. Shopkow 1997: 132–3.
11. Greenway 1996: 70.
12. Le Patourel 1976: 353–4.
13. Hicks 2009: 40–56.
14. Rowley 2013.
15. Reilly 2020.
16. Rowley 2016: 10–12.
17. Allen Brown 1984: 8.
18. Bates 2013: 92.
19. Fernie 2000: 134–287.
20. Ferguson 2013: 193-201.
21. Fernie 2000: 117.
22. West 2007.
23. Thorpe 1978.
24. Shapland 2013: 29.
25. Jamieson 2019.
26. Eaton 2000.
27. Eaton 2000: 31–57.
28. Henig: personal communication.
29. Turner *et al.* 2004: 223–317.
30. Eaton 2000: 136–7.
31. Howell 2000: 387–95.
32. Eaton 2000: 27.
33. Nancarrow 2014: 72–3, 85.
34. Drury 1982: 30–419.

35. Crummy 1981: 52.
36. Creighton 2002: 149–50.
37. Fernie 2000: 110.
38. Stocker and Vince 1997: 223–32.
39. Jamieson 2019.
40. Flight and Harrison 1978.
41. Paul Drury Partnership 2009: 12–17.
42. Potter 2001: 119–42.
43. Creighton 2002: 39–40.

Chapter 11

1. Short 2003: 191–214.
2. Stenton 1971: 687.
3. Pohl 2015.
4. Hiscock 2003: 132.
5. Alkazwini 2016.
6. Baxter 2012.
7. Poole 1993: 253.
8. Trotter 2014: 118.
9. Trotter 2014.
10. I am indebted to the late Esther Paist for the information about Anglo-Norman music.
11. McKinnon 1990: 173.
12. Lefferts 1990: 170–96.
13. Ibid.
14. Rowley 2016.
15. Dodwell 1982: 226.

Conclusion

1. Roberts 2008: 64.
2. Lefferts 1990: 170–96.
3. Dodwell 1982.
4. Hadley and Dyer 2017: 58.
5. McLain and Sykes 2019.
6. Stenton 1971: 686.

Bibliography

Primary Sources

The Anglo-Saxon Chronicles (2000) eds Swanton, M. et al., London: Phoenix Press.

Annales Cambriae (2012) ed. Williams J., Cambridge: Cambridge University Press.

Bernard of Clairvaux (1970) *Cistercians and Cluniacs: St Bernard's Apologia to Abbot William*. Collegeville, MN: Liturgical Press.

Caesar (2016) *Civil War*, ed. and trans. Damon, C., Cambridge, MA: Harvard University Press.

Chronicle of Battle Abbey (1980) ed. and trans. Searle, E., Oxford: Oxford Medieval Tracts.

Chronicle of John of Worcester, vols ii–iii (1995-8), ed. Darlington, R.R. and McGurk, P., Oxford: Oxford Medieval Tracts, Oxford University Press.

Domesday Book: A Complete Translation (2003). London: Penguin Books.

Gerald of Wales (1978) *The Journey Through Wales and the Description of Wales*. London: Penguin.

Gesta Guillelmi of William of Poitiers (1998) ed. and trans. Davis, R.H.C. and Chibnall, M., Oxford: Clarendon Press.

The Gesta Normannorum Ducum of William of Jumieges, Orderic Vitalis and Robert of Torigni (1992–5) ed. and trans. Van Houts, E.M.C., 2 vols, Oxford: Clarendon Press.

Goscelin (1850) *Vita s. Augustini*, Patrologia Latina.

Gransden, A. (1981) *Gosceli, Historia major sancti Augustini*. PL80.

Greenway, D. (1996) *Henry of Huntingdon; The History of the English People, 1000–1154*. Oxford: Oxford University Press.

Liber Eliensis (2005) trans. Fairweather, J., Woodbridge: The Boydell Press.

Orderic Vitalis (1969–80) *Ecclesiastical History of Orderic Vitalis*, ed. and trans. Chibnall, M., 6 vols, Oxford: Oxford Medieval Tracts.

Peterborough Chronicle, 1070–1154 (1958) ed. Clark, C., Oxford: Oxford University Press.

Symeon of Durham (2000) *Libellus et Exordio atque Procursu istius hoc est Dunhelmensis Ecclesie*, ed. and trans. Rollason D., Oxford: Oxford Medieval Tracts.

Thomas of Marlborough (2003) *History of the Abbey of Evesham*, eds Sayers, J. and Watkiss, L. Oxford: Oxford Medieval Tracts.

William of Malmesbury (2002) Giles, A.J. (ed.), trans. Sharpe, J. *Gesta Regnum Anglorum: The Deeds of the Kings of England*. London: George Bell and Sons.

William of Malmesbury (2007) *Gesta Pontificum Anglorum: The History of the English Bishops*, ed. and trans. Winterbottom, M. and Thomson, R.M., Oxford: Oxford Medieval Tracts.

William of Newburgh (1987) *The History of English Affairs*, Book 1, eds Walsh, P. and Kennedy, M.J., Warminster: Aris and Phillips Classical Texts.

Wright, T. (2018) *The Anglo-Norman Metrical Chronicle of Geoffrey Gaimar*. London: Forgotten Books.

Secondary Sources

Aalen, F. (2006) *England's Landscape: The North East*. London: Collins and English Heritage.

Abrams, L. (2012) 'Early Normandy', in *Anglo-Norman Studies* 35. Woodbridge: Boydell & Brewer.

Addeyman, P. 2017) *The Atlas of Historic Towns*, vol 5. Oxford: Historic Towns Trust.

Albu, E. (2001) *The Normans in their Histories: Propaganda, Myth and Subversion*. Woodbridge: Boydell.

Alexander, J.S (2007) 'The Introduction and Use of Masons' Marks in Romanesque Buildings in England', *Medieval Archaeology*, Volume 51, 63-81.

Alkazwini, A.A. (2016) 'The linguistic influence of the Norman Conquest (11th century) on the English language', *International Journal of Linguistics* 8(3): 141–51.

Allcroft, A.H. (1908) *Earthwork of England*. London: Macmillan & Co.

Allen, M. (2012) 'Mints and money in Norman England', in *Anglo-Norman Studies* 34. Woodbridge: Boydell & Brewer.

Allen Brown, R. (1984) *The Normans*. Woodbridge: Boydell Press.

Allen Brown, R. (1989) *Castles from the Air*. Cambridge: Cambridge University Press.

Allen Brown, R. (2002) *The Norman Conquest of England: Sources and Documents*. Woodbridge: Boydell & Brewer.

Allison, M. (2003) *History of Appleton-le-Moors, A 12th Century Planned Village*. Easingwold: G.H. Smith and Son.

Ancient Oaks of England, Herbaria.plants.ox.ac.uk/bol/ancientoaksofEngland/deerparks accessed 18 December 2021.

Armitage, E.S. (1912) *The Early Norman Castles of the British Isles*. London: J. Murray.

Aston, M. (1985) *Interpreting the Landscape*. London: Routledge.

Aston, M. (2000) *Monasteries in the Landscape*. Stroud: Tempus.

Aston, M. and Bond, J. (1987) *The Landscape of Towns*. Stroud: Sutton Publishing.

Austin, D. (ed.) (1982) *Boldon Book: Northumberland and Durham*. Chichester: Phillimore.

Austin, D. (1989) 'The deserted medieval village of Thrislington', *Society for Medieval Archaeology Monograph Series*, No. 12.

Austin, D. (1990) 'Medieval settlement in the north-east of England – retrospective summary and prospect', in Vyner, B.E (ed.) *Medieval Rural Settlement in North-East England*. Durham: Architectural and Archaeological Society of Durham and Northumberland.

Austin, N. (2010) *The Secrets of the Norman Invasion*. Crowhurst: Ogmium Press.

Ayers, B. (1994) *Norwich*. London: B.T. Batsford & English Heritage.

Ayers, B. (2004) 'The urban landscape', in Rawcliffe, C. and Wilson, R. (eds) *Medieval Norwich*. London: Hambledon and London.

Baker, J. and Brookes, S. (2014) *Beyond the Burghal Hidage: Anglo-Saxon Civil Defences in the Viking Age*: 84. Leiden: Brill Academic Publishers.

Baring, E.H. (1898) 'The conqueror's footprints in Domesday', *The English Historical Review* 13: 17.

Barlow, F. (1992) *The Life of King Edward Who Rests at Westminster*. Oxford: Clarendon Press.

Barlow, F. (1997) *Edward the Confessor*. Yale University Press.

Barlow, G. (2011) 'The landscape of Domesday Suffolk', *Landscape History* 32: 2.

Barnes, G. and Williamson, T. (2015) *Rethinking Ancient Woodland*. Hatfield: University of Hertfordshire Press.

Bartlett, R. (2002) *England under the Norman and Angevin Kings 1075–1225*. Oxford: Oxford University Press.

Bates, D. (1975) 'The character and career of Odo, bishop of Bayeux (1049/50–1097)', *Speculum* 50(1): 1–20.

Bates, D. (1982) *Normandy Before 1066*. London: Longman.

Bates D. (1998) *Regesta Regnum Anglo-Normannorum: The Acts of William I (1066–1087)*. Oxford: Oxford University Press.

Bates, D. (2013) *The Normans and Empire*. Oxford: Oxford University Press.

Bates, D. (2014) 'The abbey and the Norman Conquest: an unusual case?', in Licence, T. (ed.) *Bury St Edmunds and the Norman Conquest*. Woodbridge: Boydell Press.

Bates, D. (2016) *William the Conqueror*. New Haven: Yale University Press.

Bates, D. (ed.) (2018) *1066 in Perspective*. Leeds: Royal Armouries Museum.

Bates, D., D'Angelo, E. and van Houts, E. (eds) (2018) *People, Texts and Artefacts: Cultural Transmission in the Medieval Norman Worlds*. London: Institute of Historical Research.

Battles, D. (2013) *Cultural Differences and Material Culture in Middle English Romance: Normans and Saxons*. New York: Routledge.

Baxter, R. (2006) 'The Construction of the West Doorway of Rochester Cathedral', in Ayres T. and Tatton-Brown, T (eds.) *Medieval Art, Architecture and Archaeology at Rochester*, The British Archaeological Association, Conference Transactions XXVIII.

Baxter, S. (2001) Review of Roffe, D. (2000) *Domesday: The Inquest and the Book*. Oxford: Oxford University Press. *Reviews in History* 216. https://reviews.history. ac.uk/review/216. Accessed 26 April 2021.

Baxter, S. (2012) 'The making of Domesday Book and the languages of lordship in conquered England', in Tyler, E.M. (ed.) *Conceptualizing Multilingualism in Medieval England, c.800–c.1250*. Turnhout, Belgium: Brepols.

Baxter, S. (2017) 'The Domesday controversy: A review and a new interpretation', *The Haskins Society Journal: Studies in Medieval History* 29: 225–93.

Baxter, S. (2018) '1066 and government', in Bates, D. (ed.) *1066 in Perspective*. Leeds: Royal Armouries Museum.

Baxter, S. and Lewis, C.P. (2017) 'Domesday Book and the transformation of English landed society, 1066–86', *Anglo-Saxon England* 46: 343–403.

Beresford, M. (1967) *New Towns of the Middle Ages*. London: Lutterworth Press.

Beresford, M. and St Joseph, J.K.S. (1979) *Medieval England: An Aerial Survey*. Cambridge: Cambridge University Press.

Biddle, M.(ed) (1976), *Winchester in the Early Middle Ages*, Winchester Studies 1, Oxford, Clarendon Press.

Biddle, M. (1986) *The Old Bishop's Palace, Winchester*. London: English Heritage Guidebook.

Blair, J. (2001) *English Medieval Industries: Craftsmen, Techniques, Products*. London: Hambledon-Continuum.

Blair, J. (2007) *Waterways and Canal-Building in Medieval England*. Oxford: Oxford University Press.

Blair, J. (2014) 'In search of the origins of the English village', *Current Archaeology* 291: 12–23.

Blair, J. (2018) *Building Anglo-Saxon England*. Princeton and Oxford: Princeton University Press.

Blair, J. and Golding, B. (eds) (1996) *The Cloister and the World*. Oxford: Oxford University Press.

Blair, J. and Steane, J.M. (1982) 'Investigations at Cogges, Oxfordshire, 1978–81: The priory and the parish church', *Oxoniensia* XLVII: 37–127.

Bond, J. (2004) *Monastic Landscapes*. Stroud: Tempus.

Bond, J. (2007) 'Canal construction in the early Middle Ages: An introductory review', in Blair, J. (ed.) *Waterways and Canal Building in Medieval England*. Oxford: Oxford University Press.

Bond, J. (2014/15) 'Native deer in medieval English parks: Part 1 Red deer', *The Journal of the British Deer Society* Winter.

Bond, J. and Tiller, K. eds. (1997 2nd ed.), *Blenheim: Landscape for a Palace*, Stroud, Sutton Publishing, Oxford University Department for Continuing Education.

Bond, J., Clark, D., Harrison, J. and Rowley, T. (2017) 'Appleton Manor: A most remarkable house', *Oxoniensia* LXXXII: 1–34.

Bony, J. (1992) *French Gothic Architecture of the Twelfth and Thirteenth Centuries*. Berkeley: University of California Press.

Brett, M. and Woodman, D.A. (2015). *The Long Twelfth-Century View of the Anglo-Saxon Past*, London: Ashgate Publishing.

British Archaeological Association (1978) *Medieval Art and Architecture at Worcester Cathedral*. Oxford: British Archaeological Association.

Brooke, C.N.L. (1999) *Churches and Church Men in Medieval Europe*. London: Bloomsbury Academic.

Brookes, S. (2017) Domesday Shires and Hundreds of England (data set). York: Archaeology Data Service (distributor) https://doi.org10.5284/1058999

Brooks, A. and Pevsner, N. (2012). *Herefordshire. The Buildings of England*, Yale: Yale University Press.

Browett, R. (2016) 'The fate of Anglo-Saxon saints' cults after the Norman Conquest: St Aethelwold of Winchester as a case study', *The Journal of the Historical Association* 101(345): 183–200.

Burton, J. (1994) *Monastic and Religious Orders in Britain 1000–1030*. Cambridge: Cambridge University Press.

Burton, J.E. and Kerr, J. (2011) *The Cistercians in the Middle Ages*. Woodbridge: Boydell Press.

Campbell, J. (1975) 'Norwich', in Lobel, M.D. *The Atlas of Historic Towns*, vol. 2. Oxford: The Scholar Press in conjunction with the Historic Towns Trust.

Cantor, L. (1982) *The English Medieval Landscape*. London: Croom Helm.

Chaplais, P. (1987) 'William of Saint-Calais and the Domesday survey', in Holt, J.C. (ed.) *Domesday Studies*. Woodbridge: The Boydell Press.

Chapman, A. (2010) *West Cotton, Raunds*. Oxford: Oxbow Books.

Chibnall, M. (1999) *The Debate on the Norman Conquest*. Manchester: Manchester University Press.

Christelow, S.M. (2006) 'Names and ethnicity in Anglo-Norman England', in Postles, D. and Rosenthal J.T. (eds) *Studies in Medieval Culture* XLIV. Kalamazoo: Western Michigan University.

Clout, H. ed. (2007) *History of London*. 5th edition. London: Harper Collins.

Clover, H. and Gibson, M. (1979) *The Letters of Lanfranc, Archbishop of Canterbury*. Oxford: Oxford University Press.

Cole, A. (2013) *The Place Name Evidence for a Routeway Network in Early Medieval England*. BAR British Series 589. Oxford: British Archaeological Reports.

Colvin, H.M. (ed) (1963a) *A History of the King's Works* vol.1. London: HMSO

Colvin, H.M. (ed.) (1963b) *A History of the King's Work* vol 2. London: HMSO.

Colvin, H.M. (1963c) *A History of Deddington, Oxfordshire*. London: SPCK.

Combes, P. and Lynes, M.(1995) 'Hastings, Hastingaceaster and Haestingaport: A question of identity', *Sussex Archaeological Collection* 133: 213–24.

Cook, H. (2017) *The New Forest: the forging of a landscape*. Oxford: Windgather Press.

Coppack, G. (1990) *Abbeys and Priories*. London: Batsford/English Heritage.

Cowdrey, H.E.J. (1969) 'Bishop Ermenfrid of Sion and the Penitential Ordinance following the Battle of Hastings', *Journal of Ecclesiastical History* 20: 225-42.

Cragoe, C.D. (2010) 'The custom of the English Church: Parish church maintenance in England before 1300', *Journal of Medieval History* 36(1): 1–19.

Creighton, O.H. (2002) *Castles and Landscapes: Power, Community and Fortification in Medieval England*. Sheffield: Equinox.

Creighton, O.H. (2018) '1066 and the Landscape', in Bates, D., D'Angelo, E. and van Houts, E. (eds) (2018) *People, Texts and Artefacts: Cultural Transmission in the Medieval Norman Worlds*. London: Institute of Historical Research.

Creighton, O. and Rippon, S. (2017) 'Conquest, colonisation and the countryside: Archaeology and the mid-11th- to mid-12th-century rural landscape', in Hadley, D. and Dyer, C. (eds), *The Archaeology of the 11th Century*. London: Routledge.

Crossley, A. ed. (2021) *Oxford*, British Historic Towns Atlas Volume VII. Oxford: The Historic Towns Trust in association with Oxford Archaeology.

Crouch, D. (1986) *The Beaumont Twins: The Roots and Branches of Power in the Twelfth Century*. Cambridge: Cambridge University Press.

Crouch, D. (2011) *The English Aristocracy: 1070–1277*. New Haven: Yale University Press.

Crummy, P. (1981) *Aspects of Anglo-Saxon and Norman Colchester*. CBA Report 39. London: Council for British Archaeology.

Dalton, P. (2002) *Conquest, Anarchy and Lordship: Yorkshire*. Cambridge: Cambridge University Press.

Dalton, P., Insley, C. and Wilkinson L.J. (eds) (2011) *Cathedrals, Communities and Conflict in the Anglo-Norman World*. Woodbridge: Boydell.

Darby H.C. (1951) *An Historical Geography of England Before A.D. 1800*, 3rd edition. Cambridge: Cambridge University Press.

Darby, H.C. (1953) *The Domesday Geography of Eastern England*. Cambridge: Cambridge University Press.

Darby H.C. (1971) *The Domesday Geography of Midland England*, 2nd edition. Cambridge: Cambridge University Press.

Darby H.C. (1977) *Domesday England*. Cambridge: Cambridge University Press.

Davis, R.C.H. (1976) *The Normans and their Myth*. London: Thames and Hudson.

Dodd, A. (ed.) (2003) *Oxford Before the University*. Oxford: Oxford Archaeological Unit.

Dodgson, J.M. (1987) 'Domesday Book: Place-names and personal names', in Holt, J.C. (ed.) *Domesday Studies*. Woodbridge: Boydell Press.

Dodwell, C.R. (1982) *Anglo-Saxon Art: A New Perspective*. Manchester: Manchester University Press.

Donkin, R.A. (1978) *The Cistercians: Studies in the Geography of Medieval England and Wales*. Toronto: Pontifical Institute of Medieval Studies.

Drury P.J. (1982) 'Aspects of the origins and development of Colchester Castle', *Archaeological Journal* 139: 302–419.

Drury, P.J. and Rodwell, W.J. (1978) 'Investigations at Asheldham, Essex. An interim report on the church and the historic landscape', *Antiquaries Journal* 58: 133–51.

Dyer, C. (2002*) Making a Living in the Middle Ages*. New Haven: Yale University Press.

Eaton, T. (2000) *Plundering the Past: Roman Stonework in Medieval Britain*. Stroud: Tempus.

English, B. (1995) Towns, mottes and ring-works of the Conquest. In Ayton, A.C. and Price, J.L. (eds) *The Medieval Military Revolution*. New York: Barnes and Noble.

Everett L. (2007) Suffolk RCZAS – Targeted Inter-tidal Survey Report. Ipswich: Suffolk County Council Archaeological Service.

Faith, R. (1997) *The English Peasantry and the Growth of Lordship*. Leicester: Leicester University Press.

Farjon, A. (2017) *Ancient Oaks in the English Landscape*. Kew: Royal Botanic Gardens.

Ferguson, P. (2013) 'Three Romanesque Patrons and their Regard of the Past', in McNeill, J. and Plant, R. (eds). *Romanesque and the Past*. Leeds: British Archaeological Association.

Fernie, E. (2000) *The Architecture of Norman England*. Oxford: Oxford University Press.

Fernie, E. (2014) *Romanesque Architecture: The First Style of the European Age*. New Haven: Yale University Press.

Fields, N. (2006) *Rome's Saxon Shore: Coastal Defences of Roman Britain AD 250–500*. Oxford: Osprey Publishing.

FitzStephen, W. (1990) *Description of London*. ed F. D. Logan. New York: Italica Press.

Fleming, R. (1991) *Kings and Lords in Conquest England*. Cambridge: Cambridge University Press.

Fleming, A. and Barker, L. (2008) 'Monks and local communities: The Late-Medieval landscape of Troed y Rhiw, Caron Uwch, Clawdd, Ceredigion', *Medieval Archaeology* 52: 261–90.

Flight, C. and Harrison, A.C. (1978) 'Rochester Castle', *Archaeologica Cantiana* 94: 27–60.

Foord, K. and Clephane-Cameron, N. (2015) *1066 and the Battle of Hastings: Preludes, Events and Postscripts*. Battle, Sussex: Battle and District Historical Society.

Fowler, G.H. (1922) 'Bedfordshire in 1086: An analysis and synthesis of Domesday Book', *Bedfordshire Historical Record Society*.

Fradley, M. (2011) 'The Old in the New: Urban Castle Imposition in Anglo-Norman England, AD 1050–1150', PhD thesis. University of Exeter.

Fradley M. and Carey G., (2016) *Archaeo-Topographical Survey Caus Castle, Westbury, Shropshire*, A Preliminary report, Castle Studies Trust.

Gardiner, M. (2000) 'Shipping and trade between England and the continent', *Anglo Norman Studies* XXII.

Gardiner, M. (2003) 'Economy and landscape change in post-Roman and early-medieval Sussex, 450–1175', in Rudling, D. (ed.) *The Archaeology of Sussex to AD 2000*. Brighton: Heritage Books/University of Sussex.

Gardiner, M. and Rippon, S. (eds) (2007) *Medieval Landscapes*. Oxford: Windgather Press.

Gauthiez, B. (1998) 'The Planning of the Town of Bury St Edmunds: a Probable Norman Origin', in Gransden, A. (ed) *Bury St Edmunds: Medieval Art, Architecture, Archaeology and Economy*, Leeds: British Archaeological Association Conference Transactions XX.

Gelling, M. (1979) *The Early Charters of the Thames Valley*. Leicester: Leicester University Press.

Gem, R.D.H., (1986), 'Lincoln Minster: Ecclesia Pulchra, Ecclesia Fortis', *Medieval Art and Architecture at Lincoln Cathedral*, The British Archaeological Association Conference Proceedings for 1982, 9-28.

Gerrard, C. and Aston, M. (2007) *The Shapwick Project, Somerset: A Rural Landscape Explored*. Society for Medieval Archaeology Monographs. London: Routledge.

Gillingham, J. (2012) 'A historian of the twelfth-century Renaissance and the transformation of English society, 1066–c.1200', in Noble, T.F.X. and Van Engen, J. (eds) *European Transformations: The Long Twelfth Century*. Indiana: University of Notre Dame Press.

Gillingham, J. (2018) '1066 and warfare: The context and place (Senlac) of the Battle of 'Hastings', in Bates, D. (ed.) *1066 in Perspective*. Leeds: Royal Armouries.

Goldberg, E.J. (2020) *In the Manner of the Franks: Hunting, Kingship and Masculinity in Early Medieval Europe*, Philadelphia, University of Pennsylvania Press.

Golding, B. (2013) *Conquest and Colonisation*. 2nd ed. Basingstoke: Palgrave Macmillan.

Goodall, J. (2006) *Warkworth Castle* (English Heritage Red Guides). London: English Heritage.

Goodall J. (2011) *The English Castle: 1066-1650*, New Haven and London: Yale University Press.

Goody, J. (1982) *Cuisine and Class: A Study in Comparative Sociology*. Cambridge: Cambridge University Press.

Gransden, A. (1982) *Historical Writing in England: c.500 to c.1307*. Ithaca, NY: Cornell University Press.

Gransden, A. (1995) 'The composition and authorship of the *De Miraculis Sancti Edmundi* attributed to Herman the Archdeacon', *Journal of Medieval Latin* 5: 1–52.

Gransden, A. ed. (1998) *Bury St Edmunds: Medieval Art, Architecture, Archaeology and Economy*. Leeds: British Archaeological Association.

Green, J.A. (1997) *The Aristocracy of Norman England*. Cambridge: Cambridge University Press.

Green, J.A. (2004) Robert fitz Haimon. *Dictionary of National Biography*. Oxford: Oxford University Press.

Green, J.A. (2013) 'Forest laws in England and Normandy in the twelfth century', *Historical Research* 86(233): 416–31.

Greene, J.P. (1992) *Medieval Monasteries*. Leicester: Leicester University Press.

Griffin, E. (2007) *Blood Sport*. New Haven: Yale University Press.

Hadley, D. and Dyer, C. (2017) (eds), *The Archaeology of the 11th Century*. London: Routledge.

Hall, D. (2013) 'Twentieth-century varieties reflecting medieval settlement in Normandy: Combining modern and historical dialectology', *Acta Linguistica Hafniensia: International Journal of Linguistics* 43(2): 176–99.

Hall, D. (2014) *The Open Fields of England*. Oxford: Oxford University Press.

Hall, F.J. (1895) 'The arrangement of monastic buildings', *Transactions of the East Riding Antiquarian Society* 3: 78.

Hallam, H.E. (ed.) (1988) *The Agrarian History of England and Wales* vol. 2. Cambridge: Cambridge University Press.

Hardy P.T. and Wall T. (eds) (2000) *Moccas: an English Deer Park*. Peterborough: English Nature.

Harper-Bill, C. (2004) 'Losinga, Herbert de', DNB. https://exproxy-prd.bodleian.ox.ac.uk:2102/10.1093/ref:odnb/17205. Accessed 15 April 2021.

Harper-Bill, C. and Van Houts, E. (eds) (2003) *A Companion to the Anglo-Norman World*. Woodbridge: Boydell Press.

Harvey, S. (2014) *Domesday: Book of Judgement*. Oxford: Oxford University Press.

Haslam, J. (2010) *Early Medieval Towns in Britain*. Princes Risborough: Shire.

Haslam J. (2021) 'The settlement and landscape context of the Battle of Hastings', *Medieval Archaeology* 65(1): 126–50.

Hawkins, A. and Rumble, A. (1976) *Domesday Book: Staffordshire*. Chichester: Phillimore.

Hayward, P.A. (1998) 'Translation-narratives in post-Conquest hagiography', in *Anglo-Norman Studies* XXI. Woodbridge: Boydell and Brewer.

Hewitt, C.M. (2010) 'The geographic origins of the Norman conquerors of England', *Historical Geography* 38: 130–44.

Hewitt, C.M. (2016) *The Battle of Hastings: A geographic perspective*. Electronic Thesis and Dissertation Repository 3628. https://ir.lib.uwo.ca/etd/3628.

Hewitt, C.M. (2018a) 'How did East Sussex really appear in 1066? The cartographic evidence', *Digital Studies / Le champ numérique* 8(1): 91.

Hewitt, C.M. (2018b) 'Mapping the Pevensey area back to 1066: The historical environmental evidence', *Cartographica* 53: 2.

Hicks, L.V. (2009) 'Outdoor space in chronicles', *Anglo-Norman Studies*, Vol XXXII. Woodbridge: Boydell & Brewer.

Higham, N. (1990) 'Settlement, land use and Domesday ploughlands', *Landscape History* 12: 1.

Higham, R. and Barker, P. (1992) *Timber Castles*. Exeter: Exeter University Press.

Higham, N.J. and Ryan, M.J. (eds) (2011) *Place-Names, Language and the Anglo-Saxon Landscape*. Woodbridge: The Boydell Press.

Hill, B.D. (1968) *The English Cistercian Monasteries and their Patrons in the Twelfth Century*. Urbana: University of Illinois Press.

Hinton, D. (2002) *Archaeology, Economy and Society*. London: Seaby.

Hiscock, N. (2003) *The White Mantle of Churches*. Turnhout: Brepols.

Historic England (2018) *River Fisheries and Coastal Fish Weirs; Introduction to Heritage Assets*. Swindon: Historic England.

Holman, K. (ed.) (2003) *Historical Dictionary of the Vikings*. Lanham, MD: Scarecrow Press.

Holmes, M. (2015) 'Making a fast buck in the Middle Ages: Evidence of poaching from medieval Wakefield', in Baker, K., Carden, R. and Madgwick, R. (eds) *Deer and People*. Oxford: Windgather Press.

Hoofnagle, W.M. (2017) *The Continuity of Conquest: Charlemagne and Anglo-Norman Imperialism*. Pennsylvania: Pennsylvania State University Press.

Hooke (1998) *The Anglo-Saxon Landscape: The Kingdom of the Hwicce*. Leicester: Leicester University Press.

Hooper, N.A. (1991) *Great Domesday Book: Berkshire: County Edition*. Alecto Historical Editions.

Hope, St J. (1909) 'The ancient topography of the town of Ludlow', *Archaeologia* lxi: 393–88.

Hoskins, W.G. (1955) *The Making of the English Landscape*. London: Hodder & Stoughton.

Hoskins, W.G. (1973) *English Landscapes*. London: BBC Books.

Howell, R. (2000) 'The demolition of the Roman tetrapylon in Caerleon: An erasure of memory?', *Oxford Journal of Archaeology* 19(4): 387–95.

Hudson, J. (2012) *The Oxford History of the Laws of England 871–1216*. Vol. II. Oxford: Oxford University Press.

Hurlock, K. and Oldfield, P. (eds) (2015) *Crusading and Pilgrimage in the Norman World*. Woodbridge: Boydell Press.

Huscroft, R. (2009) *The Norman Conquest: A New Introduction*. London: Longman.

Impey, E. and Parnell, G. (2000) *The Tower of London: The Official Illustrated History*. London: Merrell Publishers Ltd.

Impey, E. (2020) 'A wooden castle scratched in stone: a 13th-century graffito from the castle at Caen', *castlestudiestrust.org/blog/2020/11/17* Accessed 5 March 2022.

Ivens, R.J. (1980) 'Patterns of Human Activity in the Southern Midlands of England: Archaeological and Documentary Evidence', PhD thesis, Queens University of Belfast.

Ivens, R.J. (1984) 'Deddington Castle, Oxfordshire, and the English honour of Odo of Bayeux', *Oxoniensia* 49: 101–19.

James, T.B. (1990) *The Palaces of Medieval England, C.1050–1550 – Royalty, Nobility, the Episcopate and Their Residences from Edward the Confessor to Henry VIII.* London: Seaby.

Jamieson, E. (2019) 'The Siting of Medieval Castles and the Influence of Ancient Places' *Medieval Archaeology* 63 Issue 2: 338-374.

Jervis, B. (2016) 'Objects and social change: A case study from Saxo-Norman Southampton', in Alberti, B. Meirion Jones, A. and Pollard, J. (eds) *Archaeology after Interpretation: Returning Materials to Archaeological Theory.* London and New York: Routledge.

Jervis, B., Whelan, F. and Livarda, A. (2017) 'Cuisine and conquest', in Hadley, D. and Dyer, C. (eds) *The Archaeology of the 11th Century.* London: Routledge.

King, E. (2002) 'Economic development in the early twelfth century', in Britnell, R. and Hatcher, J. (eds) *Progress and Problems in Medieval England: Essays in Honour of Edward Miller*, revised edition. Cambridge: Cambridge University Press.

John, M. (2020) 'Where are the Flemings?', pembrokeshirehistoricalsociety.co.uk/where-are-the-flemings. Accessed 2 July 2020.

Jope, E.M. and Threlfall, R.I. (1946/7) 'Recent medieval finds in the Oxford district', *Oxoniensia* xi/xii: 165–70.

Jørgensen, D. (2009) 'The roots of the English royal forest', in *Anglo-Norman Studies* 32. Woodbridge: Boydell & Brewer.

Jørgensen, D. (2013) 'Pigs and pollards: Medieval insights for UK wood pasture restoration', *Sustainability*. February 2013.

Kapelle, W.E. (1979) *The Norman Conquest of the North: The Region and its Transformation 1000–1135.* Raleigh Durham NC: University of North Carolina Press.

Keats-Rohan, K.S.B. (2009) 'The genesis of the honour of Wallingford', in Keats-Rohan K.S.B. and Roffe, D.R. (eds) *The Origins of Wallingford.* BAR British Report 464. Oxford: Archaeopress.

Keen, L. (1988) 'Coastal salt production in Norman England', *Anglo-Norman Studies* XI: 133–80.

Kelly, S.E. (2000–1) *Charters of Abingdon Abbey.* Oxford: Oxford University Press.

Kissock, J. (1997) 'Post-Conquest and pre-Conquest villages in Pembrokeshire', in Edwards, N. (ed.) *Landscape and Settlement in Medieval Wales.* Oxford: Oxbow Monographs 81.

Klukas, A.W. (1984) 'The architectural implications of the Decreta Lanfranci', in *Anglo-Norman Studies* 6. Woodbridge: Boydell & Brewer.

Knowles, D. (1940) *The Monastic Order in England.* Cambridge: Cambridge University Press.

Knowles, D. (reprint 1994) *The Religious Orders in England.* 3 vols. Cambridge: Cambridge University Press.

Knowles, D. and St Joseph, J.K.S. (1952) *Monastic Sites from the Air.* Cambridge: Cambridge University Press.

Lamb, H.H. (1977) *Climate, Present, Past and Future.* vol. 2. London: Routledge.

Langton, J. (2010) 'A common of hunting? Forests, lordships and community before and after the conquest', in Langton, J. and Jones, G. (eds), *Forests and Chases of Medieval England and Wales, c.1000–c.1500*. Oxford: St John's College Research Centre.

Langton, J. (2014) 'Forest fences: Enclosures in a pre-enclosure landscape', *Landscape History* 35(1): 10–11.

Laws, E. (1888) *The History of England Beyond Wales*. London: Bell.

Le Maho, J. (1994) 'Les Fouilles de la cathédrale de Rouen 1985–93', *Archéologique Médiévale* 24: 1–51.

Le Patourel, J. (1976) *The Norman Empire*. Oxford: Clarendon Press.

Leary, J. et al. (2013) 'The Marlborough Mound, Wiltshire. A further Neolithic monumental mound by the River Kennett', *Proceedings of the Prehistoric Society* 79:137-63

Lefferts, P.M. (1990) 'Medieval England', in McKinnon, J. (ed.), *Antiquity and the Middle Ages*. London: Longman.

Lennard, R. (1959) *Rural England, 1086–1135*. Oxford: Oxford University Press.

Lennon, B. (2014), 'A study of the trees in Savernake Forest and Tottenham Park, Wiltshire, using statistical analysis of stem diameter', *Garden History*, 42, No.2, 234-256.

Leslie, K. and Short, B. (eds) (1999), *An Historical Atlas of Sussex*, Chichester: Phillimore

Lewis, C.P. (1994) 'The French in England before the Norman Conquest', in *Anglo-Norman Studies* 17: 123–44.

Lewis, C.P. (2016) 'Audacity and ambition in early Norman England and the big stuff of the Conquest', in *Anglo-Norman Studies*, vol XL. Woodbridge: Boydell & Brewer.

Liddiard, R. (2002) *Anglo-Norman Castles*. Woodbridge: Boydell Press.

Liddiard, R. (2003) 'The deer parks of Domesday Book', *Landscapes* 4(1): 4–23.

Liddiard, R. (2005) *Castles in Context: Power, Symbolism and Landscape, 1066 to1500*, Macclesfield, Windgather Press.

Liddiard, R. (ed.) (2007) *The Medieval Park: New Perspectives*. Macclesfield: Windgather Press.

Liddiard, R. (2018) 'The landscape of Anglo-Norman England: Chronology and cultural transmission', in Bates, D., D'Angelo, E. and van Houts, E. (eds) *People, Texts and Artefacts: Cultural Transmission in the Medieval Norman Worlds*. London: University of London Press.

Lilley, K. (1999) 'Urban landscapes and the cultural politics of territorial control in Anglo-Norman England', *Landscape Research* 24(1): 5–23.

Lilley, K. (2002) *Urban Life in the Middle Ages: 1000–1450*. London: Red Globe Press.

Lilley, K. (2017) 'The Norman Conquest and its influences on urban landscapes', in Hadley, D. and Dyer, C. (eds) *The Archaeology of the 11th Century*. London: Routledge.

Linsley, S. (2005) *Ports and Harbours of Northumberland*. Stroud: Tempus.

Lobel, M.D. and Johns, W.H. (eds) (1969) *The Atlas of Historic Towns*, vol 1. Oxford: Historic Towns Trust.

Lobel, M.D. and Johns, W.H. (eds) (1975) *The Atlas of Historic Towns*, vol 2. Oxford: Historic Towns Trust.

Loyn, H.R. (1978) 'Domesday Book'. *Anglo-Norman Studies* 1: 121–30.

Maitland, F.W. (1907) *Domesday Book and Beyond*. Cambridge: Cambridge University Press.

Martin, G. and Williams, A. (2004) *The Domesday Book: A Complete Translation*. New York: Penguin.

Mason, J.F.A. (1963) 'Roger de Montgomery and his sons', *Transactions of the Royal Historical Society* 13: 1–28.

Matthew, D. (1962) *The Norman Monasteries and their English Possessions*. Westport, Connecticut: Greenwood Press.

Matthew, D. (2005) *Britain and the Continent, 1000–1300*. London: Hodder Arnold.

McClain, A. (2011) 'Parish churches in late medieval England', *Archaeology of Medieval Europe* II: 467–78.

McClain, A. and Sykes, N. (2019) 'New archaeologies of the Norman Conquest', in *Anglo-Norman Studies* 41. Woodbridge: Boydell and Brewer.

McKinnon, J. (ed.) (1990) *Antiquity and the Middle Ages*. London: Longman.

Meeres, F. (2010) *A History of Bury St Edmunds*. Andover: Phillimore & Co.

Mew, K. (2000) 'The dynamics of lordship and landscape as revealed in a Domesday study of *nova foresta*', in *Anglo-Norman Studies* 23. Woodbridge: Boydell & Brewer.

Miller, E. and Hatcher, J. (1995) *Medieval England: Towns, Commerce and Crafts, 1083–1348*. Cambridge: Cambridge University Press.

Moorhouse, S. (2007) 'The medieval parks of Yorkshire: Function, contents and chronology', in Liddiard, R. (ed.) *The Medieval Park: New Perspectives*. Macclesfield: Windgather Press.

Morillo, S. (1994) *Warfare under the Anglo-Norman Kings 1066–1135*. Woodbridge: Boydell and Brewer.

Morley, A. and Gurney, D. (1997) *Castle Rising Castle, Norfolk*. Norwich: East Anglian Archaeology.

Morris, R. (1989) *Cathedrals and Abbeys of England and Wales*. London: J.M. Dent.

Morris, R. (1997) *Churches in the Landscape*. London: Phoenix.

Morris, R. (2018) 'Church and Landscape', in Gerrard, C. and Gutiérrez, A. (eds) *The Oxford Handbook of Later Medieval Archaeology in Britain*. Oxford Handbooks Online.

Muir, R. (1997) *The Yorkshire Countryside: A Landscape History*. Keele: Keele University Press.

Muir, B.J. and Turner, A.J. (eds) (1998) *The Life of St Wilfred by Edmer*. Exeter: Exeter University Press.

Munby, J. (2011) 'Domesday boroughs revisited', in *Anglo-Norman Studies* 33. Woodbridge: Boydell & Brewer.

Munns, J. (2016) *Cross and Culture in Anglo-Norman England*. Woodbridge: The Boydell Press.

Nancarrow, J.-H. (2014) 'Ruins to re-use: Romano-British remains in post-Conquest literary and material culture', PhD thesis, University of York.

Nichols, F.M. (1882), 'Colchester Castle', *Transactions of the Essex Archaeological Society*, New Series Vol. 3, Part 1.

Nieus, J-F. (2016) 'Early Aristocratic Seals: An Anglo-Norman Success Story' in *Anglo-Norman Studies*, 38: 101.

Oggins, R.S. (2004) *The Kings and Their Hawks: Falconry in Medieval England*. New Haven: Yale University Press.

Oksanen, E. (2012) *Flanders and the Anglo-Norman World 1066-1216*. Cambridge, Cambridge University Press.

Oosthuizen, S. (2005) 'New Light on the Origins of Open-Field Farming', *Medieval Archaeology*, 49 Issue 1.

O'Sullivan, D. (2011) 'Normanising the north: the evidence of Anglo-Saxon and Anglo-Scandinavian Sculpture', *Medieval Archaeology* Vol 55, 163-91.

Ottaway, P. (2017) *Winchester: An Archaeological Assessment*. Oxford: Oxbow Books.

Page, W. (ed.) (1974) *A History of the County of York*, Vol 3. London: Victoria County History.

Palliser, D.M. (ed.) (2000) *The Cambridge Urban History of Britain* vol 1. Cambridge: Cambridge University Press.

Palliser, D.M. (2014) *Medieval York, 600-1540*. Oxford: Oxford University Press.

Palmer, J. (1995a) 'War and Domesday waste', in Strickland, M. (ed.) *Armies, Chivalry and Warfare in Medieval Britain and France: Proceedings of the Harlaxton Symposium*. Spalding: Shaun Tyas.

Palmer, J. (1995b) 'The Conqueror's footprints in Domesday Book', in Ayton, A.C. and Price, J.L. (eds) *The Medieval Military Revolution*. New York: Barnes and Noble.

Parker, E. (2015) 'Cnut's invasion of England: Setting the scene for the Norman Conquest', *BBC History Magazine*, February 2015.

Paul Drury Partnership (2009) *Rochester Castle Conservation Plan Part 1*. Teddington: Paul Drury Partnership.

Pestell, T. (2002) *Landscapes of Monastic Foundation*. Woodbridge: Boydell.

Pettifer, A. (1995) *English Castles: A Guide by Counties*. Woodbridge, The Boydell Press.

Platt, C. (1976) *The English Medieval Town*. London: Secker and Warburg.

Platt, C. (1984) *The Abbeys and Priories of Medieval England*. London: Secker and Warburg.

Plomer, W. (2006) *Kilvert's Diary 1870–1879 – Selections from the Diary of the Rev. Francis Kilvert*. London: Obscure Press.

Pohl, B. (2015) *Dudo of Saint-Quentin's Historia Normannorum: Tradition, Innovation and Memory*. Woodbridge: Boydell and Brewer.

Poole, A.L. (1993) *From Domesday Book to Magna Carta,1087–1216*. 2nd ed. Oxford: Oxford University Press.

Poore, D., Norton A. and Dodd, A. (2009) 'Excavations at Oxford Castle: Oxford's western quarter from the mid-Saxon period to the late eighteenth century', *Oxoniensia* LXXIV: 1–18.

Potter, J. (1998) 'The Benefactors of Bec and the Politics of Priories', *Anglo-Norman Studies*. vol. 21.

Potter, J.F. (2001) 'The occurrence of Roman brick and tile in churches of the London Basin', *Britannia* 32: 119–42.

Potts, C. (1994) *Monastic Revival and Regional Identity in Early Normandy*. Woodbridge: Boydell.

Pounds, N.J.G. (1994) *The Medieval Castle in England and Wales*. Cambridge: Cambridge University Press.

Pounds, N.J.G. (2000) *A History of the English Parish*. Cambridge: Cambridge University Press.

Prior, S.J. (2007) 'Strategy, symbolism and the downright unusual', in Costen, M. (ed.) *People and Places: Essays in Honour of Mick Aston*. Oxford: Oxbow Books.

Rackham, O. (1986) *The History of the Countryside*. London: J.M. Dent and Sons.

Rackham, O. (2003) *Ancient Woodland: Its History, Vegetation and Uses in England*. 2nd revised ed. Dalbeattie, Kirkcudbrightshire: Castlepoint Press.

Rawcliffe, C. and Wilson, R. (2004) *Medieval Norwich*. London: Continuum.

RCHME (1926) *An Inventory of Historical Monuments in Huntingdonshire*. London: HMSO.

RCHME (1931) *An Inventory of Historical Monuments in Herefordshire*, Volume 1, South West. London: HMSO.

RCHME (1934) *An Inventory of Historical Monuments in Herefordshire*, Volume 3, North West, London: HMSO.

RCHME (1972) *An Inventory of the Historical Monuments in City of York*, Volume 2, the Defences. London: HMSO.

Reilly, L. (1996) 'The emergence of Anglo-Norman architecture', in *Anglo-Norman Studies* XIX. Woodbridge: Boydell & Brewer.

Reilly, L. (2020) *The Invention of Norman Visual Culture*. Cambridge: Cambridge University Press.

Renn, D. (1994) 'Burgeat and gonfanon: Two sidelights from the Bayeux Tapestry', *Anglo-Norman Studies* 16: 177–98.

Renoux, A. (1991) *Fécamp: Du Palais au palais de Dieu*, Caen: Presses de CNRS

Rex, P. (2014) *The English Resistance: Underground War against the Normans*. Stroud: Amberley Press.

Reynolds, S. (1982) *Introduction to the History of English Medieval Towns*. Oxford: Oxford University Press.

Rippon, S. (2008) *Beyond the Medieval Village*. Oxford: Oxford University Press.

Rippon, S., Smart, C. and Pears, B. (2015) *The Fields of Britannnia*. Oxford: Oxford University Press.

Roberts, B.K. (2008) *Landscapes, Documents and Maps: Villages in Northern England and Beyond AD 900–1250*. Oxford: Oxbow Books.

Robinson, D.A. and Williams, R.B.G. (1983) 'The Sussex coast past and present', in Short, B.M. and Williams, R.B.G. (eds) *Sussex: Environment, Landscape and Society*. Stroud: Sutton Publishing.

Roffe, D. (2007) *Decoding Domesday*. Woodbridge: The Boydell Press.

Roffe, D. (2018) 'Castle construction, conquest and compensation', in *Anglo-Norman Studies* XLI. Woodbridge: Boydell & Brewer.

Roffe, D. and Keats-Rohan, K.S.B (eds) (2016) *Domesday Now: New Approaches to the Inquest and the Book*. Woodbridge: Boydell Press.

Roffey, S. (2017) 'Charity and conquest: leprosaria in early Norman England', in Hadley, D. and Dyer, C. (eds), *The Archaeology of the 11th Century*. London: Routledge.

Rollason, D. (2016) *The Power of Place: Rulers and their Palaces, Landscapes, Cities and Holy Places*. Princeton and Oxford: Princeton University Press.

Round, H. (1964) *Feudal England: Historical Studies on the Eleventh and Twelfth Centuries*, 2nd edition. London: Allen and Unwin.

Rowe, A. (2007) 'The distribution of parks in Hertfordshire: landscape, lordship and woodland', in Liddiard, R. (ed.), *The Medieval Park: New Perspectives.* Macclesfield: Windgather Press.

Rowley, T. (1972) *The Shropshire Landscape.* London: Hodder & Stoughton.

Rowley, T. (1981) *The Origins of Open-Field Agriculture.* London: Croom Helm.

Rowley, T. (1983) *The Norman Heritage.* London: Routledge.

Rowley, T. (2001) *The Welsh Border.* Stroud: The History Press.

Rowley, T. (2013) *The Man Behind the Bayeux Tapestry.* Stroud: The History Press.

Rowley, T. (2016) *An Archaeological Study of the Bayeux Tapestry: The Landscape, Buildings and Places.* Barnsley: Pen and Sword.

Rowley, T. forthcoming, 'Landscapes of Lordship in Late Medieval Shropshire', in McNeill J. and New E. eds, *Art, Architecture and Archaeology in Medieval Shropshire,* British Archaeological Association Conference Transactions, XLV.

Saunders, C J. (1993) *The Forest of Medieval Romance.* Woodbridge: Brewer.

Sawyer, P. (2013) *The Wealth of Anglo-Saxon England.* Oxford: Oxford University Press.

Schofield, J. (1991) 'The construction of medieval and Tudor houses in London', *Construction History* 7: 3–28.

Schofield, J. (2011) *London 1100–1600: The Archaeology of a Capital City.* Sheffield: Equinox.

Schofield, J. (2011) *St Paul's Cathedral Before Wren.* Swindon: English Heritage.

Schofield, J. and Vince, A. (2003) *Medieval Towns.* Leicester: Leicester University Press.

Schofield, J., Blackmore, L., Pearce, J. and Dyson, T. (2018) *London's Waterfront 1100–1666: Excavations in Thames Street, London 1974–84.* Oxford: Archaeopress Archaeology.

Searle, E. (1974) *Lordship and Community: Battle Abbey and its Banlieu.* Toronto: Pontifical Institute of Mediaeval Studies.

Searle, E. (1991) '"Inter Amicos": The Abbey, Town and Early Chartres of Battle', *Anglo-Norman Studies,* XIII.

Senior, J., Semple, S., Turner A. and Turner S. (2014) 'Petrological analysis of the Anglo-Saxon and Anglo-Norman atonework of St Peter's, Wearmouth and St Paul's Jarrow', *McCord Centre Report* 2014.2. Newcastle upon Tyne: Newcastle University.

Sergeant, P.W. (1899) *The Cathedral Church of Winchester.* London: George Bell and Sons.

Shapland, G. 2013. 'Meanings of timber and stone in Anglo-Saxon building practice', in Bintley, M.D.J. and Shapland, G. (ed.) *Trees and Timber in the Anglo-Saxon World.* Oxford: Oxford University Press.

Sheppard, J.A. (1976) 'Medieval village planning in northern England: Some evidence from Yorkshire', *Journal of Historical Geography* 2(1): 3–20.

Shopkow, L. (1997) 'History and Commentary: Norman Historical Writings in the Eleventh and Twelfth Centuries', in *Draco Normannicus (Standard of the Normans).* Washington DC: Catholic University of America Press.

Short, B.M. and Williams, R.B.G. (eds) (1983) *Sussex: Environment, Landscape and Society*. Stroud: Sutton Publishing.

Short, I. (2003) 'Language and literature', in Harper-Bill, C. and Van Houts, E. (eds) *A Companion to the Anglo-Norman World*. Woodbridge: Boydell Press.

Stafford, P. (1985) *The East Midlands in the Early Middle Ages*. Leicester: Leicester University Press.

Stamper, P. (2009) 'Middle Ages: Rural settlements and manors', in Driscoll, S., Hunter, J. and Ralston, I. *The Archaeology of Britain*. London: Routledge.

Steane, J. (1993) *The Archaeology of the Medieval English Monarchy*. London: Batsford.

Stenton, F.M. (1970) 'English families and the Norman Conquest', in Stenton, D.M. (ed.), *Preparatory to Anglo-Saxon England*. Oxford: Oxford University Press.

Stenton, F M. (1971) *Anglo-Saxon England*. 3rd edition. Oxford: Oxford University Press.

Stillman, N., (1980),'Castle Pulverbatch: a field survey of a motte and bailey earthwork in Shropshire', unpublished report, University of Birmingham, Shropshire HER ESA 1137.

Stocker, D.A. and Everson, P. (2006) *Summoning St Michael: Early Romanesque Churches in Lincolnshire*. Oxford: Oxbow Books.

Stocker, D. and Vince, A. (1997) 'The early Norman castle at Lincoln and a re-evaluation of the original West Tower of Lincoln Cathedral', *Medieval Archaeology* 41: 223–33.

Strutt, K.D., Barker, D. and Sly T. (2018) 'Report of the geophysical survey at Old Sarum, Wiltshire, April and July 2017', *The Old Sarum Landscapes Project Research Report*, no. 3. University of Southampton.

Studd, R. (2000) 'Recorded 'waste' in the Staffordshire Domesday', *Staffordshire Studies* 12: 121–33.

Styler, I.D. (2019) *The Story of an English Saint's Cult: An Analysis of the Influence of St Aethelthryth of Ely, c.670–c.1540*. Unpublished PhD thesis. University of Birmingham.

Swanton, M.J. (1975) *Anglo-Saxon Prose*. London: J.M. Dent.

Sykes, N. (2007) 'The Norman Conquest: A zooarchaeological perspective', *BAR International Series* 1656. Oxford: Archaeopress.

Sykes, N. (2007) 'Animal bones and animal parks', in Liddiard, R. (ed.) *The Medieval Park: New Perspectives*. Macclesfield: Windgather Press.

Sykes, N. and Carden, F. (2011) 'Were Fallow Deer Spotted (OE *pohha/pocca* *) in Anglo-Saxon England? Reviewing the Evidence for *Dama dama dama* in Early Medieval Europe', *Medieval Archaeology*, Volume 55 Issue 1, 130-162.

Tait, J. (1936) *The Medieval English Borough*. Manchester: Manchester University Press.

Taylor and Muir (1983) *Visions of the Past*. London: Dent.

Thomas, H.M. (2007) *The Norman Conquest: England after William the Conqueror*. Lanham, Maryland: Rowman and Littlefield.

Thomas, H.M. (2020) *Power and Pleasure: Court Life under King John,* 1199–1216. Oxford: Oxford University Press.

Thompson, H. (2003) *The English and the Normans: Ethnic Hostility, Assimilation, and Identity 1066–c.1220*. Oxford: Oxford University Press.

Thorpe, L. (1978) *The Journey Through Wales and the Description of Wales*. London: Penguin Classics.

Time Team (2013) 1066: The lost battlefield. Episode 275: Special 54, www.channel4.com/programmes/time-team-specials/4od. Accessed 15 January 2015.

Tourhoudt, E.V. (2013) 'The formation of parish territories in western Normandy in the XIth-XIIIth centuries', in Merdrinac, B. et al. (eds) *La paroisse, commonauté et territoire*. Rennes: Rennes University Press.

Trotter, D. (2014) 'Why are there so few French place-names in England?', *English Today* 30(2): 39–42.

Tsurushima, H. (2011) '*Hic est miles*: Some images of three knights: Turold, Wadard and Vital', in Lewis, M.J., Owen-Crocker, G.R. and Terkla, D. (eds) *The Bayeux Tapestry: New Approaches*. Oxford: Oxbow Books.

Tsurushima, H. (2016) 'Salmon, herring, oysters and 1066', in *Anglo-Norman Studies* 29. Woodbridge: Boydell and Brewer.

Turner, R.C., Allen, J.R.L., Coldstream, N., Jenkins-Jones, C., Morris, R.K. and Priestley, S.G. (2004) 'The Great Tower, Chepstow Castle, Wales', *The Antiquaries Journal* 84: 223–317.

Unwin, T. (1990) 'Saxon and early Norman viticulture in England', *Journal of Wine Research* 1(1): 61–75.

Vaughn, S.N and Fisher, P. (1991) *The Abbey of Bec and the Anglo-Norman State*. Woodbridge: Boydell & Brewer.

Verbeckmoes J. (1988) 'Flemish tenants-in-chief in Domesday England', *Revue Belge de Philologie et d'Histoire* 66(4): 725–56.

Victoria County History (1905) *Victoria County History of Sussex*, vol 1. London.

Victoria County History (2006) *Victoria County History of Somerset*, vol 9, London: VCH.

Victoria County History (2014) *Victoria County History of Shropshire*. Vol. 6.1 Woodbridge: Boydell & Brewer.

Waites, B. (2007) *Monasteries of the North York Moors and Wolds*. Stroud: Tempus.

Wardle, T. (2009) *England's First Castle*. Stroud: The History Press.

Watts, M. (2017) 'Watermills and waterwheels', in Hyer, M.C. and Hooke, D. *Water and the Environment in the Anglo-Saxon World*. Liverpool: Liverpool University Press.

Welldon Finn, R. (1967) *Domesday Studies: The Eastern Counties*. London: Longman.

Welldon Finn, R. (1971) 'Hampshire', in Darby, H.C. and Campbell, E.M.J. (eds) *The Domesday Geography of South-East England*. Cambridge: Cambridge University Press.

Welshman, R. (2019) 'The hoar apple tree of the Battle of Hastings: A new translation', Paper presented at the Theatres of War conference, Lancaster University, November 2019. academia.edu. Accessed 4 February 2020.

West, J. (2007) 'A taste for antiquities? Henry of Blois and the arts', in *Anglo-Norman Studies* 30: 213–30.

Wickham, C. (2005) *Problems in Doing Comparative History*. The Reuter Lecture. University of Southampton Centre for Antiquity and the Middle Ages.

Wickham, C. (2010) *The Inheritance of Rome*. London: Penguin.

Wickham, C. (2016) *Medieval Europe*. Yale University Press.

Williams, A. (1995) *The English and the Norman Conquest*. Woodbridge: The Boydell Press.

Williams, A. (2003) 'A bell-house and a burh-geat: Lordly residences in England before the Norman Conquest', in Liddiard, R. (ed.) *Anglo-Norman Castles*. Woodbridge: Boydell Press: 23-40.

Williams, A. (2004) 'Eadric the Wild', *Oxford Dictionary of National Biography*. Oxford: Oxford University Press.

Williams, A. (2016) 'Of Danes and thegns and Domesday Book: Scandinavian settlement in eleventh-century Berkshire', *Anglo-Norman Studies* XXXIX. Woodbridge: Boydell & Brewer.

Williams, A. (2018) '1066 and the English', in Bates, D., D'Angelo, E. and van Houts, E. (eds) *People, Texts and Artefacts: Cultural Transmission in the Medieval Norman Worlds*. London: Institute of Historical Research.

Williams, G. (2019) 'The Chew Valley hoard', *British Archaeology*, Nov./Dec. 2019.

Williams, M. (1970) *The Draining of the Somerset Levels*. Cambridge: Cambridge University Press.

Williamson, T. (2003) *Shaping Medieval Landscapes*. Oxford: Windgather Press.

Winkler, E.A. (2016) 'The Norman conquest of the classical past: William of Poitiers, language and history', *Journal of Medieval History* 42(4): 456–78.

Winkler, E.A. (2020) 'Imagining the medieval face of battle: The 'Malfosse' incident and the Battle of Hastings, 1066–1200', *Historical Research* 93(259): 2–22.

Wright, D. et al. (2017) 'Burwell Castle, Cambridgeshire', in Wright, D. and Creighton, O.H. (eds.) *Castles, Siegeworks and Settlements. Surveying the Archaeology of the Twelfth Century*. Oxford: Archaeopress 17-23.

Wyeth, W. (2018) 'Medieval Timber Motte Towers', *Medieval Archaeology*. Volume 62 Issue 1: 135-156.

Youngs, F.A. (1979) *Guide to the Local Administrative Units of England*. 2 vols. London: Royal Historical Society.

Zarnecki, G. (1972) *The Monastic Achievement*. London: Thames and Hudson.

Index

Aachen (North Rhine-Westphalia), 237, 269

Abbeys *see* monasteries

Abbotsbury Abbey (Dorset), 10

Abingdon (Oxfordshire), 138, 227
  Abbey, 10, 21, 27, 68, 174, 177, 182,
    227-8, 249
    Abbey Chronicle, 61

Acton Reynald (Shropshire), 190

Adam fitz Hubert, 80

Administrative structure:
  Anglo-Saxon, 4–7, 71, 138
    carucates, 6, 13, 153
    earldoms, 4, 5, 75, 245
    hides, 6–7, 13, 37, 71, 73, 74, 79, 103,
      182, 186
    hundreds, 1, 6, 36, 41, 42, 43, 74, 79,
      170, 245
    shires, 5–6, 59, 60, 70, 74, 115, 138,
      156, 159
    Witan, 4
  Norman, 8
    barons and baronies, 70, 71, 79–80, 130,
      169, 194, 212, 244, 257, 265, 304
    castleries, 71, 74–8
    in Normandy, 74–5
    English landholders, 73–4
    feudal system, 6, 7, 71, 88, 101, 212,
      304 *see also* barons, manors, peasants
    honours, 71, 78, 86
    intermarriage, 72–3
    manors and manor houses, 7–8, 12, 13,
      15, 48–9, 71, 86, 165
    palatinates, 71, 75
    peasants, 8, 12–13, 15, 53, 60, 74, 86,
      102, 208, 242
    rapes, Sussex, 40, 74, 76–7
    redistribution of land, 52, 53, 54, 65,
      70–80, 107, 231 *see also* colonization
    taxation, 74
  see also Church

Aelfric, Abbot of Eynsham Abbey, 19

Aelfwine, 73

Aelred, Abbot of Rievaulx, 210, 268, 306

Aethelred II, the Unready, 3, 9, 40, 41, 249

Aethelstan, King of England, 4

Aethelwig, Abbot of Evesham, 182

Aethelwine, Bishop of Durham, 60, 68

Aglionby (Cumbria), 86

Agriculture, 12–13, 16–18, 208, 218–22, 234,
  235, 248, 311
  cattle 17, 18, 219, 220, 221–2, 234,
    243, 248
  field names, 298–9
  field systems, 16–17, 86, 90
  oxen, 17, 61, 222
  pigs 17, 234, 235, 236, 238
  sheep 17–18, 207, 210, 212, 218, 219–20,
    221, 227–8, 234, 248
  see also monasteries

Ailric, 73

Alan Rufus, Lord of Richmond, 62, 86,
  202, 297

Aldreth Causeway, 68–69

Alençon (Orne), 265

Alfred, the Great, King of England, 145, 148

Allen Brown, R., 266

Alnmouth (Northumberland), 4, 166

Alnwick Castle (Northumberland), 132, 166

Alvecote (Warwickshire), 218

Amaury, *vicomte* of Thouars (Deux-Sèvres), 85

Ambleston (Pembrokeshire), 92

Anarchy, The, 97, 119, 146, 151, 161, 265

Anderitum see Pevensey

Anglo-Saxon Chronicle, 5, 10, 28, 30, 33, 37,
  42, 43, 49, 51, 54, 55, 56, 60, 62, 67, 68,
  81, 86, 110, 115, 121, 143, 153, 174, 175,
  240, 247, 295

Annales Cambriae, 88

Anselm, Abbot of Bury St Edmunds, 224,
  259, 268

Anselm, Archbishop of Canterbury, 169, 182, 224, 295
Appleton-le-Moors (North Yorkshire), 65–6
Architecture, 288, 310
    Romanesque (Anglo-Norman), 94, 182, 208, 259, 289–93
        decoration, 268, 290–3
        imitating Roman, 259, 268, 273, 280–1, 282, 291 *see also* Roman *spolia*
Arundel (West Sussex), 31, 76, 304
Ashby-de-la-Zouch (Leicestershire), 297
Asheldham (Essex), 188, 192
Ashwood (Staffordshire), 240
Aston Eyre (Shropshire), 190
Atiscross (Flintshire), 245
Auckland Castle (Co. Durham), 245-6
Augustinians, 113, 143, 176, 192, 204–208, 214, 215
Austin canons *see* Augustinians
Avening (Gloucestershire), 18
Avranches (Manche), 101
Axbridge (Somerset), 138

Baldock (Hertfordshire), 298
Baldwin, Abbot of Bury St Edmunds, 225
Balsdean (East Sussex), 32
Bamburgh Castle (Northumberland), 115, 132
Bampton (Oxfordshire), 164
Banbury (Oxfordshire), 164
Bangor (Gwynedd), 173
Barlings Abbey (Lincolnshire), 223
Barnack (Cambridgeshire), 22, 223
Barnard Castle (Co. Durham), 132, 288
Baronies 72
Baschurch (Shropshire), 166
Basingwerk Abbey (Flintshire), 213
Bath (Somerset), 181, 270–1
    Abbey, 182, 197
Battle (East Sussex), 30, 36, 42, 43, 44, 76, 225, 227
    Abbey, 42, 43–6, 172, 198, 201-2, 227
    Abbey Chronicle, 42, 201, 227
Baudri of Borgueil, 268
Bawtry (South Yorkshire), 166
Bayeux (Calvados), 41, 285
    Castle, 110
    Tapestry, **1**, 15, 16, 33, 34, 36, 37, 40, 41, 45, 47, 80, 101, 102, 110, 182, 183, 252, 256, 266, 267, 307, 308

Beachy Head (East Sussex), 297
Beaconsfield (Buckinghamshire), 161
Beauchief Abbey (Sheffield), 297
Beaudesert Castle (Warwickshire), 219, 297
Beaulieu Abbey (Hampshire), 297
Beaumanor (Leicestershire), 297
Beamish (Co. Durham), 297
Bec-Hellouin, Le (Eure),161, 170, 171, 179, 181, 194, 201, 215–17, 305
Beccles (Suffolk), 156
Beckermonds (North Yorkshire), 299
Bede, 278
Bedstone (Shropshire), 190
Belewe (Cumbria), 298
Belper (Derbyshire), 297
Belvoir Castle (Leicestershire), 288, 297
Benedeit, 304
Benedictines, 44, 94, 97, 148, 155, 181, 185, 196–8, 199–201, 203, 207, 208, 212, 213, 215, 218, 219, 224, 227, 305
Bercaries, 220 *see also* sheep
Beresford, Maurice, 167
Berkhamsted (Hertfordshire), 30, 48, 49, 51, 285
    Castle, 107
Bermondsey Abbey,145
Bernay Abbey (Eure), 180
Berry Pomeroy (Devon), 297
Bignor (West Sussex), 22
Bishop's Castle (Shropshire) 114
Bishop's Waltham Castle (Hampshire), 151
Black Canons *see* Augustinians
Bladon (Oxfordshire), 164
Bleddyn (Blein), King of Wales, 56, 87
Boeve de Haumtone, 304
Bolasis, 297
Boldon Book, 245, 256
Bonsall (Derbyshire), T'owd Man, 23
Bordesley Abbey (Worcestershire), 211, 224
Boston (Lincolnshire), 256
Botcheston (Leicestershire), 301
Boudicca, 276
Boulge (Suffolk), 296
Bourton-on-the-Water (Gloucestershire), 221
Bowes Castle (Co. Durham), 115
Bradley (North Yorkshire), 221
Bramber (West Sussex), 31, 76, 77
Brand, Abbot of Peterborough, 67–8
Brede (East Sussex), 170

Breteuil-sur-Iton (Eure), 123-4
    Laws of, 82, 89, 123
Bridgnorth (Shropshire), 128–9
Brimham (North Yorkshire), 220–1
Bristol, 29, 55, 88
Broadway (Worcestershire), 228
Brotonne Forest (Seine-Maritime), 238
Bruera (Cheshire), 298
Bruern (Oxfordshire), 298
Brut histories, 304
Bryanston (Dorset), 301
Buckfast Abbey (Devon), 213
Buckland (Oxfordshire), 18
Bucknell (Shropshire), 190
Bulverhythe (East Sussex), 32, 34, 37, 38, 39
Burford (Oxfordshire), 164, 165
Burgh Castle (Norfolk), 282
Burghal Hidage, 37
Burh, 34, 37, 40, 83, 85, 96, 102, 138,
    145, 156
    burh-geats, 102–103, 108, 117, 125, 224
Burwell (Cambridgeshire), 99
Bury St Edmunds (Suffolk), 138, 161, 224–7
    Abbey, **5**, 20, 21, 179, 182, 223, 224,
    225–7, 268
Byland Abbey (North Yorkshire), 210, 222, 224

Caen (Calvados), 22, 111, 139–40, 157, 181, 222
    Abbaye-aux-Dames, 18, 139, 179, 219, 229
    Abbaye-aux-Hommes (Saint-Étienne),
    139, 175, 179, 184
Caerleon (Monmouthshire), 71, 271, 274, 287
Caerwent (Monmouthshire), 273, 274
Caesar Augustus, 263, 268
Caesar, Julius, 262–5
Caister-on-Sea (Norfolk), 24
Caldbec Hill (East Sussex), 43, 44
Calder Abbey (Cumbria), 213, 221-2
Caldew (Cumbria), 298
Calne Palace (Wiltshire), 119
Cambridge, 140, 195, 214, 285, 296
Cangle (Oxfordshire), 298
Cannock (Staffordshire), 297
Canterbury, 9, 47, 50, 140, 181, 182, 194,
    274, 285, 286
    Castle, 110, 115
    Cathedral (Christ Church), 8, 154, 176–7,
    181, 184, 185, 196, 199, 274, 278, 291,
    293, 295, 305, 308, 309

churches, 274
    St Augustine's Abbey, 22, 24, 110, 223,
    273-4, 295, 307
Capitulare de Villis, 237
Caradoc of Llancarfan, 90
Cardiff, 88
    Castle, 88, 274
Carew (Pembrokeshire), 91
Carisbrooke Castle (Isle of Wight), 282
Carlisle (Cumbria), 23–4, 82, 86, 181, 197
Carmarthen, 130–2
Carolingian impact, viii–ix, 56, 99, 121, 158,
    179, 237–8, 252, 259, 278, 308
Carthusians, 213
Cassiobury (Hertfordshire), 81-2
Castle Acre Priory (Norfolk), 97, 199, 204
Castle (West) Bytham (Lincolnshire), 81
Castle Rising (Norfolk), 24–5, 80, 115
Castleries *see* administration
Castle Bryn Amlwyg (Shropshire) 109
Castles, 35, 37, 65, 75, 88, 95–137, 140,
    151, 156, 161, 169, 199, 215, 237, 252,
    286–7, 297
    Earth and timber, 96, 102, 103, 104,
    107–8, 117
    France and Normandy, 99–102, 110, 114
    Keeps, 36, 96, 101, 114–18, 106, 107,
    114–7, 125, 145, 156, 274
    Motte and bailey, 36, 92, 96, 97, 101–102,
    103–106, 107, 108–113, 128, 133, 136,
    154, 156, 159, 161, 274, 279, 282, 297
    see also castleries, towns
Cattle *see* agriculture
Caus (Shropshire), 75, 166–8
Cerne (Abbas) (Dorset), 296
    Abbey, 10
Cerney (Gloucestershire), 296
Chale (Isle of Wight), 192
Chapel-en-le-Frith (Derbyshire), 298
Charlemagne, Holy Roman Emperor,
    268, 269
Charles 'the Simple', King of the Western
    Franks, ix
Charlton (West Sussex), 32
Charterhouse (Somerset), 297
Chase, *see* forests
Chasewood (Staffordshire), 240
Chatham (Kent), 194
Cheddar Palace (Somerset), 121, 252

Chepstow Castle (Monmouthshire), 117, 272–4

Chester, 75, 181, 245, 270, 278, 285

Chichester (West Sussex), 76, 138, 181, 285

Chilsworthy (Devon), 297

Chipping Norton (Oxfordshire), 161, 163-4, 165

Christchurch Priory (Dorset), 192, 223

Chronicle of the Princes, 92

Church, 121, 122, 169–95, 218, 224, 231, 259, 260, 266, 272, 289
   dedications, 90, 173, 177–9 *see also* saints
   in Normandy, 9, 169–70, 174, 175, 182, 260
   organisation, 9–10, 171, 173, 180–2, 189, 305
     cathedrals, 9, 10, 140, 169, 170, 172, 181–2, 184, 196–7, 198, 231, 246
     dioceses and sees, 9, 94, 145, 157, 159, 164–5, 181
     minsters, 9–10, 189, 190, 192
     parish churches, 140, 162, 174, 188–94, 208, 215, 290–1
     treasures, 54, 170, 172–3, 174–5, 307
   see also monasteries

Chute Forest (Wiltshire), 243

Cinque Ports, 36, 37

Cippemore (Staffordshire), 240

Cirencester (Gloucestershire), 221, 296

Cistercians, 63, 204, 208–11, 212, 213, 218, 219, 220, 221, 224, 297

Clairvaux Abbey, 24, 208, 209

Clanville (Hampshire), 299

Clanville (Somerset), 299

Clare (Suffolk), 112

Clarendon Palace (Wiltshire), 121, 182, 258

Classical heroes and writers, 259, 260, 261, 262–6

Claudius, Emperor, 275, 277

Clavering (Essex), 104

Claverley (Shropshire), 307, 309

Clopton (Northamptonshire), 192

Clun (Shropshire), 75-76, 129–30

Cluniacs, 97, 143, 198, 203–204, 212, 305

Cluny Abbey (Saône-et-Loire), 203–204, 305

Cnut, King of England, 3, 4, 52–3, 73, 170, 238, 259

Cogges (Oxfordshire), 216–18

Coins, 3, 34, 52, 59, 88, 103, 259
   hoards, 58–9, 63–4
   mints, ix, 5, 40, 58, 64, 88, 138, 145, 146, 156, 159, 161, 166, 224

Colchester, 115-116, 138, 199
   Castle, 115, 275–8
   Chronicle, 277
   St Botolph's Priory, **6**, 204, 278-9

Colonization, 81–94, 123
   Breton, 71, 85, 86
   Fleming, 71, 85, 86–87, 88, 90–1, 93
   French, 71, 81–5, 88, 93, 151, 227, 260
   Scotland, 93–4
   Wales, 87–93
     Church, 172

Colswein of Lincoln, 74

Combe (North Yorkshire), 222

Combe Abbey (Warwickshire), 211

Combermere Abbey (Cheshire), 213

Comines, Robert de, Earl of Northumbria, 59

Constantine, Emperor, 268, 277

Corbet family, 166–7, 190

Corfe (Dorset):
   Castle, 115
   Forest, 243

Corfton (Shropshire), 246

Cornbury Forest (Oxfordshire), 249

Costessey (Norfolk), 245

Coventry:
   Castle, 99
   Cathedral, 182, 197

Croome d'Abitot (Worcestershire), 297

Crowhurst (East Sussex), 43

Crowland Abbey (Lincolnshire), 223

Crown-wearing, 4, 52, 56, 121

Crusades, x, 126, 171, 175, 194, 214, 261, 293, 298

Cudlow (West Sussex), 32

Curfew, 142

Danelaw, 3, 6, 12, 13, 138

Danes, 3, 4, 5, 13, 41, 52–3, 59, 60, 62, 63, 67, 68, 151, 201, 206 *see also* Vikings

Daniel of Beccles, 19

Dapifer, Eudo, 277

Darby, H.C., 11–12, 13, 240

David I, King of Scotland, 93, 265

Deddington (Oxfordshire), 79, 80, 164, 165
    Castle, 107, 108
Deer parks, 83, 96, 117, 235, 236, 237, 238,
    245–51, 253
    in Normandy, 245–6
    see also forests, hunting
Deerhurst (Gloucestershire), 170
Delamere Forest (Cheshire), 245
Denby (West Yorkshire), 18
Derby, 138
Devizes (Wiltshire), 135-6
Dinan Castle (Côtes d'Armor), 110-111
Dol Castle (Ille-et-Vilaine), 110
Domesday Book, 4, 5-7, 8, 10–13, 16, 17, 18,
    19, 20, 21, 22, 24, 26, 27, 28, 29, 34, 37,
    40–1, 48, 49, 56, 62, 63, 73, 74, 79, 80, 81,
    85, 103, 128, 138, 140, 143, 151, 153, 156,
    159, 161, 186, 211, 219, 222, 224, 227,
    232, 234, 235, 236, 240, 246, 249, 256,
    268, 272, 294, 296, 298
Domfront (Orne), 265
Dorchester on Thames (Oxfordshire), 9, 181
Doué-la-Fontaine (Maine-et-Loire), 99
Dover (Kent), 30, 37, 38, 48, 49, 50, 54, 78,
    223, 285–6
    Castle, 38, 49, 115
Downton Castle (Wiltshire), 119
Drayton (Oxfordshire), 74
Drengs, 86, 92, 93
Drewston (Devon), 301
Drogo de la Beuvrière, Lord of Holderness,
    81, 86
Droitwich (Worcestershire), 24
Dryburgh, 94
Dudley Castle, 254
Dudo of Saint-Quentin, 261, 288
Dunwich (Suffolk), 181
Durham, 5, 9, 60, 133, 244, 296, 297
    Cathedral, 4, 61, 66, 169, 176, 184, 185–6,
        197, 203, 244, 245, 256, 260, 268, 290

Eadmer, Abbot of St Albans, 274
Eadmer of Canterbury, 1, 169, 278
Eadwig, King of England, 27, 149
Eadwine Psalter, 8, 308
Earldoms, 75
Ealdred, Abbot of St Albans, 274
Ealdred, Archbishop of York, 51, 54
Ealhswith, wife of Alfred the Great, 148

Eamont (Cumbria), 299
East Mersea (Essex), 170
Eastbourne (East Sussex), 170
Eaton Socon (Cambridgeshire), 98-99
Edburton Hill (West Sussex), 48
Edgar the Atheling, 30, 47, 50, 51, 54, 56,
    59, 67, 68, 93
Edgar, King of England, 27, 51
Edric the Wild, 56–7, 68, 130
Edward the Confessor, King of England, 3,
    4–5, 8, 21, 37, 52, 71, 81, 86, 87, 88, 103,
    119, 141, 170, 227, 251, 284, 295
Edward the Elder, King of England, 6, 148
Edwin, Earl of Mercia, 56
Eleanor of Aquitaine, wife of Henry II, 29, 160
Elmham (Norfolk), 181
Ely (Cambridgeshire), 2, 68, 181, 222 see also
    Fenland Revolt
    Aldreth causeway, 68
    Cathedral, 10, 28, 67, 169, 176, 178, 196,
        219, 222, 223
    Stuntney causeway, 68, 222
Emma of Normandy, 3
Enville (Staffordshire), 299
Ermenfrid, Bishop of Sion, 201
Esger the Staller, 71
Eustace, Count of Boulogne, 54
Evesham (Worcestershire), 227
    Abbey, 176, 177, 182, 221, 222, 227–8
        Abbey Chronicle, 60, 61
Ewyas Harold (Herefordshire), 103-5, 110
Exeter, 55, 78, 190, 285
    Cathedral, 172
    Exeter Book, 270, 271
    Rougemont Castle, 55, 103, 282
Eye Priory (Suffolk), 199
Eynesbury (Cambridgeshire), 18
Eynsford Castle (Kent), 282
Eynsham (Oxfordshire), 164, 165
    Abbey 10, 19, 165, 252

Falaise (Calvados), 161
Fantosme, Jordan, 304
Farnham Castle (Surrey), 119, 151
Faulston (Wiltshire), 301
Fawsley (Northamptonshire), 13
Fécamp (Seine-Maritime), 100
    Abbey, 24, 27, 34, 40, 170, 177, 179,
        216–18, 308

Fenland revolt, 67–8, 178 *see also* Ely
Feudal system, 12, 53, 70, 71, 74, 101
Fish and fishing, 17, 19–22, 75, 246, 311
    fishponds, 21–2, 96, 121, 224, 248, 250
Fitzalan family (Earls of Arundel), 166
Flamston (Wiltshire), 301
Flat Holm, **2**, 55
Fleury Abbey (Loiret), 174
Folkestone (Kent), 78
Forests, Royal, and Forest Law, xii, 18,
    237–45, 252–3, 256
    in Normandy and France, 237–8, 248, 257–8
    see also deer parks, hunting, woodland
Fountains Abbey (North Yorkshire),
    208–209, 212, 220, 222, 224, 248
Fowlmere (Cambridgeshire), 103
Franks, ix, x, 3, 4, 56, 101, 237
Frodsham (Cheshire), 27
Frostenden (Suffolk), 53
Frosterley (Co. Durham), 256
Fulbourn (Cambridgeshire), 179
Fulk Nerra, Count of Anjou, 99
Furness Abbey (Cumbria), 213, 222

Gamblesby (Cumbria), 86-7
Gate Helmsley (North Yorkshire), 65
Gatehouses *see* burh-geats
Geoffrey, Bishop of Coutances, 51, 57, 182
Geoffrey Gaimar, 265
Geoffrey de Mandeville, 71–2
Gerald of Wales, 91, 271
*Gesta Guillelmi ducis Normannorum et regis
    Anglorum*, 262
Giffard, William, Bishop of Winchester,
    121, 149
Gilbert Crispin, Abbot of Westminster, 181
Gilbertines, 213
Gillemichael, 61
Gilmorton (Leicestershire), 81
Gisors Castle (Eure), 24
Glassonby (Cumbria), 86
Glastonbury (Somerset), 138, 224, 227, 229
    Abbey 13, 21, 27, 149, 151, 182, 219, 222
Gloucester, 4, 138, 140, 287, 296
    Cathedral, 74, 88, 221, 228
    Palace, 119, 121
Godwin, Earl *see* King Harold
Golborne (Cheshire), 27
Goltho (Lincolnshire), 15, 102

Goodrich Castle (Herefordshire), 287
Goscelin de St Bertin, 1, 265
Gough Map, 285
Grandmont Abbey (Haute-Vienne), 24
Grandmont, Order of, 213
Great Bedwyn (Wiltshire), 161
Great Wytheford (Shropshire), 190
Grinshill (Shropshire), 190
Grinstead (East) (West Sussex), 22
Grosmont Castle (Monmouthshire), 288
Gruffydd ap Rhys, Prince of Deheubarth, 95
Gulpher (Suffolk), 296
Gundulph, Bishop of Rochester, 115, 181,
    184, 194, 282
Gunthorpe (Nottinghamshire), 17
Guy de Warewic, 304
Gyrth, brother of Harold, 42
Gytha, mother of Harold, 2, 55, 263

Hadrian's Wall, 270
Hailes Abbey (Gloucestershire), 211
Hales (Norfolk) church, 193
Hampton (Worcestershire), 28
Harald Hardrada, King of Norway, 3, 33
Harbledown (Kent), 194
Harmondsworth (Middlesex), 179
Harold II, King of England, **1**, 30, 33, 34,
    42, 43, 46, 55, 57, 58, 59, 170, 171, 201-2,
    251-2, 262, 263, 285, 312
    Earl Godwin, 34, 40, 81, 170, 256
Harraby (Cumbria), 86
Harrying of the North, 59–65, 201, 266, 285
Harthacanute, King of England, 41–2
Hastings (East Sussex), 30, 31, 32, 34,
    36–40, 42, 43, 76, 170
    Battle of, 30, 36, 42–7, 57, 70, 71, 170,
        182, 248, 260, 262, 285, 312
    site of 42–4
    Castle, 37, 38, 40, 107, 110
Hatfield Chase (South Yorkshire), 243
Hatfield Forest (Essex), 243, 258
Haughton-le-Skerne (Co. Durham), 298
Haveloc the Dane, 304
Haverfordwest (Pembrokeshire), 91
Havering (London), 256
Hayling Island (Hampshire), 179
Heath (Shropshire), 190-1
Hedingham Castle (Essex), 115
Hedon (East Yorkshire), 166

Helgot de Reisolent, 301
Hemel Hempstead (Hertfordshire), 81
Hen Domen (Powys), 109
Henry I, King of England, 65, 86, 90–1, 95, 117, 128, 161, 181, 206, 207, 228, 249, 256, 266, 291, 295
Henry II, King of England, 21, 24, 29, 132, 133, 142, 145, 160, 164, 240, 241, 250, 251, 256, 257–8, 265, 295, 303, 312
Henry III, King of England, 154
Henry de Beaumont, Earl of Warwick, 130
Henry, Earl of Northumberland, 133
Henry de Blois, Bishop of Winchester, 119, 121, 149, 151, 269
Henry de Ferrers, 199
Henry of Huntingdon, 46, 53, 184, 250, 261, 265, 280, 302
Herbert de Losinga, Bishop of Norwich, 158
Herbert fitz Ivo, 80
Hereford, 75, 82
   Castle, 56, 113
   Cathedral, 179
Hereward 'the Wake', 67–8, 177
Hermann, Bishop of Salisbury, 184
Hervey, Bishop of Ely, 222
Hexham (Northumberland) 60
Historia Normannorum, 288
Historia Pontificalis, 269
Holdgate (Shropshire), 301
Holinshed, Raphael, 160
Holt (Norfolk), 245
Horses, 77, 80, 119, 221, 234, 248, 254
Horton (North Yorkshire), 221
Hoskins W.G., xi–xii, 310
Hospitals, 149, 194–5, 207
   lepers, 149, 194–5
Howton (Herefordshire), 301
Huby (North Yorkshire), 65
Hugh, Earl of Chester, 245
Hugh of Montfort, 78
Hugh de Port, 80
Hugh de Puiset, Bishop of Durham, 246
Hugh fitz Baldric, Sheriff of Yorkshire, 62
Hugh the Chanter, 151
Humphrey de Tilleul, 71
Hunting, 121, 161, 170, 235, 237, 238, 239, 240, 242, 244, 251–8
   deer, 235, 239, 240, 244, 246–8, 252, 253, 254, 256

falconry, 246, 251, 253, 256, 258
hays, 240, 246, 252
hunting dogs, 244, 245, 254–6
other game, 239, 246, 248, 254, 256, 257, 311
rituals and techniques, 252–4
wolves, 256
see also deer parks, forests
Huntingdon, 140, 285
Hythe (Kent), 37, 78

Iffley, church, **4**
Illuminated manuscripts, 290, 293, 307, 308
Industry, 22–4, 156–7, 220, 222–4
   metal working, 22–4, 221, 224
   stone quarrying, 22, 222–3
   water engineering, 21, 96, 139, 222, 224, 308
Ingarsby (Leicestershire), 81
Isle of Wight, 33, 77
Isleham (West Sussex), 32
Ivry-la-Bataille (Eure), 101

Jarrow (Tyne & Wear), 60, 297
   Abbey, 185, 203
Jedburgh (Roxburghshire), 94
Jervaulx Abbey (North Yorkshire), 297
Jesmond (Newcastle), 297, 299
Jeu d'Adam, 304
John, King of England, 195, 239, 254–8, 297
John of Salisbury, 254, 269, 306
John of Worcester, 34, 51, 60, 119, 169, 240
Johnstone (Devon), 301
Judhellus filius Aluredi (Juhel de Totnes), 86, 199
Jumièges (Seine-Maritime):
   Abbey 179, 201
   Forest, 238
Jurston (Devon), 301

Kanglecroft (Hertfordshire), 298
Kearnsey (Kent), 298
Kelso (Roxburghshire), 94
Kempley (Gloucesrshire), 294
Kempsford (Gloucestershire), 18
Kendal (Cumbria), 161
Kenilworth Castle (Warwickshire), 115-6
Kesteven Forest (Lincolnshire), 242
Kibworth Harcourt (Leicestershire), 81
Kilnsey (North Yorkshire), 220, 221

Kilpeck (Herefordshire), 136-7, 292-3
Kings Clipstone (Nottinghamshire), 256
Kingsholm Palace (Gloucestershire), 121
Kingston (East Sussex), 32
Kingswood Forest (Kent), 238
Kinver Forest (Staffordshire), 240
Kirkstall Abbey (West Yorkshire), 224
Kirkstead Abbey (Lincolnshire), 224
Knights Hospitaller, 130, 214
Knights Templar, 126, 166, 214, 298

La Haia de Perchet (Hauts-de-Seine), 246
La Zisa, Palace of (Sicily), 250-1
Lacy, de, family, 73, 80, 126–7, 130
Land redistribution *see* administrative
    structure
Lanfranc, Archbishop of Canterbury, 68, 73,
    74, 139, 143, 170, 176–7, 181, 182, 184,
    194, 200, 222, 266, 291
Langeais (Indre-et-Loire), 100
Langport (Somerset), 138
Language, 288, 294–6, 310 *see also* literature,
    music
Lastingham (North Yorkshire), 290
Launceston Castle (Cornwall), 254
Le Cangel (Essex), 298
Leicester, 138, 271
Leiston Abbey (Suffolk), 212
Leland, John, 113
Leonin, 305
Lessay Abbey (Manche), 236
Lessingham Priory (Norfolk), 215
Letterston (Pembrokeshire), 92
Levisham (North Yorkshire), 66
Lewes (East Sussex), 43, 76, 195, 203–204
    Priory, **5**, 172, 199, 223
Liber Eliensis, 2
Lichfield (Staffordshire), 181
    Cathedral, 291
Licques Abbey (Pas-de-Calais), 212
Life of St Columbanus, 237
Life of St Edmund the Martyr, 304
Lincoln, 9, 74, 138, 140, 151, 166, 181, 190,
    279, 285
    Castle, 279, 285
    Cathedral, 165, 169, 184, 268, 279–81
    churches, 282
Lindisfarne (Northumberland), 61
Lintz (Co. Durham), 297

Literature, 174, 288, 301–4, 310 *see also*
    language
Llandaff (Cardiff), 173
Llandudoch (Pembrokeshire), 213
Llanfair Waterdine (Shropshire), 190
Locatores *see* drengs
Lockton (North Yorkshire), 66, 67
London, 1, 30, 43, 47, 50, 51, 138, 141–5,
    151, 153, 161, 181, 190, 194, 285 *see also*
    Westminster
        Baynard's Castle, 141
        churches 143, 190, 214, 283
        London Bridge, 141–2
        Montfitchet's Tower, 141
        St Paul's Cathedral, 142–3
        Tower of, 115, 117, 141, 273, 282
        White Tower, 114–15, 260, 275, 277
Longville (Shropshire), 299
Lonlay (Orne), 215
Lorimer (Hampshire), 27
Ludgershall Castle (Wiltshire), 244
Ludlow (Shropshire), 125, 127–8
    Castle, **5**, 117, 125–8, 214
Luton (Bedfordshire), 236
Lyme (Regis) (Dorset), 24
Lynn (King's) (Norfolk), 83, 158, 256

Macclesfield Forest (Cheshire), 245
Magna Carta, 38
Magnus liber, 305
Mainstone (Hampshire), 301
Malcolm III, King of Scotland, 56, 88, 93
Malet family, 199
Malfosse, 44, 46–7
Malling (West) (Kent), 211
Malmesbury Abbey (Wiltshire), 28, 68,
    175-6
    Abbey Chronicle, 28
    Castle, 119
Manasses Arsic, Lord of Cogges, 216
Manorbier (Pembrokeshire), 91
Manor houses, 15, 103, 188, 215, 234,
    304, 311
Manors, 7–8, 12, 13, 15, 21, 24, 48–9, 55,
    71, 88, 161, 165, 234, 235, 240, 245, 248,
    277, 311
Mantes (Île-de-France), 62
Map, Walter, 211
Market Harborough (Leicestershire), 162

Markets and marketplaces, 5, 37, 82, 85, 93, 108, 123, 127, 128, 130, 132, 133, 135, 138, 156, 161–2, 164, 165, 166, 167, 192, 222, 226, 227, 228, 229
Marlborough (Wiltshire), 162–3
  Castle, 96, 161
Marlston (Berkshire), 301
Marmoutier-en-Loire Abbey (Indre-et-Loire), 44
Marsh Chapel (Lincolnshire) saltern mounds.
Marsh Gibbon (Buckinghamshire), 73
Martin of Bec, Abbot of Peterborough, 28
Matilda, Empress, 146, 148
Matilda, wife of William I, 56, 139
Matter of England romances, 304
Maugersbury (Gloucestershire), 228
Maurice, Bishop of London, 143
Meaux Abbey (East Yorkshire), 220, 222
Melrose (Roxburghshire), 94
Menageries, 21, 247, 250
Merchem (Flanders), 109–10
Merdon Castle (Hampshire), 119, 151
Mersea Island (Essex), 21
Milburn Priory (Dorset), 215
Middleham Castle (North Yorkshire), 115
Middlewich (Cheshire), 24, 62
Milford on Sea (Hampshire), 192
Military service, ix, 5, 6–7, 182, 214 see also
  Cinque Ports
Mills, 19, 26–7, 93, 96, 224, 246
Minchinhampton (Gloucestershire), 18, 219, 229
Moccas (Herefordshire) 232–3
Monasteries, 10, 19, 20, 21, 24, 27–8, 43, 88, 94, 119, 138, 161, 169, 170, 171, 172, 174, 179–80, 181–2, 188, 192, 196–231, 246, 248, 291, 295, 297, 304, 311
  Dissolution, 149, 201, 207, 229
  granges, 63, 188, 209, 210, 211, 213, 220–1, 222, 224
  in Normandy, 177, 179–80, 199–201, 203, 212, 213, 215, 216–8, 219, 229, 305, 308
  see also agriculture, church administration, towns, viticulture
Mondrem Forest (Cheshire), 245
Monkton (Kent), 19
Monkwearmouth (Tyne & Wear), 185
Mont-Saint-Michel Abbey (Manche), 27, 180
Montacute Castle (Somerset), 57, 58, 59

Montgomery (Powys), 88, 90, 301
Montvilliers Abbey (Seine-Maritime), 180
Morcar, Earl of Northumbria, 56, 68
Moreton Corbet (Shropshire), 190
Moreton-in-Marsh (Gloucestershire), 228–9
Morville (Shropshire), 189–90
Muchelney Abbey (Somerset), 10
Murdrum fine, 62
Music, 288, 304–307, 310
  liturgical, 174, 305–306
  non–liturgical, 30
  see also language
Muslim influence, 119, 248, 250–1, 291, 293

Nantwich (Cheshire), 24, 62
Narberth South (Pembrokeshire), 92
Neath Abbey (Glamorgan), 213
Neroche Forest (Somerset), 258
Nevern (Pembrokeshire), 179
New Buckenham (Norfolk), 97
New Forest (Hampshire), 18, 77, 240, 242–3, 244, 256, 257
Newcastle upon Tyne Castle, 132, 161
Newsham (Lincolnshire), 212
Newtown (Isle of Wight), 166
Norbertines see Premonstratensians
Norham (Northumberland), 133
  Castle, 3, 115, 132–3
Norman:
  Conquest, impact of, viii, xiii, 3, 13, 30, 33–6, 40–2, 52, 53, 59, 65, 81, 140, 169, 171–2, 173, 179, 231, 235, 245, 260, 268, 288, 289, 294, 305, 307, 310, 311, 312
  'empire', x–xi, 259–60, 261, 266–9, 272
  see also administrative structure, architecture, church dedications
Normandy, creation of, viii–x
North Cadbury (Somerset), 71
North Elmham (Norfolk), 235
Northampton, 138
Northleach (Gloucestershire), 221, 228
Northwich (Cheshire), 24, 62
Norwich (Norfolk), 3, 82, 84, 85, 138, 140, 156–9, 181, 190
  Castle, 82, 156–8
  Cathedral, 157–8, 169, 197
Notre-Dame Cathedral (Paris), 305

Nottingham, 83, 138, 296
  Castle, 83
Nun Monkton (North Yorkshire), 65

Oak trees, 235–6
Odo, Bishop of Bayeux, Earl of Kent, 50, 54,
  70, 78–80, 107–108, 182, 183, 266, 282
Offenham (Worcestershire), 222
Ogbourne St George Priory (Wiltshire), 216
Okehampton Castle (Devon), 254
Old Bracklesham (West Sussex), 32
Old Sarum (Wiltshire), 3, 159–60, 181
  Castle, 96, 159–60
  Cathedral, 159–60, 184
  Oath of Salisbury, 159
  Palace, 159
  see also Salisbury
Osmerley (Worcestershire), 211
Ongar (Essex), 246
Orderic Vitalis, 8, 52, 54, 56, 59, 60, 63, 72,
  82, 95, 151, 264, 265, 302
Osbern Pentecost, 103
Osmund, Bishop of Salisbury, 159
Osney Abbey (Oxford), 206–7
Oswestry (Shropshire), 75, 98–99
Oxford, 4, 138-9, 162, 176, 204–7
  Beaumont Palace, 298
  Castle, 73, 106
  Osney Priory, 206–7
  St Frideswide's Priory, 204–6, 207
  St George's Tower, 106

Painswick (Gloucestershire), 301
Palaces, 119–23, 237, 252
Palatinates, 75
Panborough Hill (Somerset), 27
Paris, Matthew, 274–5
Parish Churches, 188–94, 290
Paul of Caen, Abbot of St Albans, 81, 177,
  181, 274
Peasants see administrative structure
Pelham, Thomas, Earl of Chichester, 38
Pembroke, 2, 89
Penrith (Cumbria), 161
Penson (Devon), 301
Penstone (Devon), 301
Percy family, 65, 202
Perdigon, troubadour, 8
Pershore Abbey (Worcestershire), 18, 228

Personal names, 288, 299–301
Peterborough:
  Cathedral, 10, 19, 28, 67, 68, 172, 174,
    177, 182-3, 223, 291, 295
  Tout Hill, 182
Pevensey (East Sussex), 30, 31, 32, 34–6, 37,
  38, 40, 42, 76, 170, 264, 285
  Bay, 1
  Castle, 35, 96, 107, 117, 282
Peveril Castle (Derbyshire), 23
Picot de Say, Lord of Clun, 130
Pigs see agriculture
Pippin III, King of the Franks, 237
Place names, ix, 10, 40, 90, 248, 258, 288,
  296-9, 301
Planned towns see towns
Planned villages, 63, 65–7
Pleshey (Essex), 97, 136
Polesworth (Warwickshire), 211
Policraticus, 306
Pontefract (West Yorkshire), 82, 99, 103
Pope Alexander II, 170–1
Pope Nicholas II, 189
Portchester (Hampshire), 34, 37, 76, 140
  Castle, 76, 117, 282
Portland (Dorset), 78
Povington Priory (Dorset), 215
Premonstratensians, 208, 211–13, 297
Prémontré (Aisne), 212
Priories, 215–8 see also monasteries
Pulverbatch Castle, 2
Pyramis, Denys, 304

Quarr (Isle of Wight), 223
Quatford (Shropshire), 128

Rackham, Oliver, 232–3, 234
Ralph de Courbépine, 80
Ralph of Gaël, Earl of East Anglia, 56, 68,
  85, 86
Ralph of Mantes, Earl of Hereford,
  103, 106
Ralph, Bishop of the Orkneys, 265
Ralph the Crafty, 256
Ralph the Staller, 86
Ramsey Abbey (Cambridgeshire), 19, 166,
  174, 223
Ranston (Dorset), 301
Ranulf Flambard, Bishop of Durham, 133

Ranulf le Meschin, vicomte of Bayeux, 86
Ranulph de Glanville, Chief Justiciar of England, 212
Rayleigh (Essex), 106
Reading Abbey (Berkshire), 194
Redesdale (Northumberland), 256
Reginald, Abbot of Evesham, 227
Reginald, Abbot of Ramsey, 142
Reinfrid, Prior of Whitby, 201–202
Remigius of Fécamp, Bishop of Lincoln, 184, 268, 281–2
Rennes Castle (Ille-et-Vilaine), 110
Repton Castle (Derbyshire), 112
Revesby Abbey (Lincolnshire), 210–11
Rhiwallon, King of Wales, 56, 87
Rhuddlan (Denbighshire), 245
Rhys ap Gruffydd, Prince of Deheubarth, 213
Rhys ap Tewdwr, Prince of South Wales, 273
Richard II, King of England, 119, 160
Richard I, Duke of Normandy, 101
Richard II, Duke of Normandy, 3, 100, 101
Richard Scrob, Sheriff of Worcester, 103
Richard's Castle (Herefordshire), 104, 105, 110
Richardson (Wiltshire), 301
Richborough (Kent), 125
Richmond (North Yorkshire), 62, 82, 86, 244
   Castle, 38, 117-8, 288, 297
Rickmansworth (Hertfordshire), 81
Rievaulx Abbey (North Yorkshire), 208, 209–11, 268, 297
Ripon (North Yorkshire), 162
Robert, Abbot of Evesham, 228
Robert, Count of Eu, 38, 76
Robert, Count of Mortain, 24, 34, 51, 57, 70, 78, 86, 151
Robert de Beaumont, Earl of Leicester, 257
Robert de Bellême, Earl of Shrewsbury, 128
Robert de Comines, Earl of Northumbria, 59
Robert de Mowbray, Earl of Northumbria, 203
Robert d'Oilly, Lord of Wallingford, 73, 106, 206
Robert of Rhuddlan, 71, 245
Robert de Todeni, 297
Robert de Umfraville, Lord of Redesdale, 256
Robert fitz Haimon, Lord of Glamorgan, 88
Robert fitz Roger, Lord of Warkworth, 133
Robert fitz Wimarc, 104, 106

Rochester (Kent), 43, 50, 79, 194, 285, 286
   Castle, 107–108, 115, 282
   Cathedral, 6, 107, 184, 197, 199, 268, 283, 293
Rockingham Castle (Northamptonshire), 252
Roger II, King of Sicily, 261
Roger Bigod, Earl of Norfolk, 80, 204
Roger de Breteuil, Earl of Hereford, 13, 56, 68
Roger de Clinton, Bishop of Coventry and Lichfield, 190
Roger de Montgomery, 76, 88, 112, 130, 199, 204, 269, 301
Roger de Mowbray, 210
Roger, Bishop of Salisbury, 96, 135
Rolleston (Wiltshire), 301
Rollington (Dorset), 73
Rollo, ix, 41, 261
Roman de Brut, 302
Roman de Rou, 302
Romance of Horn, 304
Romanesque architecture see Norman architecture
Rome:
   Roman fortifications and ruins, 34–6, 55, 96, 103, 107, 114, 117, 131, 138, 141, 145, 149, 151, 155, 159, 269–71, 273, 274, 275, 278, 279, 282, 284, 285, 286
   Roman roads, 1, 43, 284–7
      Ermine Street, 279, 285
      Fosse Way, 279, 285
      Icknield Way, 51, 285
      in Normandy, 285
      Via Devana, 285
      Watling Street, 50, 284–5, 286
   Roman spolia, 269, 272, 273, 274–5, 276, 277, 278, 282–3
   St Peter's Basilica, 268, 278
   Trajan's Column, 266-7
   see also architecture, classical heroes
Romney (East Sussex), 31, 34, 37, 49
Romsey Abbey (Hampshire), 223
Rosamund Clifford, 250, 251
Rouen (Seine-Maritime), ix, 29, 139, 141, 161, 263, 265, 266, 285
   Great Tower, 101-2
   Saint-Ouen Abbey, 21, 170
   Sainte-Trinité-du-Mont, 179
Rowlstone (Herefordshire), 301
Royal Forests see forests

Rudheath Forest (Cheshire), 243
Rufford Abbey (Nottinghamshire), 210
'Ruin, The', 269–71, 278
Rye (East Sussex), 24, 32, 34, 170
Ryton-Eleven-Towns (Shropshire), 166

Saints, 176–9, 181, 304
    Anglo-Saxon:
        St Aethelbert, King of England, 179
        St Aetheldreda, 176
        St Aethelthryth, 178
        St Aethelwold, 10, 177–8
        St Cuthbert, 176, 179, 185, 268
        St Cuthman, 177
        St Dunstan, 10, 51, 174, 177, 179
        St Edmund, 179, 224, 268, 304
        St Frideswide, 176, 204–6
        St Oswald, 10, 187
        St Swithun, 177, 179
    Norman:
        St Augustine, 212, 278
        St Benedict, 10, 174, 208
        St Bernard, 208, 212
        St (Virgin) Mary, 176, 179
        St Michael, 85, 179
        St Thomas (Becket) of Canterbury,
            177, 194, 307, 310
        St Valéry, 179
        St Vigor, 177, 179
    see also church dedications
St Albans Abbey, 21, 81, 169, 177, 181, 203,
    246, 274, 276
St Asaph (Denbighshire), 173
St David's (Pembrokeshire), 88, 173, 273
St Dogmael's Abbey (Pembrokeshire), 213-4
St Ives (Cambridgeshire), 166-7
Saint-Clair-sur-Epte, treaty of, ix
Saint-Denis, Paris, 170, 237
Saint-Ébremond (Manche), 246
Saint-Evroult (Orne), 179
Saint-Germain-des-Prés, ix
Saint-Martin-de-Séez (Orne), 199
Sainte-Pience (Manche), 246
Saint-Valéry-sur-Somme, 30, 33, 179
Saint-Wandrille Abbey (Seine-Maritime),179
Salcey (Northamptonshire), 298
Salisbury (Wiltshire), 159, 160 see also
    Old Sarum
Salt, 24–6, 62, 138

Saltwood (Kent), 78
Sampson, Abbot of Bury St Edmunds, 246
Sandal Castle (West Yorkshire), 254
Sandwich (Kent), 33, 34, 37, 48, 78
Savernake Forest (Wiltshire), 236
Savigniacs, 210, 213
Sawtry Abbey (Cambridgeshire), 223, 230
Saxon Shore forts, 34, 282, 285
Scandinavian impact, ix, 3, 4, 59, 138, 231,
    261, 291, 310, 312
Scolland of Canterbury, 22
Scotland, 93-94.
Scottish Wars of Henry II, The, 304
Seacroft (West Yorkshire), 224
Seinte Resurrection, 304
Selby Abbey (North Yorkshire), 21, 61, 172
Selsey (West Sussex), 181
Sempringham (Lincolnshire), 213
    Order of see Gilbertines
Serlo, Abbot of Gloucester, 208
Shalfleet (Isle of Wight), 192-3
Shapwick (Somerset), 13–14
Sharnbrook (Bedfordshire), 21
Shawbury (Shropshire),190
Sheep see agriculture
Shepton Mallet (Somerset), 297
Sherborne (Dorset), 159, 181
Sherwood Forest (Nottinghamshire), 243
Shrewsbury, 75, 82, 140, 296–7
    Abbey, 166, 172, 190, 198-9, 269
    Castle, 56, 269
Sigeric, Archbishop of Canterbury, 259
Silchester (Hampshire), 285
Simeon of Durham, 133
Skipton (North Yorkshire), 287
Slepe (Cambridgeshire), 166
Slindon Park (Sussex), 234
Snettisham (Norfolk), 80
Song of the Battle of Hastings, 40, 262
Song of Roland, 307
South Lopham (Norfolk), 189
South Mimms (Hertfordshire), 110
Southampton, 29, 81, 85, 140
Southwark (London), 50, 121, 194
    Cathedral, 143
    Palace, 122
Southwell Minster (Nottinghamshire),
    283-4
Southwold (Suffolk), 20

Speculum caritatis, 306
Stafford, 82
   Battle of, 56
Stainburn (North Yorkshire), 221
Stallingborough (Lincolnshire) 18
Stamford (Lincolnshire), 138, 140
Stamford Bridge, Battle of, 3, 33, 57
Standard, Battle of the, 265
Stanhope (Co. Durham), 245
Stephen, Count of Aumale, 166
Stephen, King of England, 97, 121, 148
Stephen of Rouen, 265
Stevenstone (Devon), 301
Steyning (West Sussex), 31, 49, 170-1, 177
Stigand, Archbishop of Canterbury, 54, 180
Stogursey (Somerset), 215
Stoke Mandeville (Buckinghamshire), 297
Stoke St Milborough (Shropshire),190
Stokesay (Shropshire), 297, 299
Stowe (Shropshire),190
Stow-on-the-Wold (Gloucestershire),
   221, 228
Stratton-on-the-Fosse (Somerset), 179
Stuttgart Psalter, **5**
Sulgrave (Northamptonshire), 102
Sussex, 32
   coast, 30–2, 34, 36–7, 76
Swaffham (Norfolk), 19
Swansea, 130, 131
Sweyn II, King of Denmark, 59
Sweyn Forkbeard, King of Denmark, 52
Symeon of Durham, 61, 133, 185

Takeley (Essex), 179
Tal-y-Llychau (Talley) (Carmarthenshire), 213
Taunton Castle (Somerset), 119, 121, 151
Taxation, ix, 4, 5, 6, 8, 12, 41, 53, 59, 63, 74,
   82, 107, 156, 240
Taynton (Oxfordshire), 22
Temple Bruer (Lincolnshire), 166, 298
Tewkesbury Abbey (Gloucestershire), 7, 88, 290
Thame (Oxfordshire), 164
Thanet (Kent), 24
Thankerton (Lanarkshire), 93
Thankerton (Pembrokeshire), 92
Thaon, Phillipe de 303
Thetford (Norfolk), 112, 181, 204
Thomas of Bayeux, Archbishop of York, 151
Thorkell of Warwick, 74

Thorney Abbey (Cambridgeshire), 19, 29
Thurstan, Archbishop of York, 208
Tidenham (Gloucestershire), 19, 20
Tingrith (Bedfordshire), 297
Tintern Abbey (Monmouthshire), 210, 224
Tironensians, 213
Titchfield Abbey (Hampshire), 223
Tolland Royal (Wiltshire), 256
Tooting Bec (London), 216
Torksey (Lincolnshire), 239
Tostig, Earl of Northumbria, 3, 33
Totnes (Devon), 78, 86, 199
Tovil (Kent), 299
Towns, 89, 107, 138–68
   in Normandy, 139–40, 156
   castle towns, 123–36
      in Normandy, 123
   monastic towns, 224–9
   new (planned) ports, 166
      in Normandy, 139
   new (planned) towns, 160–7, 224, 297
      in Normandy, 161

Tristan and Isolde, 251, 303
True Cross, 57
Tutbury (Staffordshire), 296
Tulketh Abbey (Lancashire), 213
Turold, Abbot of Peterborough, 68, 177
Turstin fitz Rolf, 71
Tutbury Priory (Staffordshire), 199
Tynemouth Priory (North Tyneside) 203

Upper Smite (Warwickshire), 211
Urbanus Magnus, 19
Utrecht Psalter, 21, 253 308

Vaccaries, 18, 221–2, 243 *see also* cattle
Venison, 239, 248, 253, 254
Vesci, de, family, 166
Vikings, ix, 5, 10, 33, 37, 40, 41, 52, 59,
   138, 139, 151, 153, 174, 261, 267 *see also*
   Danes, Scandinavian impact
Villages, 13–16, 234
   planned 63, 65–7, 86, 92
Vipont, Robert de, 166
Visual arts, 307–308
Vitalis of Canterbury, 22
Viticulture, 27–9
Voyage of St Brendan the Abbot, 304

Wace, Robert, 38, 41, 302
Wadard, 50, 80
Wakefield (West Yorkshire), 244
Wales, 87-93,, 172-3
Walkelin, Bishop of Winchester, 147–8, 177–8
Wallingford (Oxfordshire), 30, 50, 73, 138,
    140, 145, 161, 285
    Castle, 73, 96, 107
Walter, Abbot of Evesham, 28, 177
Walter l'Espec, 209
Walterstone (Herefordshire), 301
Waltham (Essex), 57
    Waltham Chronicler, 174
Waltham Castle (Hampshire), 119
Waltheof, Earl of Northumbria, 5, 56, 68
'Wanderer, The', 271
Warenne family, 76, 199, 203–4
Warkworth Castle (Northumberland), 132,
    133-4
Warwick, 140, 304
Waste, 40–1, 48–9, 51, 54, 55, 56, 59, 60, 61,
    62–3, 67, 88, 112, 151, 208, 210, 240
Watchet (Berkshire), 27
Waterston (Dorset), 301
Waverley Abbey (Surrey), 208
Weald, 1
Weardale Forest, (Co. Durham), 244, 256
Weedon Bec (Northamptonshire), 216
Wells (Somerset), 181
Wenlock Priory (Shropshire), 190, 199,
    204-5
Weobley (Herefordshire), 130-1
Westham (East Sussex), 36
Westminster, 4, 22, 141, 144
    Abbey, 30, 51, 141, 221, 229
    Palace, 22, 119–21, 141, 269
    see also London
Weybridge Forest (Cambridgeshire), 243
Whatton (Nottinghamshire) 22
Wheldrake (North Yorkshire), 65
Wherwell (Hampshire), 211
Whitby Abbey (North Yorkshire), 155, 201
White Canons, see Premonstratensians
Whitland (Carmarthenshire), 213
Whorlton (Co. Durham), 297
Wiggonby (Cumbria), 86
Wigmore (Herefordshire), 75
Wigod of Wallingford, 73
William de Albini, Earl of Arundel, 97

William of Aumale, 265
William de Braose, 77
William of Calais, Bishop of Durham,
    185–6
William de Corbeil, Archbishop of
    Canterbury, 282
William II d 'Eu, 38
William de Percy, 202
William fitz Baldwin, 131
William fitz Osbern, Earl of Hereford, 54,
    77, 88, 103, 123, 179, 272
William of Jumièges, 35, 61
William of Malmesbury, 29, 46, 61, 90, 95,
    119, 159, 173–4, 175, 181, 184, 187, 201,
    250, 251, 263, 264, 290, 302
William of Newbury, 95
William of Poitiers, 42, 46, 49, 60, 70, 115,
    174–5, 182, 262–3
William I, King of England, xii, 7, 22, 23,
    30, 50, 51, 52–6, 59–63, 68, 70, 71–9, 82,
    83, 85, 86, 88, 93, 121, 122, 145, 146, 154,
    155, 159, 161, 169, 170, 171, 173, 175,
    179, 181, 182, 198, 201, 227, 240, 247,
    248, 251, 256, 259, 260, 261, 272, 273,
    285, 312
    Duke William of Normandy, 30, 31, 33–5,
        37, 40, 42, 43, 44, 47–51, 100, 119, 139,
        145, 170, 264
    'emperor', 259, 260, 262–5, 266, 268,
        269, 277
William II, Rufus, King of England, 80, 86,
    88, 108, 119, 148, 151, 169, 175, 203, 223,
    252, 257, 265, 269, 282
Williamston (Northumberland), 301
Wimarc family, 104, 106
Winchelsea (East Sussex), 31, 32
Winchester (Hampshire), 4, 9, 27, 47, 49, 56,
    119, 138, 140, 145–51, 179, 181, 190, 194,
    195, 256, 258, 279, 285, 300, 301 see also
    hospitals
    Bishop, 123
    Castle, 107, 117, 145, 269, 282
    Cathedral, 22, 27, 121, 145, 146, 147–8,
        164, 169, 174, 177–8, 291, 196, 223,
        244, 268–9, 289, 305, 308
        Winchester Annals, 147, 149
    churches, 146–7, 149, 190
    Hyde Abbey,148–9
    Palace, 119, 121, 145, 146

St Cross Hospital, 149-50
St Giles Fair, 150-1
St Mary's Abbey, 148
School of Illumination, 7
Wolvesey (Bishop's) Palace, 119, 121-2,
    145, 146, 149, 269
Windsor (Berkshire), 49, 50, 161, 181
    Forest, 18
    Castle, 161
    Palace, 119, 121, 161
Wirral Forest (Cheshire), 243, 245
Wiston (Lanarkshire), 93
Wiston (Pembrokeshire), 91, 92
Witney (Oxfordshire), 121, 164
Wizo the Fleming, 92, 93
Woodland, 232–7, 242
    ancient 235–6
    wood pasture, 234–6, 243, 248
Woodstock (Oxfordshire), 164-5
    Palace, 119-121
    Chase, 238
    Park, 249–51
Wool *see* sheep
Woolmer Forest (Hampshire), 243

Wootton (Oxfordshire), 79–80, 164
Worcester, 42, 138, 194, 285, 296
    Cathedral, 169, 172, 181, 186–7, 196, 295–6
Wren, Christopher, 143
Wroxeter (Shropshire), 269–71
Wulfstan, Archbishop of York,
    Bishop of Worcester, 102, 181, 182,
    186–7, 295–6
Wychwood Forest (Oxfordshire), 249

Yarmouth (Isle of Wight), 166
Yarmouth (Great), (Norfolk), 158, 256
Yeavering (Northumberland), 119
York, 5, 9, 22, 33, 40, 59, 60, 63–5, 81, 138,
    140, 151–5, 156, 166, 181, 190, 194, 195,
    239, 285
    Baile Hill Castle, 151, 154
        Clifford's Tower, 154
    Cathedral (Minster), 151, 154–5, 203
    churches, 155, 190
    King's Fishpool, 22, 153
    St Mary's Abbey, 65, 155, 202–3, 208
    York Castle, 151, 153
Yvelines Forest, 237